# LARGER THAN LIFE

# LARGER THAN LIFE

*Donald Gordon and the Liberty Life Story*

Ken Romain

Jonathan Ball Publishers
Johannesburg

First published in 1989 by
Jonathan Ball Publishers
P O Box 2105
Parklands
2121 Johannesburg

(011) 880-3116/7/8

ISBN 0 947464 08 5

Designed and typeset by Book Productions, Pretoria
Printed and bound by National Book Printers, Goodwood, Cape

# Contents

# Foreword by Donald Gordon

Since Ken Romain first produced his draft of *Larger than Life*, I have had the opportunity of reading and reflecting on the past four decades of my life which represents the period from the commencement of my training as a chartered accountant in 1948 to my emerging as founder chairman of one of South Africa's acknowledged leading institutions, uniquely positioned on the international scene. These forty years have been of great moment to me and have almost exactly coincided with the tenure of office of the present South African government which assumed power in the same year as I commenced my career. This period which spans my entire adult life has been an era of great political and economic trauma, difficulty and change during which South Africa has been subjected to international isolation, sanctions, disinvestment and innumerable other pressures resulting in, and from, a somewhat abnormal society. This period has created great opportunities, immense challenges and constant frustrations for many of us as we have sought to build constructively and progressively and, at the same time, to conform to the highest standards of behaviour as dictated by the needs of our changing society and the general principles prevailing in the Western world in the latter part of the twentieth century.

For those in the higher echelons of the business and financial community, these conflicting forces helped, ironically, to create many business leaders of greater determination and focus than would usually be generated in a more stable environment. Throughout this period it has been the fundamental approach at Liberty Life to create opportunities out of adversity and, with hindsight, our aspirations and dynamic growth have been advanced by reason of the optimistic and positive attitude that has always been part and parcel of our business philosophy.

In recent years there has been substantial and critical comment, from both public and private sources, concerning the perceived concentration of economic power in South Africa. I have, for a long time, been a proponent of the approach that concentration of economic power is inevitable and of some importance to the development of South Africa's resources in the best way consistent with the special needs and requirements of our unique environment. I predicted in 1982, at the time of Liberty Life's 25th Anniversary, that by the end of the decade there would be five or six dominant groups which would have a vital influence on the economy. This forecast has proved accurate and, at the end of 1988, no more than six defined groups had actually emerged in this dominant role. Each such group has as core components a major bank, an important life insurance company and key allied industrial and mining interests. The structure which has evolved in South Africa is reminiscent of the Zaibatsu System which had developed in Japan over a long period and whose existence at the end of the Second World War was the catalyst that enabled Japan, after being the first target of nuclear warfare, to rise from the ashes into perhaps the most powerful economy in the world today.

South Africa is too small and lacking in skilled human resources to afford a fragmented financial and industrial system which would be totally incapable of either financing or managing the special needs of the times. These major business giants have collectively proved themselves able to cope with the multitude of challenges and difficulties caused by sanctions, disinvestment and other destabilising political activity. Such major groupings are equipped to provide the necessary financial and human resources and expertise to deal with the special pressures to which South Africa has been subjected; also to contemplate vital new ventures of a size and scope which would otherwise be impossible by diffused pockets of capital and enterprise. The dominant groups of this country have become employers of major importance, exercising strong leadership and constituting an exemplary role model in terms of enlightened labour relations and a behavioural pattern which stands comparison with best Western standards. In this way their influence has played a major role in stimulating the positive course into which South Africa's political momentum is currently evolving as well as facilitating a new focus on social responsibility.

In looking back on some of the corporate transactions which have propelled Liberty Life into becoming a leading corporate player, both in South Africa and in the United Kingdom, and on which Ken

Romain has concentrated in the pages of *Larger than Life*, I am conscious of the number of transactions which have connotations of disinvestment. I should make it clear that I have a great abhorrence in principle of the motives underlying political disinvestment and its soulmate, sanctions, and that I am convinced that all the companies with which we have been involved in this connection since 1972 would have disinvested with or without the intervention of Liberty Life.

Fortunately, most of our involvement with this emotive activity has been with companies in the insurance industry where our primary motivation and objective has been the rationalisation of the life insurance industry in line with the Report of the Franzsen Commission of Inquiry into Fiscal and Monetary Policy. Once there was official recognition of the need for a greater measure of local participation in and the rationalisation of the South African insurance industry, Liberty Life took a corporate decision that it was necessary to amalgamate the financial resources of a number of the highest quality medium-sized companies to create one major life company which would constitute a serious competitive force to challenge the two dominant South African life insurers located in the Cape, and at the same time to play a lead role in the development of South Africa's life insurance industry applying the considerable international expertise we had accumulated.

In being the catalyst for combining the resources of four high-quality companies: Liberty Life, Prudential Assurance Company of South Africa and the South African operations of the Canadian-based Manufacturers Life Insurance Company and the Sun Life of Canada, we have achieved our goals. The Charter Life Insurance Company, the erstwhile offshoot of the Guardian National Insurance Company, a subsidiary of the Guardian Royal Exchange Assurance of London, was also subsequently included as a 60 per cent owned subsidiary of Liberty Life with Guardian National remaining with a 40 per cent interest. These highly complex corporate transactions, combined with powerful organic growth arising from a high degree of innovative product design and marketing dynamism, created a life insurance group with high quality South African and international assets now valued at more than R17 billion. Taking into account off-balance sheet investment portfolios and real estate administered on behalf of institutional clients and self-administered pension funds, directly managed associate companies in which we own more than 30 per cent of the equity and our mutual fund interests, total assets under the Group's direct control currently exceed R25 billion. If one includes other associated companies in which the Group has either joint control or has a dominant equity shareholding of the order of 30 per cent or more the total South African based and international assets over which The Liberty Life Group has significant influence exceed R85 billion.

The Liberty Life Group also had direct involvement in returning control of two major, non-insurance corporations to South African ownership: The Premier Group Holdings and The Standard Bank Investment Corporation. The Premier Group, which we control jointly with Johannesburg Consolidated Investment Company and Anglo American Corporation, offered Liberty Life a unique opportunity in 1983 of an involvement at the top level in the food and consumer-orientated sectors of the economy. This included the simultaneous acquisition by Premier of a 35 per cent interest in The South African Breweries. We thus also acquired a significant indirect position in South Africa's leading beverage-based consumer-orientated group, whose interests embrace not only dominance in the beer and beverage industries but also have extensive interests in the hotel, retail, furniture, clothing and textile industries. Since then The Liberty Life Group has also acquired a significant direct stake in The South African Breweries. Liberty Life's major strategic interest in banking is now represented by the largest single shareholding in The Standard Bank Investment Corporation and their joint control of The Liberty Life Group through Liblife Controlling Corporation. This link has been a major factor in the Standard Bank becoming, indisputably, South Africa's leading bank following the final disinvestment by the London-based Standard Chartered Bank in 1987. Both of these key investments were vital to Liberty Life's strategic positioning in South Africa and enabled it to achieve an interest in the economy in line with those of its major competitors. The concept of close linkage of banks and life insurance companies is now becoming a major feature of the international financial services industry and Liberty Life led in this development.

We were able to negotiate the South African repatriation of Premier Group and Standard Bank Investment Corporation, and our other international acquisitions, on favourable terms before the impetus of disinvestment had become a factor involving major competition and higher prices being paid for the later opportunities that presented themselves. In all these cases we were a reluctant participant in the events leading up to international investors withdrawing from South Africa. Nonetheless, our activities in this area have undoubtedly been greatly beneficial to the economy and have saved an enormous quantum of external dividend flow from South Africa over the years. By way of example, I firmly believe that control of South Africa's leading bank should be in local hands. Stripped of the emotionalism of the present times, this should be indisputable. All this corporate activity was undoubtedly the foundation for Liberty Life's dynamic and accelerating growth over the past decade.

I nonetheless regret that Standard Chartered Bank, one of the United Kingdom's leading banking institutions, finally disposed of their South African interests, although we were aware that political considerations were not necessarily the major reason for their disinvestment. I am, however, gratified that Liberty Life has succeeded in maintaining a most cordial connection and friendship with Standard Chartered Bank which supported TransAtlantic Holdings strongly in the difficult early years of its international development. I also take considerable pride in the fact that we have maintained excellent relationships with each and every one of the international groups we have dealt with in this connection. In the case of Guardian Royal Exchange, I still sit on the main London Board following the disposal of the major portion of their interests in The Liberty Life Group in 1978.

Perhaps the most important event in my business life was the restoration to South African control of Liberty Holdings from the Guardian Royal Exchange which had acquired control of the fledgeling Liberty Life from its founders in 1964. The amount of R27 million expended in the reacquisition of control is now worth over R800 million and the annual saving of dividend payments abroad now closely equates to the R27 million repurchase price. This example of the favourable aspects of disinvestment, from a financial and economic point of view, has been of substantial benefit to the South African economy, particularly as the Guardian Royal Exchange retained over 10 per cent of the equity of Liberty Holdings as well as their controlling interest in Guardian National Insurance Company. The complex transaction enabled Liberty Holdings ultimately to acquire a 44 per cent interest in this very profitable and important undertaking which plays a leading role in the South

African fire, accident, personal lines and marine insurance industry. I remain Chairman of this company; a further indication of our success in maintaining excellent international relationships.

It will be clear from the relevant chapter in *Larger than Life* that my efforts to dissuade the Guardian Royal Exchange from disinvestment from The Liberty Life Group were totally sincere. I took this approach notwithstanding the advantage the planned reduction of their commitment would confer on us. It was only later that I began to recognise the positive benefits to us and to the economy that could accrue from their somewhat unfortunate policy on South Africa.

And so the objectives of official policy and of the Franzsen Commission Report were achieved and posterity will, no doubt, acknowledge the great benefits to the Republic of reacquiring control of some of our best businesses at that time. Those companies which have had the foresight, acumen and the will to continue with their South African involvement in this time of trauma and crisis will find themselves favourably positioned in one of the leading economies in the world of the future. This, I say, notwithstanding the temporary psychological and other problems encountered in the short term as a consequence of the activities of the international disinvestment lobby, and the senseless follow-my-leader attitude of major international corporations in withdrawing from South Africa for negative and political reasons at such an important moment in South Africa's social evolution.

At a very early stage, Liberty Life took a strategic decision that, as insurance is essentially an international business and that as we had come on the scene late in the day, rather than developing a small regional insurance company battling against the might and dominance of companies sometimes more than 100 years older than Liberty Life, we should concentrate our business activities on a wider international basis. This decision was implemented notwithstanding all the difficult political and financial constraints under which we have operated internationally over the past 27 years. We were also very conscious at the time of the enormous impediments to this course of establishing ourselves in more mature economies, but we were confident that our fresh and flexible approach could have some relevance in other countries restricted by hidebound traditional attitudes.

Immediately following the listing of Liberty Life in 1962, we participated in the establishment of The Abbey Life Insurance

Company, which was to become the largest listed insurance company formed in the United Kingdom since the Second World War. Ironically, as one of the string of incredible coincidences that have occurred throughout my career, Abbey Life was destined to establish the first major relationship with a leading commercial bank in the United Kingdom on very similar lines to the relationship we had established with Standard Bank Investment Corporation a decade earlier, and which has had such positive consequences for both Liberty Life and Standard Bank Investment Corporation in South Africa. Abbey Life has recently become a listed subsidiary of Lloyds Bank, a major British clearing bank, and, in the fullness of time, in my view, this is bound to co-ordinate the distribution systems of the two institutions to achieve even greater success in the years to come. Incidentally, the take-over bid made by Lloyds Bank for Standard Chartered Bank in 1986 was a major factor in Standard Chartered Bank's subsequent withdrawal from South Africa – another twist of fate affecting Liberty Life's destiny.

Sadly, following our association with the Guardian Royal Exchange in 1964, we were obliged to dispose of our interests in Abbey Life and therefore participated in none of the fruits of the development of this dynamic company after that time. Nonetheless, we take great pride in the achievements of Sir Mark Weinberg and Mr Sydney Lipworth and in the remarkable success of the concepts we conceived together in the very early days of Liberty Life. Both have achieved great things personally and Sydney Lipworth is now Chairman of the Monopolies and Mergers Commission, a position of the greatest importance and prestige in the United Kingdom and internationally; and, of course, Mark Weinberg was knighted for his wide achievements within 25 years of the tentative early days of Abbey Life. He goes from success to success and is today a doyen of British society and the business establishment.

Following my fourteen years of association with the Guardian Royal Exchange, having become their first foreign-based director in 1971, and their relinquishing control of Liberty Holdings in 1978, our strategy for directly internationalising the business of Liberty Life again became a priority. Our pre-occupation with this objective was much reinforced by the enormous experience we had gained of international markets during the Guardian Royal Exchange era. I had personally also gained great insight into the workings of the United Kingdom and other international markets, and had achieved a wide spectrum of business and personal relationships in all the major English-speaking countries of the world. This led into our acquiring a dominant near 30 per cent interest in the Sun Life Assurance Society, a major and respected United Kingdom based life assurer, and a controlling stake in Capital & Counties, a leading listed international property company specialising in office and retail orientated real estate in the United Kingdom. This is an area of the market in which we have acquired particular expertise following our absorption of Rapp & Maister and Real Estate Corporation, two leading listed South African real estate companies, which Liberty Life acquired during the seventies. It was at that time that my association with Michael Rapp really began. Since then, he has remained my closest confidant and colleague, notwithstanding his subsequent relocation to London. The background to these events is well documented in *Larger than Life*.

Thus in the space of thirty years, we have built up a major institution, very strongly positioned in the South African environment to play an important role in the great opportunities that lie ahead following the new political dispensation which, in the medium term, is likely to emerge from the highly fluid and rapidly changing political scenario now prevailing in our country.

The role to be played by the South African life insurance industry is seminal to the future development of this vital region on the southern tip of Africa. I foresee that the life insurance industry, in which Liberty Life is so powerfully positioned, and its consort, the pension fund industry, are likely to become the major providers of a vast quantum of the necessary long-term capital for the optimum development of the entire sub-continent. At the same time, the life insurance industry, with its highly sophisticated marketing structure and investment expertise, continues to enhance the promotion of long-term savings in South Africa where the rate of overall savings has declined and no institutionalised social security system exists. The banks, too, will play a major part, but the role of providing permanent capital will be largely the responsibility of the life insurance and pension fund industries which will act both as direct investors and also, indirectly, as investors of last resort in developed corporations, thereby freeing risk capital for entrepreneurs and like individuals to develop the new opportunities that will arise.

I have never believed that the life insurance industry, apart from its position in mature and proven situations, should be involved in providing direct risk capital, but rather that it should be encouraged to use other institutions and enterprises to filter the funds generated from the life offices' fiduciary situations into the mainstream of enterprise development. I believe that the major role that South African life insurers must assume is to channel the savings of the man in the street into enterprises and initiatives, including those necessarily generated by the public sector, of vital import to our economy and its infrastructure. It is in this that I believe the South African life insurance industry has played, and will continue to play, a vital role.

I am extremely thankful for the opportunities that this great country has offered to us in providing an environment in which it was possible to visualise the concepts which would eventually emerge as The Liberty Life Group of today. We have taken full advantage of these circumstances, I hope fairly and justly, in the best interests of our country and the community in which we operate.

In this connection, I have always found the financial regulatory authorities extremely helpful and supportive and the official approach, in my view, has generally been conducive to innovative attitudes and a free enterprise society. The support and understanding of the office of the Registrar of Financial Institutions in particular have been of great importance to the attainment of our aspirations, and I take considerable pride in the degree of trust and confidence they have always demonstrated in Liberty Life and in me personally. This, I hope, has been reciprocated in full measure.

In similar vein, I can only express the greatest appreciation of the encouragement from the various members of the South African Treasury and Reserve Bank with whom we have had to consult and work in the course of our innumerable and often complex requirements for which their approval, assistance and support were required. We have maintained excellent relationships with successive Ministers of Finance over the past two decades or so, and they have shown great understanding for what we were doing and the role we play in the economy. In this context I would like particularly to mention The Honourable The Minister of Finance, Mr Barend du Plessis. I am now in my sixtieth year and he is the first Minister of Finance in my lifetime who is younger than me. I hope we have reciprocated his support and that of Dr Chris Stals, Special Economic Advisor to the Minister of Finance and the man nominated to be the Governor of the Reserve Bank, by virtue of the contribution that we have tried to make in the general interests of the country.

The tax environment in which Liberty Life operates as a life insurer has always been fair and realistic, and has usually attempted to apply the principles of the 'level playing field'. Consequently, when the tax rates in recent years had escalated to uncomfortable levels because of the temporary requirements of the economy, we were loath to complain of their impact while the formula was being appropriately restructured to deal with the complexities of modern day life insurance. We have always made our contribution honestly and, in some cases, against what we saw to be our own interest, to help create a tax environment appropriate to the vast needs of this country in terms of its inevitable heavy commitment to social responsibility and defence. We were amongst the first to make positive recommendations as to the role of pension fund taxation in relation to the country's tax base at a time when new taxation sources were desperately required. Notwithstanding that the overall tax load may well have increased, our suggestions were directed towards the restructuring of the taxation basis of the life insurance and pension fund industries in the interests of creating a more equitable environment for the development of pension fund and life insurance business in the public interest.

Looking back on Liberty Life's achievements over thirty years, the fun and satisfaction I have personally had in developing Liberty Life to its present status has been totally and undeniably absorbing. I doubt whether anyone has enjoyed any challenge more than I have. It has been gratifying in every way and I cannot believe my good fortune in being pointed at the right time into this particular field of enterprise. For me, perhaps, it was more than the achievement of the impossible dream.

So many people in so many situations and places have played a part in achieving what has been accomplished that I feel daunted by the task, for the first time, of publicly recording and acknowledging their contribution. First and foremost, I need to acknowledge my long-suffering immediate family. Although they have reaped tremendous material advantages from the success of Liberty Life, to a great extent they have been left to their own devices during the extended period over which I have had to devote virtually my entire energy to developing Liberty Life – my all-consuming mistress. Nevertheless, none of them has ever complained and I am deeply grateful for the involvement, love and affection with which I have been rewarded by the entire family over the past thirty years. My wife Peggy's support and her dedication to the family have ensured that our children have grown up to be worthwhile human beings; for this and all that she has given to us, I shall be forever grateful.

I also owe a great debt of gratitude to all those who have supported me throughout our endeavours with good heart and great loyalty. Many of them have devoted a substantial part of their lives to Liberty Life and to its destiny and I salute them, particularly people like Gail Benjamin and Maureen Hart – the two closest props of my business life who have received relatively limited financial reward for all their efforts. They are supremos in their fields and have been my secretaries, aides and confidantes for almost a quarter of a century. Gail still remains in office but Maureen, seven years ago, went on to concentrate on her personal life following her marriage to John Kilroe, the current Chairman of Shell SA. Other people, like Isaac More – my long-suffering driver, have also remained totally loyal and patient with a very demanding person.

From my stalwart colleagues – past and present – in Liberty Life itself I have received total loyalty. The ever-enthusiastic Farrell Sher and incredibly loyal Humphrey Norman have given their all in my personal support. And there are many, many others whom I am reluctant to mention by name for fear of upsetting many hundreds that I might fail to mention. Many of their names are recorded in the pages of *Larger than Life*.

There are many people in the wider world who have had a deep and lasting impact on Liberty Life and on my personal development, and who have made great contributions to our achievements. The foremost of these is my Mother who, until her death five years ago, never allowed me to lose my humility. She never allowed me to forget who I was or where I came from, and I revere the impact of this on my life, attitudes, balance and self-esteem. From my Father, I learned the tenets and philosophy of hard work and, to this day, he is the only man I have ever known who worked harder and more intensely than I do myself. Sadly his rewards were as meagre as mine have been bountiful.

I have had the privilege of meeting and associating with the rich and the famous and many of the business leaders of the world; and, since I am gregarious and thoroughly enjoy social occasions, I have gained much, both intellectually and personally, from these contacts. My innumerable mentors and advisors have had an indelible impact on my life. Notable amongst this category is Ernest Bigland, who gave me such enormous support and who played an undeniable part in all that has gone into *Larger than Life*. He was himself much larger than life.

I have also derived great inspiration from the example of other men such as Harry Oppenheimer and Anton Rupert, both of whom I now regard as my personal friends and for whom I have enormous respect and affection; and other luminaries such as Julius Feinstein to whom I was articled and who is still senior partner of Kessel Feinstein, our lead auditors; Henri de Villiers – Liberty Life's deputy chairman and my closest colleague at the Standard Bank; Gavin Relly, Chairman of the Anglo American Corporation; Ian Mackenzie, the former Chairman of Standard Bank; Ted Roy, Chairman of Liberty Life from 1964 to 1972 during the period in which I relinquished that position; and, of course, Sydney Lipworth and Mark Weinberg.

There are many others such as Michael Rapp, Johann Rupert, Louis Shill, Monty Hilkowitz, Louis Miller, Meyer Kahn, our solicitors Michael Katz and Len Berkowitz, stockbroker Max Borkum and all my Board colleagues in The Liberty Life Group and associate companies who have played such vital roles in Liberty Life's success story – the list goes on and on.

Liberty Life has also been deeply influenced by some of our major competitors who, not always intentionally, have provided a stimulant and example for our development. In spite of all the years of confrontation in earlier times with Jan van der Horst, Chairman of the South African Mutual, I have no difficulty in admitting to an ungrudging sense of admiration for this man who has done so much for the South African insurance industry, the Old Mutual, and the South African economy.

My other erstwhile major competitor in the South African market, Professor Fred du Plessis, also played a role in the development of his company, Sanlam, Liberty Life and the insurance industry in general. Notwithstanding the strong competitive interface, I had a very great respect and affection for Fred and was devastated at his untimely death in a road accident early in 1989. This was a sad loss for South Africa and for all of us in the insurance industry.

My sincere appreciation also goes out to all those who have contributed directly to *Larger than Life* in which we have tried to encapsulate some of the corporate philosophy and thinking that has driven Liberty Life to the heights it has achieved, and also to act as a permanent record and reference work for those younger people entering the industry or the financial sector, whether in South Africa or abroad.

Finally, may I express my deepest gratitude to the long-suffering Ken Romain. In difficult circumstances he has worked immensely hard and has produced a remarkable record of some of the most exciting and most notable events in the thirty years of Liberty Life's existence. I should say that, until the final stages of his drafting, he had virtually no access to me and that, in these circumstances, I am sure that all his readers will better appreciate what has been achieved. I must also thank Hylton Appelbaum who performed a sterling and untiring role in bringing this project to fruition.

I believe we have made sure that the spirit of Liberty Life will flourish and grow. The basics and the foundations have been conscientiously put in place. For my own part, I intend to stay with Liberty Life for as long as I am fit and able and until it is necessary to pass the baton to my successors. But I will not stay beyond my usefulness. My ambition is for the company to maintain its position as the quality company it has become. With the spirit and the calibre and the enthusiasm of the people who make Liberty Life what it is, the years I have spent in the development of this great institution will, I fondly hope, not have been in vain.

DONALD GORDON
July 1989

# Author's Preface

This book, *Larger than Life*, is not, and is not intended to be, a conventional corporate history of the Liberty Life Association of Africa Limited. Rather, it is an episodic history, an attempt to capture the drama and the fascination of what is arguably one of the most extraordinary business accomplishments of the post-World War II era; certainly one of the most remarkable world-wide in the financial sector and in the field of life insurance and financial services.

It is the story of the creation, in the space of thirty years, of a financial institution that has had an indelible influence on the life insurance and financial services industries both in the Republic of South Africa and in the United Kingdom, and whose impact has repercussions even beyond these geographic limits.

In order to achieve authenticity for *Larger than Life*, it has been necessary to include certain confidential and sensitive material – documents, statements and so forth from a multitude of people. It is believed that it would be far more instructive and useful to the reader and students, aspirants and observers of the financial scene in South Africa, the United Kingdom and elsewhere, that such material should be included. However, because of the desirability of scrupulous adherence to accepted principles of confidentiality, the utmost care has been taken to give interested parties an opportunity of commenting and consenting to the inclusion of certain sensitive matters. It is sincerely hoped that this has been achieved and that nobody will be offended by the objective of having a more complete and accurate record of the Liberty Life saga.

By its nature and by its intent, this volume has extensive chronological gaps. These are covered by quoting from the institution's Annual Reports for 1987 and 1988, straddling its thirtieth anniversary year. The corporate profile of the Liberty Life Group, and a year-by-year summary of its progress, are placed in an Appendix.

# Acknowledgments

This book would not have been possible without the involvement, encouragement, effort, time and support of a large number of people. I shall not have the space to name all of them, but I particularly want to thank those many busy businessmen who made time to talk to me and my tape recorder, or on the telephone, and those who bothered to read the draft, or draft chapters, and put me right where I had gone wrong.

First must come Donald Gordon, who let me loose amongst Liberty Life's records and archives, and who has accorded me a degree of independence that I think is quite exceptional in a commissioned work; and who, in what is the busiest business life that I have ever been closely associated with, has given me a remarkable amount of time. Next his daughter Wendy Appelbaum, without whose staunch advocacy the project would never have seen the light of day, and his wife Peggy, who has allowed me to play havoc with holidays and weekends whilst remaining delightfully kind to me personally.

The names that follow are strictly in alphabetical order, for it would be totally invidious to attempt in any way to indicate who has given me more aid and comfort than anyone else.

My very sincere thanks to Archie Aaron, Raymond Ackerman, Bob Aldworth, Hylton Appelbaum, Piet Badenhorst, Oliver Baring, Julian Benson, Morris Bernstein, Hugo Biermann, Robert Bigland, Tony Bloom, Max Borkum, Harry Brews, Nigel Bruce, Margot Bryant.

The Earl of Cairns, Lily Cane and her son, Joel, Cecil Carrington, Mike Carstens, Wolf Cesman, Tim Collins, Sir Brian Corby, Yves D'Halluin, Henri de Villiers, Peter Dugdale.

Steve Ellis, Julius Feinstein, Charles Fiddian-Green, Raymond Fine, Leslie Frankel, Rudi Frankel, Harold Fridjhon, Doug Gair, Rex Gibson, Bill Giemre, Sam Goldblatt, Harold Gorvy, Manfred

Gorvy, Dick Goss, Harry Gottlieb, Sir Peter Graham, Peter Greenfield.

Morry Haifer, Charles Hambro, Steve Handler, Hans Hefer, Basil Hersov, Monty Hilkowitz, Helmut Hirsh, Murray Hofmeyr, James Inglis, Meyer Kahn, Dennis Kaplan, Sid Kaplan, Michael Katz, Sol Kerzner, Derek Keys, Maureen Kilroe (nee Hart), Natie Kirsh.

Basil Landau, Patric Lee, Piet Liebenberg, Ben Lipshitz, Sydney Lipworth, Wynand Louw, Bertie Lubner, Ian Mackenzie, the late Ian MacPherson, Issy Maisels, Dennis Marler, Roy McAlpine, Bruce McInnes, Garry McLeish, Joel Mervis, Mike Middlemas, Bob Miller, Harold Morony, Barry Mortimer, Steve Mulholland, Gerry Muller, Hugh Murray, Tertius Myburgh.

Bernard Nackan, Johan Nel, David Nohr, Humphrey Norman, Perry Oertel, Julian Ogilvie Thompson, Sir Angus Ogilvy, David Palmer, Joe Pamensky, Ted Pavitt, Shlomo Peer, Hennie Pelser, John Perkins, the late Fred du Plessis, Sydney Press.

Dennis Raeburn, Michael Rapp, Gavin Relly, Pat Retief, Alan Romanis, Hugh Rubin, Roy Sable, Philip Sceales, Monty Schapiro, Julian Schlesinger, Tim Sewell, Farrell Sher, Louis Shill, Gerald Stein, Conrad Strauss, David Susman.

Eric Tenderini, Jan van der Horst, Julius van Velden, John von Ahlefeldt, Gordon Waddell, Richard Wagner, Keith Wallace, Albert Weinberg, Sir Mark Weinberg, Bomber Wells, Dorian Wharton-Hood, Ray Wheeler, Brian Whitehouse, Peter Wilmot-Sitwell, Bill Wilson, Mark Winterton, John Worwood, Peter Wrighton, Basil Wunsh, Taki Xenopoulos, Brian Young and Rod Zank.

Within Liberty Life itself, for support, services and simple help far beyond the call of duty, my sincere thanks to Gail Benjamin, Avril Ord, Lauren Schutte, Ron Pierce and Mike Lee. Finally, to my editor, Frances Perryer, grateful thanks for a job well done.

# 1 The GRE Buy-back

The history of Liberty Life is punctuated by mega-deals, from the 1972 takeover of the South African operations of Manufacturers Life of Canada, which doubled the company's size overnight, to the 1983 acquisition of joint control of the Premier Food Group, simultaneously achieving effective control of South African Breweries, in an audacious deal that shook the South African business establishment to its very foundations. Then on to the tactical takeover of the United Kingdom's listed property giant, Capital & Counties, by Liberty Life's overseas associate, TransAtlantic, followed in 1988 by the restructuring of First International Trust as the holding company for the Group's offshore investments, involving a record R484 million rights issue. In 1986 there was the R300 million takeover of the Prudential Assurance Company of South Africa and the R2,2 billion flotation of Liberty Investors Limited.

Of all these events, probably the most important and dramatic deal was the 1978 management buy-back of control of Liberty Life from Guardian Royal Exchange. This deal, though it involved less than R30 million, was central to the momentous events that followed. It meant that, after fifteen highly fruitful if somewhat tumultuous years under the wing of GRE and its often autocratic chief executive, Ernest Bigland, Donald Gordon was once again in sole control of his own destiny, and that of his creation, the Liberty Life Group.

Yet Gordon himself did not actually sign the Heads of Agreement that sealed the triumphal return of the country's third largest financial institution to South Africa. That vital document was signed on his behalf by his colleague and friend, Michael Rapp, who by that time was already Gordon's business partner, most senior executive director and closest confidant.

That the deal was possible, that it could even be contemplated, is characteristic of the almost incredible success story that is Liberty Life.

Back in 1964, Guardian Assurance of London, then (and still) one of the largest and most important international composite insurance giants, had bought 75 per cent of Liberty Life, mainly from the small group – Donald Gordon, Louis Shill, Hugh Rubin, Brian Young and Sydney Lipworth – who had founded the company seven years earlier. The following three years saw several changes. Sydney Lipworth resigned as a director of Liberty Life soon after the Guardian took control, and with his wife Rosa emigrated to the UK, where he in due course joined Mark Weinberg (now Sir Mark) as an executive director of the Abbey Life Assurance Company, which achieved great success, and indeed revolutionised the UK life insurance industry, in the sixties. Louis Shill left Liberty Life in 1965 to take command of the Sage Holdings financial services group. In 1967, both Rubin and Young retired from Liberty Life. Thus, in a very short time, Gordon was left to carry on Liberty Life as undisputed supremo, to drive it relentlessly to the great heights it was destined to achieve over the following two decades. Control of the fledgeling assurer (assets were R3 million) cost Guardian under R2 million, and this was paid through the securities rand (the precursor of the financial rand of today) for an actual outlay of some £750 000, a minuscule fraction of Guardian's then world-wide assets of £1 billion.

By 1978, after twenty years of exponential growth, Liberty Life, and its holding company, then Guardian Assurance Holdings (now Liberty Holdings), controlled assets of some R700 million. This represented around 10 per cent of the assets of the Life Fund of Guardian Royal Exchange. Thus, in terms of GRE's Life Fund, in one instance, and in terms of the overall GRE scene, in another, as we shall see, the Liberty Life tail was beginning to wag the GRE dog.

The merger of the Royal Exchange and the Guardian was itself a momentous event in the history of the British insurance industry, bringing together as it did two major insurance companies each straddling great international insurance empires. The Royal Exchange Assurance, the senior of the two components of this historic marriage, was established by Royal Charter in 1720, virtually coinciding with the birth of the insurance industry as we know it today. Its London headquarters is the famous Royal Exchange, which still stands as a major landmark cheek by jowl with the Bank of England in the very heart of the City of London. The Royal Exchange is close to the actual site on which the modern world's insurance industry was conceived and evolved by the doughty merchants of the late seventeenth and early eighteenth centuries.

The other component, Guardian Assurance, was a mere stripling by comparison, having been formed as a registered company as recently as 1810. But by 1968, when the merger was consummated, the two companies were of similar size, though the Royal Exchange, if only by virtue of its greater age, was the more senior and prestigious. However, as it was the Guardian that had taken the initiative in the negotiations, it was the Guardian's name that took precedence over that of the Royal Exchange – hence Guardian Royal Exchange rather than Royal Exchange Guardian. Guardian's chief executive, Ernest Bigland, had had to move smartly to win this, to him, very important nuance, which was strongly resented for many years by some of the Royal Exchange stalwarts. However, in less than a decade, the Royal Exchange element of the directors had reasserted their dominance in the GRE Boardroom – that is the way things work in the City of London.

The merger worked out very well over time, and it is salutary to remember that when one talks of the Guardian Royal Exchange Assurance, one is talking of the inner core of the British financial establishment.

Crucial to the fifteen years of collaboration and success between the giant GRE and its small but explosively growing South African subsidiary, was the relationship that had developed between GRE's Ernest Bigland and Liberty Life's Donald Gordon. Between the two was an age gap of seventeen years, a massive "culture" gap (City of London laid-back versus Johannesburg get-up-and-go) and sufficient other differences to make their relationship, which developed into one of close and abiding friendship, a remarkable one indeed. The use of the term "South African subsidiary", above is deliberate; but, although legally accurate, it is by no means illustrative of the way the relationship worked. In practice, Bigland gave Gordon total autonomy, to a degree that indeed belied the "subsidiary" status, and the occasional disagreement, though mostly on principle rather than style, was always amicably settled by consensus and in good faith. Gordon responded by according considerable deference, and great respect, to the man who had become his mentor and his friend.

Bigland initiated Gordon into the ways and culture of the City of London, and his younger colleague, "Donald", for his part, imparted to Bigland some of the cult of the entrepreneur, and introduced him to the finer nuances of lateral business thinking and financial engineering.

The unusual, even unique, relationship worked, indeed it prospered mightily, beyond the wildest dreams of either of the two men. Bigland's tremendous pride and total involvement in Liberty Life were as if it was his own creation, and its notable success was the high peak of Bigland's business career as much as it was Gordon's.

But this was about to end. Ernest Bigland would reach the age of sixty-five in December 1978 and his retirement as managing director and chief executive of Guardial Royal Exchange was mandatory. It was accepted with the great dignity which characterised the man, but it nevertheless completely altered the equation – and the relationship between GRE, Liberty Life and Gordon.

This aspect was important, but there were others. In 1976, Johannesburg's sprawling black township of Soweto had erupted in rioting that saw hundreds of deaths; there was world-wide condemnation, and the political aspects of financial involvement in the Republic again became an issue on a scale not seen since the time of Sharpeville in 1961. In an atmosphere in which anti-South African political pressures were mounting, the imbalance of the Guardian's Life Fund became an issue within the GRE. It was a relatively simple matter: the assets of a life fund, geographically and in currency and maturity terms, should closely match its liabilities, in similar terms. And the Guardian's Life Fund, in which the small initial investment into South Africa had been of little consequence, had next to no liabilities in geographical South Africa nor, in currency terms, in the rand. Since the investment had by then grown to represent an important proportion of the total and was expanding at an exponential rate, the Life Fund was in a state of potential considerable imbalance, particularly in the long term, should political problems seriously destabilise the South African economy. Moreover, the GRE had a far-flung business empire, and political pressure was beginning to be exerted in particular against high-profile business operations of multinational companies operating within the Republic.

Given the will, of course, ways could have been found to transfer all or part of the stake in South Africa "up the line" – out of the

Guardian's Life Fund elsewhere in the greater GRE group. But the cash – some £10 million or so would have been involved – was not immediately or conveniently available. And the will to stay heavily committed to an increasingly unpopular South Africa was completely lacking on the part of several influential members of the Board of Guardian Royal Exchange, who became agitated by any criticism of its policy. Let it be said that Bigland was certainly not a member of the "soft-option" lobby. But there were other powerful influences at work within GRE which could have rocked it to the core.

Gordon's growing influence and power at Court, as the Boardroom at GRE is known, and his position on the main Board, was another factor. It was a matter of extreme concern to a considerable echelon of GRE's senior management, as well as to some of the executive directors, in relation to whom he was senior in terms of GRE Board service and influence. There was even talk of Gordon becoming chief executive of GRE on Bigland's retirement. There were also doubts in many minds as to whether anyone other than Bigland could effectively control Gordon. All this was anathema to a number of members of senior management, who also felt threatened by DG's independent affluence, his entrepreneurial drive and his undoubted flair in the insurance world.

Thoughts of "disinvestment" had been in the air as early as 1976. Indeed, the then executive director and general manager of GRE, Peter Greenfield, who after retiring from GRE remains a director of the Liberty Life Group and a close colleague and advisor to Gordon to this day, prepared an internal "note" for Ernest Bigland dated 4 March 1976.

His covering letter read: "I attach a note giving details of our South African holdings, but because of the situation in Southern Africa various views have been expressed by GRE directors concerning our interest in Liberty Life. By any standards the original investment in South Africa has been outstandingly successful for which considerable credit goes to Donald Gordon and his team. Any fundamental change in our present position can only be successful if it is supported both here and in South Africa.

"From time to time Donald has expressed views about moving to a position where South African shareholders have a majority stake. Clearly the timing of any such move is of considerable importance to

GRE and indeed we must expect to receive some benefit for moving from a position of control."

Greenfield's "note" set out the position in detail. The GRE shareholdings in Liberty Holdings (then named Guardian Assurance Holdings) were given as 26,2 million shares in the Life Fund, 8,6 million under "General Fund", and 7,3 million shares under "Other", representing the minority South African shareholders, for a total of 42,1 million, which would rise to 53,4 million ordinary shares on completion of the then current Rapp & Maister Real Estate Corporation takeover, which would completely reshape Liberty Life's profile in real estate from that date forward.

He then made the following observations: "The Guardian Life Fund holding of 26,2m shares has no corresponding Life Fund liability in South Africa. This asset has a market value of over £20m which does not match a like liability and under the new Department of Trade Regulations the value of this asset is substantially reduced for solvency purposes.

"The UK General Fund is in a similar position in that it has only limited liability in South Africa and again the value of the asset is, under the regulations, substantially reduced for solvency purposes.

"Bearing in mind the aspects referred to above and the political and economic situation which could develop in South Africa it is necessary to consider our strategy with regard to our Liberty holding. There are no grounds on which the Guardian Life Fund would be justified in increasing its investment in Liberty Life, indeed there are many good reasons for the Life Fund reducing its holding.

"A transfer of Liberty Holdings shares from Life Fund to General Fund should not produce exchange control problems but would produce a large capital gains tax liability for the Life Fund. However, similar reasons for not increasing the holding of the Life Fund also apply to the General Fund.

"Disposal of Liberty Holdings shares:

"(a) for Cash

"Small disposals would probably be treated as portfolio investments. The proceeds would be in securities rand which remain blocked but are saleable abroad at a discount of 25 per cent.

"The size of our holding in Liberty Holdings is such that both in the UK and South Africa it is considered a direct investment and not a portfolio investment and is subject to the restrictions imposed by the exchange control regulations in both South Africa and the UK.

"A substantial disposal for cash would also present greater difficulties in the present political and economic climate. I understand that it is unlikely that the [South African] Reserve Bank would permit remittances of direct investment proceeds through the official foreign exchange market and nor are they eligible for dollar premium in the UK.

"(b) for Shares

"The disposal or exchange of Liberty Holdings shares for shares in another company could, on a strict interpretation, suffer from some of the constraints applicable in (a). However, if a specific opportunity should arise or be created then in view of the size of the operation I consider that we should pursue how we can achieve special dispensation."

While Donald Gordon may indeed have expressed views such as Peter Greenfield noted regarding the return of control to South Africa, DG himself does not recall this. Clearly then, the issue was of no real concern to him at that time, even though it was exercising minds at the top of the GRE.

Of far greater moment to Gordon was the situation looming up as Bigland's retirement came ever closer. DG was unhappy at the prospect of being "controlled", however lightly, by anyone other than the man he had come to trust and respect, and whom he regarded as his intellectual equal.

After much thought – Gordon does nothing that he has not thought through as thoroughly as is humanly possible – he wrote, on 8 December 1977, a personal letter to the then Chairman of GRE, Tim Collins, with which he enclosed a three-page *aide-mémoire*. In this, Gordon set out in considerable detail his ideas as to the way GRE should be managed after Bigland. His views were revolutionary, even in the South African context. Seen against the background of the always conservative approach of "The City", DG's suggestions were virtually heretical.

Simply, Gordon proposed a "troika" – the division of GRE's massive world-wide affairs into three separate and distinct areas: Financial and Investment, Administration and Personnel, and Insurance Operations, including Reinsurance and Life – with each area being headed up by its own managing director. Each member of this triumvirate would be precisely equal in rank, and any dispute would be settled, in the early days at least, by Bigland, who, on his retirement, was to step upstairs to be deputy chairman.

Gordon did not, of course, name names. But nobody could have been in the slightest doubt that one of them should be that of Donald Gordon. The other two were Peter Dugdale – who eventually got, and still has, the top executive job at GRE – and Peter Greenfield, whom many saw as the front-runner at the time.

The proposals went down like the proverbial lead balloon. A multitude of objections were raised, but the most telling of them, which Bigland emphasised in a letter to DG dated 4 January 1978, was that one of the three would very soon emerge as top dog. And again, it would seem, there was absolutely no doubt in the minds of any of the protagonists as to whom this would be – Donald Gordon.

As always, Gordon fought hard, but fairly. He went over to London in January 1978 and battled with Collins, with Bigland, with all and sundry. But he was unable to beat the system. He returned home, to write to Bigland on 3 February about "the very traumatic week" that he had just spent in London. And, one would not be surprised, to begin to give some serious thought to the options that were open to him as the prime mover in GRE's most important overseas asset.

"Not so," he says to-day, "I was disappointed, of course, at first, as I still think that a company of the size and complexity of GRE could only have benefited from the proposals that I had put forward. That's all in the past, of course, but with all due modesty it is intriguing to speculate as to what might have been the outcome over the past ten years or so had my proposals been accepted.

"I was serious, and I was prepared at that time to move to London if need be. Anyway, disappointed as I was, I came back to Johannesburg determined only to develop Liberty Life to its fullest potential – and within the greater Guardian Royal Exchange Group."

In London, however, they saw it differently. As Greenfield recalls it, "GRE was, and still is, a pretty conservative institution, and, to me, it was surprising that Donald Gordon had stayed with us so long. I thought that he may well have felt inhibited – there were always things that he wanted to do, and that he had to fight for. I, in fact, supported Donald's troika proposals, although I knew full well that we'd have a troika for a week – and then it would be DG all the way. Simply, though, I think the way the establishment saw it was that we had a tiger by the tail – and, had the tiger had its own way, well, he might have proved a bit difficult to control. Anyhow, as the dust began to settle, we in London began to give very serious thought indeed to the future of our South African involvement – and to that 'note' I had addressed to Bigland two years earlier."

Writing many years after these events, in November 1986, Greenfield recalled that: "I was convinced that the gestation period (of the buy-back deal as a whole) was definitely elephantine, as far as GRE were concerned. DG was also aware that a parting would result in time unless the troika idea succeeded. However, I was a little surprised (when I found in my files my 'note' of March 1976) by how firmly and how long before the sale my views had been expressed to Bigland and the Chairman, Tim Collins."

By early 1978, therefore – from whichever side of the Equator one is viewing matters – a parting of the ways was inevitable.

The pace began to quicken, with Ernest Bigland flying to Johannesburg on 27 February 1978. His discussions with Donald Gordon over the next few days, before he flew on to Cape Town on 2 March for a brief holiday, were mostly concerned with relations between Johannesburg and London after his retirement. Peter Dugdale had been appointed to succeed him, and it must have required all of Bigland's tact and persuasive powers to convince Gordon that a satisfactory relationship could be evolved.

"It was not an easy situation," DG recalls. "I had worked happily and very productively with Ernest all those years, and now they had put someone I hardly knew, someone they had imported from Canada, into a position nominally senior to myself, or at least in a position theoretically to call the shots. Yet I was technically the senior; not only was I managing director of GRE's most important international asset, but I had been on the main GRE Board for the past six years, and Dugdale was not even a director at the time. Fortunately, he was a very charismatic man with a great sense of humour, but that alone could not necessarily make for the sort of dynamic business relationship that was needed, or that I was accustomed to."

So, if the question of "buy-back" or "disinvestment" was discussed on this visit, it was in a very minor key. "If it was mentioned, I didn't take it seriously," says DG, "I couldn't imagine that London could possibly be seriously considering selling us out." And, so he says, he put the matter to the back of his mind, as being totally unthinkable.

But it was not to remain in abeyance for long. In March, Peter Greenfield arrived on what was ostensibly a routine visit to attend the year-end Board meetings of the three Group companies, Guardian Assurance Holdings, Liberty Life and the short-term arm, Guardian Assurance SA, of all of which Gordon had by now assumed the chairmanship. During this visit, in private talks with Gordon which, Greenfield acknowledges, had been pre-planned between Bigland and himself, Greenfield (at least as he himself thought) made it very plain that Guardian Royal Exchange was indeed serious about reducing its South African involvement. And he also made it clear that it was the view of Bigland and himself – the two GRE directors most closely involved with Liberty Life – that disinvestment could only be successfully achieved if a deal were evolved with which Gordon himself was completely comfortable. Even so, DG was shocked. He saw the decision to disinvest as totally bizarre and, somewhat uncharacteristically, it was some time before he actually appreciated the fantastic opportunity that had so nonchalantly been thrown into his lap.

For a long time, DG found it impossible to believe that London really planned to dispose of its Liberty Life interests, but shock turned into anger as the concept of the proposed rejection filtered finally into his mind. "My impression, looking back, is that Greenfield fairly casually mentioned to me that there might just be the opportunity for a large piece of Guardian Holdings to be acquired. And he thought that, perhaps if I used some ingenuity, I could find a way. I didn't really take it seriously. It was beyond my comprehension that a sell-out could be in their minds. We'd made such a massive contribution to the success of GRE, particularly in the life area, that the concept of even contemplating the disposal of even a fraction of such an irreplacable asset was quite inconceivable to me.

"I knew Bigland regarded Liberty Life as the jewel in the Guardian Royal Exchange crown and I felt very let down by both him and Tim Collins. Collins and I had never really established a close relationship. We respected each other, but I always felt he was cautious, or possibly nervous, when I was around. I could never explain this but put it down to his natural shyness.

"In retrospect, I now totally accept that Bigland's action in this matter was to maintain the equilibrium of the new GRE management structure under Dugdale, given the rather withdrawn and laid-back attitude of the Chairman, Tim Collins, who in Bigland's view could have had some difficulty in coping with the dynamism and thrust of GRE's burgeoning South African subsidiary. Bigland's objective was to prevent disruption and conflicts of personality arising in the future, in circumstances where a somewhat conservative British institution at a relatively mature stage of its development would be exposed, without his intervention, to Liberty Life's unusually dynamic approach.

"Bigland and I had developed a unique and highly successful *modus vivendi* over a very long period of years and it might have been difficult, certainly in the short term, for Collins or Dugdale, or anyone else for that matter, to assume the London end of that relationship. He was also obviously eager to give me the opportunity of having a free hand to take Liberty Life onwards to its exciting destiny."

On 2 April 1978, Donald Gordon flew to London on what proved to be an unusually long visit. He attended the GRE Board on 5 April, and he had a number of talks, both formally and privately, with Ernest Bigland, Peter Dugdale and Tim Collins. When Gordon flew out of London to New York on 26 April, he was in no doubt that Guardian Royal Exchange was serious in its intentions regarding Liberty Life, and equally sure that the situation could be resolved in one way, and in one way only – by control passing to himself and his colleagues. And this, one should appreciate, was long before the international concept of management buy-outs became generally acceptable.

Overall, though, Gordon was still far from happy with the situation. "I told them they were mad, that they were irresponsible even to think of disposing of the jewel in GRE's crown. I was angry and I felt rejected at the mere thought, after all we had achieved together, that such a thing was seriously proposed. I made this very clear, and I made it even clearer that, after fourteen years of a happy and mutually prosperous association, there was no possible circumstance in which I would get into bed with any other partner. If they wanted to sell control of Liberty Life to any outside party I did not approve of, then I would have no part of it – I simply wouldn't be around any more."

All this and more was thrashed out in those dramatic – and frequently traumatic – April talks. But the principle was settled: Gordon would go back to Johannesburg and put that well-known ingenuity to work. The amount of money involved, some R30 million, was in the stratosphere by the standards of the day, but DG was determined not to falter.

He returned to Johannesburg on 5 May – and immediately the

midnight oil began to burn at Guardian Liberty Centre. All those in Liberty Life's top echelons are accustomed to working under pressure, but the pressures, trauma and excitement of the weeks that followed are still remembered as something special. Most of the work was done by Gordon himself and his closest colleague, Michael Rapp, but the inner circle involved in the brainstorming that followed also included Farrell Sher and Roy McAlpine, both now executive directors of Liberty Holdings, and Mark Winterton, now joint managing director of Liberty Life. Monty Hilkowitz, Winterton's predecessor, and Gordon's long-serving secretary, Maureen Hart, who worked with him throughout the GRE era, were also very much in the thick of things.

One major complication at the time was that the holding company's own control of Liberty Life was about to be strengthened, involving a further capital injection. In earlier years, the South African interests of Manufacturers Life of Canada and of Sun Life of Canada had been acquired for, in part, the issue of Liberty Life shares. Between them, the two Canadian companies held in total 1,7 million shares in Liberty Life. Fortuituously, but also inconveniently, negotiations had started earlier in the year with both companies, and in March 1978 it had been agreed in principle that Guardian Holdings would buy these shares in Liberty Life at R9 a share, or some R15,3 million. This would raise the holding company's stake in Liberty Life to 65 per cent.

While these deals were being negotiated, the matter of financing that R15 million arose, and it was decided by Liberty Life's team, for various good reasons, to do it through an issue of non-redeemable preference shares, since the object of the exercise would be defeated if it became necessary to issue equity capital. The obvious source to approach was Barclays Bank, Liberty Life's lead banker for over twenty years. "I called Bob Aldworth (then Barclays' MD)", says Gordon, "only to be told that Barclays would not be interested because they were over their ceiling for providing preference share capital for that year. Apparently, they had just handled an issue of R100 million of similar type finance for the Anglo American group. I said to Aldworth, with pointed and considerable anger, that we too were very important clients of Barclays, and they shouldn't concentrate all their efforts on Anglo American at the expense of other clients. That same afternoon Nedbank – or rather its subsidiary, Union Acceptances Limited (UAL) – took the whole R15 million issue. This followed a lunch with UAL's then managing director, Johan Nel, whom I told in some detail of my morning's disenchantment with Barclays. He went back to his office and by 2.15 pm they had jumped into the breach without fuss or hesitation."

Rather amusingly, the lunch with Nel had been designed to mend bridges and smooth feathers ruffled by the Liberty Life acquisition the previous year of control of First Union General Investment Trust from under the nose of Union Acceptances, and of Old Mutual.

Had Nedbank at that time not been firmly ensconced in the orbit of the Old Mutual, it is not inconceivable that the whole history and orientation of South Africa's major financial institutions could have been vastly different from the pattern that has actually emerged. Nedbank could well have been offered the opportunity of participating in the management buy-out that was instead offered to – and grabbed with alacrity by – Standard Bank. But the Old Mutual connection made this virtually impossible.

The sale of the Canadians' Liberty Life shares to Guardian Holdings and Nedbank's financing of these transactions were to become of considerable significance when the Gordon/Rapp think-tank finally came up with a feasible scheme – which, quite remarkably, was achieved within the space of two weeks. Recalls Greenfield, who flew out to Johannesburg on 22 May to be presented with a fully workable plan: "I just couldn't believe that even Donald Gordon and Michael Rapp could have come up with such a comprehensive scheme in so short a time. So I thought that they must have been working on it from much earlier. Obviously, they spotted a window, and took it." This was certainly not the case, but one could not blame Greenfield for thinking so.

In essence, the plan involved the purchase, from Guardian Royal Exchange, of 21,5 million of its shares in Guardian Holdings. This was the number of shares that, when added to those shares already personally held by Gordon and Rapp, would give them control of GAH, and through it, of Liberty Life, thanks to Guardian Holdings' 65 per cent holding. Control would be exercised through a new company, which would be named Liblife Controlling Corporation. Cash flows and dividend flows were precisely calculated and re-calculated, and these indicated that the maximum price that could be paid for these 21,5 million shares was R1,25 a share, a matter of R27 million, a truly massive sum at that time, and perhaps equal, in 1989 money terms, to at least R300 million.

But before this could be presented to Greenfield and, later, to the Board of GRE, three major problems had to be solved. First, where to borrow a sum of that magnitude in their private capacities; second, how to repay the enormous debt they were contemplating assuming; and third, how to persuade GRE to accept R1,25 for a share then trading at R1,45, to say nothing of any enhanced value that might reasonably be attributed to control.

The second problem had to be solved before the first could even be addressed. What eventually evolved was a refinement of the preference share scheme that had been devised for the take-out of the two Canadian companies. This involved a double layer of preference shares; indeed, a triple layer if one took into account the preference shares in Liberty Life itself, and yet another if one included the preference shares in Fugit, the investment trust subsidiary even lower down in the chain. It was complicated and ingenious, and in the event this imaginative financing proved so effective that all of the R21,5 million issue of redeemable prefs was redeemed within four years, instead of the seven years that it had originally been calculated would be needed to clear Gordon and Rapp of the very heavy debt burden that they were proposing to take on.

Next came the question of the banker. Who was to be invited to be the institutional funding partner in the future control of the Liberty Life Group? "Our natural source of finance would have been Barclays," says Gordon, "but I was, at that time, so upset and annoyed with Aldworth over my previous request for preference share financing that I refused to go back to them on any account. We carefully considered Nedbank as it had been so helpful when Barclays was not, but were put off by the close links it had with the Old Mutual, and the possibility of interference from that source. Of course, Old Mutual was not only Liberty Life's major competitor, but the relationship between their Chairman, Jan van der Horst, and myself had been somewhat soured by the Fugit affair a year or so earlier. We then considered Volkskas, and the possibilities of access into the Afrikaans market that such a link would open up. I phoned the Chairman of Volkskas (then Dr Hurter) and asked him for an appointment to come and have a cup of tea. However, at this time, and very unfortunately for Volkskas as events turned out, they were in the throes of internecine war with Bankorp and Sanlam. Whatever his motives, it was fairly obvious to me that at that moment in time Dr Hurter found it inappropriate for him to meet with me. We were left with Standard Bank, with whom we had had virtually no business dealings at all up to that time.

"Time was moving on, and I was due back in London the following week. [That was for Ernest Bigland's retirement festivities, culminating in a farewell party on 8 June, but vital discussions would take place at the same time.] So, I think it was on the Tuesday morning, 6 June, I arranged a meeting with Henri de Villiers, then managing director of Standard Bank [now Chairman of Standard Bank and deputy chairman of Liberty Holdings and Liberty Life]. We met in my office at around 7 am. I put to him the proposal that we should acquire control of Guardian Holdings and that we would need funding of some R25 million – we had to have a margin for error. As a quid pro quo Standard could acquire 25 per cent of the equity of Liblife Controlling for R2 million. Rapp and I would put in R2 million and R4 million respectively for our equity shares of 25 per cent and 50 per cent." These amounts were settled by Gordon and Rapp transferring personal shareholdings in Guardian Holdings to Liblife Controlling Corporation.

"As the 50 per cent shareholder, I was to have a casting vote and be entitled to the chairmanship for life. De Villiers, who had been a merchant banker earlier in his distinguished career, quickly grasped the essentials and the magnitude of the opportunity and, subject to the bank Board's approval, the partnership was sealed – the partnership between Standard Bank and Liberty Life which was to have such a dramatic effect on the evolution of the South African financial sector and all the mergers that followed."

It is amusing to note that in Donald Gordon's diary for 6 June 1978, the entry – for 7.30 am, not 7.00 – is "Andre" de Villiers, rather than "Henri". This confirms, beyond a shadow of doubt, that any previous business contact between the two had been tenuous indeed. Gordon notes that De Villiers makes a point of always being early for important appointments; "and on that momentous occasion, we both were at the office well before the appointed time."

From De Villiers, confirmation is immediate. "Prior to June 1978, our contact with Liberty Life, and with Donald Gordon, had been minimal, even adversarial [a reference back twelve years in time to the early battles in the mutual fund industry between National Growth Fund, with which De Villiers had been associated, and the pioneer mutual, Sage Fund, which Gordon and Shill had created]. But this proposition was a natural. As a merchant banker by training, maybe I think differently to conventional commercial bankers, so, from the very outset, I had no problem at all with this deal – so long as we, Standard, got the right share of the action."

In the event, Standard emerged with 25 per cent of the equity of Liblife Controlling – the "right share" in De Villiers' view – but there were, he recalls, "a few problems over this". Nonetheless, he sees it, in retrospect, as: "An incredible deal – it was not just the sum involved, though R25 million was not chicken feed in 1978 – but for Liberty Life, and Standard, it was so much bigger, so much more important, than was visualised at the time. Everything that has happened since flowed from this deal. DG emerged as top dog – he could now do just what he wanted and he was answerable to nobody – not even to the Standard Bank. When I sold the 1978 deal to my Board, on the basis that our advances were well, indeed very well, secured and that we were also in for 25 per cent of something big – something that could only get bigger – I said then that it wasn't the end of the line. But, even then, I didn't anticipate Standard taking joint control of the Liberty Life Group in 1983. Except, of course, that we haven't really got true joint control; DG is life Chairman, and our full influence is scheduled to take effect only after his retirement, when we will have the right to nominate the Chairman. That's the way Donald wanted it."

After that digression, the chronicle returns to 6 June 1978. There was that seminal morning meeting with De Villiers, and then at 6 pm Gordon caught the plane to London. There, on 8 June, he attended an emotional farewell party for his friend Bigland. And, in many hours of intensive and gruelling negotiations, mainly between himself, Bigland (who maintained a powerful position within Guardian Royal Exchange as deputy chairman) and Dugdale, the main points concerning GRE's disinvestment from South Africa, which Gordon still maintained was both unwise so far as GRE was concerned and disloyal to himself personally, were hammered out.

When Gordon returned to Johannesburg on 19 June, terms were broadly settled: Guardian Royal Exchange would sell control to a consortium controlled by DG and backed by a "major South African financial institution". Michael Rapp had not been mentioned to GRE at this stage, and neither had the name of the major financial institution concerned. Minor details like price and financing remained to be ironed out. Meanwhile, the deal, in broad principle, would go before the Guardian Royal Exchange Board on 27 June.

Back in Johannesburg, Gordon and Rapp prepared for the final battles. They re-worked their homework: R1,25 remained the maximum price they could pay – and get out of debt by redeeming the preference share capital advanced by Standard Bank within a reasonable time-span. Standard Bank, subject to its Board's approval, remained their chosen financier, but its participation was still to be confirmed. When, on 28 June, Gordon received the news that the Guardian Royal Exchange Board had given its approval to the final negotiations, he arranged another session with De Villiers. This was on 5 July, and De Villiers still seemed very much onside, if not indeed excited by the whole prospect.

Gordon and Rapp flew to London on Sunday 16 July 1978 to what was quite possibly the most important week in their lives to that date. On the Monday, they worked and reworked their figures. As Gordon recalls: "All the figures had been checked and re-checked, but in a situation like this one wants to check again. And Michael and I had arrived in London without a calculator between us. So we sat for hours, working every possible combination and permutation in longhand." Rapp's recollection is more succinct: "The blighter made me work them all out – at least three times – on paper – and still he wasn't satisfied until he had rechecked my arithmetic for himself yet again."

That afternoon, Gordon went alone to see Tim Collins, and strongly expressed his views. "I told him again, but for the last time, that they were mad, that this was an ill-conceived deal, one that was not in the best interests of the Guardian Royal Exchange. I told him that I wanted no part of it, that they were forcing decisions on me that I would much prefer not to have to make. I was going to have to take on burdens and responsibilities far greater than I wanted. But, if GRE was still determined to sell, Collins had to know that I was the only possible buyer; I told him again that I would not get into bed with anyone else. And I tendered my written resignation from the Board of Guardian Royal Exchange – I had to have freedom to negotiate at arm's length and have no conflicts of interest. On this, I made my position absolutely clear."

On the morning of Tuesday 18 July, Gordon woke around 4 am. "By 4.30, I was wide awake on a perfect English midsummer's day, and there was a lot on my mind. So I started to pace up and down in the apartment lent to me by the GRE. Michael and I had arranged, when we parted about midnight the previous evening, after battling to complete our final calculations, that we would reconvene at about 8 am, but here was I up and about and raring to go, and he was still fast asleep and probably snoring contentedly. So, as the dawn turned to bright daylight, I telephoned him at his flat: 'Get over here immediately, you're late for our meeting and we've a hell of a lot of work to do.' 'Sorry, Donald,' said a sheepish Michael in a very sleepy voice. 'My watch must have stopped at 4.30 am: I've overslept. I'll be right over.' When Michael arrived about thirty minutes later, still blissfully unaware of the hour, and having driven across half of London in record time, he remarked how lucky he had been with traffic – no hold-ups at all." This was a good and early start to another day's hard bargaining, mainly on the question of price. DG didn't have the heart to tell Rapp until a few weeks later that he had actually started work before 5 am on that particular summer's day: "Michael was never known to be an early riser."

During the morning of that Tuesday, when the question of price was being toughly negotiated, Gordon excused himself at precisely 11 am to make an important telephone call. Unbeknown to the GRE negotiating team, it was to De Villiers in Johannesburg, where the clock was one hour ahead of London. In that precious hour, the Standard Bank Board had met, in true banking tradition, at exactly 11 am South African time – and had agreed within that hour to the Bank's proposed financing of the deal. Gordon had his money and his backing, and he returned to the fray with Dugdale and Bigland like a giant refreshed, but still without disclosing the nature of his telephone conversation. "They thought I'd got my second wind – they didn't know what had hit them."

By the evening, the negotiating committee of Dugdale, Bigland, Greenfield, Rapp and Gordon had reached agreement on the broad general terms. The price was to be raised from R1,25 to an effective R1,35 by means of a special 10 cent dividend to be declared by Liberty Holdings, a change which, of course, would not affect the Gordon/Rapp financing position at all, though it would reduce the net assets that they were buying by some R5 million. Many more details remained to be ironed out, but the battle on price appeared, to Gordon at least, to be over for the moment.

However, deals of this magnitude are never consummated in one session, particularly not in the City of London with a conservative and traditional insurance company. On the following day, as Gordon recalls, the atmosphere changed. "We began, again and again, to go over the same points; points that I had assumed were agreed. The atmosphere changed from one of cordial, if tough, negotiations, to one approaching acrimony."

Greenfield's recollection is that, although the Guardian Royal Exchange Board had agreed to the deal in principle on 27 June, leaving the details, and especially the all-important "detail" of price, to be settled by the committee that was negotiating on 17 and 18 July, some members of the GRE Board became "a little restive" when they learned that the committee had settled at an effective price of only R1,35. The background to this is that the Guardian Holdings share price in Johannesburg, possibly on rumours of something important about to happen, had run ahead to R1,75 by Friday 14 July. The quotations of both Guardian Holdings and Liberty Life were suspended, at the request of the companies, on Monday 17th, but the R1,75 closing price still stood.

Another factor, according to Greenfield, was that both he and Bigland were part of the negotiating team. "Because of our long association with DG, we were rather seen, by some elements on the GRE Board, to be 'Gordon men'; and, of course, Bigland, having retired as MD, was no longer an executive director."

So the pressure was on, and whatever the real reason, the Guardian Royal Exchange Board, that Wednesday, set up a reinforced negotiating sub-committee, comprising Dugdale, Bigland and one Bill Ritchie, a Scottish accountant who was a long-standing non-executive GRE director and a partner in the eminent accounting firm of Touche Ross.

After that tough Wednesday, Gordon, never the most patient of men, and who resented Ritchie querying matters and agreements that he thought were already settled, woke in a truculent mood. "I was not going to be pushed around any more," he recalls, "so I decided to disappear for the day." He left the flat (GRE's luxurious guest flat in Whitehall Court, Westminster) and went about his own affairs. When he got back that night, there were endless messages waiting for him – all of them from GRE, Dugdale and Bigland.

Next day, Friday 21 July, Gordon answered a call from Dugdale, who was very concerned as to where Gordon had been the previous day, and complained plaintively that "we waited around the whole day for you so we could continue the talks." "I told him that I was fed up with all the bickering and that as far as I was concerned, the matter was clear-cut. Either GRE goes ahead at R1,35 or the whole thing is over and I am out. I'm going back to Johannesburg tonight; Michael Rapp is here if you need to query any details, and I will be at the end of a telephone from Monday if he can't sort everything out." With that, DG caught the Friday evening plane back to Johannesburg without any further contact or discussion. While this may well have been an excellent negotiating ploy, to a large extent it was also a reflection of his resentment and impatience, which were very real.

On the Saturday, both Rapp and Greenfield recall playing very bad golf together. That game may have been important, however, because Rapp remembers telling Greenfield that Guardian Royal Exchange was pushing Gordon too hard, and could easily lose him altogether. Greenfield remembers this, but says that he did not take it too seriously. "Remember," he twinkles, "I had by now been associated with DG for fifteen years, and had seen all the strategies and posturings before. Both Rapp and Gordon are consummate negotiators, and together they make a truly great team. Perhaps I should call it rather a 'great act' – I really don't know which of them most deserved the Oscar."

On Sunday, Monday and Tuesday, the international telephone lines between Johannesburg and London were humming. Eventually matters were settled – and, with hindsight, settled to the satisfaction of all concerned. The effective price of R1,35 (including that 10 cent special dividend) may have been a bit on the tough side, as some press comment at the time pointed out, but Rapp's recollection is that "we didn't think at the time that we were getting it cheap". Gordon feels the same, and repeats his *bon mot* of the time: "Why should I have paid Guardian Royal Exchange for my own goodwill?" Greenfield's comment is that: "We were in the right ball park – at the most we were arguing over another 10 cents." The 10,4 per cent of Liberty Holdings that Guardian Royal Exchange retained, and still retains, is today worth over R180 million, and yields almost R6 million a year in dividends.

The 21,5 million shares purchased from the GRE were augmented by shares already owned by Gordon and Rapp to achieve their control position. The number of Liberty Holdings' shares held by the top company, Liblife Controlling, was approximately 23 million in total, now increased to around 23,7 million, or 52 per cent of the issued equity at the 1988 year end.

In this early management buy-out prototype, the Liberty Life

Group's senior executives were given the opportunity of acquiring 15 per cent of the equity in varying proportions. All those who have stayed with the Group for the past decade have become multimillionaires. Liberty Life today is run probably by more millionaires and multimillionaires than any public corporation in the Republic. Monty Hilkowitz stayed only seven-and-three-quarter years and thus realised only a small part of his participation before he left for Australia, a decision that was to cost him about R12 million, a remarkable measure of the unprecedented success that followed the GRE era.

Later on, younger executives would be brought into the circle to provide Liberty Life with a uniquely motivated elite. Many of these are destined to achieve undreamed of financial rewards over the next decade.

By Wednesday 26 July, the Heads of Agreement that had been drawn up the previous week and fine-tuned by telephone were finally signed in London. Peter Dugdale signed "for and on behalf of The Guardian Royal Exchange Assurance Limited", a major public company in the United Kingdom. Michael Rapp signed "for and on behalf of Donald Gordon", a private citizen of the Republic of South Africa. The contrast was, and remains, a striking commentary on the sheer force in the world financial community that Donald Gordon had already become in his own right.

One final condition was imposed by the Guardian Royal Exchange Chairman, Tim Collins. Donald Gordon was to withdraw his resignation from the Guardian Royal Exchange Board. He was indeed happy to do so, and he remains there to this day.

The deal that returned control of Liberty Holdings and thus of Liberty Life itself to South Africa – and, even more importantly in terms of what would follow, effectively to Donald Gordon personally – was a crucial event in that institution's tumultuous and dynamic affairs. Its almost incredible progress over the next decade, particularly in the United Kingdom, flowed directly from the dramatic events of the 1978 European summer. For those directly involved, both in London and in Johannesburg, even Wimbledon, Royal Ascot and all the other distractions of the "London Season" were overshadowed by the significance of Liberty Life's change of control and return to South Africa.

That is why this episode is chosen as the starting point of this saga.

Certainly, so far as the Liberty Life Group's senior executives were concerned, a whole new world of opportunity was opened up by the deal, and by their inclusion, by Gordon and Rapp, in that management buy-out. The Group's stalwarts – those who, working alongside DG, have helped to make the Group what it is today – such as Monty Hilkowitz, Mark Winterton, Steve Handler, Farrell Sher, Roy McAlpine, James Inglis, Alan Romanis, Wolf Cesman, Lewis Neuberger, and many others, all benefited greatly from the events of 1978 when they were given that unprecedented opportunity to participate indirectly in the equity of the new Liblife Controlling Corporation.

All have prospered mightily as a consequence; and, apart from Hilkowitz, all these senior executives are still in Liberty Life's service – more than a decade later.

Ernest Bigland continued to serve as joint deputy chairman of Liberty Life until May 1984, when he duly retired from all the Liberty Life Group boards at the Annual General Meeting following his attainment of the mandatory retirement age of seventy. He died suddenly in December 1985 of a rare strain of leukemia. Donald Gordon was the only non-family member present at the small funeral in a freezing, snow-bound English country churchyard. So ended the remarkable relationship of two men from totally disparate backgrounds who had met and respected each other and who did great things together. "It was perhaps the most meaningful business relationship of my life. I shall never forget Ernest," Gordon says many years later, still with great feeling and emotion.

# 2 Planting the Acorn

This book, recording some of the epic events in the history of Liberty Life, is inevitably also the story of Donald Gordon, for it was he who conceived it, breathed life into it, and, by the sheer force of his will and determination, built it to be a major force in the life insurance and financial services fields of two of the world's leading financial centres, London and Johannesburg. Donald Gordon's dazzling performance over the past thirty years is virtually unrivalled in the world of life insurance, and has few parallels in any other financial field. As an innovative genius, he has revolutionised life insurance in South Africa, and has had a profound impact on the industry in the United Kingdom. The extent to which his companies, and the fortunate early investors in them, have prospered is astounding. An investment of R1 000 made thirty-one years ago is today worth over R4 million, and some of those early investors, or their heirs, to this day enjoy the fruits of that fabulous fortune.

The outstanding achievements of Donald Gordon, financial engineer extraordinary, which unfold in these pages, provide all the ingredients of a spectacular and dynamic career.

Liberty Life Association of Africa Limited was incorporated on 10 September 1957, twenty-seven years after Gordon himself was born. The company was registered to undertake life assurance business on 22 August 1958 and its first policy was issued on 1 October 1958. At the first Board meeting, held in Johannesburg on 8 October 1957, there were only two directors, Donald Gordon and Sydney Lipworth. The company was initially operated by a total staff of three: Gordon, his first secretary Mavis Venables, and Louis Miller, the master life insurance salesman whom DG had persuaded to join the fledgeling company from the up-market Prudential.

Brian Young was due to join the company on 1 November 1958 and Hugh Rubin early in 1959, at the same time as Lily Cane, the ever-loyal bookkeeper whose son, Joel, a chartered accountant, works closely with DG to this day as a deputy general manager of Liberty Holdings. Sydney Lipworth remained a non-executive director until his resignation in the wake of the Guardian takeover in 1964. His advice and support, however, played a major role in the difficult formative years. He emigrated to the United Kingdom in 1964 and made a great success in life insurance, as is recorded elsewhere in these pages. In September 1987, having greatly distinguished himself in his career, he was appointed Chairman of the Monopolies and Mergers Commission, one of the most prestigious and influential business positions in the UK.

Donald Gordon was born in Johannesburg on 24 June 1930. His father, Nathan, born in Kovno in Lithuania, had arrived in South Africa in 1918, at the age of twenty-two, a refugee from the pogroms of those times. Soon afterwards he married his cousin, Sheila Shewitz, and set up home in Johannesburg. "He worked very hard all of his life," Gordon recalls, "but for virtually no material reward. He ended his working career as a credit manager with Advance Laundries. In the mid-sixties, when he retired, he was earning about R250 a month, and his pension, after a lifetime of hard and devoted work, was a mere R28 per month. The injustice of this always rankled with me, and must have been a factor, if a subconscious one, in leading me into life insurance and pensions. My father was the only man I have known who was capable of working harder than me. I am happy that, towards the end of his hard life, he was able to see that Liberty Life would be a success."

Donald, their second child, was educated at King Edward VII School (KES) in Johannesburg, an establishment for which he still feels considerable affection and loyalty. The school was across the road from the Gordon home in Johannesburg's Yeoville suburb, and the young Donald only left home for classes as the bell began to toll at 8 am. He was a relatively studious boy, very steady if not outstandingly brilliant, and he matriculated well in 1947, gaining a first-class pass with distinctions in mathematics, physical science and geography.

Interestingly, in view of his immense success in finance and insurance, he would have preferred to have been a physicist or a scientist. In an interview some years ago, he said: "My bent was towards chemical engineering. This seemed to make sense. It fitted in with my flair and the particular subjects I was good at, mathematics, science and geography. But going to university would have been an unacceptable financial strain on the family. So, somewhat reluctantly, I went into articles as a chartered accountant, which I hated for the first three months until I realised I had to buckle down to it and try to make a success of my career if I was to get anywhere in life. After this major change in mind set, I got a big kick out of accountancy, which turned out to be the foundation of my life's work."

He joined accountants Isaacs & Kessel (still, as Kessel Feinstein the auditors to Liberty Life, an indication of the extent to which loyalty plays a part in his business philosophy). During the course of his articles, he studied the theoretical side of accountancy at the University of the Witwatersrand (Wits). Accountancy professor Tommy Cairns is on record as having said, several years later, that, of all the students who had passed through his hands over the years, "only three stood out as being of really exceptional ability." They were Derek Keys, a classmate of Gordon at KES and now Chairman of the giant mining house, General Mining Union Corporation (Gencor), Mark Weinberg (also educated at KES, but a year behind Keys and Gordon), the founder of Abbey Life and of Hambro Life, and now, as Sir Mark, Chairman of Allied Dunbar in London – and Donald Gordon. DG nowadays reluctantly acknowledges only Keys as his superior as an accountant, but points out that: "Of course, at school, Weinberg was our junior by a year."

It is an amazing coincidence that the lives of the three have remained intertwined. Gordon played a major role in the formation of Abbey Life, the keystone of Weinberg's fortune, and Keys is today on the Board of TransAtlantic Holdings, the company that Gordon created in 1980 as the holding company for Liberty Life's extensive international interests.

Given Cairns's accolade, it is not surprising that the young Gordon made rapid progress at Kessel Feinstein. In January 1950, some months before his twentieth birthday, he was made responsible for one of the firm's more important audits, that of the Standard General Insurance Company, the South African subsidiary of the large Italian insurance group, Assicurazioni Generali, of Trieste. That audit, for which he was to retain responsibility until 1957, was of crucial importance to his career, and had a strong influence on his final area of specialisation – the life insurance industry.

He found Standard General's records in poor shape at that time. As he puts it: "I just about rewrote the records in the first year. In the process I learnt about as much as anyone could about insurance accounting and just what could go wrong." Gordon became totally engrossed with insurance and quite fascinated with its various aspects, and such was his impact on Standard General's managing director that, in 1952, he was offered the position of general manager in charge of administration at a salary some fifteen times his then stipend as an articled clerk. He had by this time passed all the examinations needed for qualification as a chartered accountant, but still had a year to go before his articles would be completed, to entitle him to put the letters CA (SA) after his name. Even so, the temptation of a salary of some £3 600 per annum, plus his compelling interest in insurance, persuaded him to accept the offer – only to be turned down a few weeks later because the full Board of Standard General thought that, at twenty-two, he was too young for the job. He still remembers the intense disappointment he felt at the time, and marvels at the dramatic effect this twist of fate had on his whole future.

Gordon duly completed his articles and qualified as an accountant in 1953. In 1954, aged only twenty-four, he was offered a partnership in Kessel Feinstein, which he accepted, although he had already made up his mind that his ultimate career would be outside the accountancy profession. He continued to head the Standard General audit until he retired from practice. Insurance was getting seriously into his blood.

It was round about that time, Lipworth recalls, that DG began to think seriously about forming his own company. Lipworth was a year behind Gordon at KES (and thus a contemporary of Weinberg), and he was studying law at Wits. They were neighbours in Yeoville, and frequently bussed to the city together. "It was in 1953 or 1954, on top of the bus," Lipworth remembers, "that Donald first mentioned to me his idea of starting an insurance company. At first, it was going to be a form of pension fund, but it soon evolved into a full-blown life company. I told him not to be daft. But, over the years, he would keep coming back to it, and gradually his ideas crystallised."

By 1956, DG was firmly committed to his dream – he was determined to start his own life insurance company. He drew up a document setting out his proposals for the formation of a new company. It was a quite remarkable paper, and in it he foreshadowed many of the factors and developments that were to prove vital to the success of the fledgeling Liberty Life in the exciting years that lay ahead.

He strongly emphasised the advantages of establishing a new life office in Southern Africa. First, he noted that interest rates, the lifeblood of life assurance activity, are normally higher in young, developing countries than in older, developed economies. Then there was the point that profits arising from life assurance activities were reasonably favourably taxed. He next drew attention to the tremendous growth that had taken place in recent years in the pension fund field, and noted that with legislation pending to control pension funds, "an unprecedented flow of wealth, and also of cash" would be diverted to local insurance companies. At that stage, the life market was dominated by the three Cape Town-based mutual insurers, the Old Mutual, Sanlam, and Southern Life; with African Life, the Prudential, and Sun Life and Manufacturers Life (both Canadian), also very much in the picture.

And, although inflation was hardly an issue in the mid-fifties, he foresaw that it would rapidly become one, and pointed out that there would be an ever-increasing demand for life insurance as money continued to depreciate and people came to recognise the need for more and more life cover. Next came the telling point that, despite their natural advantages, most existing South African insurance companies were hampered by very high rates of administrative expenditure. These high costs, he postulated, were the result of the shortage of trained people in the insurance industry, and also a reflection of the lack of any incentive to trim overheads because of the wide margin of profitability and the virtual non-existence of effective competition.

He spelt it out: "In the event of a company managing to contain its expenditure at economic levels and making the best use of the prevailing high interest rates, a tremendous amount of life and pension fund business could be written on highly competitive terms with even the oldest established overseas companies. In spite of a fairly general lack of efficiency in the administration of life assurance offices in this country, it is a well-known fact that life assurance companies show very substantial returns to their shareholders, which but emphasises the immense possibilities with efficient management."

Then, many years before its introduction into the international insurance world, DG foreshadowed linked insurance. "It has long been the criticism of life insurance that policyholders are always paid out in depreciated currency. It is proposed to attempt to overcome this drawback by utilising the loan value of the policies of those desiring to participate in investment in terms of real assets such as property and equity shares. This arrangement will not only have the effect of minimising to a large extent the corrosive effect of the depreciation of money but will also decrease future premium payments by the policyholders."

In the event, of course, as linked policies developed, the returns generated from the equity or property investments were utilised to increase the value of the policy itself, rather than to reduce premiums. But Gordon, even before his company came into being, was looking well ahead.

Looking back, twenty-one years later, DG summed up his initial approach to insurance in an interview with the *Financial Mail*. "I was fascinated by the challenge and the mathematical aspects of the life insurance industry. At that time the life insurance industry was somewhat dozy. There was no particular expertise in management or investment and virtually no innovation. What was being done had been done for the last fifty years or more. Nobody had ever tried really to reassess the situation or reappraise the possibilities. The standards of marketing were plainly poor, the quality of the sales representatives was mediocre at best, and the image of the industry wasn't all that progressive, in fact, it was downright dull. I understood the fundamental principles (of life insurance) very clearly. Basically, you take premiums, invest them to get an optimum return, and take off your expenses and mortality costs. We immediately decided to go to the only market I knew, to the people whose needs I understood and identified with. We went straight for the upper market, the business and professional market."

At the time, the Liberty Life approach was regarded as a complete impertinence and it drew considerable criticism from the existing majors. They, DG recalls, "lashed into Liberty Life mercilessly for its sheer cheek in tackling the sophisticated, top-bracket market that they all craved."

Another early advantage stemmed from Gordon's perceptions of profit-sharing. "From the very outset, I appreciated that there was no real scientific and equitable system of passing back to policyholders the benefit of investment results on a year-to-year basis. Nobody was making any constructive effort to pass on these benefits in any way at all. To a large extent investment didn't go much further than gilt-edged and fixed-interest type investment. It was around that time that the whole concept of equity investments was just beginning to come into its own. Prior to this, their suitability and acceptability as life insurance based assets was anathema to the established life insurance industry: equities were regarded as totally unsuitable. They were considered far too risky and volatile actually to be used for the purposes of policyholder security.

"Two basic factors influenced me: that in those days there was no real motivation to run life insurance companies economically and efficiently; and that there was no real attempt to put some dynamism into investment with policyholders' interests in mind. We saw the possibility to develop a highly efficient operation without the wastage caused by the then calibre of insurance company management and staff.

"I saw a tremendous opportunity in that field, and also a tremendous opportunity in terms of putting real investment expertise to work."

Early in 1957, Donald Gordon took the plunge. In probably the most momentous decision in a life that would see many major decisions, he resigned from Kessel Feinstein to devote all of his very considerable energies to getting his life insurance project off the ground. It was a friendly parting, but some of the senior partners were highly sceptical – and showed no hesitation in conveying their views to the brash twenty-seven-year-old who was preparing to take on the South African and international giants.

Although the big rival companies were indeed well established, they were not highly effective at that stage, and therein lay DG's chance, if he could only get the backing he needed.

One of Liberty Life's main rivals, then and now, is Sanlam; it was until early 1989 headed by the late Professor Fred du Plessis, a respected academic when DG was about to start Liberty Life. Asked for his perspective, he commented: "Going back quite a bit, I was interested in the whole financial sector as a professor of money and banking long before 1971 [when he joined Sanlam], and I think that, looking at it from that particular perspective, I would make two comments.

"One is that undoubtedly at the time of the start of Liberty Life there was almost an archaic situation in the life insurance business.

"The second point I would like to make is that undoubtedly

Donny is one of the sharpest brains in business that we have in this country and I've got every respect for the way he took the chance. It's one thing to have an opportunity, but it's quite another thing to grasp that opportunity and to make the most out of it, and he certainly did that."

The senior partner of Kessel Feinstein, Benjamin (Benny) Kessel, was very encouraging, and backed his faith in the young man to the tune of £1 000, becoming one of the seven subscribers to the Memorandum and Articles of Liberty Life when that concern was incorporated on 10 September 1957.

Precious few others, however, shared either the vision of Du Plessis or the faith of Kessel, and the young Gordon received very little other encouragement as he pounded the pavements of Johannesburg, Durban and Cape Town in search of backers to share his vision of those "tremendous opportunities".

Looking back, in the 1978 *FM* interview, DG's comment was: "I think the mere fact of ever getting that £42 000 together was a major achievement, perhaps the most difficult challenge I have ever taken on. At that point, I was certainly not a salesman and I was really far too conservative by nature to be able successfully to persuade people to put up money for a long-term business like life insurance. I told them that it would be perhaps twenty years before they would see any return on their money (some days, when I was particularly brazen, I dared reduce my estimated time-scale to fifteen years, but never to ten years!). This was hardly the recommended way to raise venture capital [another modern financial term unheard of thirty years ago], but my conservative training was too deeply embedded to allow me to cut corners." Not even in the attainment of his dream.

"I probably approached hundreds of people and 98 per cent of them listened carefully. Some politely declined, but others were openly derisory. It took nine months; nine months of disappointment and frustration, trying to get the money together. This was a pretty disheartening time, and it probably accounts for my obsession over the years of always over-capitalising my businesses. In the theme of Scarlett O'Hara, I never wanted to be short of capital again."

In truth, that period was more than disheartening. The going was so tough that even the indomitable DG was on the point of giving up. He was, he once recalled, "within an inch" of accepting a position with the late Philip Frame's Consolidated Textiles. However, at their last negotiating meeting the tough old textile tycoon had a change of heart. "I've decided not to appoint you," he said, "you will never be happy working for anyone other than yourself – you have to be captain of your own ship. Much as I would love to have you with me, I recognise the signs." Gordon secretly agreed with the older man.

Stories of those heart-breaking months are legion, and mostly, no doubt, apocryphal. Rudi Frankel, of Tiger Oats, has quite a vivid recollection of going for a long walk with his young acquaintance and listening carefully to his well-presented plans. Indeed, he firmly believes he was the first to be approached, and records the incident in his own excellent history of Tiger Oats, *Tiger Tapestry*, which was published in 1988. "Donald Gordon came to see me in 1957. We went for a walk and he explained to me his ideas concerning Liberty Life and proposed that I should join him in that venture. Being unsure, I consulted the late Alec Fine, senior partner of our auditors. He had had experience of an insurance company, but it was a slow-going one so he said 'No, leave it alone. There's no money in that.' It was a great pity – to say the least – that I took his advice." Ironically, Alec Fine was the Chairman of Standard General when its Board turned down the proposal to appoint the young Gordon as general manager in 1952.

Another who turned down DG's invitation to take shares was Michael Rapp, later to become one of Gordon's closest associates – and a multimillionaire as a result. Rapp, then twenty-two and newly started in his father's then modest construction business, Rapp & Maister, was enthused with Gordon's ideas, and brashly asked his father for a loan of £100 in order to take up 100 shares. His father said he was irresponsible, so much so that he was tempted to lend Michael the money so that he could lose it, learn the most essential of business lessons (that a fool and his money are soon parted!) early in life, and never be tempted to such lunacy again!

Another of the better stories – and one which also has the merit of being fully authenticated by correspondence – concerns Bertie Lubner, now joint Chairman of the international glass and timber giant, Plate Glass & Shatterprufe Industries. A close friend of DG from childhood, Lubner was then already an established businessman.

In a letter dated 21 August 1957, Gordon wrote to Lubner: "I was upset not to have heard from you following our recent telephone conversation. But you will find attached the memo on the proposed new insurance company (which has now been registered). I think the possibilities are outstanding as you will judge for yourself and I hope you will find your way clear to coming in with me. For the moment, please treat the whole thing as confidential, but if you would like to interest someone else, I would be grateful."

Some twenty years later, in a letter dated 1 December 1976, Lubner finally got around to replying. "Dear Donny, On going through some old personal files I came across a letter and proposal document, copy of which is enclosed, which I am sure will be of interest to you – in fact, I must apologise for not having replied to this letter earlier.

"Actually, I do not think there is any merit in your proposals because whilst the idea may sound good, I, frankly, feel that you have neither the ability or the experience to take on all the many insurance companies who, after all, have been so many years in the field.

"I would, therefore, suggest that you stick to auditing which will provide you with a very good living, and with no complications. However, if you do want to speculate a bit I suggest you spend a bit more time on Cloud Investments, particularly if the syndicate each put in a few more rands per month. What a mug I was!!!"

Lubner relates an amusing anecdote about Cloud Investments, the private investment company of DG and a few friends, which would become a major early shareholder in Liberty Life. His father Morrie, virtually the founder of Plate Glass, was listening to Bertie, Donny and their friends talking about their little investment company, and the money they were going to make. The older man interrupted them: "I'll give you a name for it – Cloud. Your heads are there already, but it sounds to me as if your feet are also firmly planted in the clouds."

Shill has another, and probably more accurate, version of "Cloud". He remembers: "The name Cloud was derived from the initials of the original participants – Clive Rosenberg, Lou (Shill and Doppelt) and Donny."

It is interesting to note that, over the years, Liberty Life has become the largest shareholder in the Lubner's flourishing international enterprise.

But mug he was, indeed, as were the many others who turned the young Gordon away empty-handed. For an original shareholder in Liberty Life, had he merely held on to his shares and not taken up his rights issues, would have seen his investment of the equivalent of R1 000 in 1958 grow to some R4,2 million by 1988. And an avid follower of rights issues, of which there have been many, would have seen that same R1 000 soar to almost R12 million, had he backed his original judgement to the not inconsiderable tune of another R2 million – the bulk of it in the major 1986 issue – over the years.

But, back in 1957, the crystal balls were cloudy, and Gordon, despite his herculean efforts and those of his associates, was having considerable difficulty in getting Liberty Life's capital base up to the statutory minimum of £50 000 (then R100 000) that was required before an insurance company was permitted to start writing business.

Capital came in painfully slowly, and, in the main, in penny packets. The seven original subscribers, in September 1957, who included Gordon himself, as well as Kessel, Young and Rubin, put up £1 000 apiece, for a total of £7 000. On 2 January 1958, another £3 000 dribbled in, including £200 from DG's own private company, Donshel Investments (Pty), and £1 000 from Lipworth. Total by the end of January 1958 – a princely £10 000.

In the next five months, DG put in overtime at hard selling. The result was that a further 19 000 shares were allotted on 2 June 1958, of which 1 000 went to his father, Nathan, 1 000 to Jack Berman, soon to become a director, 1 000 to Louis Shill, and – to help make up the biggest individual investment in Liberty Life – another 4 000 to Young, who was the only "moneyed" young man in DG's original group. The balance came in packets of £1 000 each from twelve brave investors. This brought the total capital subscribed to £29 000, to be further augmented, on 18 June, by another £2 000, including £1 000 from Louis Miller, the star insurance salesman who was to play a vital role in Liberty's early years. Total by June 1958, only £31 000, still £19 000 short of target.

One of those brave early investors, who took up 1 000 shares, was a Dr Savill Binder. Recalls Gordon: "He was my wife's family doctor, a GP, whom I had never met until Peggy fell pregnant. Well, we certainly couldn't afford a gynaecologist in those days and when he came to see her, he and I started talking. He enquired what I did, and when I told him I was in the process of forming a life insurance company, and told him of my hopes and aspirations, he turned to me and said: 'Well, that sounds fine; I would like to invest in your new company.' I was astonished, for up to then nobody, but nobody, had actually asked me for shares.

"Taking a deep breath, I said: 'Well, that's great, how much would you like to invest in my company?' 'I would like to put in £3 000,' he came back. That would have made him the biggest single investor in Liberty Life outside the founding group, and I thought it was far too much for a doctor to put at risk. 'No,' said I, 'that's far too much, I couldn't allow you to do that.' Anyway, I restricted him to 1 000 shares, and he gave me his cheque there and then. Well, he held them all the way through, right up to his death a few years ago.

"That's only part of the Binder story. About mid-1987, following Savill Binder's death, I received a letter from his son, asking my advice. Over 90 per cent of his family's wealth, he wrote, was tied up in Liberty Life shares, and did I think he should reduce the holding? 'Well,' I replied to him, 'if it was anyone else but you, I would say, particularly with the market as high as is it, maybe you should take a bit of profit and diversify. But with your father I have had a long-standing tradition – I always prohibited him from ever contemplating the sale of one single share and I think I should say the same to you.' That was just before the October Crash – and the shares have probably appreciated 25 per cent since then. When I saw Savill's widow, Freda, some time later, she said: 'Donald, I am so grateful that you persuaded my son not to sell our Liberty Life shares. They have put all my children through the best education and have given us all a marvellous life style.'"

A more amusing, but alas apocryphal, version of Dr Binder's investment, is that he and Donald Gordon first met on the night of 3 November 1958, when Peggy was about to give birth to the Gordons' first child, Richard. She, apparently, was determined that the child would be born on her birthday, the following day – which he indeed was. This story has it that it was while the doctor and the father were awaiting the somewhat delayed birth that they got talking, and Binder decided to make the investment that would transform the Binder family fortunes. But, sadly, the Register of Allotments shows that the conversation must have taken place some months earlier, for the 1 000 shares shown in the name of Savill Binder were allotted on 2 June 1958!

There was only one other occasion when an investor actually asked if he could please buy shares in Liberty Life. "This was in 1962, just before the listing," Gordon recalls. "It was in Switzerland, at the Swiss Reinsurance Company of Zurich, that I met this American, one Shelby Cullom Davis. He was much older than myself, in fact, many years later he finished up at sixty-five years of age as US Ambassador to Switzerland. He was then the leading broker in trading insurance shares on Wall Street, and we met over lunch at the Swiss Re, went back to our hotel in a car together, and then spent the evening together – talking insurance, philosophy and everything else. I think we stayed up till well past midnight; anyhow, we clicked as people, and I invited him to come to South Africa to see Liberty Life and the country for himself.

"I didn't really expect to hear from him again. But, within a couple of days of returning home, I received a phone call from Shelby. 'If you were serious about our coming to South Africa, my wife and I will be on tonight's Swissair flight.' He and his wife Katherine came, stayed with Peggy and me for two days – and asked if he could buy 3 000 shares. And, I remember very well indeed, he paid in dollar travellers' cheques. It probably came to about $8 000 in those days." And so started a life-time friendship – one of the many which arose out of Liberty Life.

On 30 June 1958, a further 14 000 £1 shares were allotted, of which 1 500 went to DG's Donshel Investments, to bring his direct personal stake to 2 500 shares. In addition, he, as founder, had an option on 8 000 shares, and this, when it was exercised in April 1962, proved to be the foundation of his richly-deserved personal fortune. Brian Young took up another 1 500, taking his total holding up to 6 500, and providing a very solid foundation for his own family's fortune, even though he would eventually leave Liberty Life, in unhappy circumstances, in 1967 following the disruption of Gordon's relationship with Louis Shill and the dispute over the future of Sage Fund.

Thus, after nine months of massive and intensive effort, Donald Gordon, sometimes supported by Louis Shill, had managed to secure only £45 000 of capital for Liberty Life. Shill recalls: "I personally raised some of the founding capital from Cape Town investors who still remain grateful, indebted and invested." Even if that was a bit better than the £42 000 Gordon was to refer to in that 1978 interview cited above, it was still a daunting £5 000 short of the minimum required before Liberty Life could legally start to write life insurance.

So, in July 1958, DG went to Pretoria to the Office of the Registrar of Financial Institutions, that uniquely South African government department that controls all matters financial, from unit trusts, to building societies and banks – to insurance companies, both long- and short-term. It is an almost impossibly difficult brief, but, perhaps because of that, the department tends to attract particularly able civil servants. Gordon, in 1958, was fortunate that one of them was Naas van Staden, later himself to become Registrar, but then in charge of long-term insurance affairs.

Gordon was not exactly going cap-in-hand to Van Staden, but he was by no means in a position of strength. The outstanding amount required by Liberty Life, he explained, was due in terms of partly-paid shares, and would be in the company's coffers by the end of the year. Could he kindly have a licence to commence operating as a life assurer? Well, history shows that Van Staden was sympathetic, and Gordon's later comment was that "he went way beyond the call of duty to help and assist."

The then Registrar of Financial Institutions, Van Staden's immediate superior, was Rudolph de Villiers, a distinguished incumbent. Clearly, Van Staden could only act through De Villiers, who would eventually come to be on very friendly terms with both Gordon and the UK Guardian's Ernest Bigland, who would come onto the Liberty Life stage a few years down the road.

On 22 August 1958 Liberty Life was duly registered as a life assurer, and its first policy was issued on 1 October that year. It was not until 19 December 1958, however – in keeping with Gordon's undertaking to Van Staden – that that final tranche of capital was issued. Then, 5 000 shares were allotted, to bring the total to that magic £50 000 mark. Of these, 4 000 went to Standard Bank Nominees (Transvaal), and Brian Young's recollection is that it was his father who provided the vital last piece of finance – on the strict understanding that he would be refunded "as soon as possible".

The final point to note in this financing tale is that this last batch of shares was issued at a premium – albeit of only a humble sixpence – presumably on the strength of the 83 policies that were actually on the books of the new company by 1 December 1958.

If raising the money to gather together a capital base large enough to qualify Liberty Life to market life assurance was to prove a major problem, another, almost equally serious, was how actually to sell the product.

Gordon was not without experience of the direct selling of life insurance, over and above his audit experiences with Standard General. During 1956 he had been recruited as a part-time sub-agent by one Bob Miller, then head of the Johannesburg branch of the

Prudential, and until his retirement in November 1988 the managing director of North City Brokers, a major arm of Liberty Life's broker sales force.

Miller's own story is an interesting one. A schoolmaster for some years, he was introduced in 1951 to the Prudential by his father-in-law, who was with that company, probably the leading up-market life office in those days. "Basically, he didn't like the way I was keeping his daughter on a schoolmaster's salary; he thought, quite rightly, that she was entitled to better things." At first Miller did not enjoy selling life insurance: he quickly proved to be very successful but found the job somewhat unfulfilling, a rather odd attitude given the very considerable financial rewards and the high regard in which insurance consultants are held these days. So he enrolled with the University of South Africa for an LL B – "Selling life insurance in the mornings, studying in the afternoons; that year, 1953, I came near the top of the Prudential's sales list, and I also passed my law examinations."

Shortly after, he was offered a management job. It proved to be the niche he was seeking. "By 1956 I had built up one of the biggest and best Prudential teams in the world – not just in South Africa. The prime part of the job was to recruit salesmen, and I wanted only quality people. I therefore concentrated on university graduates."

One of those that he approached was Donald Gordon, whom he knew as an auditor. "I offered him a Prudential special part-time agent's contract," says Miller (whose other claim to fame in the Liberty Life story is that he also recruited, but as a full-time Prudential employee, one Dorian Wharton-Hood – the man who, following the 1986 takeover of the Prudential of South Africa by Liberty Life, is now joint managing director of the enlarged concern).

Gordon, according to Miller, brought in some useful business. "He proved an excellent salesman, dealing mostly with fellow-professionals." Then, early in 1957, Gordon told Miller that he had decided to start his own company – "so I won't be able to place any more business with the Prudential. I'm confident I'll make a million one day – how about coming in with me to run the sales side?"

Miller turned the offer down. "I never thought they could possibly succeed. What chance had a completely new company of selling against established giants like Old Mutual, Prudential and Sun Life of Canada? And anyway, as manager of the Prudential's best branch, I was probably earning a good deal more than the general manager of the Prudential himself, and I just couldn't afford to take the risk."

But Miller had a younger brother, Lou, whom he had recruited to the Prudential (from pharmacy!) a few years earlier. Lou was a brilliant salesman, and better placed, career-wise, to take a chance. So Miller recommended Lou to Gordon for the job. This dynamic association was clinched on a Johannesburg street corner following a chance meeting in September 1958.

It turned out to be an all-important development, for all Liberty Life old-timers are unanimous in their view that Lou Miller's enthusiasm, zest, sheer determination and selling skills played a very major part in Liberty Life's success in those tough early days. His untimely death, in an aircraft accident near London in 1972, is to this day regarded as a Liberty Life tragedy, and DG still gets emotional when he relates the circumstances.

Louis Miller became a shareholder of Liberty Life (with 1 000 £1 shares) and on 19 December 1958 he was confirmed as the recipient of Liberty Life's first staff housing loan. The Board resolved: "That the bond granted to Mr L Miller of £5 500 be and is hereby confirmed, and that Mr Donald Gordon, a director of the company, is authorised to complete all formalities relative thereto. It was recorded that the rate of interest on this bond was 6 per cent per annum chargeable monthly in arrear as from 1 December 1958."

Even before the official starting date of 1 October 1958, Miller had begun to sell life insurance for Liberty Life. In view of his critical importance in those early days, it is not surprising that there are many Liberty Life legends about this redoubtable salesman, and quite a few concern "The First Policy", to which we shall return in a moment. One of the better stories reflects the widely held belief that Miller sold best when he faced a challenge.

In the early days of retirement annuities, February was the RA month (and to a certain extent it still is, as that month is the last one of the fiscal year). One February in the early days, probably 1962, Miller wanted a tennis court at his home. So he approached Gordon with a straightforward deal. If he, Miller, produced R50 000 of annualised RA business during February (for which he doubtless had ample prospects already lined up), would the company pay for his new tennis court?

Gordon, never anybody's fool, knew he was being conned,

impressive though the self-imposed target was. "Any idiot can sell R50 000 of RAs these days," he said, "but for R100 000-worth you've got yourself a deal."

Miller duly produced not R100 000, but R110 000 of business, an almost incredible feat at a time when the maximum tax deductible contribution to an RA was R600 a year per individual. That tennis court was well deserved – Miller sold over 200 RAs to "buy" it.

The tennis court is a true story, perhaps embellished a little over time. But The First Policy is another matter. Fact and fiction combine to confirm that it was sold by Miller, on 18 September 1958, to Taki Xenopoulos, the colourful Greek-South African entrepreneur who built up his own Fontana food and retailing empire in the years that Liberty Life itself was growing.

The legend (and Gordon insists that it is true) has it that Miller, who had grabbed a handful of the first 500 proposal forms to come rolling off the printing press, returned thirty minutes later with The First Policy, having met his prospect on a street corner and asked him if he would like to be the first policyholder in a brand-new insurance company. Fiction continues that Miller suggested that one day, Taki's picture would be framed and hung on the walls in the foyer of what would by then have become a great insurance giant; it goes on to note that many, Gordon himself included, suspected that Miller used the same technique to sell scores more policies; even that, "many people probably mistakenly believe they hold the first policy in the company".

Fact is much more prosaic; it is simply that The First Policy was sold by a tried and trusted life insurance technique; sell to those you know and who know you. As Xenopoulos, who then owned one small food store, was to recall, many years later: "Louis Miller was a fantastic salesman and he and his wife Hazel were customers of mine. He had approached me a number of times over the years about insurance, and I'd bought a Prudential policy from him. He came again to me when Liberty Life started, and he did indeed tell me that I would be the first policyholder, but that wasn't why I bought. Basically, I think I just bought more life assurance from Louis because he was a very nice person, a dynamic salesman and a charming personality – and, most importantly, somebody I trusted." Later, many years later, when both were successful businessmen, Taki remembers a conversation with Donald Gordon. "He said to me: 'Taki, it's a pity you didn't keep your policy, because by now your statue would be in the foyer of our new building in Braamfontein.' My reply, I think, was that I had surrendered it for that very reason – I didn't want my statue in Braamfontein, or anywhere else."

So, over the years, fact and fiction in this respect are not all that far apart; there's not that much difference between a picture and a statue!

Something quite remarkable about The First Policy is not that it, itself, does indeed figure in Liberty Life's Actuarial Control Register as the very first entry on the first entry date of 1 October 1958, but that nobody around Liberty Life, let alone Xenopoulos himself, recalls that he took out not merely one, but three separate Liberty Life policies around that time. There is that very "first" entry, a non-profit whole-life policy for £5 000; then at number 14, also with the entry date 1 October 1958, there is another £5 000 non-profit whole-life for Xenopoulos,T. This is followed by number 33, on 1 November 1958, for a non-profit whole-life policy for £15 000, a not inconsiderable sum for those days.

Xenopoulos cannot remember why he went so deeply into the new company, but clearly Miller was a salesman of genius. Xenopoulos remembers being concerned, however, presumably at the extent of his commitment to Liberty Life. "I was discussing life insurance with a friend and was asked: 'Why are you insured?' 'For peace of mind,' I replied. Then the friend said: 'If you want peace of mind, Taki, how can you possibly be with this tiny new insurance company that is run by a bunch of amateurs. They're not professionals and they look undercapitalised – if you're after peace of mind, surely that defeats your whole purpose.'" The "friend" was subsequently identified as one Neville Phillips, then a Sun Life salesman who would eventually, though involuntarily, join Liberty Life in 1974 with the Sun Life takeover. He remained with the company until his death in 1987.

Taki mulled this advice over for a while – and then opted out. The Register notes that all three policies were surrendered in January 1962. So far as can be ascertained, these were Liberty Life's first surrenders, so Taki Xenopoulos has two claims to fame.

Finally, in the matter of The First Policy, there is the question of what really is First. Is it the first entry in the Register? If so, the honour does indeed belong to Xenopoulos. Or is it the policy that carries the first number, that is 58 09 001 (which presumably translates as the first policy issued in September 1958)? If this is the case, even though the entry is the third in the Register, the honour of truly being the first policyholder of Liberty Life should be accorded, most fittingly, to one "Gordon, D".

For the record, the first ten policies issued, by number, were, after Gordon's 58 09 001: 002, Brian Young; 003, Taki Xenopoulos; 004, D Kuper; and 005, M Kuper (the Kupers and their company, I Kuper & Company, held 3 000 Liberty Life shares). These were the only "58 09s". Then followed, as "58 10s", 006, M Mayer; 007, James Bond not then having achieved fame, was Xenopoulos's second policy; 008, N L Tsourou; 009, H D Vollmer; and 010, B L Ornallas.

Having now granted Donald Gordon, the founder of Liberty Life, his rightful place as Liberty Life's first policyholder as well, it is time to return to other events that concerned him in those critical early years.

In September 1957, soon after he had taken the first step towards independence by incorporating his new company, he met Peggy Cowan. It was at tennis, one Saturday afternoon. The courtship was brief. "I didn't fancy him much at first, but my brother-in-law Harry Cohen (a director of Plate Glass) knew Donny well. 'Peggy,' he told me, 'that man is brilliant, fantastic, you really must marry him.' It was my brother-in-law who talked me into it."

In December, Donny invited Peggy to accompany him to Witbank for the weekend. He was staying with his friend Louis Shill; she with a cousin, and Brian Young was also in the party. They went swimming that Saturday afternoon. Peggy again: "I'd just been over to the South of France, and had got myself quite a tan – and the most stunning bathing costume you've ever seen, a very sexy white one. I must have made an impact, because Louis and Brian encouraged Donald, saying that I was the perfect wife for him." That Sunday evening, in the car on the way back to Johannesburg, with a back-seat passenger in the shape of a local bank manager's nineteen-year-old daughter whom they had been asked to give a lift, DG proposed. "I hope the girl in the back was asleep – anyway, I said 'Yes' and we woke my mother to give her the news when we got home about 11.30 pm." That was 12 December 1957; they were married on 21 January 1958 at the Transvaal Automobile Club, in Johannesburg's northern suburb of Houghton. The best man was Louis Shill.

"At first," Peggy recalls, "Donny said perhaps he'd better give up the idea of Liberty Life; he wouldn't be earning, he wouldn't be able to keep me; maybe he'd better stay in practice instead. I wouldn't hear of it and by then I was as fired up with enthusiasm as he was. So I convinced him to go ahead, that we had little to lose, and everything to gain. In the worst case, he could always go back to auditing, anyway."

"So then he wanted the wedding and honeymoon over as soon as possible so that he could get on with Liberty Life. But he did spare two weeks for a wonderful Garden Route honeymoon that took in Plettenburg Bay, the Wilderness and Cape Town." Plettenburg Bay was to play an important role in the future of Gordon and Liberty Life as the focus of the Gordons' bi-annual holiday pilgrimage to the coast. Many deals would be conceived and constructed on the veranda overlooking "Gordon's Bay", the name by which the beach below the Gordons' Plettenburg Bay home would become known.

Then back to the sheer slog of raising the capital and preparing for the launch. "His uncle, Jack Berman lent him, free of rent, a little office to work from, and I would go in at lunchtime and in the evenings to do the typing [Peggy continued working, at Anglovaal, and they virtually lived on her salary]. He drew up his own policies, every document, he did everything himself; there was no one to help him but me."

By April 1958, with a little capital in the bank, Liberty moved into an office on the fifth floor of the old Provident Assurance House, in Johannesburg's Fox Street. Peggy continued to help, but . . . "As luck would have it, I had fallen pregnant on the honeymoon – at the time, that seemed the biggest blow of all." She continued to work until August, and their son Richard Michael was born on 4 November 1958, virtually coinciding with the start of business at Liberty Life.

As it happened, all three of DG's children had to compete with Liberty Life for his attention. In September 1960, Wendy Donna was born, to be followed by Graeme John in May 1963, and DG concedes grudgingly that it was not until all his children were approaching adulthood around 1980 that time became a less disputed commodity. Notwithstanding the relative paternal neglect in their early life, all three have a great affection and admiration for their father.

Wendy makes this very clear in an interview published in *Style* magazine in November 1988: "As his daughter I speak from a position of privilege. Fathers tend to dote on their daughters and Donny is no exception. As a father he is exceptional – it's not that

I've never done anything wrong, he is simply too clever to wear rose-tinted spectacles, but he is always completely empathetic, understanding and forgiving.

"He understands everything and has the ability to turn problems into advantages. He is always incredibly optimistic and positive and always sees the bright side of any situation. For example, Donny is an insomniac – he sleeps about three hours a night. The average person would consider this a disability. Not him – he sees this as a gift which allows him a daily five-hour advantage over the rest of the world. He, therefore, can cram two of the average person's working days into one of his! He can be totally exhausting!

"Although I have been married for seven years, my father still plays a strong 'father role' in our lives. When Hylton and I married we built a little house at the bottom of Donny's garden. When it became too small for us and we decided to move he was distraught and was really worried that he would not see us often enough.

"Anyway, we bought a new house not too far away. Donny was, by now, going through anguish so we decided to sell the new house and alter the old one at the bottom of the garden.

"Donny is the typical besotted grandfather and adores having his family in close physical proximity. He often drops in to see his grandchild, either on his way to or from the office. Nicholas calls him Donny, though he says, tongue-in-cheek, that he would prefer his grandchildren to call him 'the Chairman' because it's more respectful. The problem is that sometimes I'm not sure whether he is joking or not!

"It's sometimes really difficult having so successful a father, especially in terms of time. When I was a child and Donny was building Liberty Life the constraints on his time were such that I could never have as much of his time as I wanted. After I grew up, however, he always made a point of keeping me abreast of the developments in his business life, and often he'd ask my opinion – not that I ever kidded myself that he'd agree with me unless I agreed with him first.

"I've always found his world fascinating and have learned to be very tight-lipped about what I hear from him. He wanted me to go into business and was appalled when I wanted to study medicine instead of a B Com. In the end I opted for a BA. I tried working for him for a short while, but it was not a good idea. Temperamentally we're too alike, and it was difficult being the only person who worked for him who wasn't scared of him.

"The most amazing thing about him, in my opinion, is his positive spirit. He is enormously generous in every way, and never wants to hear anything bad about people because he genuinely wishes everybody well. Hylton works for both Liberty Life and for Donny personally and they often spend time in the evenings and over weekends discussing social responsibility programmes and various charities, which areas form part of my husband's responsibility. Donny is deeply concerned with, and moved by the plight of those who have been less fortunate than he and he does an enormous amount to redress some of the inequities in society. He is very modest about these activities and is, therefore, unheralded."

Back in mid-1958, Mavis Venables had joined Liberty Life as the first full-time member of staff and DG's secretary, a position she was to fill with distinction and devotion for the next eight years. That he has had only three secretaries in thirty-one years – Mavis Venables, then Maureen Hart, and now his present secretary, Gail Benjamin – speaks volumes for the loyalty and devotion that Gordon inspires. He may reduce them to tears on occasion, and they may infrequently tender resignations which are never taken seriously or accepted, but his secretaries stay with him. Gail Benjamin has now served her seven years' apprenticeship with great accomplishment, having joined Liberty Life in mid-1982 when the company moved into the new Head Office in Ameshof Street, Braamfontein. DG regards Gail as a true professional and a heaven-sent successor to Maureen Hart, who called all the shots at Liberty Life for almost seventeen years. Maureen left Liberty Life to marry John Kilroe, who in 1988 was appointed Chairman of Shell SA. This was competition of a sort that not even DG could overcome, and he took great joy in giving Maureen away in marriage to John in 1983. By that time, she was regarded – and is still – as a member of the Gordon family.

For most of that first difficult year, 1957, Gordon was battling to raise the capital that was required before the company could commence trading. But Liberty Life was also a corporate entity, and the early Board minutes provide some interesting insights.

The very first Board meeting, held at Johannesburg on 8 October 1957, had essential business to transact. Its first resolution was that "Mr Donald Gordon be and he is hereby appointed Chairman." He and Sydney Lipworth were the only two directors, and they went on to open a bank account – at the Netherlands Bank, Fox Street – and to authorise payment of preliminary expenses of £391 8s.

That the first item concerned the purchase, from Palladium Stationers, of statutory books and rubber stamps (for £3 3s 6d), is of more than passing interest, given Gordon's meticulous concern that everything about Liberty Life should always be scrupulously correct and properly approved.

Lipworth was strictly a non-executive director – he had been called to the Bar in 1956 and needed to earn his living. He recalls: "I was non-executive from the outset. In fact, I had to get the Bar Council's permission to join the Liberty Life Board, because the Council had a ruling that advocates should not be directors of commercial undertakings. I had no money at all and Donald had to lend me the money to buy my directors' qualifying shares." So an early consideration was the augmentation of the Board, and as it happened, at the next formal meeting, on 2 January 1958 (no second New Year's Day when there's work to be done!), it was first noted that one of Liberty Life's very few errors had already been committed.

"It was recorded that in terms of Article 91 of the Articles of Association of the company, the company had appointed only 2 (two) directors and not the necessary 3 (three) as is required by the said Article." The "error" was rapidly rectified by the appointment first of Jack Berman (himself an early shareholder, with 1 000 shares, whose sojourn on the Liberty Life Board was very brief, for he resigned by agreement in 1959) and then of Louis Shill, who would play a major part in the development of the group in the crucial early years.

On 30 April 1958 the Chairman welcomed Berman and Shill to their first meeting, and the Board then proceeded to approve the group's first investment decisions. Gordon has always been of an ultra-conservative bent, and these inaugural investments could hardly have been more cautious. The first one was the investment of £2 000 in Electricity Supply Commission 1978/83 Local Registered Stock (5 3/8 per cent) – the first tiny step in what would, over the years, become an enduring and mutually satisfactory association between Liberty Life and the big parastatal, Eskom. Next came the momentous decision to place a total of £13 500 on call at rates between 5 per cent and 7 per cent.

And, as a precursor to the very close interest and control over investment matters that Gordon would continue to exhibit over the years to come, "It was resolved that in future all loans and investments could be made under the authority of the Chairman and any one other director . . ."

The Board appointed Mr H N Murfin as the company's first actuary. He was subsequently replaced by Messrs Shepley & Fitchett, one of Johannesburg's leading actuarial partnerships, on 20 April 1959, having resigned "as a result, primarily, of a dispute regarding fees". The dispute could not have been all that serious, for the Chairman was then "authorised to thank Mr Murfin for his past efforts on behalf of the company".

Next, the Board authorised the Chairman to "settle all matters" in connection with the reassurance treaty to be entered into with the Swiss South Africa Reassurance Corporation. This early link with the SwissRe was to prove of vital importance when it came to selling those early life policies.

The Board's last duty that day was to authorise the purchase, from the Chairman, of his Renault Fregate motorcar TJ 140160 for £700 – and to charge him £3 a month for the private use of it. The next stage in the Chairman's motorcar progression would be to the second-hand Riley ND 1242, bought for £1 001 in March 1960. It would be several more years before the purchase of his first Rolls Royce. That proud landmark in the life of a man who greatly appreciates and enjoys his motorcars would come in 1969. The term "his first Rolls Royce" is used deliberately, because it was his own; none of the Chairman's motorcars, after that 1960 Riley, have belonged to the company, as Gordon owns all his own cars, and does so to this day.

In June 1958 the first tentative links with other financial institutions were forged when current accounts were opened with the South African Permanent Mutual Building Society, the United Building Society and the Standard Bank of South Africa (Witbank Branch), while further sums of capital, as it came slowly to hand, were invested, mostly in local government stock. The first venture into actual share purchase was modest, and suitably cautious: on 16 June, the Board approved the purchase of 500 preference shares in Rand Carbide, for £362 10s. (It was not until 4 December 1959 that Liberty Life first dipped into the actual equity market, and then the purchase was of 200 shares in the sugar bluechip, Sir J L Hulett & Sons, at 77/6d a share.)

The team that was to carry Liberty Life through its formative years was now almost complete. Brian Young and Hugh Rubin were both working for the company as full-time executives, and would join the Board in June 1959 and July 1960 respectively. Monty Schapiro, a respected and established insurance broker and Chairman of the short-term broker, S A May, joined the Board as a non-executive director in June 1959 – largely, as he jokingly recalls, "to boost up the average age of what was thought to be an overly young Board, as I was, and still am, seven-and-a-half years older than Donny."

It was at that Board meeting, on 23 June 1959, that a lengthy minute dealt with the appointment of a managing director – one Donald Gordon. As both Chairman and MD, he thus consolidated his position at the helm of the ship that he had launched, and had piloted through some very early storms. Having made the appointment of managing director, the Board immediately proceeded to the protection of its investment. "The life insurance policy taken out by the company on the life of the managing director on a five-year term basis for £10 000 (with a further £10 000 accident benefit) was confirmed. It was resolved that a further £10 000 five-year term policy be taken out by the company on the life of the managing director."

Evidence of the frugal early approach to remuneration is provided by the Board minutes for 15 July 1960, when the matter of directors' emoluments was tabled.

"At the meeting of 8 July 1960, the three non-working directors, Messrs H L Shill, M S Lipworth and M Schapiro were delegated to investigate the position in regard to the increase of emoluments of the executive directors, and at a meeting on 15 July 1960 they recommended that Messrs D Gordon, B P Young and H Rubin receive annual emoluments, inclusive of all expense allowances, etc, of £3 500, £2 500 and £2 500 respectively, commencing with effect from 1 July 1960, these amounts being exclusive of any directors' fees paid [these were a somewhat ungenerous £200 per annum]. As from 1 July 1960, no commission would be payable to any of the working directors on any new insurance business introduced to the company by them. Commission on business introduced prior to 30 June 1960 to remain unaffected."

When South Africa converted to decimal currency in 1961, the pound sterling became two rands, so Donald Gordon's 1960 stipend was equivalent to R7 000. Even allowing for the rampant inflation of the intervening years, and the more recent dramatic devaluation of the rand in sterling terms, it was by no means a generous payment.

Even less so was the R5 000 a year paid to each of Liberty Life's other two "working" directors.

In February 1959 Liberty had moved into its first "proper" offices, a very modest suite, "Offices Nos 415-429 (inclusive)" in Loveday House, on the corner of Loveday and Marshall Streets in downtown Johannesburg. It was from there that the first Annual Report and Accounts, that for the thirteen-month period from 26 November 1957 to 31 December 1958, was published. It showed a profit of £629.

Looking back, many years later, Lipworth says: "We were very proud of the fact that we broke even in that first year. It was largely due, of course, to the fact that nobody, neither Donald, Hugh, Louis nor Brian, took any meaningful salary. But we had very, very tight administration and control over expenses that set a pattern for the future. Also, we had no claims in that period, and we had the income from our capital, which was invested. Anyway, we somehow turned the corner that first year, and we must have been the only new company in the whole history of life insurance, world-wide, to do that."

Indeed, Liberty Life was probably unique in the annals of life insurance in returning a profit in its first year. The conventional wisdom in those days was that it took many years – possibly as long as twenty – of losses before a life company could break even. But first Liberty Life, and then its offshoot, Abbey Life in the United Kingdom, would prove otherwise.

# 3 Towards a Listing

Despite the manifold problems of Liberty Life's first year, the end of 1958 saw 106 policies on the books for an aggregate sum assured of £765 000. The allotment on 19 December 1958 of 5 000 shares at 20s 6d, a premium of sixpence a share, brought the issued capital up to the required minimum of £50 000, much to Gordon's relief, even though this constituted a paper-thin buffer on which to start a life insurance company, however small. The minimum practical capital necessary in 1989 would be at least R10 million, and then with little prospect of success in the highly competitive conditions of today.

Perhaps it was because of the problems he faced in raising that relatively small initial capital that Donald Gordon has since been greatly preoccupied with capital base. He freely admits that Liberty Life is over-capitalised, but that is a fault that allows him to sleep comfortably at night. Liberty Life, he has always felt, should have the best possible capital base relative to its size; it should, if at all possible, be the best capitalised life insurer in the business (and it has certainly been that for very many years); it should, in the capital sense, be, in his own words, "idiot proof for at least three generations after my death or retirement. In that, I think I might just have succeeded, with over R3 billion of capital cover, not counting a further R2 billion of policyholders' free reserves at the 1988 year-end. That's as large as any I know of in the Western world. Almost as large as the Prudential of Britain," he twinkles, with obvious pride.

The first Report and Accounts comprised nine typed foolscap sheets stapled together (a far cry from today's beautifully produced and lavishly illustrated corporate image builder). However, in a number of important aspects it set guidelines for the future.

First, the cautious, conservative investment approach that would always be a Liberty Life – indeed, a Donald Gordon – hallmark. "A very conservative policy of investment has been followed by your directors. In particular, it has been their policy to invest in gilt-edged stocks to a much greater degree than is required by statute. At the same time advantage has been taken of the high ruling interest rates and an overall return of approximately 6 per cent per annum has been achieved." Liberty Life was still far too small to be exposed to any downside risk whatsoever. The preoccupation with equities and real estate, and hedge assets in general, would come much later. Over the years, investment policy obviously had to widen, but conservatism has always remained the keynote.

Talking to the *Financial Mail* in 1978, DG underlined this. "We've always been terribly conservative. I have probably allowed the company to develop far too slowly, particularly in the early stages. It was always a step by step approach. My inborn conservatism would never allow me to do anything which I couldn't see the end of."

And, talking to the author in 1988, he carried the philosophy further. "One of the important original concepts was that of being the most investment orientated company of them all. My personal belief was that a life insurance company should be an insurance company on the liabilities side, and carefully balance out its risks, of course, but on the asset side it should be very much akin to a merchant bank, with their traditional clinical and professional approach to investment, and always with an eye to the strategic possibilities. By contrast, the conventional wisdom was to have a balanced investment portfolio right across the board so nothing can go wrong; the snag with that approach is that you are always in the middle of the pack – very boring and very ordinary. With the Liberty Life formula, much more is achievable, but there must be a highly incisive focus to reduce errors of judgement to the minimum.

"We believed, from the very beginning, that our policyholders would want us to do better than other companies, and that was a very important concept of the difference between them and us. We actually did our promotional effort by stressing the investment aspect, with investment leading all our promotion from the front, as it were, and not the other way around, with a total concentration on the life insurance factor. Another aspect was the concept of a more equitable distribution of the profitability of investments made on behalf of policyholders, and the logical thing for that was to pass on the benefits of our concept of a 'partnership in investment' directly to our clients. That quickly led to linked insurance, first to mutual funds, and inevitably from there in short order to the utilisation of internal investment funds developed specifically to achieve policyholders' expectations and aspirations. The benefit to shareholders was thus incidental to the satisfaction of our clients, the policyholders."

Next, and crucial to selling life insurance policies in those early days, was Liberty Life's policy on reinsurance. "It has been the policy of your directors to re-assure a high proportion of the risk and in pursuance of this policy, the company at 31 December 1958 retained a net risk of only £47 500." This, out of an aggregate sum assured of £765 000, is a retention of only 6,2 per cent. Indeed, in those very early days, the policy was for Liberty Life itself to retain a maximum of only £500 of risk per individual life. As the company grew, retentions, of course, were steadily increased, but in the early years it was of the utmost importance to be able to assure prospective policyholders that the vast bulk of the risk would not be shouldered by the infant Liberty Life, but passed on to the massive Swiss Reinsurance Company. Later others, including the Mercantile & General and the Victory, both of London, and the Hollandia, of Amsterdam, also played a major role in accommodating the explosive expansion of Liberty Life's business.

Next, tight control over expenses enabled the directors to report: "The life revenue account discloses the fact that in spite of all establishment and preliminary expenses being written off, a life fund of £2 739 was established. This achievement, in the first year of operation of a life insurance company, is a feature of no mean significance which augurs well for the future of the company."

"Tight control over expenses" has remained a feature of Liberty Life to this day and, even if DG no longer counts the petty cash every night – as his colleagues aver that he did in the early days – expense control is rigidly maintained. Cost consciousness, and hence low expense ratios, have played an essential role in Liberty Life's success over the years.

The directors' comments, ending with: "In summary, the progress of the company gives every cause for satisfaction and certainly exceeds the most optimistic expectations of your directors", are highly significant after only three months of active operations. That things were going so well, and that the youthful Board felt sufficiently confident to express its optimism in such definite terms, did indeed "augur well for the future". One other interesting detail of that first Directors' Report is that it unequivocally acknowledges

Gordon as the founder of the company, though without actually naming him. "At an extraordinary meeting of shareholders held on 8 October 1957 an option was granted until 26 November 1969 to the founder of the company to take up a maximum of 8 000 shares of £1 each in the company at £1 per share."

On 15 November 1960, the option was transferred. The Board minute reads: "Mr Gordon referred to the above option which had been granted to him at the first meeting of the shareholders of the company. He notified the meeting that he had disposed of all his rights, interest and title to the option in favour of Liberty Trust (Proprietary) Limited, their nominees or assigns. Mr Gordon disclosed that he was interested as a director and shareholder in the latter company and tabled the nature and extent of his interest in it. Messrs H L Shill, B P Young and H Rubin informed the meeting that they were also interested as shareholders and directors in Liberty Trust (Proprietary) Limited and tabled the nature and extent of their interest."

Although his closest colleagues now also had an interest in the option, there is no doubt that its eventual exercise, on 28 April 1962, was one of the cornerstones of Gordon's personal fortune. But his real opportunity arose following the reacquisition of control of Liberty Life from GRE in 1978.

Imaginative innovation has always been a feature of Liberty Life, and this was apparent right from the start. One of the first policies offered was a life insurance policy with disability benefits attached at no additional outlay. The concept was of a divided policy; one part of it was a disability benefit policy, the other a normal whole-life with-profits policy. While a claim on the former would naturally affect the level of the bonus rate on the latter, cover against disability was of considerable appeal in the professional and managerial market in which Liberty Life had chosen to operate. The cost of the disability cover was included in an extremely cost efficient manner.

Even so, the going was difficult. The big, established rivals fought hard, and not always cleanly. Sun Life of Canada was strongly entrenched in the professional field. Brian Young, and quite a few others, recall having to sell against the slogan: "Why not make sure by insuring with Sun Life of Canada rather than with Liberty Life of Doornfontein!" – a somewhat unsalubrious suburb of Johannesburg. One variant had it that the slogan was "Liberty Life of Witbank", in acknowledgement of the fact that, for the first few years, Louis Shill continued to live in Witbank, in the eastern Transvaal, commuting to Johannesburg on a weekly basis. Brian Young also came from Witbank.

On the other hand, the new company did have a few things going for it, apart from the sales star, Lou Miller. As Young puts it: "All of us concerned had good reputations, and we all had our professional contacts, many of whom proved to be prepared to back us, even if for relatively small amounts. And we took pains to explain our view of how a life company should be operated, that the life expectancy tables then in general use were outdated, that sensible investment policies would generate superior profits; that expenses could be kept down, that we were young, lean and hungry while the opposition had grown fat, complacent and lazy. In the end, it all paid off, but it was by no means easy – far from it."

By mid-year, the company was looking towards territorial expansion. An agent, Ted McKune, was appointed in the Cape, and he was to run the Cape Town operation successfully for many years. He showed great courage in holding the fort in the very backyard of the established insurance giants of Southern Africa. For Natal, however, with its large English-speaking population, the decision was taken to open a full branch office within the company's first year. The Board resolved, on 3 August 1959, "That the company enter into an agreement of lease with the Johannesburg Building Society in respect of offices Nos 819 and 820, J B S Building, Corner West and Field Streets, Durban, commencing on 12 August 1959, for a period of two years."

And the next Board meeting, on 11 August, took matters a stage further. Under the heading "Allotment of Shares", it was noted: "Further to the company's sales promotion in Natal it was agreed that certain shares would have to be allotted in that area with the provision that allotment should be as restricted as possible. The negotiations with the prospective allottees were left to the discretion of the managing director. The shares were to be allotted at a premium of 2/6d per share."

So Gordon went off to Durban to try to sell a "restricted" number of shares, and at a premium of 12,5 per cent that looked distinctly cheeky to some – after all, the company had been trading for barely one year. A meeting of prospective investors was convened, and Gordon waxed lyrical about the company's prospects. He must have been very convincing, because 6 500 shares were allotted at that 2/6d premium, during September and December, plus a further 3 500 to Cloud Investment, the private investment company in which Gordon, Shill, Young, Rubin and others were shareholders.

Two typical Liberty Life stories stem from that sales campaign. The first concerns Dr Reuben Shatz, then a young and struggling medical practitioner to whom Gordon had been introduced. "We're just starting up in Durban," DG told the young doctor, "and there will soon be plenty of life insurance medicals. You can have all the medicals you can handle if you take up 500 shares." Shatz, unhappily, did not have £562 10s, but he could scrape up £112 10s – "Would that do?" Well, perhaps it would. And Dr Shatz remained a shareholder until his untimely death in 1983, by which time scrip issues, all of which he retained, had pushed his holding up to 3 000 shares, worth the equivalent of R150 000.

The second is one of the many "missed the boat" stories that surround the Liberty Life saga. A wealthy furniture manufacturer, one of the leaders of the Durban community, was another that Gordon met. This pillar of society was very impressed by Gordon's presentation, and hastened to say that he would happily take up 5 000 shares, but that "he'd be damned if he would pay a premium of one penny a share, let alone 2/6d, for shares in a company that had hardly got off the ground." Gordon stuck to his guns, insisting on the premium – or no shares. And that was that: another potential multimillionaire had missed the boat.

That first Durban office, incidentally, proved to be one of Liberty Life's few early disappointments, largely because of staffing problems, and because of the lack of the "personal confidence factor" in Gordon and his colleagues that was proving so important to success in the Transvaal. The branch was closed at the end of the two-year lease. Durban would later become part of Liberty Life's success story, however, when Gordon appointed Harry Brews as Durban agent on 1 August 1962.

Brews, for years a top golfer, was a prefect at KES when Gordon was in the lower forms. DG still remembers "how Harry kicked my backside when he was officer commanding the school's cadet battalion". How fate turned the tables! DG also remembers his involvement in the trauma of Brews's many emotionally-charged marriages. Brews is still at Liberty Life as deputy general manager, investment marketing, but will be retiring in 1989 after twenty-seven tumultuous years with the company. Albert Weinberg, Brews's pragmatic number two, who also helped to keep Harry on the straight and narrow, retired on schedule a few years ahead of his impetuous colleague, but at the end of 1988 was still active in the Group as a consultant to the Liberty Life subsidiary, Charter Life.

From his experiences with Harry, with Louis Miller's marital sagas, not to mention the marital problems of many other Liberty Life stalwarts, Gordon's second profession might almost have been that of marriage counsellor. He claims he was nearly as successful at that as he has been at life insurance; perhaps there is a tenuous connection between the two!

Liberty's first "trading anniversary" late in 1959 provided the peg for the first of the many laudatory press comments that would fill four bulging press cuttings books by the late eighties. There were brief mentions in the *Cape Times* and the *Natal Mercury* of 24 September, and a longer piece, well worth quoting, in the now-defunct *Rand Daily Mail* of 16 October 1959, written by the doyen of South African financial journalists, Harold Fridjhon. Headed "Maiden year", the article reads: "A year-old life assurance company, Liberty Life Association of Africa, which started business in 1958, has reason to be satisfied with the results of its maiden year of operation.

"Policies for sums assured exceeding £2,4m have been written, and the company modestly claims that this might be a record for the first year's business of a new life office in South Africa.

"The management tells me that the cost ratio of this business was very favourable because of the high average sum assured per policy written. This is attributable to the fact that most policies were effected with business and professional people.

"Favourable conditions prevailing in the long-term gilt market last year have enabled the company to invest at a return exceeding 6 per cent. The portfolio consists mainly of government, municipal and other local authority stocks and, to a lesser extent, in mortgages and first-class industrial preference shares."

For the company's full financial year, to 31 December 1959, new sums assured totalled £2,74 million, and net premium income, after deduction of necessarily heavy reassurance premiums, amounted to £47 750. The profit for the year, the first full year of operations, was £1 829.

The event that was to prove a vital turning point in the fortunes of the company – and the real flywheel of its success – was first noted as a very low-key minute of a Board meeting that, most unusually, spread itself over two Fridays, 8 and 15 July 1960. It was headed "The Professional and Executive Retirement Fund". It heralded the advent of retirement annuities, but the word "Annuity" had been omitted!

The Professional and Executive Retirement Annuity Fund (Peraf) was first minuted thus: "The managing director outlined what steps had been taken in regard to the establishment of the aforementioned Fund and after discussion all matters undertaken in connection with the establishment of the said Fund together with the appointment of the company as managers, were confirmed."

Gordon himself spelt out the advantages of RAs, as the new product came to be widely known, in an article published under his own name in *Business News* in 1962.

"The establishment of pension funds by companies for their employees has for many years been an accepted feature of our economic life, but it was only recently that this social boon was extended to include those who are not eligible for participation in organised pension schemes.

"This was made possible by Income Tax Act No 58 of 1960, which brought into being the means to establish approved retirement annuity funds to enable any person to provide for his retirement in later years with the help of tax concessions."

There is no doubt that RAs were attractive. But it is a tribute to Gordon's foresight that it was he, and only he, in the whole of the South African insurance industry in 1960, who fully grasped their possibilities, as well as recognising their special appeal to the top income bracket business and professional market that Liberty Life had made its target.

Looking back, talking to the *Financial Mail* in 1978, Gordon didn't completely see it that way, although he did acknowledge its importance. "The development of retirement annuities was a big turning point. Most of the companies here took it very low key because it had been very much a dead duck when the principle started earlier in the UK.

"For a long time there was no growth at all in this field in the UK, but, being a chartered accountant, the tax implications struck me very forcibly indeed. In a way, it was an opportunity lost, because had I had the backing, in the early stages of retirement annuity development, we could have done much more. About 1961, the company was tiny, with assets well under R1m. We didn't have the backing and the respectability to be able to do justice to this exercise. Had we then had the image and the backing of the Guardian Royal Exchange, we could have swept the market. However well we did, we must have lost three out of four prospective policies, just by the opposition saying well, who the hell is this company, a lot of young chartered accountants playing silly buggers."

For all that retrospective modesty, RAs did serve to put Liberty Life on the map. And, in a development that would have a major impact on the life insurance industry in the United Kingdom as well, they brought Mark Weinberg into the industry, and into Liberty Life's orbit.

Liberty Life began marketing RAs in the latter half of 1960, but interestingly, in view of the importance that they were to assume, no further mention of the new product was made in the Board minutes for that year after the initial mention in July. However, Brian Young recalls: "I remember spending a Sunday afternoon on the lawn of Donald's home in Melrose going through the whole concept. We gave the new retirement annuity fund the name of the Professional and Executive Retirement Annuity Fund. All the executives were there and it was in the very early days of the new legislation having come into force. At that particular meeting we cleared up most of the problems and we were out selling almost immediately. Apart from the early start, the other advantage we had was that all our connections were in the higher income field. It was pretty easy to sell to professionals when you could tell them: 'Now look, the government is paying half your premium for you.'"

By 31 December 1960, the impact of RAs was seen in the fact that net premium income for the year then ended was almost doubled at R188 950, from the previous year's R95 500. Profits, however, largely reflecting the costs of launching the new product, fell back from R3 658 to R3 278.

It was in 1960 that Mark Weinberg came on to the scene. He had been through Wits University's Law School with Liberty Life non-executive director Sydney Lipworth, and the two were close friends. Young recalls that the two of them had gone through their B Com and LL B years "without ever failing to get a first in any subject". Weinberg had spent from 1957 to 1959 in London taking a Master of Laws degree and had been thinking of settling there. But he returned to Johannesburg in the middle of 1959 to work with a firm of attorneys, Hayman, Godfrey & Sanderson. Although all three of them had been at the same school, Lipworth re-introduced Weinberg to Gordon and he acted as Liberty Life's lawyer in helping to formulate and register Peraf.

Weinberg remembers working closely with Gordon on the Peraf rules during 1960: "We made a number of trips to Pretoria together to persuade both the Registrar and the Income Tax authorities to approve the rules, which were to play such an important role in Liberty Life's success." In the event, recalls Gordon: "Mark became fascinated with the concept, and with life insurance generally – with consequences, in the years to come, that would have a massive impact on the industry in the United Kingdom." Indeed, for it was during this period that Liberty Life decided to back the formation of Abbey Life. From late December 1961 to May 1962, Weinberg spent all his time in Liberty Life's offices, "learning from Donny Gordon how to run a life assurance company."

Weinberg, as a solicitor, had had no direct exposure to life insurance, although it was obviously in his blood. His father, who had died when Mark was very young, had been a life insurance salesman, and his brother-in-law to be, one Smokey Simon, was a top agent with Sun Life of Canada. Initially, at Liberty Life, Weinberg was concerned mainly with the presentation and marketing of RAs. He recalls: "They weren't very strong on the presentation side of things; their presentation was just a roneoed three-page letter. I was keen on glossy covers and good paper; after all, the only thing policyholders saw was that paper, and I thought they should have value for their money. I worked a lot on the marketing side and that's where my own feeling for life insurance, and marketing it, was developed." That "feeling" for marketing life insurance was later to be put to very good use indeed.

Weinberg also got some experience of the sales side. "Soon after Weinberg joined Liberty Life," says Young, "I remember going with him for a week to Bloemfontein selling RA contracts with our local agent there, a man called Issy Goldblatt. Whenever I see Mark we still pull each other's leg about that trip, but working with Issy was where he got his first sales experience." Issy Goldblatt was certainly a great salesman, and he has maintained his relationship with Liberty Life over all these years.

Weinberg's other major contribution to Liberty Life in the time he spent with the company was in connection with the listing that was to come in June 1962. "Working with Donny, I had a lot to do with the production of the prospectus. As a lawyer, and now being involved with, and increasingly enthusiastic about, life insurance, I could use a lawyer's language to describe life insurance."

Another important event of 1961, and one that emphasised Gordon's international outlook, even in those early days, with the company barely three years old, was the decision taken on 7 April 1961 to establish a London branch. "A detailed discussion took place on the desirability of establishing a London branch office and for the purpose of financing this, the allotment of 10 000 shares of R2 each to a reinsurance group. The minimum price to be paid would be R2,25 per share. Any reinsurance facilities granted to the Allottee should not be of an absolute, permanent nature."

On 26 May 1961, after visits to London by Gordon and Schapiro, the Board was advised of an "Agreement with General Reinsurance Syndicate (Alherma Investments and Hollandia Reinsurance Company)". Gordon was able to tell the meeting "that the technical problems involved with the deal were gradually being ironed out, and that he was particularly delighted by the co-operative attitude of the Swiss-South Africa Reinsurance Company Limited". Maybe he was "particularly delighted", but the truth is that the great Swiss reinsurer, at that stage, was not even prepared to back the tiny Liberty Life to the tune of £10 000 – very much to their regret in later years.

Gordon went on to note that "it had been agreed in principle with all concerned that the Hollandia would commence its participation in our reinsurance treaties [the name by which contracts with reinsurers are known in the industry] with effect from 1 July 1961 on identical terms" with those of the Swiss Reinsurance. The link with Hollandia was sealed by the allotment to them, on 25 September 1961, of 10 000 Liberty Life shares – not at the R2,25 minimum specified by the Board, but at R2,40 a share.

By the end of 1961, net new business premium income had advanced only modestly, from R139 000 to R142 500, although total premium income, after reassurances, moved up from R189 000 to R251 000. The directors, however, were confident enough to suggest that a "reasonable dividend would be declared in the near future".

Not only that, but they were sufficiently satisfied with progress seriously to consider another, and very major, leap forward. Despite the extreme youth and immaturity of the company, and notwithstanding the fact that there was no precedent, and no dividend record, the directors dared to contemplate the listing of Liberty Life on the Johannesburg Stock Exchange.

Shortly before the publication of the 1961 Report, there was a Board meeting on 2 February 1962. Under the heading "General" appeared the following: "A general discussion ensued on the possibility of acquiring a listing for the shares of the Company on the Johannesburg Stock Exchange. The matter was left in abeyance pending the acquisition of further information."

The *Financial Mail*, reviewing the 1961 accounts in May 1962, just prior to the listing (obviously, the "further information" had been acquired, and had proved satisfactory) waxed quite lyrical. "After some of the unimpressive insurance company accounts recently reviewed, it is a pleasure to examine those of Liberty Life. A small South African company and a young one – the December 31 1961 accounts give the picture after only 3 1/4 years of operation – Liberty Life has nevertheless succeeded in quickly establishing itself on a sound foundation." Commenting on the strength of the Life Fund, and the "unimpaired capital and reserves of R164 805", the *FM* went on to note: "That this should have been achieved so rapidly – a life office often takes seven to ten years to offset the heavy costs of acquiring its initial portfolio – is a tribute to its young and energetic management team and to ruthless pruning of administration costs."

The stage was now set for the listing of Liberty Life, the first listing of a life assurance company in the history of the Johannesburg Stock Exchange. One last preliminary was the issue, by way of rights, of another 22 000 shares at R2,50 a share, to bring the authorised and issued capital to a round figure of R200 000. It was noted that: "Although the directors considered that the capital of the company was already adequate for its business requirements, it was decided to increase the issued and paid-up capital to the full authorised capital of R200 000 in order to comply with the requirements of the Johannesburg Stock Exchange for a primary listing of shares. Accordingly, in May 1962 22 000 shares were offered to and taken up by existing shareholders for cash at R2,50 per share, by way of a one-for-four rights issue and applications for excess shares."

The pre-listing statement was published on 3 June 1962 – three weeks before Donald Gordon's thirty-second birthday. It was not an invitation to the public to subscribe for shares – none were available

– but was issued "for the purpose of giving information to the public with regard to the company". This it did admirably well, but the report of the consulting actuaries went even further. This independent Statutory Report provided the most glowing confirmation, were such needed, of the outstanding achievements of Gordon and his colleagues over the preceding three-and-a-quarter years. It is worth quoting at some length:

"The Life Assurance Fund is required to cover the actuarial liability under unmatured policies and includes any surplus. The actuarial liability is the amount which, together with future premiums and interest earnings, will provide for the future payment of death claims, maturity values and annuity payments as they fall due, as well as the expenses of operating the company.

"In South Africa, a relatively stringent minimum basis of computing actuarial liabilities is obligatory under the Insurance Act of 1943 (as amended): the assurance company is required to assume that the net rate of interest earned by it will be limited to 3 ½ per cent and that the mortality amongst its policyholders will be in accordance with the A1924–1929 ultimate mortality table, which was drawn up on the basis of mortality experience amongst assured lives in Britain during those years. Moreover, the Insurance Act does not permit the company in calculating its actuarial liabilities to take full allowance for the high procuration and new business costs which are general: these costs are allowed for in the premium rates charged and are recouped by the company from the payment of future premiums under each policy. The effect of the stringent statutory requirements and the restrictions on the allowance in respect of new business expenses is that a new life assurance company is invariably expected to draw on its capital for a period of from seven to ten years after its establishment in order to cover its actuarial liabilities on the basis required by the Insurance Act.

"In this connection, we report that, at the last valuation of the company's actuarial liabilities which was conducted by us on the basis laid down by the Insurance Act, for the year ended 31 December 1961, only 3 ¼ years after the commencement of life assurance business, a surplus of R33 066 was disclosed as having arisen during the year. This surplus was sufficient not only to enable the company to absorb entirely the extent to which establishment and procuration costs since inception had required financing out of shareholders' funds in order to meet the statutory actuarial requirements, but also to strengthen free reserves by the transfer of R7 000 to investment reserve and to leave the Life Assurance Fund as reflected in the balance sheet in excess of statutory requirements.

"The effect is that the Life Assurance Fund of R269 930 in the Balance Sheet at 31 December 1961 fully covered the Company's actuarial liabilities to policyholders, calculated on the statutory basis, leaving its capital and shareholders' reserves of R164 805 entirely unimpaired. We understand that the capital and capital reserve have subsequently been increased by further issues of shares, to raise total capital and shareholders' reserves to R235 805.

"The adoption of a more realistic basis of valuation, consistent with current interest rates and mortality experience, would have resulted in a substantially greater surplus, but the adoption of the statutory basis has the effect of strengthening the Life Assurance Fund and of deferring to the future surpluses which would otherwise have been reflected at this stage.

"The fact that the capital and shareholders' reserves remain intact after meeting the statutory actuarial requirements after only 3 1/4 years of assurance business is, in our view, an exceptional achievement, reflecting the company's efficient management and strict economy in administration, and the high class of business written by it.

"On the basis of our experience in regard to insurance companies developing on conservative bases and given continuation of the experience to date, future actuarial valuations should disclose growing surpluses in the years to come, which should, after the provision of competitive bonuses to participating policyholders, make an increasing contribution to the funds available for distribution to shareholders."

Apart from this richly deserved praise and appreciation from the consulting actuaries, the pre-listing statement was straightforward. Interestingly, the sponsoring stockbrokers were Max Pollock & Freemantle, and not Davis Borkum Hare, with whose senior partner, Max Borkum, Donald Gordon was to build a close personal relationship over the years. And the London manager was listed as one Mark Aubrey Weinberg, who, DG recalls, "got married the day before the listing and went off to London to commence his new career. He had met Sandra Leroith, a beautiful lady who was a daughter of a prominent Johannesburg architect, in the middle of work on the listing. We were just getting to the closing stages of the documentation and I well recall one evening when he was supposed to be at my house at 7 pm, and he turned up at 11. He didn't apologise for being late, but leaned nonchalantly against the mantelpiece and announced phlegmatically that he was getting married – in that detached manner that is so distinctively a Mark Weinberg characteristic. I was surprised, to say the least, as we had all been working very hard, and at all hours. 'How do you ever manage to see the girl?' I asked, before congratulating him." Sadly, Sandra died in London at a very young age, but she played an important role in Mark's early introduction to the London scene.

When the JSE opened for business on Monday 4 June 1962, the opening price of Liberty Life's R2 shares was an unexciting R2,70, to give the company the very modest initial market capitalisation of only R270 000.

A somewhat unexciting start for a new listing in a high-glamour business. Who could foresee that this low-key beginning was in fact the debut of perhaps the most exciting performance stock ever to be seen on to the Johannesburg Stock Exchange? But at this stage nobody took the slightest notice, and hardly any dealings took place for some considerable time until the Schlesinger Organisation, through its African Life subsidiary, subscribed for 30 000 new Liberty Life shares at R10 per share in November 1962.

From then onwards, the game was on, and shareholders were given the roller-coaster ride of the century. Great fortunes were made – and missed. Those who stayed aboard hit the jackpot, and the stalwarts prospered mightily.

# 4 Into UK – Abbey Life

Shortly before Liberty Life's successful listing on the Johannesburg Stock Exchange, Mark Weinberg returned to London as Liberty Life's representative, and to prepare for the launch of a new life insurance company specifically designed to attack the sleepy United Kingdom market. Donald Gordon, from the outset, had seen the desirability of an international approach to life insurance, and the two men were to combine to create a company which would have some impact on the UK life insurance scene. Neither, in all honesty, had the slightest idea of how great an impression would in fact be made. But hope springs eternal in the human breast.

If the South African life insurance market was proving encouragingly vulnerable to an innovative and entrepreneurial approach, then the United Kingdom market seemed wide open to new attitudes and determination. Liberty Life had begun to roll on a product adapted, and improved, from the UK-model of retirement annuities, which had proved to be a virtual non-event in the UK environment. Gordon and Weinberg had sensed that, after years of stagnation, the UK market was ready for Liberty Life's type of innovation. In any event, it all seemed a great challenge and adventure for both men, motivated as they were by "the impossible dream".

In the words of one long-time Liberty Life man, Albert Weinberg (no relation): "Mark Weinberg's early experience with Liberty Life, after the couple of years he had earlier spent in London, made him realise just how archaic the life insurance business in the UK had become. The range of policies, and the approach, had not changed in decades and the selling of life insurance was so low key that Britain was one of the most under-insured countries in the Western world. Abbey Life was planning to market a relatively new concept – life insurance policies linked to unit trusts, under which a policyholder could watch his policy value grow by tracking the price of the units in the daily press."

Gordon was simultaneously planning to introduce the idea to South Africa – it was, in fact, to be Liberty Life's next major breakthrough in policy innovation. But Liberty Life still had to create the necessary mechanism, as no unit trusts existed in South Africa at that time. The first such trust was to be launched in 1965, when Donald Gordon, supported by Louis Shill, took the lead by forming South Africa's first mutual fund, Sage Fund. The thinking behind an equity link had been spelt out in Gordon's original memorandum produced in 1957, preceding the formation of Liberty Life. He and Weinberg had endlessly discussed such an approach, and in discussing it, had refined it into an exciting concept. They knew it was only for want of determined and imaginative promotion that it, along with many another initiative, had fallen flat in the stodgy UK market.

The extent to which the UK market needed a fresh approach, and the magnitude of the impact that Weinberg, stimulated and motivated by Gordon and Liberty Life's early success in South Africa, was ultimately to have on it through Abbey Life, can be best appreciated by reference to a UK authority on the life insurance industry.

Professor Barry Supple, in his major work on the Royal Exchange Assurance published in 1970 and sub-titled "A History of British Insurance 1720–1970", was very conscious of what were, at the time he was writing, some very important developments, presaging a groundswell of changing attitudes.

"The growth of life business is perhaps the best example of the response of insurance to the advent of relative affluence and inflation. This was reflected in the renewed tendency for the public to save an increasing proportion of rising incomes by taking out life policies: between 1946 and 1960, for example, ordinary life premiums as a percentage of total personal income in the UK rose from 1,54 to 2,52. Given this boom, in the eight years after the War ordinary premium income grew at the spectacular rate of 10,4 per cent per annum, compared with 4,4 per cent in the inter-war period and 3,4 per cent in the years before 1914. And the high rate continued: between 1953 and 1967 the annual growth rate of ordinary premiums was some 9,7 per cent. Sums assured by ordinary policies grew from £2 590 million in 1945 to £12 867 million in 1962 and £16 100 million in 1966. In the first five years of the sixties alone the annual level of new sums assured more than doubled.

"Associated with this development has been an increasing emphasis on group pension business and the self-employed pension business, which was given very considerable tax advantages by financial legislation in 1956.

"In general, by the late 1950s and 1960s the higher bonuses derived from the new profitability of investment activity meant that policyholders as well as offices were concentrating on the investment aspects of life insurance, particularly in the context of the rising price of equities.

"Indeed, by the late 1960s a small but growing number of offices were experimenting with life policies whose value was explicitly linked to that of equities, through unit trust funds. This was an obvious response to the manifest pressures of rising prices, a booming stock market and new consumer attitudes.

"In addition, however, it was stimulated by the mechanism of competitive innovation, for the decade of the 1960s had seen a spectacular increase in the unit trust movement, and the unit trusts themselves had begun, most successfully, to innovate by the issue of life policies linked to their units in schemes for regular savings. Some of the established life offices had responded first by associating themselves with similar schemes, and then by combining the equity element with traditional endowment policies. At the end of the decade it was not yet clear how far this new fashion would carry the life industry as a whole, or whether it would be justified by trends in the value of equity capital.

"But it had already demonstrated two important lessons: first, that life policyholders and companies alike had become dominantly concerned with investment in the context of apparent long-run inflation; second, that the forces of competition and emulation were still strong enough to give a new shape and direction to the industry."

The largest single factor in that "new shape and direction" that Supple perceived in 1970 was Abbey Life – and Abbey Life was conceived and planned in Liberty Life's offices in Johannesburg in the closing months of 1961. Liberty Life, Abbey Life and the driving force and outstanding skills of Donald Gordon and Mark Weinberg were to change the shape of the life insurance industry in the UK – just as Liberty Life itself was beginning to do in South Africa.

Another measure of the impact of the new shape and direction on the United Kingdom life insurance industry is provided by Sun Life

Assurance, the major UK life assurer in which TransAtlantic Holdings, Liberty Life's UK associate, had built up an indirect 29,9 per cent stake by the close of 1988. In the beautifully-illustrated *The Sun Life Story – 1810-1985*, published to celebrate that company's 175th anniversary, Jack Minnitt, Sun Life's archivist, pays an unintended compliment to the influence of the men who had done so much to introduce and make acceptable entirely new concepts of life insurance.

"In the early 1970s, unit linked policies were still a novelty, a strange hybrid offered in the main only by new, specialist companies. Within less than 10 years, unit linked assurance had become very big business indeed, and Sun Life had been one of the first of the established offices to recognise its potential when, in January 1977, we launched Solar Life Assurance to market these new contracts.

"Initially, most of the establishment treated the unit linked concept with considerable caution. This was small wonder, for it was a pretty radical departure from one of the traditional tenets of life assurance; the promise of a guaranteed return. In its place, the unit linked contract offered the policyholder the chance to obtain an appreciably better deal, through backing his own judgement in specific sectors of the investment market from a range chosen by the assurance company's own experts. That the time was ripe for this development is proved by the dramatic growth of unit linked business, both for the insurance industry as a whole and for Sun Life in particular."

The first mention of Abbey Life in Liberty Life's records is in a low-key Board resolution dated 4 January 1962. Most suitably, considering the new era Liberty Life was entering, the resolution appeared on the very first page of Liberty Life's second directors' minute book – volume two.

"It was recorded that the company had been approached by promoters of a new British life insurance company (the Abbey Life Assurance Company Limited) with a view to Liberty Life obtaining a participation in the capital of Abbey Life, as well as to assist them technically. On the basis of Abbey Life undertaking to give Liberty Life a first participation in their reassurances above their retention it was resolved that the Liberty Life Association of Africa Limited acquire 5 000 shares of £1 each at par in the Abbey Life Assurance Company Limited."

Weinberg recalls that late in 1961, he had finally decided to settle in the UK. "I was wondering what to do with my life and I talked to Donny, Hugh Rubin and the others. The upshot was that they would be interested in establishing an office in London. I said that it didn't make sense to operate as a branch of a South African life company but that I, with their support, was prepared to start a new UK life company. After the Reserve Bank had said 'Yes' in principle, the decision was taken instead to start Abbey Life, and I actually physically started Abbey Life as a shell in December 1961 while I was in Johannesburg learning all about how to do it, so to speak."

Another link between the two companies came on 16 February 1962, when Abbey Life was given a 25 per cent participation in the prime risk retentions of Liberty Life, thereby reducing the need for Liberty Life to reinsure with the professional market, an arrangement confirmed on 7 March 1962, when Liberty Life's retentions on its own risks were increased from R2 000 to R3 000 "subject to a further increase of R1 000 in the event of satisfactory arrangements being concluded with The Abbey Life to acquire an interest in the basic retentions of Liberty Life." This "reverse reinsurance" arrangement never actually came into effect, for a Board resolution of 14 November 1963 records that it was "cancelled *ab initio* by arrangement" with Abbey Life.

On 9 May 1962, it was resolved by Liberty Life: "That Mark Aubrey Weinberg be appointed as the London manager of the company," and that is how Weinberg appeared in Liberty Life's pre-listing statement of 3 June 1962. It is interesting to note that there was no mention at all in that document of Liberty's £5 000 investment in Abbey Life, nor of the impact that that company might make on the UK life insurance market. Clearly, the thoughts of Donald Gordon and his colleagues were wholly concentrated on Liberty Life, its listing and its immediate progress. The fledgeling Abbey Life, at that point, was regarded very much as a secondary issue, to be placed, for the time being, on the back burner.

Indeed, it was not until 18 July 1963 that Abbey Life warranted another mention in Liberty Life's Board minutes. Then: "The Chairman reported on the results of his trip to London, with particular reference to the progress of Abbey Life Assurance Company Limited. 12 000 shares of £1 each in the Abbey Life were available at approximately £1 2s 0d per share, and it was resolved that an application be made to the South African Reserve Bank for permission to purchase these shares out of the Liberty Life's funds in the Republic."

Reserve Bank consent was duly forthcoming and the shares were purchased, for £1 1s 7d each. Liberty Life's stake in Abbey Life thus became 17 000 shares, or 34 per cent of the then £50 000 issued capital, at a total cost of some £17 950.

By June 1962 Mark Weinberg was back in London, preparing for the launch of Abbey Life in October that year. As he recalls: "I had had a lot to do with the launch of Liberty Life on the Johannesburg Stock Exchange, and I flew back to England – hopefully permanently, which was what I wanted – the day before the actual listing. I spent the next three months getting Abbey Life ready to roll." As with Liberty Life four years earlier, it wasn't easy; Weinberg, this time with Gordon's staunch support, faced similar problems over raising the additional capital required, in creating a sales force, and in opening up new connections.

Despite all the problems, the Abbey Life Assurance Company opened its doors for business in September 1962. It was small, but it was well-connected – to South Africa's only listed life assurer; and it had a good address at 1-3 St Paul's Churchyard, London, EC4. Also, it had at the helm men of high intelligence and unbounded energy and ambition.

While Abbey Life's growth was eventually to be quite phenomenal, the first couple of years – as indeed the similar period had been for Liberty Life – were really hard slogging, disappointment and frustration. Only those very few men who have started great institutions from scratch can really know the toughness, the challenge and the trauma of the early years – and the thrill of the final breakthrough. Exceptional men, such as Weinberg and Gordon, have had their fair share of this experience. So much so that when, less than two years down the line, the Georgia International Life Insurance Company, of Atlanta, made an offer of 35/- per Abbey Life share, all concerned were basically ready to accept. Of course, a capital profit of 75 per cent in two years was pretty good going in an era when capital profits were rare and extremely difficult to come by, but it capitalised Abbey Life at barely £100 000, so it was hardly a case of its having set the Thames on fire. Even so, it was the very first capital gain that Liberty Life had ever achieved.

Abbey Life's slow initial progress is underlined in a report by Guardian's assistant actuary, S W Pressman, to his chief, the actuary, F B Tucker, dated 29 April 1964, when Guardian was wondering just what to do with the indirect stake in it that it had just acquired via its takeover of Liberty Life:

"Abbey Life Assurance Company Limited. The above company was established in 1961 and commenced business about September 1962. The managing director is M A Weinberg, B Com, LL B (Rand), LL M(London). He is aged about thirty-five [actually, Weinberg was then only thirty-three], South African born, and was a member of the Johannesburg Bar. He was closely associated (as a solicitor) with Donald Gordon in the formation of the Liberty Life and came to London to start the Abbey Life.

"The company's authorised capital is £75 000 of which £61 500 has been issued (£56 500 fully paid and £5 000 10 per cent paid). 27,6 per cent is held by the Liberty Life and the balance by various individuals. Weinberg has an option to purchase 5 000 £1 shares at par by December 1971.

"Operations are virtually a one-man affair – apart from Weinberg there is an accountant and a total staff of four or so. Business is received from certain brokers, from a financial paper which circularised its subscribers (and is treated as an agent) and direct as a result of newspaper and financial press reports earlier this year. Weinberg's wife, who has press agent experience, is currently seeing brokers regarding policies for women and will subsequently 'attack' women's magazines. Weinberg does not wish to develop an inspector force (at this stage, at any rate) and is therefore confining his attention to new business sources which require the minimum of servicing.

"Reassurances are placed with the Victory, who underwrite all business except the straightforward. (The Abbey Life are not LOA members and therefore have no Association Registry facilities.) Attempts have been made to interest brokers in placing sub-standard business with the Abbey Life, the underwriting again being done by the Victory.

"The allocation of profits is 'as determined'. Surprisingly, 75 per cent of conventional business is with profits. No bonus rate has yet been declared. New gross annual premium income for 1964 is expected to be about £50 000 (£15 000 in 1963). The consulting actuaries (Bacon & Woodrow) had been pressing for an increase in the paid-up capital, but following an approximate valuation at 31 December 1963, they are reported to be pleasantly surprised at the position and to have said there would be no difficulty in demonstrating solvency.

"In the past, Weinberg had made occasional private visits to South Africa, the last six weeks ago. He doubts whether such visits will continue in the future. The Abbey Life act as a 'front' and a pillar-box for the Liberty Life, handling the rare queries that arise.

"There have been occasional enquiries in the past from American sources as to whether the Abbey Life is available for purchase."

During this period, Weinberg, as the managing director resident in London, was the main driving force, as Pressman had noted, but Gordon's part was not inconsiderable. As co-founder and 27,6 per cent shareholder, he devoted as much time as possible to Abbey Life, but obviously the newly listed Liberty Life was his main concern. The two men are almost complete opposites in character and style, however, so it is probably just as well that the bulk of their dealings were by telephone and correspondence.

Weinberg reminisces: "Donny was a director of Abbey Life for the two years from 1962 until 1964, when we sold out. He would come over to London every few months for a Board meeting, and in general we got on very well, but in time a little tension developed between us. Nothing serious, and anyway, the company was always the main thing, for both of us. I have a very different style of running a company from Donny's. No-one, least of all me, can fault Donny's way of running his company – it's just different.

"Donny's way of running a company arises out of the fact that he is an accountant, and he is immensely concerned with detail. He thinks everything through; he is like a chess player. When Donny used to look at a balance sheet, he used automatically to add up the figures to make sure that the printer had got them right. He has a mind like a computer. I'm much more fundamentally a marketing person and therefore I'm thinking much more conceptually and so I'm not worried about whether or not all the figures add up. Neither of us are right or wrong, but as a result of our totally divergent approaches, I don't think we could have worked together for very much longer than we did. At 6 000 miles distance, everything was fine; he ran his company successfully and I ran mine – but I wouldn't really have enjoyed having Donny too close to me. In many respects, then, the parting of the ways when it came was actually a very appropriate development."

The two men, now in 1989 major figures in their own right in the

UK insurance industry, still meet occasionally. Says Weinberg: "We are very relaxed with one another whenever we do get together," while Gordon has a great admiration for Weinberg's achievements, and believes him to be a true genius. He readily acknowledges their different styles, and easily concedes that he is an accountant – first, second and last. On the conceptual front, it would be a fascinating debate as to which of the two was the more inventive and innovative. But it is incontrovertible that it was Gordon who stimulated Weinberg to enter the life insurance industry in the first place and gave him his introduction to the intricacies of the business.

They are still pretty competitive; outside observers can detect something of an "edge" between the two individuals who have possibly done more than any others to transform life assurance, world-wide, in little more than two decades. Perhaps Weinberg resented the fact that he wasn't the first in the life insurance business – but, of course, Gordon was always one year his senior.

The "parting of the ways" between Abbey Life and Liberty Life had its genesis in Liberty Life's March 1964 deal with the UK's Guardian Assurance Company. This gave Guardian 75 per cent control of Liberty Life, and thus an indirect 20,7 per cent stake in the infant UK life assurer, with the inherent possibility of a conflict of interest on Guardian's own turf in the UK. This, of course, was not an immediate problem; Abbey Life was in the new field of linked assurance, a field eschewed by the staid, established, old-time assurers, of which Guardian was a leader. And Abbey Life was far too small to be of real concern, anyway, to Liberty Life's new controllers.

The basic lack of concern about Abbey Life – on the part of either Guardian, or Liberty Life, for that matter – is illustrated by the paucity of either correspondence or Board time devoted to the topic. Clearly, all concerned were content to let Weinberg get on with his job while they proceeded with the vastly more important task of meshing Liberty Life into Guardian's worldwide operation.

The first, somewhat casual, mention came in a letter from Gordon to Ernest Bigland, then Guardian's general manager, dated 20 April 1964, in which Gordon referred to a forthcoming visit by him to London in June that year: "There are many purely Liberty Life problems for me to go into, particularly in relation to the Abbey Life, which will probably not involve the Guardian at all." And a Liberty Life Board meeting in May 1964 merely confirmed that

Abbey Life was on the managing director's agenda for discussion in London the following month.

During Gordon's June visit, Abbey Life clearly came up for discussion, for Bigland, writing on 23 June to put the meetings on record, said: "It was agreed that no further action should be taken about our present shareholding or relationship with the Abbey Life at this stage but the position could always be reviewed in the future."

Weinberg recalls that, just prior to that visit, he had met Bigland over lunch on the introduction of Noel Benjamin, another ex-South African lawyer resident in London. It was, he remembers, a frustrating meeting. "There we were, a little offshoot of Liberty Life, and they had now been acquired by Guardian. What did Guardian want to do about us? Well, Bigland was polite, but he couldn't seem to even focus on what the relevance of Abbey Life was. Why should they bother to take over this little company or even think seriously about it? So no discussions ever took place. If they had, I would probably have been willing to go along with Donny into Guardian at that time."

Unbeknown to Weinberg, Guardian had in fact shown some spark of interest in Abbey Life prior to his lunch with Bigland. Pressman had submitted the report to Tucker referred to above, and in an inter-office memo dated 29 April 1964 Tucker had in turn referred it to his superior, Bigland.

"Re Abbey Life. Following our conversation yesterday Mr Pressman has obtained a substantial amount of information about this company and has written a brief report which I enclose with press cuttings and also their provisional balance sheet and accounts as at 31 December last. This, I think, will give you a good general picture of this company.

"Pressman also obtained extensive information on their ratings, prospectuses and quotation pamphlets which I will not bother you with but if the need arises to make a detailed investigation of the company we have the information.

"In Pressman's report you will notice that the Consulting Actuaries are said to be pleasantly surprised at the estimated financial position at 31 December last year – it would be interesting to see what the position was.

"You will also notice their estimated increase in new annual premiums for 1964 at the substantial figure of £50 000.

"The Liberty Life apparently owns 27,6 per cent of the shares and as the Guardian owns 75 per cent of the Liberty Life it effectively has a 21 per cent interest in the Abbey Life.

"I do not know what form the discussion between you and Mr Weinberg will take but I have had a few random thoughts, as follows:

"1. If we allow the Abbey Life to continue in competition with Guardian we shall get a 21 per cent interest in their success. It would not therefore be sound for us to encourage the company by allowing the business which could come to us to go to them because we should lose the chance of 100 per cent profit in return for 21 per cent. This situation is different from the Liberty Life where we cannot compete with them in South Africa and are therefore using them as an effective branch of our Life Fund.

"2. As you will see the Abbey Life are intensively engaging in unit trust linked sales which the Guardian, as a matter of policy, does not transact, so that it could be said that they are not in direct competition with us unless we should change our policy.

"3. Again the Abbey Life engages (and this seems to be one of its main attractions) in permanent sickness insurance which we do not transact but in my opinion, which I have held for a number of years, the Guardian ought to engage in this new field which in a matter of a few years or so will become normal trading in the life insurance industry. If we did do so I think the effect would be to cut severely the activities of the Abbey Life since the Guardian is a superior company in the matter of financial standing. However, to undertake permanent sickness insurance requires a special 'know-how' which we ourselves do not have at the moment and could not possibly hope to acquire out of our own staff which, as you know, is very short in numbers. Let me say that we have the theoretical know-how but not the practical know-how. It occurs to me therefore that if the Abbey Life had such know-how (although they will have acquired it in a very short time) it might be appropriate for us to buy this know-how and then possibly let the Abbey Life be sold to the American source at a good price. I do not know how true the point in Pressman's report about the Americans is but I believe that a very good price would be paid for an existing life company, no matter what its age is, as an established base to commence operations.

"I trust that Pressman's report and my comments will give you a reasonable background before your meeting."

Since, as Weinberg recalled it, Bigland seemed unable even to focus on the relevance of Abbey Life to the mighty Guardian when they met a few days later, Tucker's carefully disguised enthusiasm was wasted.

Even so, Bigland dropped Benjamin a cordial note on 7 May 1964: "Dear Mr Benjamin, Thank you very much for a most enjoyable lunch today. I was pleased to have the opportunity of meeting Mr Weinberg. I will certainly see that he meets Mr Tucker and I hope we may be able to do some business together."

And to Tucker, the following day, Bigland wrote: "I met Mr Weinberg yesterday and suggested that you would get in touch with him (hope in the near future) to have a discussion about whether we can do any business together. I told him we might be interested in a sickness contract and as it is a rather complicated one tied up with a unit trust I think he had better explain the details to you. I did not go into any detailed points but I did hint that if we came to any agreement which might substantially increase their business it might mean that we would like to reconsider the financial association, ie through the Liberty Life we now have a 20 per cent interest in the Abbey Life."

So there was, at that stage, a real, if somewhat dim, spark of interest. But it was soon to be doused by the lackadaisical approach typical of the City of London in those distant days, and by the overriding importance to the British of the precious summer holidays. Tucker to Bigland, 22 May 1964: "I am afraid that I have not been able yet to make an appointment with Mr Weinberg because of several pressing matters, holidays and so on, and during the next fortnight I shall be involved with the Actuaries Congress in London and Scotland. It seems, therefore, that the earliest date I can make will be early June, unless you would like someone else to see him in the meantime. I do not think the matter is very urgent and perhaps it could wait."

But wait it could not, for matters continued to drift until August, when Weinberg was approached by an American insurance company, Georgia International. He immediately flew out to Johannesburg to discuss the matter with Gordon. The official documentation totally fails to capture the excitement of the issues involved.

On 24 August 1964, Gordon wrote (in Bigland's absence on holiday) to Guardian's company secretary. "Mr Roy [Liberty Life's then Chairman], who has now returned from overseas, has mentioned to me that you had been approached by an American company looking for a United Kingdom outlet and that your view was that this might offer a solution to the problem of Abbey Life. In principle, I think we should disengage ourselves from the affairs of Abbey Life at this stage, for the reasons we discussed in London. Coincidentally, I have only this morning received a communication from Mr Weinberg informing me that he has been approached by the Georgia International Life Insurance Company, who are interested in acquiring all the shares in Abbey Life. I understand the suggested consideration is somewhere between 30/- and 35/- per share or on a share-for-share basis based on this price. As Mr Weinberg apparently believes this will offer him an exceptional opportunity, subject to your agreement I would be inclined to accept such an offer as and when it is made. I have no further details available but he will be contacting me in the next few days. As the matter is likely to be one of urgency, I would very much appreciate your cabling me on your attitude as soon as possible."

On receipt of that letter, the company secretary immediately cabled: "Thanks letter 24 August willing agree possible sale Abbey Life shares. – Fireguard." And he followed up with a letter: "I cabled you yesterday regarding the Abbey Life about which incidentally Mr Benjamin telephoned me yesterday. It is a strange coincidence that there should be more than one American company active in this direction for my possible contact was an entirely different source from the Georgia International Life."

And, also on 27 August, Benjamin cabled Gordon: "G are satisfied in principle. M W has firm offer for 33 shillings which he thinks will be improved to 35/-. He is visiting Johannesburg for personal reasons in any event. Will advise you on detail after he returns London regards. Benjamin."

All this was sufficient for Liberty Life's Board to be primed at its meeting on 1 September 1964. Under the heading: "Offer for the purchase of the shares in Abbey Life Assurance Company Limited", it was minuted: "Mr Gordon informed the Board of his discussions in regard to the future relationship between the Abbey Life Assurance Company Limited and the company, and of the attitude of the Guardian in this connection. He indicated that an informal offer of £1 15s 0d per share had been received by the company for its 17 000 shares of £1 each in Abbey Life. Mr Gordon informed the meeting that in his view a number of unneccessary complications could be obviated should the company accept such an offer, if and when it is formally made. He further expressed the opinion that the price offered was attractive in view of the progress of the Abbey Life to date. It was also recorded that the Guardian had agreed in principle to the sale of the shares. It was therefore resolved that, in the event of a formal offer being made to the company, it should dispose of its 17 000 shares of £1 each at not less than £1 15s 0d per share."

On 10 September, Bigland wrote: "I am sure we are right to consider the sale of your shares in Abbey Life subject to a formal offer and I hope that this will go through." And on the 17th he reiterated: "I am glad we both agree that it would be sensible to sell the Liberty Life's holding in Abbey Life if, as we trust, a formal offer is received." Finally, on 13 October 1964, Gordon was able to inform Bigland: "The sale of the Abbey Life shares has now been completed at £1 15s 0d per share, which has resulted in a very useful capital profit accruing to this company. Of the proceeds, £21 000 has been remitted to South Africa in terms of our existing undertaking to the exchange control authorities, and the balance has been retained in the United Kingdom and has been invested in long-dated British Government securities giving us a tax-free return of over 6 per cent."

It was, of course, an exceedingly small deal, involving a total of only £98 875, of which Liberty Life's share was a mere £29 750. The real drama was in the excitement of the moment – and the "what might have been", had Tucker made time to see Weinberg when the latter "would probably have been willing to go along with Donny into Guardian".

At the time, however, Weinberg saw the deal as crucial to the future of his battling company. "I was terribly keen for the deal to go ahead – I really needed the sort of backing the Americans could give me." So it was not really just for "personal reasons", as Benjamin had put it, that Weinberg flew to Johannesburg. It was to sell the deal to his colleague and partner, Donald Gordon, and to make certain that he would not block it.

While the documents of that time make it plain that neither Guardian nor Liberty Life were other than very willing sellers, Weinberg's recollection is that, in reality, it was nowhere near so clear cut. "I remember Donny raising the question of whether they, Liberty Life, could hold on to some shares, maybe 20 per cent. I telephoned the Americans from South Africa, and they said 'No, definitely, not.' For them, it had to be 100 per cent, or nothing. They were planning to build up a world-wide insurance group, and Abbey

Life was their first overseas step. To have even a 20 per cent outside shareholder just was not on.

"I agreed with them, because I think there are only two good numbers in the world, and they are zero and 100 per cent. Occasionally, I've got involved in 50 per cent, but for me it has never worked out. Donny, on the other hand, thinks any number between zero and 100 per cent is good, and I believe he actually thinks that almost any number is better than 100 per cent! Donny likes 50 per cent here and 20 per cent there and so on; they are all different depending on the circumstances, but I just don't understand the logic of minority shareholdings. Anyway, in this case Donny was saying: 'OK, we're selling out, and we're all very happy with the deal. But let's hold on to 20 per cent.'

"I think his reasoning was sound. Liberty Life had done their deal with Guardian, and were now very adequately capitalised. So it made a lot of sense to want to hold on to a 'ticket' that might be worth something in time; it could well prove worth hanging on to. But anyway, when I phoned the Americans and they were adamant, Donny agreed to sell. So far as I was concerned, he was completely supportive – certainly, as I remember, not obstructive in any way."

So the deal went through, and Weinberg continued to run Abbey Life, with enormous success, until his new masters sold out. With hindsight, he reckons that Ernest Bigland lost, for Guardian, the opportunity of a lifetime. "If Bigland had just snapped his fingers, he could have bought Abbey Life for less than £100 000 at any stage right up to the time I did the deal with Georgia."

Gordon himself sees the Abbey Life affair – with hindsight, of course – as one of his few "major blunders". Talking to the *Financial Mail* in 1978, fourteen years after the event, about Abbey Life and Weinberg, he said: "He came into Liberty Life to get the background on what we were doing. Mark is incredibly bright; he has a brilliant mind, and a photographic memory and it did not take him very long to get to grips with the basics. He then went over to the UK to start Abbey Life, which we backed. The company battled along in the same way as the early days of Liberty Life. In 1964 – which turned out to be one of the major blunders of my career – because the Guardian at that time felt that it would be difficult to integrate Abbey Life into the Guardian group, they rather imposed on us to sell our interest. Weinberg came out to South Africa late in 1964 with an offer from Georgia International, a US life company, to buy our shares. We made a profit of about £12 000. I remember being in London in 1968 and opening my *Financial Times* to see that Abbey Life had been resold to IT&T for the equivalent of $64 million!" Told by the *FM* that it was the Guardian's mistake, rather than his, Gordon went on: "I should have said no to the Guardian. I didn't know how strong their objection was. They saw it as an inability to absorb this particular situation into their operation. It was terribly small and insignificant at the time as far as they were concerned."

"Small and insignificant" Abbey Life certainly was then, so much so that it is perfectly reasonable that the varied recollections of those concerned do not exactly match. It was by no means an important deal, so Gordon is being very unkind to himself when he calls it a major blunder. But the figures are horrendous.

Let Weinberg have the final word. "There were actually two American companies involved when the deal finally went through – IT&T and Georgia International. In 1964, IT&T actually bought half of Abbey Life from Georgia International for under £50 000, and then they bought the other half, in 1970, for about £12 million. They eventually sold it off, in two tranches, in 1985 and 1986, for £520 million. It really was not a bad deal for them!"

Weinberg left Abbey Life when IT&T bought control in 1970. He was supported by his old friend, Sydney Lipworth, who had joined Abbey Life five years earlier as an executive director, following his resignation from the Liberty Life Board in 1964 at the behest of the Guardian after its acquisition of control of Liberty Life earlier that year. Together they formed, with the backing of one of the most blue-blooded of London's merchant banks, Hambros, a new life insurance venture, Hambro Life. When that company was eventually floated on the London Stock Exchange, it became the largest listed insurance company to be floated in the UK since World War II. The company was ultimately acquired by the British American Tobacco Company in 1984, and Weinberg still continues as Chairman. Charles Hambro, a colleague and contemporary of Gordon on the Guardian Royal Exchange Board, is now Chairman of both GRE and Hambros Bank – yet another of the incredible coincidences that have been part of Donald Gordon's life and career.

Although Sir Mark Weinberg has been out of it for many years, the first company he and Donald Gordon created, Abbey Life, is now valued on The Stock Exchange, London, at over £1 billion. That was just prior to a 57 per cent controlling interest being acquired by Lloyds Bank Group in December 1988 consequent on the merger of Abbey Life with the financial services operations of Lloyds Bank. This made Abbey Life a major force in the UK, with immense resources and distribution capabilities to back it.

It is remarkable that Abbey Life's recent development has so closely followed Gordon's own strategic plan for Liberty Life, which has been evolving steadily over the past decade, and that the concepts involved are so similar to those being developed for TransAtlantic Holdings, which Gordon founded in 1980 as Liberty Life's offshore holding company in the UK. It is nonetheless amazing how fate writes its own script and in what strange ways the circle is sometimes completed or the triangle closed.

# 5 Seeking Big Brother

While there is no gainsaying the fact that Liberty Life's June 1962 Johannesburg Stock Exchange listing was not an immediate and overwhelming success, it is worth noting that it was a highly skilful financial manoeuvre, which really became the catalyst for the acceleration of the momentum of development.

The share, obviously, was very tightly held and in fact there were no dealings in June, when the nominal price of 270 cents put a market capitalisation of R270 000 on the company. In July, a price of 360 cents was recorded, and R5 was registered in both August and October (with a dip to R4 in September). With few sellers around, the price was somewhat artificial, but even so it enabled Donald Gordon to negotiate a double-the-market price of R10 when he did a deal with African Life in October. The sale then of 30 000 new shares to the Schlesinger Group's life company, which increased Liberty Life's issued capital to 130 000 shares, put a price tag of R1 300 000 on a company which four months earlier had been valued by the market at a mere R270 000.

The "calculated strategy" that Gordon referred to in the 1978 *Financial Mail* interview had paid off. As he put it then: "By 1962, we had made some sort of impact and we went for a listing on the Johannesburg Stock Exchange that June. It was a calculated strategy. We went on to the market with 100 000 shares at R2,70 and soon thereafter along came African Life and offered to buy 30 000 new shares at R10 a share. This was terribly attractive and very flattering, as we were really still a small struggling operation." Lipworth, many years later in an interview with the author, also noted that an early flotation was part of the founders' game plan: "One of the objectives was to float the company as soon as possible so that we could market the shares. We did it as soon as we could, soon after we had made a hit with retirement annuity policies. Once we were on the market, the next thing was to find a Big Brother."

Gordon and his colleagues had long since recognised the need for the greater muscle that a Big Brother could provide. While "Liberty Life of Doornfontein" was doing pretty well – indeed, very well, with premium income having advanced from 1959's R95 500 to R188 950 for 1960 and R250 840 for 1961 – the relatively modest increase of 1961 over 1960 confirmed that the knocking tactics of the young Liberty Life's competitors were making the going tough. Credible backing was what was needed and, with Liberty Life successfully listed on the JSE, Gordon set about seeking just that.

He first aimed high – as he would indeed continue to do throughout his career. Then, as now, South Africa's biggest single commercial operation was the Anglo American Corporation of South Africa, and it then, somewhat surprisingly considering its wide ramifications thoughout the economy, had no interest in life insurance. Gordon approached Cecil Carrington (who would later become a director of Johannesburg Consolidated Investment Company and of South African Breweries before retiring in 1986), who was in those days the head of Anglo's Investment Research Department.

In that capacity, Carrington had developed an investment module that worked well on quoted companies, and when he had used the module to indicate other areas at which Anglo American should be looking, it had pin-pointed life insurance. He was therefore in a receptive frame of mind when DG came to see him. "Gordon", recalls Carrington, "made a most impressive presentation, stressing, in particular, the need for a group as large and diversified as Anglo American to be in life insurance. Having in mind the indications of our investment module, I was easily sold on the idea of our taking a stake in Liberty Life, and sent the proposition 'upstairs'."

"Upstairs" was one Bill Wilson, who in 1962 was Anglo's managing director. It is an Anglo oddity that it has almost never had anything so mundane as a "managing director". Almost invariably, the chief executive at Anglo American is the Chairman. Harry Oppenheimer briefly graced the MD's title before formally taking over from his father, Sir Ernest, but Wilson was the only "outsider" ever to be MD of Anglo. He put the putative Liberty Life deal before Anglo's ruling body, the Executive Committee (Exco), where it was turned down – flat.

Carrington, who was very keen on the deal, was extremely disappointed. "As I recall, it was the legendary R B Hagart who finally squelched it, saying that life insurance 'was too far removed from the traditional business of Anglo American', but I regard this decision as possibly one of Anglo's most significant lost investment opportunities. After all, it wasn't as if Gordon was looking for capital to start up – there was Liberty Life, up and running, and already successful."

It is certainly ironic to note that, when Anglo American did eventually make its belated entry into the life insurance industry in 1974, it did so by buying the Schlesinger Organisation and, with it, African Life – by then, long since having sold its Liberty Life shares to Guardian at R19 per share.

Another of life's little ironies is the fact that Wilson, who turned down Liberty Life and Gordon in 1962, was, in his capacity as a director of both Edgars and Edcon, to be Gordon's prime supporter in the control battles for those companies in 1982.

After being turned down by Anglo American, Gordon continued to try to find a wholly suitable Big Brother. "I went everywhere," he recalls: "I went to Fred Haslett [known affectionately as 'The Fox'] who in January 1988 retired as the highly respected Chairman of South African Eagle, the South African subsidiary of Britain's Eagle Star, and I even went to Sanlam, the Afrikaans mutual life insurer, then, as now, second only in size to Old Mutual. There, I was rejected by the famed Dr Andreas Wassenaar himself."

So it was back to the drawing board, and hence to African Life. While African Life was by no means the ideal partner for Liberty Life, largely because, in 1962, the reputation of the Schlesinger Group was somewhat lacklustre, it was, however, well established and reasonably acceptable in the eyes of the man in the street.

African Life had been started from scratch in 1904 by one of South Africa's great early entrepreneurs, Isadore William Schlesinger. I W, as he was almost universally known, was an American and he remained such throughout his life, although he was to make his fortune in South Africa, and build up one of the country's biggest personal business empires – largely on the back of the insurance company, African Life. African Life was never able to get to the top of the South African life insurance league, but its importance lay in introducing new concepts into life insurance in the country. But things were not as promising as they appeared to be on the surface. The great I W had died in 1949, to be succeeded by his twenty-six-year-old son John, whose talents were more closely attuned to the international social scene than to the cut-and-thrust of the

Johannesburg business arena. By the early sixties, the Schlesinger Organisation was but a shadow of its former self, and the real power was vested not in the easy-going Johnny Schlesinger, but in the tough and thrusting Mandy Moross, a young and determined go-getter who was just over a year younger than Gordon himself.

At first, of course, everything went smoothly. It was a very good deal indeed for Liberty Life. For only 23 per cent of its equity, which entailed no effective diminution of the control situation, it received a much-needed cash injection of R300 000 and gained a broader capital base, a matter which, as mentioned earlier, was always of concern to DG.

The Liberty Life Board was informed on 23 October 1962. "Proposed deal with The African Life Assurance Society Limited. Mr Gordon reported to the meeting on his progress in respect of discussions he was currently having with the African Life Assurance Society Limited in regard to their acquiring 30 000 shares in the company at R10 per share. He informed the meeting of the nature of the proposals and the supplementary details that would constitute any agreement, should such come into being. The proposals were discussed at great length, and the meeting duly authorised him to continue in his discussions and to reach agreement in principle, broadly in terms of the discussions to date."

Less than two weeks later, on 3 November 1962, a joint announcement from African Life and Liberty Life said: "Mr John S Schlesinger, Chairman of the African Life Assurance Society Limited, and Mr Donald Gordon, Chairman of the Liberty Life Association of Africa Limited, today jointly announced that an agreement had been concluded between their companies whereby African Life is to acquire a 23 per cent interest in the equity share capital of Liberty Life for a consideration of R300 000 with effect from 1 January 1963.

"The additional capital accruing to Liberty Life will enable it to increase substantially the scope and nature of its operation. Both companies will benefit by the fact that they will be working in close collaboration. There will be no change in the control and management of Liberty Life as a result of the above arrangements."

Liberty Life had found its "Big Brother", but it is interesting to note which is the giant now. Notwithstanding the merger of African Life with Southern Life in the eighties, the combined company, Southern Life Association Limited, is significantly smaller than Liberty Life, even excluding the acquisition by Liberty Life of the

Prudential of South Africa in 1987. Bearing in mind that Southern Life was the third largest life office in South Africa, closely followed by African Life in fourth place, until a decade ago, this provides a vivid measure of the dynamic growth of the former protégé compared to its erstwhile "Big Brother".

Also on 3 November, Harold Fridjhon wrote a report in the *Rand Daily Mail*, under a photograph of Gordon and a three-deck headline to emphasise the importance of the event to the business community, "Schlesinger buys R300 000 interest in insurance co.":

"The African Life Insurance Society, the R75-million fulcrum of Mr John Schlesinger's empire, is to pay R300 000 for a 23 per cent interest (R10 per share) in the infant but dynamic Liberty Life Association of Africa, which has Mr Donald Gordon as its Chairman.

"Liberty Life, which started business on 1 October 1958 with a capital of R100 000, has made spectacular progress. The price which African Life will pay for its shares gives Liberty Life an effective value of R1,3 million for its 130 000 R2 shares.

"Mr Donald Gordon, the Chairman and managing director, is 33. All the directors have professional degrees in accountancy and law.

"Mr John Schlesinger will become a director of Liberty Life, and as he is 39, his presence will not materially affect the average age of the Board."

The Directors' Report for the year ended 31 December 1962, presented to the fifth Annual General Meeting of the company, was able to strike a high note: "The year under review has been one of exceptional progress in the development of your company and has recorded its transition from a relatively small life insurance office into a publicly accepted institution.

"Notable among the factors contributing to a highly successful year have been the outstanding operating results, the listing of the company's shares on the Johannesburg Stock Exchange and the establishment of a close relationship with the African Life, which has become an important minority shareholder in your company."

In getting R10 for the new shares, Gordon had driven a hard bargain, perhaps setting the pattern for all the deals to come. And the Johannesburg Stock Exchange was impressed, but not unduly so. Liberty Life's price rose to match the figure paid by African Life in November and December of 1962, but remained stubbornly below it for almost the whole of 1963, falling in fact back to R8,50 in May and

June. It was not until January 1964, when the share touched R14, that it rose substantially above African Life's entry level.

The new partnership got off to a good start with a luncheon party hosted by the new partner, Johnny Schlesinger, at the old Carlton Hotel in Johannesburg. Recalls Monty Schapiro: "It was a great lunch. On our side, we felt that Donny had done a super job. We were about to take off, and everyone was a bit euphoric. The Schlesinger people were happy too, and we were all really celebrating – both sides thought there was plenty to celebrate, as indeed there was. For us, it seemed that the early struggles were a thing of the past.

"Later on, Johnny made a speech, welcoming Liberty Life into the Schlesinger fold and all that sort of thing. He spoke of the 'honeymoon' that our two companies were about to embark on. I've never been famous for my tact, and when I interjected that 'usually, on a honeymoon, someone gets screwed', Schlesinger wasn't all that impressed."

Indeed, the honeymoon did not last long. There were problems at the very first Board meeting attended by Johnny Schlesinger's cousin, Alfred, who had been appointed to the Liberty Life Board in his stead. That was on 22 January 1963, when: "The Chairman welcomed Mr Schlesinger to his first Board meeting since his appointment on 17 January 1963." A capitalisation issue had previously been under consideration, and Gordon spoke strongly in favour of it.

The minute reads: "As had been previously discussed, the Chairman outlined proposals for the capitalisation of a portion of the share premium account and the utilisation of such amount as was required for the purpose of issuing to shareholders capitalisation shares in the proportion of three new shares for each five shares held at some specified date in the near future in conjunction, if possible, with the issuance of the company's annual balance sheet. The Chairman outlined in some detail what appeared to him to be the benefits of such a course, and in particular stressed that he felt this could be of advantage in furthering the company's image."

"Big Brother" put his foot down, firmly. "Mr Schlesinger pointed out that in his view and that of his colleagues, such a step at this stage of the company's development would be inadvisable and would possibly have an adverse effect on the company's prestige, particularly with participating policyholders and the industry in general. No decision was taken in the matter, and it was felt that members of the Board should have the opportunity of further discussion relative to this problem before taking the matter any further." Later, at the Board meeting on 14 November 1963, the proposed capitalisation issue was ditched altogether. "The advantages and disadvantages of the company declaring a capitalisation issue of its share capital were discussed at length. It was finally agreed that the advantages of such a step at this stage would probably not warrant the expense and work involved and it was accordingly resolved that this matter be shelved for the moment."

Up to the advent of African Life and the Schlesinger influence, Liberty Life had been a happy ship. Life was tough, of course, but the young team pulled well together. They worked hard, and although Gordon mostly ruled the roost, they played hard as well, and they had fun. "Board meetings", recalls Schapiro, "were always held at 6 pm, outside working hours. We would let our hair down and have a few drinks. In the early days, there was always something to celebrate – a few more policies sold. It was a happy company, even in the days when we were battling to get established."

While the interference at Board level was, to say the very least, irksome to Gordon (who would certainly have had his own way in the matter noted above had it merely been the "founders" who were present at those Board meetings), even more serious problems were arising from his personal relationship with Mandy Moross. Or, rather, from the lack of any real personal relationship between the two men.

From the beginning, they were doomed not to get on, bound to clash. Moross, the younger of the two if only by a year, was arrogant and, at that time, one of Johannesburg's most successful financiers. He had run, almost single-handedly, the R200 million Schlesinger Organisation for some ten years, and he took instructions from nobody, not even his nominal boss, Johnny Schlesinger. Gordon was running a relatively mini-company, worth barely R500 000 before African Life took an interest in it, and altogether of little moment in Moross's busy life. But Gordon, too, is not without a touch of arrogance, and he had his own not inconsiderable record of success. And he was no more accustomed to being told what to do than was Moross.

Louis Shill reminisces: "They were like chalk and cheese, but the biggest irritation was that our affairs, which were obviously of paramount importance to us, were regarded by Mandy as trivia. And he made no secret of it. Another thing – quite amusing to look back on, but important at the time – was the bickering about who went to see whom, and where. Mandy always wanted Donny to go to him at his office, but Donny dug his toes in as often as he could."

In London, Mark Weinberg was getting on with the job of running Abbey Life, and he had a different perspective of the developing situation in Johannesburg. "Donny had done the deal with Schlesinger, but Donny never rests on one deal – there is always the next one coming along. An important factor in the Schlesinger equation, and especially in Donny's dealings with Mandy, was that Donny, so far as Mandy was concerned, started low on the ladder. Starting low, each time Donny had to deal with someone, he was always dealing from weakness. Then, the moment Donny takes a step, he reassesses his position and takes the next step from the greater strength that he has built. That's been the pattern of his career; moving upwards from comparative weakness. Fundamentally, he has always been weaker than the man he has been dealing with right up until he has reached the heights that he commands now."

These penetrating observations were made in 1987, but they are also very pertinent to the situation in 1963. Weinberg also notes that Moross was more than a little patronising in his attitude towards both himself and Gordon, something that did not go down too well with either of them. "Mandy always used to say – and he used to include me in it as well, but maybe he was entitled to because their interest in Liberty Life gave them an indirect interest in Abbey Life – he used to refer to Donny and me as 'his boys'. That sort of thing would come up at, say, a dinner; Mandy would say, 'oh, my boys are here'. I'm sure that when I wasn't around Donny on his own would just be referred to as 'my boy'. It didn't worry me, but I would imagine that Donny didn't like it terribly much."

Gordon himself prefers to play down the issue. Talking to the *Financial Mail* in 1978, he merely noted that, after African Life had bought into Liberty Life: "We carried on for eighteen months like this, with African Life having a 23 per cent stake. By early 1964, the incompatibility between myself, I suppose essentially, and Mandy Moross, became clear. When Guardian appeared on the scene in 1964 and made an offer at R19 a share for control of Liberty Life, I rather prevailed on African Life to go out."

Well before the Guardian "appeared on the scene", however,

Liberty Life was actively seeking a bedmate more compatible than African Life. Schapiro remembers: "The thing with African Life just wasn't working out, and I thought anyway that what we really needed was to be associated with a major overseas company. I was in fact very anxious to do a tie-up with the Norwich Union, because I was very close to them."

The first overseas nibble came even before the Schlesinger "marriage of convenience" celebrated its first anniversary. At a Board meeting on 21 August 1963, it was resolved: "That in view of certain correspondence entered into with the Lincoln National Insurance Company, the Chairman would proceed to the United States to ascertain whether any arrangement could be concluded with that company, with a view to furthering Liberty Life's interests in South Africa." The minutes also noted another matter that would be of importance to Liberty Life's future: that, while in the US, the Chairman "would look into the methods of operation of the insurance industry and mutual funds, with a view to acquiring information which could be applied to the furtherance of the company's business". The next Board meeting authorised payment of the Chairman's travelling expenses of "R1 673,30 incurred during his recent trip to the United States". This must rank among the most fruitful expenditures Liberty Life ever made.

The approach from Lincoln National, of Fort Wayne, Indiana, a major US life insurance concern, warranted serious consideration. On his way, DG passed through London, and asked Mark Weinberg to accompany him to Fort Wayne.

"Would I come along with him to help with the legal side, Donny asked me," recalls Weinberg. "I had broken my ankle a few weeks before and I was laid up in plaster. So I asked my doctor if I could travel, and he said he would take off the plaster, but I wouldn't be able to wear proper shoes. We were leaving on the Saturday afternoon, so I rushed around the shops and finally found a pair of soft blue suede shoes. Off we went to Fort Wayne and arrived there on the Sunday afternoon – a miserable town, and nobody greeted us. Next morning we went in to Lincoln, and they greeted us very civilly and we had some very constructive discussions, but somehow I felt there was rather a frosty atmosphere, particularly so far as I was concerned. We spent three days there and they were sufficiently interested to send one of their top executives out to Johannesburg a couple of months later. On his last night in Johannesburg on that trip, he had a bit too much to drink, and he confided in one of my colleagues. 'I couldn't stand that chap Weinberg, he was so peculiar. Can you imagine someone walking around in daytime in a pair of blue suede shoes?' Clearly, the theory was that I was a sexual deviationist of some kind or other. So I wasn't at all sorry to hear eventually that the deal with Lincoln didn't go through!"

Gordon has his own version, essentially similar but a little more detailed. "Mark's suede shoes probably wrecked that whole deal. Those mid-Westerners in Lincoln National were very conservative. When Tom Watson, who later became president of the company, came out to South Africa, he told us, after a couple of drinks, many stories about how concerned Lincoln National was in those days about staff morality, and how their strict standards were maintained. Then along comes this odd-ball in his powder blue suede shoes; they were horrified – no wonder the deal didn't come off!"

One suspects there is a degree of poetic licence in the recollections of the two gentlemen concerned, for the negotiations with Lincoln National lasted several months. Indeed, they prospered, and about the middle of December 1963, DG was to take another trip to Fort Wayne, again via London, when he hoped to finalise a deal with the Americans.

In the meantime, Monty Schapiro, who was a director of the short-term brokers S A May, as well as being on the Board of Liberty Life, had been trying to find an overseas buyer for the shares of the former company. He had enlisted the support of his friend, Noel Benjamin. "I had asked him about finding a buyer for S A May, and he happened to be the personal attorney for a man called Lowndes." Noble Lowndes, of course, was a major figure in the pensions business in the United Kingdom, and Schapiro and he eventually did a deal over S A May. In the course of his talks with Lowndes, Schapiro mentioned Liberty Life, and the fact that they were also looking for a partner. "I introduced Donny to Lowndes, and they had a talk that didn't get far. But later, Lowndes phoned Benjamin and said: 'Look, about this man Gordon from Johannesburg who came to see me – maybe he should go to see my friend Bigland, of the Guardian.'" That was the imposing Ernest Bigland, then general manager of Guardian Assurance, a major British composite insurer.

So, on a wet Sunday evening in December 1963, Donald Gordon

met Ernest Bigland in London. He never did get around to making that return visit to Lincoln National in Fort Wayne.

Ironically, in 1985 a transaction was in fact put together with Lincoln National, in which they acquired 20 million shares in Liberty Life's TransAtlantic Holdings at £1,50 per share for an investment of £30 million. "First instincts should always be followed," notes Gordon wryly, for after an unconstructive period of association, it was amicably agreed that Lincoln National's shares in TransAtlantic would be placed at their purchase price with a number of other investors. So ended two attempts at an alliance with Lincoln National, both of them unproductive.

Back in Johannesburg, the Liberty Life Board met at 10 am on 3 March 1964. "The Chairman formally notified the meeting that the Guardian Assurance Company Limited of London had intimated their intention of making a bid for the shares of the company at R19 per share, subject to the major shareholders agreeing to accept this price for their shares and the necessary arrangements being made in relation to future management.

"It was resolved, on legal advice, that the directors should immediately communicate this information to shareholders and the Johannesburg Stock Exchange, in the normal way. Mr Schlesinger indicated that he was not voting in favour of the Resolution and requested the Chairman to delay the announcement until 12 noon this day to enable African Life to consider their situation. It was agreed that the announcement in the form submitted to the meeting, would be submitted to the Stock Exchange at 12 noon under these circumstances."

Gordon, as he has commented, "rather prevailed on African Life" and, despite Schlesinger's objections, the announcement was duly made. And in any event, African Life, in less than eighteen months, stood to make a profit of R270 000, almost doubling its initial investment of R300 000. Nobody should complain at that, but Moross for many years sought an opportunity to retaliate for what he regarded as a calculated insult. In the end, he succeeded, as will be related later.

By 23 March, the matter was settled. "On behalf of certain of the major shareholders of the company Mr Gordon informed the Board that negotiations for the passing of the control of the company to the Guardian Assurance Company Limited had been successfully concluded and it was resolved that an announcement be made forthwith in terms of the draft submitted to the Johannesburg Stock Exchange, the press and the company's shareholders."

The preliminary announcement had been greeted with banner headlines. The *Rand Daily Mail*, on 4 March: "UK Company may acquire Liberty Life. Guardian Assurance Company of London is negotiating with the major shareholders for the purchase of a controlling interest in Liberty Life Association at a price of R19 a share. If these negotiations are successfully concluded, Guardian Assurance will, subject to exchange control and other consents being given, offer to acquire the remaining shares at the same price.

"Guardian has assets of £600 million. It has insurance interests in Canada and Germany. Liberty, the only quoted insurance company on the Johannesburg Stock Exchange, was registered in September 1957. Authorised capital was 100 000 shares of R2, half of which had been issued. In 1961 a British investment subsidiary of a reinsurance group took up 10 000 shares. This holding was no doubt increased by 2 500 shares as a result of a subsequent one-for-four rights issue at 250 cents.

"By May 1962, the remaining shares had been issued – including 8 000 to the founder, Mr Donald Gordon, and the 22 000 shares absorbed by the rights issue – and Liberty Life was able to publish its pre-listing statement. Capital was increased later that year by 30 000 shares, issued to African Life at R10 for a 23 per cent holding.

"Liberty Life's maiden dividend of 10 cents was declared in May 1963. An increased 16 cents was declared last month from a surplus which rose from R70 000 in 1962 to R153 000 in 1963.

"A buyer's price of R18 yesterday at the close raised the market price by R5 per share."

The London press, for the very first time, became aware of Liberty Life's existence. On 3 March 1964, the *Evening News* reported "Guardian Bid", and this was followed by the *Financial Times* and *The Times* the next day.

Under the headline "Guardian Assurance Bid", *The Times* noted: "If Guardian Assurance is successful in its negotiations, announced yesterday, to acquire a controlling interest in Liberty Life Association of Africa, the group will have its first foothold in South African life business. Guardian has, of course, branches throughout South Africa, transacting fire, accident and marine business, but until now has had no life assurance interests there.

"Guardian is offering R19 for the R2 shares it is hoping to

purchase. Issued capital of Liberty Life is 130 000 shares of R2 each. The company was formed in 1957 by a group of professional men to provide a specialised life assurance service for the professional and executive classes. The company's shares were listed on the Johannesburg Stock Exchange in 1962 and in the same year African Life Assurance Society – the largest non-mutual life assurance company in Africa – acquired 23 per cent of the ordinary shares at R10 each. Liberty Life in its turn has a 25 per cent interest in Abbey Life Assurance, a company formed in this country in 1961."

Confirmation of the deal brought further headlines on 24 March, the *Rand Daily Mail's* banner reading: "Four Young Men Hit R2m Insurance Jackpot". Under it, Harold Fridjhon declaimed: "Just over seven years ago four young chartered accountants – they were in their twenties – raised R100 000 to start an insurance company. Yesterday it was announced that Guardian Assurance had bought control of the company, the Liberty Life Association, for about R2m.

"The partnership which Liberty Life has now formed with Guardian, one of Britain's major insurance groups with assets in excess of £550m, is the climax to a success story that has continued unbroken for six years."

There were, of course, fears that the change of control might lead to the disappearance of Liberty Life from the JSE lists, but the *Financial Mail* of 26 March laid this ghost.

"Fears that Liberty Life would disappear from the Johannesburg Stock Exchange lists as a result of shareholders accepting a foreshadowed bid of R19 a share by Guardian Assurance Company have, I am glad to say, turned out to be groundless. Guardian, having completed negotiations with the major shareholders for acquisition of a controlling interest at that price, will extend the offer to the public but will only offer to acquire 60 per cent of their holdings at the price. Although shareholders will be allowed to offer more than 60 per cent, acceptance of the excess will be at the discretion of Guardian.

"I should have been sad to see this share disappear from the lists because it is the only one that enables an investor to take an undiluted interest in the life insurance industry.

"Should shareholders accept Guardian's offer? I would be inclined to resist the temptation to take a profit for three reasons: that Liberty Life has a dazzling growth record, that arrangements have been made for continuance of existing management (which has shown great initiative), and that the company should benefit from joining an insurance group with world-wide interests and a useful network of South African branch offices.

"At the offer price of R19, dividend yield is only 0,8 per cent and earnings yield 6,2 per cent. But if Liberty Life can maintain its astonishing growth rate, these yield figures are not unreasonable. The bigger a company becomes the harder it becomes to maintain very fast growth. However, I would expect the law of diminishing returns to slow Liberty Life later rather than sooner."

The anonymous author (probably editor George Palmer, who was to become a personal friend of Donald Gordon, and who would work for the Liberty Life Group for a couple of years in the eighties), offered the most excellent advice.

# 6 Into Guardian

On Saturday 14 December 1963, Donald Gordon arrived in London. He was on his way to Fort Wayne, Indiana, hopefully to conclude a deal with Lincoln National Insurance Company, with whom negotiations had been under way since August 1963, and which were now looking very promising. His hopes of getting African Life, and Mandy Moross, off his back – and replacing them with a more compatible, and far more powerful, American "Big Brother" – were running high.

But a meeting had been arranged. Ernest Bigland, chief executive of Guardian Assurance, one of the UK's largest composite offices, an ambitious and forceful man, had been toying with the idea of adding a life arm to his Group's extensive short-term insurance interests in South Africa. And a mutual friend had suggested that he should talk to one Donald Gordon, who headed up South Africa's fastest rising life insurance star, Liberty Life.

The following day was wet and cold, a typical English winter Sunday. The two men met at 7 pm at Bigland's favourite London club, the Bath, which would be the scene of many an accomodation between them in the years to come. Gordon recalls: "I first met him on a rainy night in London. I walked into the Bath Club – it was the first time I'd been there – and there he was, wearing a black overcoat. About the first thing he said to me was: 'Well, I know you think British executives never work, but here I am on a rainy Sunday night – so now you know how I work.' And I said: 'That's marvellous, it suits me totally.' And we immediately got on, really quite incredibly well. Surprisingly, perhaps, for two men from such totally disparate backgrounds, but we clicked as people right from the start.

"Anyway, we talked endlessly about Guardian taking a dominant stake in Liberty Life, and that night we agreed to do a deal on the basis of the 1963 balance sheet, which would be ready by February

1964. We shook hands on it, and that was that. I cancelled my flight to America and went straight back to Johannesburg and on to a particularly merry Christmas at Plettenberg Bay."

At that first meeting, price was discussed only in general terms, with the final figure left subject to the balance sheet and results for 1963, but Gordon returned to his hotel with a pretty good idea that the figure would be an acceptable one. After all, price was not of fundamental importance – backing was the critical factor. Donald Gordon and Monty Schapiro were both staying at the Mayfair Hotel, and, as coincidence would have it, that weekend Schapiro had concluded his deal for Noble Lowndes to take control of S A May. "That evening", recalls Schapiro, "we got together and compared notes. I was cock-a-hoop with my deal and Donny was equally pleased with what he had just achieved. We were both ecstatic about the Guardian deal – not about the potential price, but the prospect of a major international partner which was just what the company needed so badly at that stage."

An internal Guardian memorandum, undated and unsigned but probably drafted by Bigland after that first meeting, confirms that Gordon had indeed made a favourable impression. Headed "Liberty Life Association of Africa Ltd", it read:

"We have been approached by the Board of the above company with a view to the purchase of a controlling interest.

"The company was founded in 1957 and is amongst the most active life assurance companies in South Africa.

"Recently there has been a number of failures of small life companies which have affected the competitive position of the Liberty Life.

"To date the policies have largely been sold by a direct sales force remunerated by way of commission, the total salaried staff amounting to about 20 people, but it is now desired to expand the operations of the company, particularly in the broker field.

"For the above principal reasons the company seeks such an association as will reflect favourably on its status and financial standing.

"The capital of the company is as follows:

| | |
|---|---|
| Issued share capital in ordinary shares of R2 each | R 260 000 |
| Capital and Revenue Reserves | R 331 000 |
| Life Fund | R1 145 000 |

"The progress achieved by the company is shown in the following tables:

| | Premiums | Expense Ratio | Life Fund | Surplus |
|---|---|---|---|---|
| | R | % | R | R |
| 1958 | 26 368 | 26,4 | 5 478 | – |
| 1959 | 95 492 | 28,2 | 29 544 | – |
| 1960 | 188 946 | 23,9 | 111 392 | – |
| 1961 | 250 839 | 19,2 | 269 930 | 31 866 |
| 1962 | 473 646 | 12,7 | 575 368 | 67 365 |
| 1963Est | 770 000 | 10,2 | 1 145 000 | 120 000 |

"The 'With Profit' policyholders are entitled to not less than 80 per cent of the profits attributable to the 'With Profits' business, which accounts for 60 per cent of the company's portfolio, the profits attributable to the non-profit account flowing to the equity. The present earnings of the company attributable to the shareholders are therefore as follows:

| | |
|---|---|
| Actuarial Surplus | R120 000 |
| Other Investment Income | R 20 000 |
| | R140 000 |
| Allocated to policyholders | R 70 000 |
| | R 70 000 |
| Dividend 1963 | R 20 000 |
| Reserves | R 50 000 |
| | R 70 000 |

"The above profit of R70 000 attributable to shareholders represents earnings of 27 per cent on the issued capital. At the price of R20 per share which has been suggested by the company this figure represents an earnings yield of 2,7 per cent.

"Life Funds are specially taxed in South Africa and the present liability amounts to approximately 9 per cent of the company's interest income and 6 per cent of the company's dividend income, which has been provided for before striking the surplus.

"The shares are quoted on the Johannesburg Stock Exchange but at the present time the directors and their families control approximately 50 per cent of the capital and the African Life Assurance Society 23 per cent. The African Life acquired their shares at R10 per share in January 1963 but it is understood that there has been little co-operation between the two companies and it is desired to terminate this association.

"Accordingly it is proposed that in the first place the Guardian should make a bid for the African Life holding at a cost of approximately £300 000 and that subsequent thereto the Guardian should make an offer to all other shareholders to purchase up to 60 per cent of their interest at a price of not less than R20 per share, equivalent to £600 000. Thus giving the Guardian a holding of approximately 70 per cent of the company's issued capital at a cost of £900 000. We understand that the price of R20 per share has already been offered by a US group.

"The management would retain 20 per cent, with 10 per cent remaining with the general body of shareholders. It would be proposed to maintain the quotation of the company's shares on the Stock Exchange.

"The company has placed favourable reinsurance business with other companies carrying a premium income of at least £100 000 and such business could be offered to the Guardian on renewal.

"The actuarial valuation is drawn up in accordance with rigid conditions laid down by the South African Insurance Act 1943, requiring calculations to be based on an assumed rate of 3 1/2 per cent net and employing A1924/29 Mortality Table.

"The reasons for the measure of success attained by the company in such a short time are:

"1. Favourable expense ratio.

"2. Excess of earned rate of approximately 6 per cent over the assumed investment rate of 3 1/2 per cent net.

"3. Careful selection of risks.

"It is suggested that if the deal should be approved the transaction should be made subject to the following conditions:

"1. Production of the audited accounts for 1963.

"2. Management agreement to retain the present directors and to fix their remuneration.

"3. Obtaining any permissions necessary in either country.

"4. Undertaking by the controlling shareholders to cede the Guardian enough shares to give the Guardian control.

"Under South African insurance legislation it is not possible for the Guardian to commence life insurance business except through a local subsidiary company. The establishment of a new life company involves the customary actuarial strains and establishment costs would be very heavy."

Meanwhile, over in Johannesburg, frantic efforts by all concerned saw preliminary figures produced – and despatched post-haste to London – by early February. The 1963 Annual Report was dated 20 February 1964, three weeks earlier than that for the previous year.

"We didn't hear anything for a while", muses Gordon, "and we were beginning to get a little concerned, for we really wanted to get the Guardian behind us. I heard afterwards that Bigland put the proposition to the Guardian Board one Wednesday and it was thrown out. But he brought it back to the Board the Wednesday afterwards and this time he was very persistent; I was to learn over the years just how persistent he could be! The Board finally passed the Resolution in principle to buy control of Liberty Life.

"He phoned me from London to tell me the news and said he would come out to Johannesburg in a few days to settle all the details. 'But before I come,' he insisted, most emphatically, 'I want you to know that we must have total certainty on the price; otherwise I'm not going to come at all.'

"And he said to me: 'We will offer you R17 a share for your company.' I said: 'R17 a share! Come off it, Mr Bigland, that's just not on. You know I want at least R20.' So he countered: 'No, R19 is my absolute limit, and at that I'm going right past my authority. R19 is the very top we will pay.'

"So I said to him: 'I know you'll pay R20, but if one rand a share means so much to the great Guardian Group, you can have it for R19 a share.' And that was that."

Towards the end of February 1964, Bigland came out to Johannesburg for what was to be the first, and probably the most fruitful, of many very productive visits.

Gordon again: "We got down to business as soon as he arrived; we negotiated the transaction, and we put it all down on just one sheet of paper. The whole deal, the Heads of Agreement, management continuity, the lot – and it was all completed in less than a day, and everything was done perfectly amicably – even to his acceptance of the condition that I was only prepared to undertake to stay on for one year. What I actually said was that I'd stay on for a year and see how we got on.

"That was on the Monday, but for the rest of the week we argued, we hassled, we almost fought. It got to such a pitch that Bigland and Louis Shill had one of the most flaming business rows that I've ever seen in all my life. I remember it clearly. We were all driving to Pretoria to meet the Registrar of Insurance, when Louis at one point completely and totally lost his temper, and it looked as if the deal might fall through."

Shill maintains that Gordon exaggerates somewhat, and that, as always, he never lost his cool, but he well remembers that week of bitter wrangling. "It really wasn't a 'flaming business row', I'd much prefer to refer to it as a heated business discussion. And you should remember we were really very junior businessmen; Bigland was an important figure, and we all rather looked up to him." Even so, the reason for the row, given hindsight and remembering that it was a battle between grown-up and very successful businessmen, seems unbelievably petty.

It was all about position. Gordon was Chairman and chief executive of Liberty Life, although he did not then still have the title of managing director, while Bigland was "merely" general manager of Guardian. And Guardian was buying control of Liberty Life, making it a subsidiary. How then could the chief executive of a subsidiary have a higher rank than the chief executive of the parent company?

Even at a distance of barely a quarter of a century, it is difficult to recall the extraordinary status consciousness of the City of London in general, and of the insurance industry in particular, in the early sixties. Throughout the insurance industry, and the banking industry as well for that matter, the chief executive was styled "general manager". And, although he was a powerful figure (and a general manager with Bigland's forceful personality was powerful indeed: his Board's rejection of the Liberty Life deal on its first presentation was one of only two such rebuffs that he suffered in his whole career), he was nonetheless staff. He was not on the Board, he was not a director – and he did not even take luncheon with the directors unless he was invited.

"Up to that point, in companies such as the Guardian and the Royal Exchange, the general manager never had lunch in the directors' dining room by right. Every day, one or two directors would come in – they were the Signatory Directors – to sign all the important documents. They would come in at half-past eleven, they would be given a proof Mint half-a-crown piece as traditional taxi money, and they would sign the documents, and then go into the directors' dining room and tuck into a five or six course meal, with wines to match, of course. They seldom or never invited any of the executive in, not even the general manager."

This recollection of Gordon's matches up, almost perfectly, with some pertinent comments by Supple. He, writing about Royal Exchange Assurance and its Court, was painting the picture as it prevailed at the turn of the century. Even so, and notwithstanding the fact that two world wars had intervened, irrevocably changing many aspects of life in class-bound Britain, the position of management in the insurance industry and in banking had changed but little.

"On the whole, therefore, the Corporation's directors were established businessmen with a stake in other commercial, manufacturing or financial affairs. This, together with their function at the Royal Exchange, generally established a clear line of demarcation between directors and officers, for the latter naturally tended to be professional insurance men, with long experience in the sole employment of the Corporation.

"Indeed, as long as the managers were simply heads of departments there were powerful reasons for the division between directors and officials. For the Court was responsible for the supervision of departmental affairs, and it would have been invidious to include among its number the very officials whom it was notionally supervising and even checking.

"Membership of the REA Court was not a sinecure. Apart from the stockholding qualification of £1 000, which ensured a substantial stake in the affairs of the Corporation, the supervisory duties of the directors were taken very seriously. Considerable thought was devoted to the membership of committees, and regular and conscientious attendance was expected. The Court itself met every week on Wednesday at noon, and absentees were fined 10s (which was divided among those present), while those arriving late or leaving without permission of the Chair, had to contribute 5s and 2s 6d respectively to the poor box."

Supple later comments on the position of one Mr Wilkinson, who in 1966 became general manager of the Royal Exchange Group. "Subsequently, in 1968, he was appointed managing director – the first manager in the modern period to be elected to the Court of directors." That Supple made that comment in those terms – incorrect though it was in a general sense, though perfectly accurate when applied solely to the Court of the Royal Exchange – underlines both the importance of the appointment, and the fact that it was unusual.

Thanks to Gordon, however, Bigland had made the vast transition from mere employee to executive director four years earlier than Wilkinson. Within months of returning from Johannesburg in 1964, and after much powerful lobbying, he was appointed a director of the Guardian, while retaining the title of general manager. And on 5 May 1965, Bigland was able proudly to cable Gordon: "Arising out of McKinsey report directors approved following appointments. Myself managing director, Caddick general manager (home), Reece general manager (investments), Trinder general manager (overseas). Only real change setting up United Kingdom control. Felt you would like prior notice of changes. Our position remains exactly as at present."

"Bigland always used McKinsey, the management consultants, to get his way with the Guardian Board," recalls Gordon. "No doubt he had used the same arguments that I had used with him to convince first McKinseys, and through them the Guardian Board, that it was vital for him to be appointed as managing director – and particularly so as I had that title."

And so a piece of City of London history was made. Executive directors became acceptable throughout the insurance industry. And the big clearing banks soon followed the precedent.

Gordon hastened to send his congratulations: "It was with considerable pleasure that I received your cable this morning informing me of your appointment as the managing director of the Guardian Assurance Group.

"If I might say it, I believe the new developments will have a most beneficial effect on the Group's future and I am fully aware of the degree of gratification to you personally in having achieved this unprecedented recognition of your loyalty to the company and your efforts on behalf of all of us associated with it. I can only sincerely hope that the new situation will succeed in releasing you to some extent from the tremendous responsibilities and burdens you have carried over the past few years."

But, as he signed himself "Kindest regards, Sincerely, Donald", he was chuckling at the recollection of the battles on this issue a little more than a year earlier – and he manfully resisted the temptation to have the words "Managing Director" typed beneath his signature.

Back in Johannesburg, in that last week of February 1964, there was, however, nothing to chuckle about; the cherished deal was almost on the rocks. "I was Chairman of Liberty Life at that point and the row was all about their wanting me to become general manager. In truth, it was just Bigland, of course, but he said it was the Guardian Board. I stated unequivocally that whilst I would give up my role as Chairman of the company, in no circumstances would I go down to general manager. 'I am the managing director of the company, and that's how it's going to be.' This argument raged for a week, and the deal almost fell down there. I just wouldn't budge, and I've already told you how totally Louis Shill was on my side. He was outraged by the whole affair. Bigland was saying that it is totally inconceivable for a British insurance company to have a director who is also the manager: 'You cannot have a managing director, it's just not on. No British institution has such a situation; they are all run by general managers.'

"Bigland was insistent. 'I'm not on the Guardian Board because it's accepted in British institutions that managers can't be directors; it's morally wrong, there's a conflict of interests, and anyway, it just wouldn't work. And what about my own position? I'm general manager – how can you be a managing director, when I'm only a general manager?'"

"I stuck to my guns", recalls Gordon, "and all my colleagues continued to support me. Bigland eventually capitulated. He went away and some months later, he was able to cable me, as previously mentioned, that he had been appointed a director of the Guardian. For the first time in the history of the British insurance industry a general manager of a major insurer had been so appointed – this honour fell to Ernest Bigland of the Guardian.

At that stage, the title of managing director had yet to be conceded by the Guardian Board. Change came slowly in the City of London. But Bigland was a man of great determination and he had decided that he would not be outranked by Gordon. He would eventually reach the rank of deputy chairman of the GRE – but the other deputy chairman, a non-executive director, was always marginally his senior. So the prized chairmanship always eluded Bigland, despite Gordon's personal support for him in that role.

Having made British institutional history, Bigland rested briefly on his laurels before taking his next step. Gordon again: "At first, he was a director and general manager. Later, he manoeuvred himself into being appointed the first managing director of any major British financial institution, let alone insurance company. Today, all Britain's institutional boards are studded with executive directors and managing directors. Everybody's a managing director, chief managing director, even executive deputy chairman or executive chairman, when a few years ago they were merely general managers and deputy general managers."

At this point, Gordon waxes quite lyrical. "I suppose I was actually a major catalyst in that seminal revolution of London's institutional structures."

Indeed, he was. Without his insistence that, as founder, he would settle for nothing less than being titled managing director of the mighty Guardian's newest and least significant subsidiary, there would have been no reason for the long settled order of institutional life in the City of London to have changed at all, and Britain's institutions could well still be in the state that Supple found them in at the turn of the century.

All was thus eventually settled, amicably, and on Tuesday 3 March 1964, DG was able formally to notify the Liberty Life Board that the Guardian "had intimated their intention of making a bid for the shares of the company at R19 per share".

The formal document finalising the deal is dated 21 March 1964. It was addressed to the general manager of the Guardian, and was signed for and on behalf of Liberty Trust by Gordon, and for and on behalf of the present holders of the ordinary share capital of Liberty Trust by Shill, Rubin, Young and Gordon – and "Monty Schapiro by his attorney Noel Benjamin". It was "Confirmed and agreed for and on behalf of Guardian Assurance Company" by Ernest Bigland.

Then began an exchange of letters that was to fill four large box files over the ensuing fifteen years – an exchange that is totally absorbing to read, and one which vividly illustrates the characters and the personalities of the two colleagues as they each pushed the other to heights that neither was likely to have achieved without that historic association. It became a great friendship, between both the two men, and their wives and families: far more than just a business friendship. "Bigland", says Shill, "was Donny's mentor. He taught Donny the ropes, how to succeed in the London 'big time', and in the international arena." And Gordon taught Bigland the rudiments of entrepreneurship.

Gordon himself saw Bigland as something of a father figure. "I looked up to him, and I developed an enormous respect for his business ability, and for his acumen. But in those early days, I was always somewhat overawed by him, and even more so by the Guardian Board."

This chronicle, in Gordon's opinion, gives a somewhat unbalanced view of their relationship, particularly as it tends to concentrate on areas of disagreement rather than on the much more frequent periods of strong accord. "People will read into it that we were constantly in a conflict situation; but it wasn't that at all. It was a great love-hate relationship in many ways, and towards the second half of our relationship I think there was a great affection – there really was. We both had great concern over many aspects of the Guardian Royal Exchange, and we used to meet often, over dinner, and discuss at great length what could be done, what should be done." Even so, they did, on rare occasions, agree to disagree.

An obvious early consequence of Guardian's assumption of control was the need to reconstitute the Board of Liberty Life, and this was formalised at meetings on 7 April and 14 May 1964. Alfred Schlesinger had already resigned, obviously in a huff, at the 23 March 1964 Board meeting when the conclusion of the Guardian deal had been formally announced. "A letter from Mr S A Schlesinger was tabled tendering his resignation from the Board of directors with immediate effect."

At the 7 April meeting, "The Chairman outlined to the meeting the position regarding the future of the Board of directors in view of the acquisition by the Guardian of the controlling interest of the company. He explained that it was necessary to arrange for the future representation of the Guardian on the Board, and indicated the views of the Guardian as had been discussed with him. In view of the situation, Sydney Lipworth and Monty Schapiro tendered their resignations from the Board of directors with immediate effect. These were accepted with great regret by the Chairman, who indicated at considerable length his feelings in this regard and thanked the two resigning Board members sincerely and emotionally for their services to the company."

It was inevitable, of course, that Lipworth and Schapiro, as the two non-executive directors, would be asked to go, and both accepted the situation with good grace, though with very considerable regret. It had been a happy Board, and all had enjoyed some good times together. But they didn't like being dealt with quite so summarily. Looking back, Schapiro's comment is that he was "fired with enthusiasm".

Then: "Mr E F Bigland, the general manager of the Guardian Assurance Company Limited of London, and Mr F R Edwards, group manager for Southern Africa, were appointed to the Board in replacement of the retiring directors."

At the 14 May meeting, with Gordon still "in the Chair", the final reshuffle took place. "Mr E J G Roy was elected a director of the company and was unanimously declared to be Chairman of the Board of directors. Mr Gordon congratulated Mr Roy on his new appointment and also welcomed Mr Edwards, who was attending his first Board meeting. Mr Roy requested that Mr Gordon remain as Chairman for the continuation of the meeting.

"Mr Gordon then proposed that the Rt Hon Lord Blackford [the aristocratic and somewhat autocratic Chairman of Guardian Assurance], and Mr J C McGough [the financial director of C G Smith, a leading Natal sugar company], who had already intimated their willingness to accept office, be appointed as directors of the company. The appointments were unanimously agreed to, subject to the receipt by the company of their formal acceptance of appointment."

The new Chairman, Ted Roy, was Guardian's local director. He was to become a close friend and loyal supporter of Gordon, and he stayed on the Board until 1976, when he reached mandatory retirement age, although he had handed the Chair back to Gordon in May 1974. The two men were barely acquainted before Roy became Chairman, but they were to become a formidable team, and Roy's loyal support was invaluable in the achievements that were to come.

On the surface, all the Board changes went smoothly, but behind the scenes Bigland and Gordon staged the first of their many contests of will by correspondence.

The first sighting shot was in the form of a cable from Bigland on 7 April. "Your letters 1st and 3rd received. [Sadly, these two letters, obviously the first to be written by Gordon to Bigland, are missing from the files.] Only urgent point directors. In view our discussions consider it most important that the two outside directors should resign at meeting 9 April. Would give wrong impression if re-elected now [obviously a reference to the Annual General Meeting] and then resigned very shortly afterwards. Would like you to submit my name and Edwards to fill vacancies. If done this way will be clearly understood and logical and you can make suitable remarks in your Chairman's speech. Hopeful one of our senior directors here will also accept appointment. Will write fully with suggested names for later appointment soon as possible."

Gordon replied on 8 April: "I am in receipt of your cable of 7 April, dealing with your suggestions regarding the Board of directors. I tried to contact you on the phone in this regard but unfortunately was unable to do so, and was left with no option but to proceed along the lines you indicated.

"I discussed the position in great detail and as tactfully as possible with Messrs Lipworth and Schapiro, who unhesitatingly tendered their immediate resignation from the Board. However, although accepting the situation that on a full re-constitution of the Board they would have had to resign in any event, they had thought that they would have had the opportunity of resigning in the near future at their convenience, with as much face-saving as possible. I am afraid these gentlemen were rather upset at what they considered to be rather harsh treatment and what they termed "rather a summary dismissal at short notice" after many years of loyal service to the company. All this was rather regrettable and unfortunate, particularly in view of Mr Schapiro's position as managing director of S A May, who are very substantial business producers for our company as well as being connected with the Lowndes group. They have both affirmed their loyalty to the company and to me, which I think was meant with sincerity. I have tried to redeem the situation as far as possible by reference in the Chairman's speech to be given at the Annual General Meeting on 9 April. However, I also feel that a personal note from you to each of them would certainly be of assistance in restoring the status quo, if you feel this could be helpful."

This letter crossed one from Bigland to Gordon, also dated 8 April. "On the question of directors, I cabled you early this week. I am very sorry that I do not feel I could agree to your suggestion that the two outside directors (Mr Schlesinger has, as you say, already resigned) should be re-elected at your Annual General Meeting tomorrow. Whilst I know they are both most able men and have been very valuable to you in building up the company, the fact remains that we have now completed our negotiations, it is known and understood by the public that your company is now associated with the Guardian, and as I said in my cable I do feel it would give the wrong impression if at the Annual General Meeting we did not bring our interest into prominence. Equally, I think it might well be much more misunderstood if, having re-elected them, we then in a comparatively short time asked them to resign. For these reasons and to make it perfectly clear what we were doing I said in my cable that I would like you to ask them if they would offer their resignations (or not put up for re-election) and that in their place you should appoint Mr Edwards and myself. I hope this can be done without any difficulties and I know I can rely on you to handle it in the most tactful way and offer our thanks to them on your behalf and ours for what they have done for the company in the past and for, I trust, agreeing to the suggestion that they should now make way for our nominees."

Having very firmly put down his foot on the issue of the outside directors, Bigland turned to more general Board matters. "I fully agree with your views about a prestige Board. I have received a long letter from Mr Edwards with some suggestions of several names that we might consider but from all reports I have received the name of Mr Roy, our present local director, stands extremely high, and I think he would really make a most excellent Chairman. However, I will be writing to you fully about this and the other suggestions very shortly. Mr Edwards has persuaded Mr McGough, who is the financial director of C G Smiths in Durban, to accept an appointment in due course. He is a very nice and able man and will put you into the market in that part of South Africa. I think this is probably sufficient at the moment from South Africa, but as I said in my cable I hope also that we can persuade one of our directors here to accept an appointment. Lord Melchett is a little reluctant to agree as he says that his company has very few interests in South Africa and that he would not normally have reason to make visits there."

In his reply, on 13 April, Gordon accepted Bigland's suggestions with good grace. "I have had good reports of Mr Roy and my only reservation as regards him taking the chairmanship is that he is relatively unknown by the public at large. However, the fact that he resides in Johannesburg is a considerable advantage and I am perfectly satisfied, if he is your choice. I am sure Mr McGough of Messrs C G Smith will be a definite acquisition to us and I am looking forward to making his acquaintance. I am disappointed that Lord Melchett is reluctant to commit himself, as I have no doubt that he would have been an ideal booster to the public image of our

Board. Nevertheless I am sure that your final choice will be equally advantageous. Looking at the situation as a whole my only reservation is the absence of a suitable Afrikaans name and suggest this may be remedied by possibly appointing one or two Afrikaners such as Mr Harold Abrahamse as alternates to the London directors."

All that remained was for Bigland to smooth those feathers that were so clearly ruffled by his somewhat peremptory "sighting shot", that cable of 7 April.

This he did in a letter dated 15 April. "The question of future directors of the Liberty Life gave me much concern and I, too, endeavoured to contact you by telephone but as this seemed so difficult and uncertain I sent you the cable. I am extremely sorry if our decision has caused any difficulties because I am most anxious that you and your colleagues should not at any time feel that we make arbitrary decisions which are prejudicial to your interests and also because I do know how very much Mr Lipworth and Mr Schapiro have helped you in the past and I would be most anxious that any changes should be made in the happiest possible atmosphere.

"I was, however, only following up the general discussions we had when I was with you, when whilst I agreed that the Annual General Meeting should take place as arranged, I did say that I felt this would be the right time for the outside, non-working directors to drop off, and I understood you to tell me that in fact you thought they would be agreeable to do so, knowing the new set-up, and that obviously the Guardian would wish their nominees to be on the Board. If I could have kept them on and added our own directors I should have been only too glad to do so but I felt this would make the Board far too top heavy.

"I am glad you have been perfectly frank with me in your comments and I enclose letters to Mr Lipworth and Mr Schapiro which I should be grateful if you would pass on to them. You will be over here in June and we can discuss the matter in rather more detail. If it has caused you any difficulties or misunderstandings I can only express my sincere regret."

So the wrangle over the non-working directors fizzled out. Gordon to Bigland on 20 April: "The question of the resignation of Messrs Schapiro and Lipworth has now been satisfactorily resolved, and I am sure that your very appropriate letters will completely eliminate any last vestige of unhappiness on their part. As mentioned to you,

I am in no doubt that this was an emotional problem more than anything else."

And the matter ceased to be an issue with Bigland's reply on 28 April. "I was very pleased to hear that the difficulties over Mr Schapiro and Mr Lipworth have now been settled. I do realise also that there was a rather special relationship between them, yourself and your other directors, all of whom have made the Liberty Life what it is, and it was not quite the same as dropping off a Board which was merely an ordinary public company."

For the remainder of 1964, the new relationship proceeded very successfully and relatively smoothly, with one major exception. In their report dated 26 March 1965 to Liberty Life's Seventh Annual General Meeting – the cover of which bore, for the first time, the proud message "A Member of the Guardian Assurance Group" – the directors were able to tell shareholders that: "The year under review has probably been the most significant in the history of your company and has again recorded gratifying operating results. A number of important developments have taken place, which in the long term are likely to have a major bearing on the future of the company.

"An event of much significance in the early part of the year was the acquisition of a 75,03 per cent shareholding in the company by the Guardian Assurance Company Limited of London. The linking of our future to that of an insurance company of the standing and financial resources of the world-wide Guardian Group, one of the world's leading international insurance organisations, has brought about a situation whereby the South African insurance public is now offered the benefits of a progressive South African registered company with locally orientated management and supported by the vast experience and resources of its British holding company. The Guardian, established in 1821, has operated in South Africa in the non-life field for over 75 years but has never in the past entered the life assurance field in this country. It is now the intention that Liberty Life will be the South African life member of the Guardian Group. On this basis, the company has immeasurably enhanced its future prospects."

And the first fruits of the newly acquired muscle that the merger brought were very evident from the figures for the year ended 31 December 1964. Total assets rose from R1,9 million to just over the R3 million mark, the Life Fund nearly doubled in rising from R1,1 million to R2,1 million, premium income less reinsurances rose from R806 000 to R1,3 million, with new business premium income soaring from R371 000 to R617 000. The operating surplus for the year was up from R132 000 to R250 000.

Behind the scenes, however, that "one major exception" to the smooth running of the relationship was beginning to cause ripples. The issue revolved round the formation of a mutual fund, which would be South Africa's first. Such a venture had clearly been under contemplation by Gordon and Shill since at least mid-1963, and on Gordon's August 1963 visit to the United States to talk with Lincoln National he had also been authorised by the Board to "look into the methods of operation" of American mutual funds. To what extent this had been discussed with Bigland during the February/March 1964 takeover negotiations is by no means clear, and anyway the matter was very much a side issue, of no great importance at the time. Both Gordon and Shill maintain that it was at least "mentioned somewhere along the line", but it is obvious from the correspondence that the question of a mutual fund had not impressed itself on Bigland's mind at all. Certainly it was not among the eight or nine matters that Mr Pressman, a senior Guardian actuary, was briefed to discuss when he was sent to Johannesburg as Bigland's troubleshooter in May 1964.

Be that as it may, the fact is that, by the time of Gordon's first official visit to London in June 1964, the issue had advanced, for Shill and himself, to the stage when it required to be discussed with their new parent. Bigland's first mention of the matter, in a letter dated 23 June 1964 confirming the items discussed during Gordon's visit, is pretty vague. "Item 7: Unit Trusts/Life Policy. It was agreed that we would have some discussions with Mr Power of Syfrets when he is over here shortly to see if we can come to some arrangement to start a unit trust in which Liberty Life and possibly you personally could have some interest and which we could link on the sales side for the sale of life policies."

Bigland had been listening, but with only half an ear. While Gordon was certainly proposing to link life policies to his unit trust – for the first time in South Africa – he had no intention whatsoever of having either John Power, or Syfrets, as his partner.

In a letter to Bigland dated 21 July, he was much more explicit. "You will recall our discussion in relation to the possibility of Liberty Life taking some participation in a unit trust management company to be set up. I have a feeling that an appropriate opportunity would be presented to us, in terms of stock market conditions, between now and the end of the year to enable us to get this scheme launched. I have in mind to induce London & Dominion Trust Limited to take a substantial participation in this scheme and to undertake its management. I have discussed this idea with them in broad principle and they have shown a considerable amount of interest in it. Should our discussions come to fruition and in addition receive the blessing of the South African authorities and the Registrar of Insurance, it will be necessary to set up the company with an initial capital of not less than R600 000. I feel it would be advantageous for Liberty Life to take up a participation in this capital to the extent of, say, R100 000; the balance of R500 000 would then be taken up between London & Dominion Trust and my group, through Cloud Investment Corporation.

"The basic thinking would be that the trust would not necessarily be opened to the public in the foreseeable future but that the units would be utilised primarily by Liberty Life for the funding of some type of equity-linked life assurance policy. London & Dominion Trust would, on the other hand, be able to market the units for the benefit of their clients, such as pension funds, etc. I believe on this sort of basis a reasonable volume of unit trust sales would be generated which, of course, would give the life sales of Liberty Life of an equity-linked nature a tremendous fillip."

It just so happened that the United Kingdom was in the throes of a postal strike at this juncture and correspondence was subject to serious delay. On 27 July 1964, in fact, Bigland routinely replied to a routine letter of Gordon's dated 14 July.

On 30 July, Gordon sent Bigland a most comprehensive and highly detailed "Memorandum on the Formation of a Unit Trust Management Company" and accompanied it with a letter in which he further stressed the advantages of the scheme, and its linked-insurance aspects. In particular: "Our being first in the field would enable us to make an important impact on the market before our competitors could have an opportunity of providing an answer to the new scheme. I feel that there is much to be said for the prestige to be gained by our being first to introduce this revolutionary idea onto the South African market and this certainly will enhance and promote our reputation for progressive thinking and for being market leaders in the Republic."

On 14 August, Bigland replied. He was by no means enthusiastic: "I would say that I am a little doubtful about the future of such trusts in the South African market", and "I would not oppose the start of such a trust but I think it would have to be set up in a particular way and be very carefully managed and controlled". Nevertheless, he agreed to go ahead. The vital thing, however, was that he accepted Gordon's, and his colleagues', proposed equity participation.

"We would be quite happy with the management being in the hands of London & Dominion Trust, they are well known to us, and in fact when I was in South Africa last year I had a long talk with Mr Jewell and went through our portfolio of investments with him: he keeps in quite close touch with Fred Edwards. If they are appointed then I think they should take up a controlling interest. I would be agreeable, subject to your Board's views, to the Liberty Life joining in as you suggest for, say, R100 000, the balance being taken up by your group, Cloud Investments."

The Liberty Life Board's views were clearly favourable, and at their meeting on 1 September 1964 the following was minuted: "Proposed formation of a unit trust management company. A memorandum dealing with the proposals that the company participate in the formation of a unit trust management company was tabled. The memorandum had previously been circularised to Board members, and the reaction of the Guardian as set out in a letter addressed to Mr Gordon by Mr Bigland dated 14 August 1964 was read to the meeting. After a full discussion of the proposals and their implications, and in view of the prestige that would accrue to the company as being the first to introduce an equity linked life insurance policy to the South African market, it was unanimously resolved that the company agree in principle to the investment of R100 000 in the proposed scheme. It was recorded that the Netherlands Bank of South Africa Limited, London & Dominion Trust Limited and Institutional Investments Limited (as Cloud Investments had been renamed) had all agreed in principle to collaborate in the proposed development. Mr Gordon was appointed by the Board to investigate this matter further on behalf of the company."

There would be a few disagreements about matters of relative detail before the eventual launch of the unit trust in June 1965, but Gordon had clearly won his battle and had established that, although Liberty Life was indeed controlled by Guardian, he himself was not. He was – and has so remained throughout his business career – an entrepreneur and an individualist. He was nobody's man but his own; he had not left the safe haven of an accountancy practice to finish up at somebody's beck and call. A few detours on the way were inevitable, perhaps, but a true entrepreneur he would always remain.

Essential to this approach, of course, is an eye for the main chance, but DG has always only looked to his own interests after first jealously guarding those of Liberty Life.

But the entrepreneurial approach was anathema to institutional thinking in the London of the early sixties, particularly in an insurance industry where no general manager had yet achieved Board status. Indeed, there are those who would aver that the situation prevails to this day. Gordon was therefore extraordinarily fortunate to have found, in Bigland, something of a soulmate. At least, Bigland was prepared to support the heresies that Gordon expounded, and was even prepared, if somewhat reluctantly, to back his ventures into "institutional entrepreneurism". And, again fortunately for Gordon, Bigland was a sufficient force in Guardian to carry the dissidents with him – not always happily, perhaps, but they did toe the line, especially when the outcome was inevitable.

As the launch of the unit trust drew nearer, both Gordon and Shill became increasingly excited about the prospects for equity-linked business. They became wholly convinced that, particularly with the head start that it would have over all its rivals, Liberty Life could sweep the field.

But they were also aware that Bigland did not fully share their enthusiasm. Although he had been very far from blocking the progress of the scheme, he had all along been lukewarm, stressing the snags and problems, urging a low-key and small volume approach to unit trust sales; demanding indeed that they be heavily restricted. And he had shown concern that the impact of equity-linked policies might adversely affect the sales of conventional life insurance, which in his view, quite correctly, was (and probably is) more profitable. But an industry must evolve and progress, or die. And with rising inflation, the old concepts of the life insurance industry were simply not meeting modern requirements.

Although he had got his way over the unit trust issue, Gordon was not at all sanguine about winning this leg of the game plan. So he hit on what seemed a sensible compromise; why not propose a new life company, to undertake only unit-linked business in partnership with

Liberty Life? It would, of course, be entrepreneurial. And what if it were to be turned down? Since early 1965, he had anyway been reviewing his own position. Life at Liberty Life, though satisfying in many ways, was somewhat less fun nowadays than it had been when they were struggling – but independent. Maybe he just wasn't cut out to be even a relatively large cog in such a very big wheel as the greater Guardian Group. And, in any event, he had undertaken only to stay on for one year.

At a Board meeting on Friday 30 April 1965, Gordon outlined his views on "the rather unorthodox innovations proposed" and volunteered to take them up with Bigland. The latter's cabled response is not preserved, but on 3 May Gordon wrote: "I thank you very much for your cable of the 30 April, and very much appreciate your early attention to this matter, which both the Board of Liberty Life and myself consider to be of prime importance. In the circumstances I have decided to come to London this weekend and will be arriving on the BOAC flight leaving Johannesburg on Saturday night."

Their discussions were intense, and animated, but by no means acrimonious (Bigland started his next letter: "Dear Donald, I very much enjoyed seeing you over here again. . ."). But they ended in deadlock.

Gordon had left a memorandum, dated 12 May 1965, with Bigland: "Following our discussions of the past few days, and with a view to securing the optimum benefits in the long term for the Guardian Group, and satisfying the natural aspirations of the writer on a permanent basis to the mutual advantage of all, it is suggested that. . ." He then went on to describe, in full detail, his proposals for a separate life company, in which he and his colleagues would have a 50 per cent equity stake.

This time, Bigland was to dig his toes in. Politely, because he didn't want to close any doors, but very firmly. "I am sure you know that I do understand the reasons behind your suggestions, not only that you think it is an excellent scheme but also you would like to feel you had the added incentive of further financial interest in its success. Equally from my side, as I have explained to you, I must really look at it entirely from the point of view of whether it is of benefit to the Guardian. Frankly, after going through your memorandum and considering all you said whilst you were here I honestly cannot feel that there is any real benefit accruing to the Guardian by our agreeing to start a new company for this business jointly with yourself and your own interests. The principal reason for saying this is that we already have the organisation and the vehicle through which this business can be handled, ie Liberty Life . . ."

Gordon responded on 26 May: "Both Mr Shill and I fully appreciate the underlying reasons for your unhappiness at the proposed changes but believe strongly that our special situation *vis-à-vis* Liberty Life and indirectly the Guardian Group should be placed on an equitable basis. We would not be honest if we did not admit that we feel rather stultified at being a very small cog in a very large group . . . I am fully conscious of my moral obligations to Liberty Life, its policyholders, staff and shareholders (in particular the Guardian Group) and it is with a view to reconciling all basic conflicts that I put up the suggestion that we promote the new mutual fund linked policy through a new life company, in which the Guardian would participate to the extent of 50 per cent of the equity with ourselves . . . Should you deem it appropriate to replace me eventually from my executive duties at Liberty Life, I am prepared to accept this position, however very reluctantly and with as little dislocation as possible, as Liberty Life is still very much a 'personality' company."

Bigland tried to keep the door open, and shifted his ground quite a bit on 2 June after a couple of cables and some frantic telephoning. The first cable: "Your letter 26 May. Very sorry that cannot feel your suggestions ultimately benefit Guardian. . . As compromise would be prepared consider participating new company for life-trust business if Guardian shareholding 75 per cent as with Liberty Life. If this is of any interest let me know. Will write you fully and agree one of us should visit earliest. Sure that between us we can find a solution."

Gordon responded immediately by telephone, with a counter-suggestion that he and Shill might go along with a 65 per cent/35 per cent shareholding split, but not 75/25. Bigland promptly shot off another cable. "Pleased hear my suggestion of interest. You will remember extreme difficulties over agreeing conditions Liberty Life/Guardian unless we held 75 per cent. Exactly same position applies here could not contemplate block of shares held outside over 25 per cent without restrictive conditions. Agreeable start new company immediately subject other arrangements satisfactory if we agree basic shareholding."

Letters then crossed in the none-too-rapid airmail of the times. Bigland's, dated 2 June 1965, reiterated his 75/25 offer and went to some pains to spell out his reasons, including having "no controlling rights" and the problems in the event of a disagreement, effectively refusing to budge further. Gordon, on 4 June, had already rejected the compromise offer. "While I am fully aware of the underlying reasons for your insistence on a 75 per cent participation for Liberty Life and/or the Guardian, we for our part would be falling short of our primary objective, ie an equitable 50 per cent participation in the proposed new company. My suggestion on the phone the other day regarding a share option arrangement in this sense does also not meet our real psychological problem, which can only be permanently solved by a 'partnership' concept rather than by a 'controlled' concept."

That seemed to be the end of the road, and a fairly short road at that. Letters and cables continued to fly back and forth and early in July, in response to an appeal from Ted Roy, Bigland flew out to Johannesburg. Roy, incidentally, fully supported Gordon's position in this matter, much to the chagrin of his principal, Bigland.

The meetings were stormy. Bigland was greeted with a draft press announcement which, in the event, of course, was never released: "The directors of Liberty Life Association of Africa Limited (a member of the Guardian Assurance Group) announce that Mr Donald Gordon, the managing director, and Mr L Shill, whilst continuing as directors of the company, will over a period be released from their executive duties to enable them to concentrate on the development and promotion of Investors Mutual Funds Limited and unit-linked life assurance contracts with Liberty Life Association of Africa Limited. The Guardian Assurance Group and the Board of directors of the company are making arrangements for the future detailed management of the company so as to ensure the continuation of its activities on the same lines as at present."

That potential time-bomb defused – and there is no doubt but that it was a time-bomb, for its effects on Liberty Life's rating on the Johannesburg Stock Exchange would have been dramatic – the principals proceeded to hammer out a fragile compromise on the basis of a memorandum that Gordon and Shill had also prepared. This, essentially, set out the basis on which the two would gradually "withdraw" to their new company whilst maintaining somewhat tenuous links with Liberty Life and with Guardian.

Bigland, seemingly, had little option but to accept the new arrangements, albeit unhappily. Back in London, he wrote on 15

July 1965, "I am sure you know how sorry I am that our association that started last year will not be quite so close in the future, although through your directorship I do hope that in fact there will be little change except in the day-to-day management.

"It too gives me much pleasure that, despite all our difficulties and problems, our personal relationship and that with your other directors stays the same.

"I am afraid it was probably inevitable that at some time you would feel that you wanted more scope for your great abilities and I am sure that we will in fact be able to greatly help each other's future intentions and go forward together."

He went on to say that he was sending out Caddick and Pressman to sort out the details of the new arrangements.

On 23 July, Gordon replied: "I would like to record how very much I appreciated your whole attitude, during our negotiations in Johannesburg, and your understanding approach to our problems. I am also very sorry that our association might not be quite so close in the future but at the same time I am in no doubt that the proposals we are now working on will be of considerable benefit to Liberty Life, ourselves and Investors Mutual Funds."

But the new accord was clearly fragile, and it began to fall apart when Caddick cabled Bigland on 26 July: "Following lengthy discussions with both parties, including Roy, consider undermentioned new scheme between Liblife and Investors Mutual Funds only satisfactory method of achieving satisfactory withdrawal of Gordon and Shill. Gordon and Shill, while remaining directors of Liblife, would give up their executive duties as replacements become available but within a reasonable time. Gordon, if requested, would act for as long as required as part-time financial investment director of Liblife. Guardian will acquire Liblife shares of Gordon and Shill and Institutional at a price basically related to current market value to be notified as soon as possible."

Since the above was much as had previously been agreed, it must have been the complicated commission and agency arrangements that followed that raised Bigland's ire. These included a "chief agency contract", "overriding commissions", and the supervision by Investors Mutual Funds of existing Liberty Life agents.

On 27 July, he cabled Gordon: "Your letter 23rd received but gravely concerned receive message Caddick about suggested terms of agreement which cannot be said to be in any way in line with sentiments expressed your letter 23rd and mine 15th. Most anxious assist you in any way possible but you will remember during my visit that full Board considered wrong Liberty Life sell major part holding in IMF and agreed only satisfactory basis was all partners IMF make agreed percentage available to you and Shill. Also agreed that you and Shill would set up your own promotional organisation without encroaching on Liberty Life organisation.

"Proposals now put forward virtually put whole Liberty Life organisation under your control which I cannot believe is intended... Do feel strongly that only possible way we can come to agreement is for you to discuss position fully at this stage with IMF on lines already agreed... Sure you will understand my alarm at present proposals which are far beyond anything even contemplated during our discussions."

That exchange of cables indicates that a very considerable degree of misunderstanding was bedevilling an already difficult situation – hardly surprisingly when negotiations are conducted at 6 000 miles distance – but it is also apparent that Bigland was losing patience.

He next made an offer to purchase Gordon's and Shill's Liberty Life shares, as agreed, but on terms which elicited a furious cable from Gordon: "Greatly disappointed at your approach to share valuation which falls substantially short of fair value and price envisaged during our recent negotiations bearing in mind our proposed present and future relationship. Would wish to obviate valuation by Deloittes if this can be avoided which would only strain future relationships unnecessarily. We would appreciate indication of your approach to our future arrangements as discussed with Caddick as we now find ourselves in a most unsatisfactory position."

Bigland's response, in his letter of 3 August 1965, was tough. He confirmed that both Gordon and Shill would be welcome to stay on the Liberty Life Board, but giving up executive duties "in your case in six months and for Shill three months". And, on the question of share purchase, he merely said: "I have already made you an offer." And he was equally unbending concerning the future commission and agency arrangements between Liberty Life and IMF.

Neither Gordon nor Shill were satisfied. That was the end of the line: their future – and they both saw it as a bright one – was going to be with IMF. So far as Liberty was concerned, they regarded themselves as being under notice, of six months and three months, respectively.

Says Gordon, looking back nearly a quarter of a century later: "Louis and I were going to go out of Liberty Life, into the mutual fund. I had been trying to work out with Ernest some mechanism whereby I could remain associated with Liberty Life on a part-time basis, but that my major interest was going to be IMF. And so I went over to London, basically to finalise all the arrangements, and I suddenly had cold feet about the whole set-up. I realised that I was, basically, just too emotionally involved with Liberty Life to pull out. After all, it was my baby, I had founded it. So I allowed Ernest to persuade me not to leave, after all the fighting."

The "persuading" took place, almost inevitably, for Bigland and Gordon, at the Bath Club, and initially in the sauna (as Gordon remembers, "to soften me up"). Afterwards, he returned to his room at the Savoy Hotel, and scribbled out his "final" terms – the notes are barely legible now – on three sheets of that renowned hotel's famed light-blue flimsy airmail notepaper. They were broadly confirmed by Bigland in a six-page letter dated 26 August 1965. It was very much a "come home, all is forgiven" type of epistle.

Gordon's decision was now finally made; he had thrown in his lot with Liberty Life and the Guardian; and it was clearly the correct decision, for the strides that he and Bigland would make together in the next thirteen years were to be tremendous.

After all the trauma, Gordon felt that he needed a short break. So, with Bigland's encouragement, he would fly to Las Palmas and take a few days relaxation by returning from there to South Africa by sea. "I got onto the Union Castle boat, and then I had the most incredible run of good luck. You know that sweepstake on the Daily Run – well, in the five days I was on board, I think I won the 'Sweep' four times and came second once. The other passengers wanted to throw me overboard, and my champagne bill came to an absolute king's ransom. I remember phoning Peggy from the ship and saying 'What the hell are you up to?' I was thinking of that old adage about lucky in love, unlucky at cards, or is it vice versa? But seriously, I wondered that if I was being so lucky with the gambling, perhaps what I'd just done in London was the biggest mistake of my life."

It was no mistake. Given hindsight, Gordon was right to stay with Liberty Life; right for himself, right for Liberty Life, and right for Guardian.

For Shill also, it has turned out in the long run to have been the best decision. According to mutual friends, however, Shill did not think so at the time, and it is said that he felt that Gordon had let him down; and that this feeling was a major contributory factor to the sad breach between the two men that was to develop in a few years' time. In the event, however, Shill has built Sage Holdings, the successor to IMF, into a major financial institution in its own right. Possibly everybody's luck was running the right way back in August 1965.

And the great partnership between Guardian and Liberty Life, between Ernest Bigland and Donald Gordon, was firmly on track. It would develop over the next thirteen years into a corporate relationship of unique stature. The personal relationship of the two men blossomed into a bond of friendship and mutual respect which on any basis was as remarkable as it must have been pre-ordained.

# 7 Mutual Fund Pioneers

The "Memorandum on the Formation of a Unit Trust Management Company" that Donald Gordon enclosed in his letter of 30 July 1964 to Ernest Bigland was to play a big part in changing the investment scene in South Africa. It was, in many ways, a remarkably prescient document.

The memorandum is noteworthy for several reasons, the most important of which is that unit trusts (or mutual funds, the terms are interchangeable), as such, did not exist in South Africa at that time; hence the scheme proposed was, in the South African context, quite revolutionary, and of some considerable importance.

Second, the document's clearly spelt-out intention to link the new units to life assurance policies was another absolute South African first, fairly obviously, since unit trusts were not then in existence, but nonetheless a major conceptual breakthrough. The very intention to equity link was a totally new concept to South Africa; apart from the retirement annuities that Liberty Life had pioneered, almost all South African life assurance at that time was conventional; no whisper had yet been heard of the heretical notion of linking life assurance with equities, in any form. True, it had been tried overseas, mostly in the United Kingdom and to a lesser extent in the United States; but it had had no real success and had by no means taken off. If anything, it had rather a bad image, especially in the UK, as indeed had unit trusts themselves at that time.

That this would all change dramatically over the next decade or so, especially in the UK, under the pioneering influence of Abbey Life, is beside the point. What Gordon was proposing, in 1964, was a seminal innovation in the South African context.

Bigland's initial reaction, on 14 August, was, even to put a slight gloss on it, lukewarm: "In the first place we must consider the background to unit trusts in South Africa. The position has obviously been prejudiced by the failure of Unit Securities & Trust Co, and

Selected Securities Fixed Trust [two very lacklustre closed-end trusts. Bigland was making the error, quite common at the time, of confusing closed-end trusts with unit trusts, or mutual funds] and taking a personal view I would say that I am a little doubtful about the future of such trusts in the South African market. However, there are special circumstances as far as Liberty Life is concerned and I accept the fact that it would probably be a useful advertisement medium and would no doubt assist the sales of your life policies."

He went on to insist that any management company should be "strictly limited to the dealing in units tied to Liberty Life policies" and the private clients of the consortium partners, adding "we would be most strongly opposed to the units being generally available to the public and their sale being actively promoted by paid salesmen". And, after noting the limited nature of the South African equity market, Bigland went on: "I would further suggest another very definite restriction and it is that the rules of the trust should clearly define limits for the more speculative type of holding. . .".

Bigland's conclusion was less than encouraging: "You may feel that our suggested restrictions would make such a trust of rather more limited interest but we do think that unless it is set up on the strictest possible lines it would not achieve its object and could cause us difficulties if there was any substantial, major change in your market." But, even so, he added his grudging blessing: "To summarise, we are not now opposing the idea and would be quite happy to support you in going ahead but we trust on the lines set out in this letter."

Behind Bigland's opening remarks was a quite common confusion concerning the nature of unit trusts and mutual funds. The situation in South Africa was governed by the Unit Trust Control Act of 1947, which basically permitted only "closed-end" funds, until it was changed by amending legislation in 1962 and 1963. Closed-end funds had a fixed, usually relatively small, capital, and because of this were controlled by quoted parent companies. It was to two unsuccessful South African closed-end trust controlling companies – which indeed were poorly perceived at the time – that Bigland was referring.

There had for some years in South Africa been calls for changes in legislation to permit the more modern concept of "open-ended" trusts – the so-called "mutual funds" that were proving so highly successful overseas, particularly in the UK and the US, whence Gordon had gone to study their *modus operandi* in 1963. And as

Gordon's memorandum spelled out, the major real difference between the outmoded and unpopular closed-end unit trust and the open-ended unit trust, or mutual fund, was the fixed, relatively limited, capital base of the former, as compared with the unlimited capital base of the latter, which could, and indeed does, fluctuate in response to the demands of investors, or unitholders.

The Office of the Registrar of Financial Institutions was well aware of the need for change, a fact that it is pleasant to be able to record in an age when it is far more fashionable to attack civil servants than to praise them.

It is a demanding office, and it is of no small consequence to the Liberty Life story that it was graced, in the years of Liberty Life's early growth and rapid development, with two co-operative and highly competent registrars. These were Rudolph de Villiers, who retired in 1970, and his successor, Wynand Louw, who filled the post with distinction until April 1981.

"I had joined the Department of Finance", recalls Louw, "in March 1957 and was transferred to the Financial Institutions Office. Soon after I got there, my predecessor called me into his office and said: 'Look, there is some pressure in Parliament to change the Unit Trust Control Act – we need to amend it to allow for open-ended trusts.' I remember that very well indeed, because I had no idea what on earth he was talking about.

"I told him that, and he just looked at me and handed me a booklet. It was written by one Edward du Cann, later to become a prominent member of the Conservative Party in the United Kingdom, who then headed up a large UK mutual fund group. Anyway, I had this little book, about 100 pages or so all about open-ended trusts, and I got hold of a pile of back issues of the *Financial Times*, which was the only London paper we had available in the office in those days. For months, I ploughed through the *Financial Times* – I just grabbed each new issue as it came in – and in the end I wrote a memorandum suggesting the changes that I thought were needed to the old Act. No, I didn't go overseas to study the subject – I just did all my homework in the office in Pretoria, with Du Cann and the *Financial Times* as my mentors. And the Amending Acts of 1962 and 1963 were almost totally based on the memorandum that I wrote."

A good deal of credit is due to Louw, and to De Villiers, for the South African legislation controlling mutual funds is widely regarded as a model of its kind.

"After all that hard work", says Louw, "nothing happened for a couple of years. We just sat back and waited for all those 'interested parties' to come forward."

Well, of course, Gordon and Shill were working away at the matter, and once they had Bigland's grudging go-ahead, they were ready to proceed to the next step – the trust deed. "The Act merely laid down all the basic guidelines", says Louw, "and the vital document, the trust deed, which sets out the precise rules for one specific trust – what its charges could be, its investment parameters, all that sort of thing, all absolutely vital – had to be worked out between the applicant and my department. The very first applicants were Donny Gordon, whom I knew slightly, and Louis Shill, whom I met for the first time when they both came to my office about the middle of 1964, to thrash out the trust deed of what was to become Sage Fund." More accurately, The South African Growth Equities Fund – the acronym would evolve later.

As Louw recalls, the trust deed that was agreed for Sage Fund provided the guidelines for the other trust deeds that were to follow over the next few years, so that, apart from pioneering the movement in South Africa, Gordon and Shill, and their legal team, did a good deal of spade-work for the competition. But that is the lot of the pioneer the world over.

By late 1964, a consortium of investors had been formed, and a Liberty Life Board resolution on 19 October 1964 put the matter on record. It was resolved:

"1. That further to certain correspondence between Mr E F Bigland and Mr D Gordon, the company agree to subscribe for 25 per cent of the capital of the proposed management company, being 150 000 shares of R1,00 each, to be issued at R1,10 per share.

"2. That the company enter into a promotional agreement with Netherlands Finance & Investment Corporation Limited (a subsidiary of Nedbank), London & Dominion Trust Limited, Industrial Underwriting & Investment Company Limited and Institutional Investments Limited (hereinafter referred to as "the Consortium"), and that such promotional agreement should, inter alia, give effect to the following, which has been agreed to by all parties to the Consortium:

"That a unit trust management company be formed and sponsored by Liberty Life Association of Africa Limited, Netherlands Finance & Investment Corporation Limited, Institutional Investments Limited, Industrial Underwriting & Investment Company Limited and/or London & Dominion Trust Limited (London & Dominion Trust Group) with each group contributing 25 per cent of the equity share capital and being entitled to equal representation on the Board of directors. Each group is to contribute maximum expertise to the furtherance of the trust's interests and to do so at such nominal expense to the management company as will not overtax its resources in the early stages. It is understood between the parties that no additional shareholders will be introduced without the approval of all parties and that the trust would operate on conservative investment lines and initially on a limited scale. It is envisaged that units would not be available to the general public until all the parties agreed otherwise and would not be marketed in the accepted sense. However, units would be available to customers of the Netherlands Bank and to clients of London & Dominion Trust. Liberty Life would have a preferential right to units to be used for its own purposes, in particular to be sold in conjunction with life insurance.

"Netherlands Bank are to undertake the banking business of the management company and to act in the capacity of trustee to the trust. London & Dominion Trust are to act as investment advisors although the Board would not in any way be obliged to act on any such advice and would be at liberty to seek such other additional advice at their entire discretion. London & Dominion Trust for the time being are to provide general office facilities where it is uneconomic for the trust to have its own such facilities although it is envisaged that at the earliest possible time an acceptable full-time manager is to be appointed. It is accepted that London & Dominion Trust would be entitled to deal at 'arm's length' with the management company in respect of the acquisition of securities etc. However, this envisages no obligation on the management company to deal in this way and would certainly do so only on ordinarily accepted financial principles.

"3. That Messrs E J G Roy and D Gordon be appointed to the Board of directors of the proposed management company to represent the interests of this company therein."

The press release introducing South Africa's first mutual fund was hardly a model of its kind. Two startlingly new ideas, each of them representing a total breakthrough in financial thinking so far as South Africa was concerned, just dumped on the table. What was an "open-end trust", and how could it, whatever it was, provide "in conjunction with" life insurance, "a hedge against the slow but constant diminution of the purchasing power of money"? The latter was the euphemism insisted on by the Financial Institutions Office: the obvious alternative, a reference to "hedging against inflation", was a sensitive issue at that time.

Far more thought and effort than had gone into the press release had been devoted to briefing the *Financial Mail*, and its article "Presenting SA's First Mutual Fund" on 23 October 1964 was to set the tone and pattern of the bulk of the considerable volume of press comment that was to appear over the next nine months, until the fund opened for business in June 1965. That the article, some twenty-five years later, still reads well as a sensible and thoughtful exposition of the merits and problems of mutual funds, is a tribute to the briefing skills of Gordon, which have always been the hallmark of his style and his personal impact in relation to Liberty Life's public image.

"Two years ago Liberty Life became the first life insurance company in South Africa to be listed on the Stock Exchange. This week, while merchant bankers, life assurance company chairmen and investment company directors slumbered, it scored another first: leading a consortium which proposes to launch the Republic's first open-end trust.

"An open-end trust, or mutual fund as it is called in America, is an investment trust with a diversified holding of quoted shares, fractional interests of which are made available to the public as units, at a price related to the quoted value of the stocks held in its portfolio. But unlike ordinary investment trust companies, a mutual fund's capital, and its portfolio, expand and contract as demand for units changes.

"As units are sold, the proceeds are used to purchase additional securities. In this way a large number of investors are able to pool their resources and enjoy the benefits of expert investment supervision, plus a wider spread of interest than most shareholders can achieve with their own slender savings.

"Under the amended Unit Trust Control Act of 1963, the management company is itself required to have a big stake in the trust, as well as have the substantial finance necessary to allow it to buy back units from unit holders who may wish to sell. Unlike a closed-end investment trust quoted on the stock exchange, sellers of mutual fund units do not sell through the market but offer units back to the management company, at a price based on the market value of the underlying portfolio on the day of sale.

"To provide additional protection for unit holders the Act requires the securities constituting the trust's portfolio to be vested in a separate trustee (in this case, presumably the Netherlands Bank) of undoubted standing. Nor may an open-end trust invest more than 5 per cent of its portfolio in any one company, or invest in any one company more than 5 per cent of that company's issued capital. And to ensure diversification, and the stability of large-scale operations, a new mutual fund must start off with a portfolio consisting of at least R500 000 in cash or securities.

"The consortium's management company intends to go for a wide spread across the share market, concentrating on first-class growth stocks. Mines, being wasting assets, will probably be excluded. But mining finance shares will be in, and so will industrials.

"Gilt-edged securities do not offer growth, so for the moment will probably not feature in the portfolio.

"Of course, the man who buys mutual fund units, backed by expert investment supervision plus diversification, cannot expect these advantages for nothing. He pays for them in the form of a small premium over the unit's market value when he buys. That premium is normally calculated as a fixed percentage mark-up on the value of the units bought, probably 4 per cent in this case. When the investor sells back units he no longer wants to hold to the management company there is, however, no charge.

"So for administering the trust, the management company earns this premium, plus an annual service charge paid by the fund and calculated as a fraction of the market value of its portfolio, valued every six months. The management company, for its part, meets all costs, including the salary of the investment advisor and other staff. The trust, however, pays any tax it is liable for, and its auditors' fees.

"Normally a mutual fund pays out to unit holders all the income it receives in dividends from investments, although the consortium probably intends to plough back capital gains.

"The tax position is straightforward: mutual funds are taxed as if they were public companies, but are not liable for tax on their dividend income. Unit holders, on the other hand, will pay tax on dividends paid on their units in the usual way.

"Mutual funds have been the major factor turning the United States into a 'share holding democracy'. They have grown in

America at an astounding rate. In 1939 mutual fund portfolios were valued at $450m. By 1957 they had grown to $9 000m, and this year they are in the region of $30 000m. By comparison, the less flexible closed-end trust has been far less popular.

"Of course the best time to start a mutual fund is at the beginning of a long bull trend. No doubt the consortium wishes devoutly that this was October 1960, not 1964. Admitting this, they are quick to point out that over the long haul the point of entry into the market diminishes in significance. In any case they take a bullish view of the long-term prospects for South Africa's leading growth stocks.

"Nevertheless, a note of warning has to be sounded: there is absolutely no guarantee that an investor who buys unit trusts tomorrow will find they are worth any more in five, ten or twenty years time. They could easily be worth much less. But that is a risk which all investors take (including the consortium itself) whether in equities, gilts, property or what have you.

"In America the mutual funds field a veritable army of agents, giving their units a 'hard sell'. This is not the consortium's intention. Quite the opposite. First, they emphasise that they do not want holders who are looking for quick profits. Secondly, they intend restricting channels of sale to investment customers (whatever that might mean) of the Netherlands Bank; to existing clients (on what date?) of London & Dominion Trust; and to new policyholders of Liberty Life.

"Ability to link life cover with mutual fund units will undoubtedly give Liberty Life a tremendous advantage over competitors. Liberty Life's agents will certainly have something extra to sell prospective policyholders, something that will provide a hedge against the inexorable decline in the purchasing power of money. So far the main protection against paying in good money and getting out bad, has been the 'with profits' policy. But this protection is restricted by the traditional investment policies of life insurance companies, and the fact that they do not regularly revalue their assets in order to pass on capital profits.

"We would guess that another selling point that Liberty Life's representatives will explain to policyholders who are prepared to have part of their regular monthly premium invested in mutual fund units, is the so-called Rand Cost Average. This sounds complicated, but is really quite simple; if equal amounts of money are invested regularly, the investor will buy units at a variety of prices, depending on share market fluctuations. He will obviously get more units for the same amount of money when share prices are relatively low, than when the market is high.

"For example, if the units cost 100 cents each, only 100 units can be bought for R100. But 125 units can be bought if their price falls to 80 cents and 200 units if they drop to 50 cents – with the interesting result that the average cost of the units bought is always below the average price paid. This is a particular advantage from buying regularly even the few units which most small savers could afford.

"Whilst investors, big and small, will welcome the initiative shown by the consortium, stock brokers may take a more jaundiced view. A mutual fund is likely to give business to a narrower spread of brokers than had the same investment been made by a large number of individual investors. Secondly, mutual funds tend to be one-way business. Like other institutional buyers, mutual funds tend to lock-up good shares.

"A more fundamental problem is the possibility that eventually the share market may become dominated by a small number of institutional investors, mutual funds included. Obviously a pattern of share values determined by the decisions of a handful of investment managers controlling vast sums may well be less stable than the more random pattern established by a multitude of small investors making their own individual, and sometimes unaccountable, personal decisions. This is, however, a small risk to accept for bringing South Africa, too, closer to a democracy of shareholders.

"Mr Rudolph de Villiers, Registrar of Unit Trusts, is to be congratulated on the skill with which he has re-designed legislation which gives promoters the elbow-room they need, and the public the protection it deserves."

In the months preceding the actual launch of the new mutual fund, as has already been chronicled, there was increasing tension between Gordon and Shill, on the one side, and Bigland, on the other. All of the people on the spot in Johannesburg were growing more and more enthusiastic about the prospects of the new medium – to the extent, as we have seen, that Gordon at one stage even contemplated leaving Liberty Life to devote himself to the new venture. Bigland, on the other hand, and most of the time 6 000 miles away in London, remained basically cool, ever urging caution and a very conservative approach – and still propagating a policy of strictly restricted sales.

In the end, as was to become almost the norm in contentious matters with his nominally "controlling" company, Guardian, Gordon got his own way. When Investors Mutual Funds Limited, the consortium's management company, began its advertising campaign ahead of the 14 June 1965 launch, the advertisements proclaimed, in contrasting bold type: "It has been decided that the issue of units will not be restricted as was previously announced but that they will be made freely available to the general public."

The launch was preceded by a press conference on 11 June 1965, addressed by Donald Gordon, who was thirteen days short of his thirty-fifth birthday. Amusingly, his opening greeting was a simple "Gentlemen": the composition of the Johannesburg press corps has changed dramatically to become progressively more feminine over the past two decades, but there were no ladies present at this important conference in the Netherlands Bank boardroom.

"In introducing the South African Growth Equities Fund we would not be honest if we suppressed our pride at being privileged to introduce the first mutual fund to South Africa. We stand on the threshold of a vast new era in investment with the introduction of a medium which will offer a unique service to the South African public and which has already been tried and proved overseas.

"The potential of the movement and its impact on the South African economy will be proved over the next few years but, hazarding a guess, I would be disappointed if in five years from now the industry did not embrace assets of between R75 million and R100 million. It will be the objective of both ourselves and the industry to derive these funds primarily from sources which would not ordinarily find their way into the risk sector of the economy. As a further result of the promotional campaign that will be launched, the principles of sound investment will be propagated, thereby lifting much of the veil of suspicion and mysticism from Stock Exchange activities.

"We are conscious of the enormous opportunities and challenges, particularly our responsibilities to the general public. We face a difficult and expensive re-education programme to bring this new concept to the man in the street and we therefore welcome the other mutual funds which will shortly be following and who will be able to share the burden of the educational programme with us. It is sincerely hoped that we will have the full support of the financial and popular press in the promotion of the infant industry in the national interest. One service in this connection in which your cooperation would be appreciated is the publication of the daily sales prices of our units in your financial pages. As a start it is appropriate to announce that the opening sales price of the units of The South African Growth Equities Fund will be 104 cents for Monday, giving a yield of 3,85 per cent. This price will be recalculated daily after the close of the Johannesburg Stock Exchange and will be notified to you before 5 o'clock each evening for the following day.

"I do not intend elaborating on the general aspects which we hope are clearly set out in our published prospectus, which has been approved in detail by the Registrar of Unit Trusts. However, there are one or two aspects on which I would like to comment further. Firstly, turning to our initial published portfolio, although it is somewhat orthodox in its composition it will, I am sure, basically secure our objective of a balanced, true barometer of South Africa's growth. It is in this sense that we offer participants in The South African Growth Equities Fund a stake in the growth potential of the Republic of South Africa.

"Although we claim little credit for this particular aspect, from our point of view, the timing of the commencement of our operations has been ideal. We believe that the underlying strength of our stock market is sounder than for a number of years past. The recent reaction in prices has enabled us to acquire securities in some of South Africa's leading companies on very reasonable terms. As long-term investors, this is a particularly advantageous situation.

"It was somewhat of a temptation to us to follow the American pattern of high management charges. However, on a full analysis of all relevant factors and considering the relative cost structures of the two countries, we are convinced that the charges applicable to American mutual funds are presently too high and are inapplicable to the South African investment scene. In the interests of the industry I express the hope that the other mutual funds which will follow us will take our lead in this regard. It is essential for us all to have the goodwill of the public and this must be earned.

"In support of our claim that investment risk is reduced to a minimum through mutual funds, I would like to quote from *Investment Companies, 1965*, produced by Arthur Wiesenberger, America's leading commentator on investment companies, who writes as follows:

"'Despite a 15 per cent rise in the Dow last year, one out of every four stocks listed on the Big Board declined in price. (Among the losers: Alcoa, American Telephone & Telegraph, General Foods, Gillette, Minnesota Mining, US Steel and other reputable blue chips.) In contrast, none of the 145 broadly diversified mutual funds covered in our year-end study on management performance declined in 1964! If you seek reasons for the ever-growing popularity of mutual funds, you need go no further.'

"We would like to publicly mention the company's great indebtedness to its consortium members, who have given so freely of their valuable time and expertise in bringing our fund to the operational stage. All the facilities of Netherlands Bank, London & Dominion Trust and Liberty Life have been freely contributed to do everything possible to ensure the success of the venture."

Thus was Sage Fund launched on its pioneering way. That, within four short years, the "industry", as Gordon chose to term it, was to be accused of responsibility for the share market setback of 1969 was not the fault of Gordon, or of Shill, who by that time would be in command. Sage Fund survived, and grew into the prosperous Sage Holdings of today. And the mutual fund industry, after its early setback, has flourished greatly. The share market crash of October 1987 had a minimal impact on the movement's popularity, and the South African investing public now has a range of some thirty funds, controlling assets exceeding R5 billion, to choose from. It all started with Sage Fund.

With the fund launched on what was to prove a highly successful path, and Donald Gordon having firmly and finally decided that his own future lay with Liberty Life rather than with the new venture, it was clear that the time had come for Louis Shill to move on to run the mutual fund management company, Investors Mutual Funds, on his own.

In Gordon's interview with the *Financial Mail* in 1978, he acknowledged that "the most driving co-founders of Liberty Life were Louis Shill and Sydney Lipworth". Lipworth had left Liberty Life when Guardian took control. It was now Shill's turn to move over to run what was, to all intents and purposes, another "joint venture". But in Shill's mind it was his own command, although Gordon was firmly ensconced as Chairman at that stage.

On the face of things, Investors Mutual Funds was a four-party consortium, with 25 per cent of its shares held by each of Netherlands Bank (now Nedbank), London & Dominion Trust, Liberty Life and Institutional Investments (Gordon and his colleagues, including Shill). Effectively, however, it was very much a Liberty Life concern: Liberty Life's 25 per cent, added to the 25 per cent of Institutional Investments, which had controlled Liberty Life before the Guardian deal, represented a seemingly homogeneous 50 per cent bloc, and this fact the "outside" partners, Netherlands Bank and London & Dominion – happily conceded in agreeing that DG should be Chairman.

Shill's "transfer" was formalised at a Liberty Life Board meeting on 4 November 1965. "Mr Gordon indicated the background of various discussions that had taken place between Mr Roy, Mr Bigland, Mr Shill and himself, regarding Investors Mutual Funds and the promotion of the Sage Growth Assurance Plan, culminating in the proposal that Mr H L Shill should be released from his executive duties at Liberty Life with a view to him taking up an appointment as executive director of Investors Mutual Funds Limited. As Mr Shill's activities will be basically concerned with promotion within the latter company, it was noted that in so far as these activities would involve the promotion of the Sage Growth Assurance Plan, he would remain closely associated with Liberty Life. It was confirmed that with effect from 30 November 1965, Mr Shill be and hereby is released from his executive duties at Liberty Life.

"Mr Roy proposed a vote of appreciation to Mr Shill for his devotion to the company's interests over the past few years and expressed the hope that the company's association with Mr Shill would continue in the years to come, to the mutual benefit of Liberty Life and Investors Mutual Funds." Shill, however, remained a director of Liberty Life.

From the beginning, things went well for Sage Fund, probably far better than the founders had envisaged (one amusing, if irritating, early problem was to persuade the press not to dub it "Sagef"). The successful early sales of Sage Fund units received another boost in October when Liberty Life launched the Sage Growth Assurance Plan – the life assurance/mutual fund link that had been at the centre of Gordon's, and Shill's, thinking when they decided to go for a mutual fund, and which was another resounding first for Liberty Life in the South African life insurance market.

Given hindsight, which of course one now has, the principle of linking to equity-type securities was probably the most important of all the Liberty Life-led innovations, for it has completely transformed the South African life insurance market (as did Abbey Life and its Mark Weinberg-led successor, Hambro Life, in the United Kingdom). Equity links placed the thrust of life insurance on investment, rather than on cover; indeed, on living, rather than on dying – a quite major transformation of the focus of a centuries-old industry in the space of less than one decade.

Again, as in the interregnum between the announcement of the mutual fund and its launch, the public needed to be educated, as well as informed. Once again, the *Financial Mail* sprang into the breach. On 24 September 1965, in an article headed "Insuring against Inflation" (it is good to see that the *FM* was even then calling a spade a shovel) and accompanied by a photograph captioned "Donald Gordon . . . insurance pioneer", it wrote:

"The word 'breakthrough' has been much abused, by journalists as well as salesmen and PRO's. Yet there are times when it is appropriate, and the new insurance scheme to be introduced next month by Liberty Life Association (part of the world-wide Guardian group) seems a case in point.

"The scheme is called the Sage Growth Assurance Plan and its essence is to link endowment assurance with the units of a mutual fund. [The idea was not uncommon in the UK, but none of the big insurance companies there offered policies linked to the purchase of units at that time.] But it is brand new in South Africa, as are mutual funds themselves.

"In the case of the Sage Plan the sum assured is geared to the growth (or otherwise) of units in the South African Growth Equities Fund (Sage). As each premium is paid, an amount of it, usually the entire premium, is allocated to the purchase of Sage units on behalf of the policyholder. The benefits on death or maturity consist of the units allocated, plus a small cash sum in most cases to make up the balance of the sum assured.

"To take an example. A man aged 40 takes out a policy with a premium of R100 a year over 25 years. In this case the nominal sum assured (ie what he would get if he dropped dead the day after) is R2 696. The total of his premiums over the period (ie R2 500) is allocated to the purchase of Sage units. At the end of 25 years he gets these units plus R196 in cash (the difference between R2 696 nominal sum assured and R2 500 allocated to units). If he died before the policy matures, his beneficiary or estate would get the units already allocated, plus the difference in cash to make up the nominal sum assured. Thus if he dies in the first year his estate would get the units bought for R100 plus R2 596 in cash.

"The great attraction of this scheme is that it is the first in South Africa which provides protection against capital erosion caused by the fall in the value of money. Clearly, however, everything depends on the extent to which units, in fact, appreciate in capital value over the life of the policy. This is a matter on which potential policyholders will have to take their own view.

"Broadly, however, it seems a reasonable bet that they will grow, over the long haul, at least as fast as the economy as a whole, probably faster. On that assumption the 5 ½ per cent a year chosen by Liberty Life for illustrative purposes seems fair. In the case of the example already given, the R2 500 worth of units purchased would be worth R5 593 at maturity assuming a 5 ½ per cent growth per annum. (In fact the average growth rate of today's Sage portfolio over the past ten years would have been about 8 per cent.)

"Some members of the public may feel that it would be risky to put all their eggs into one basket, namely, equities. They should remember, however, that all forms of saving and investment, including life assurance, involve risks; and perhaps the most certain thing in this uncertain world is that the value of money will continue to fall. If one starts with that viewpoint the Sage scheme has obvious advantages compared with conventional with-profits life policies. At the present rate of bonuses paid by Liberty Life, for example, a R100 a year conventional life policy would yield only R4 200 odd after 25 years.

"One possible drawback of the scheme is that the life cover it provides in relation to the premiums may be less than that offered by conventional non-profit policies (although greater than with-profit ones). This suggests that it may be sensible for those attracted by the Sage Plan to take out a policy under it at a rate of premium corresponding to the extent to which they are prepared to regard their payments as savings rather than strictly as premiums for life cover. This could be combined with term assurance which would provide the necessary cover until such time as the Sage policy had accumulated sufficiently in value for cover no longer to be necessary.

"From the company's point of view, its expenses will be defrayed from income from dividends on the units, which will not accrue to the policyholder.

"It will be interesting to see what response there will be to this

The young Chairman ... Donald Gordon on his Wedding Day, 21 January 1958, shortly after he had become founder Chairman of the newly-incorporated Liberty Life Association of Africa Limited.

THE LIBERTY LIFE ASSOCIATION OF AFRICA LIMITED
(Incorporated in the Union of South Africa)

BALANCE SHEET AT 31ST DECEMBER, 1958

| | £ | £ |
|---|---|---|
| SHARE CAPITAL | | |
| Authorised 100,000 Shares of £1 each | 100,000 | |
| Issued 50,000 Shares of £1 each, fully paid (Note 1) | | 50,000 |
| REVENUE RESERVE | | 629 |
| Profit and Loss Account | | |
| TOTAL SHAREHOLDERS INTEREST | | 50,629 |
| LIFE ASSURANCE FUND | | 2,739 |
| CURRENT LIABILITIES | | 10,055 |
| Balance of Purchase Price of Investments acquired | 3,572 | |
| Sundry Creditors, Provisions, Agent's Balances and Deferred Commissions | 6,483 | |
| | | £63,423 |

| | £ | £ |
|---|---|---|
| INVESTMENTS - At Cost (Notes 2 and 3) | | 34,149 |
| Union Government Stocks | 10,571 | |
| Electricity Supply Commission and Rand Water Board Stocks | 7,916 | |
| Municipal Stocks | 3,178 | |
| Quoted Preference Shares | 6,984 | |
| Mortgage Loan | 5,500 | |
| FIXED ASSETS | | 914 |
| Furniture, Fixtures, Equipment and Motor Vehicle | | |
| At Cost | 1,055 | |
| Less Depreciation | 141 | |
| CURRENT ASSETS | | 28,360 |
| Amount due by Reassurers, Outstanding and Deferred Premiums and Accrued Interest | 8,743 | |
| Balances with Bankers and Building Societies and Cash on Hand | 19,617 | |
| | | £63,423 |

The above Balance Sheet and attached Accounts together with the notes thereon are certified in terms of our report of even date.

JOHANNESBURG.
24th February, 1959.

ISAACS, KESSEL, FEINSTEIN & CO.
Chartered Accountants (S.A.)
Auditors.

On Behalf of the Board

D. Gordon DIRECTOR

Liberty Life's first financial statements as at 31 December 1958 – a very far cry indeed from the multi-billion rand figures of today.

THE LIBERTY LIFE ASSOCIATION OF AFRICA LIMITED
(Incorporated in the Union of South Africa)

LIFE REVENUE ACCOUNT FOR THE PERIOD 1ST OCTOBER, 1958 (DATE OF COMMENCEMENT OF INSURANCE BUSINESS) TO 31ST DECEMBER, 1958

| | £ | £ | | £ | £ |
|---|---|---|---|---|---|
| PREMIUMS (Net of liability to Reassurers) | | 13,184 | COMMISSIONS | | 6,171 |
| INTEREST ON INVESTMENTS | | 131 | EXPENSES OF MANAGEMENT | | 3,486 |
| | | | ESTABLISHMENT EXPENSES PRIOR TO COMMENCEMENT OF INSURANCE BUSINESS | | 919 |
| | | | AMOUNT OF LIFE ASSURANCE FUND AT 31ST DECEMBER, 1958 | | 2,739 |
| | | £13,315 | | | £13,315 |

PROFIT AND LOSS ACCOUNT FOR THE PERIOD 26TH NOVEMBER, 1957 (DATE OF CERTIFICATE TO COMMENCE BUSINESS) TO 31ST DECEMBER, 1958

| | | | | | |
|---|---|---|---|---|---|
| INTEREST ON INVESTMENTS | 1,275 | | PRELIMINARY AND SHARE ISSUE EXPENSES WRITTEN OFF | 776 | |
| DIVIDENDS ON PREFERENCE SHARES | 199 | | Less Share Premium Received | 125 | 651 |
| | 1,474 | | | | |
| Less Attributable Expenses | 200 | 1,274 | | | |
| SURPLUS ON SALE OF PREFERENCE SHARES | | 6 | BALANCE PER BALANCE SHEET | | 629 |
| | | £1,280 | | | £1,280 |

Donald Gordon still found time to be the family man – an outing with his wife and young children at Johannesburg's popular Zoo Lake Restaurant: (from left) Graeme, Peggy, Richard, Wendy and Donald (circa 1970).

The children grown up – Richard, Wendy and Graeme at their parents' 30th Wedding Anniversary party in 1988.

The 'Founding Directors': (from left) Sydney Lipworth, Louis Shill, Donald Gordon, Brian Young, Monty Schapiro and Hugh Rubin. Together again at Gordon's 50th birthday party at Sun City shortly after its opening in 1980.

Maureen Kilroe (née Hart), Donald Gordon's faithful and energetic secretary for almost seventeen years and now a close family friend, pictured with Gordon at his 50th Birthday party. Following her retirement and relocation to Cape Town in 1982, she married John Kilroe who is currently Chairman of Shell South Africa.

Louis Shill – 'one of the most driving co-founders' who left the executive team of Liberty Life to direct Liberty Life's original mutual fund offshoot, Investors Mutual Funds, management company of the Sage Fund. Shill turned IMF into the listed Sage Holdings and into an empire of his own after resigning from Liberty Life's Board in 1967.

Sir Mark Weinberg – founder of Abbey Life and now Chairman of Allied Dunbar, a major life insurance subsidiary of BAT Industries, one of the largest multi-national corporations in the UK. In July 1989 BAT became the target of a £13 billion take-over bid by a consortium led by Sir James Goldsmith.

Ernest Frank Bigland, managing director and later deputy chairman of the world-wide Guardian Royal Exchange Group. First mentor, then close friend of Donald Gordon: 'It was perhaps the most meaningful business relationship of my life.' Bigland remained a director and deputy chairman of Liberty Life until his retirement in May 1984. He died suddenly in December 1985.

Michael Rapp is a director of virtually all the companies in the Liberty Life Group. Following his relocation to the UK in 1986 he became executive deputy chairman of Capital & Counties. Rapp has been one of Gordon's closest associates and friends since he joined the Group in 1975 after the take-over of Rapp & Maister Holdings.

Friendship endures – Sydney Lipworth and Donald Gordon share some memories at the Gordons' 30th Wedding Anniversary party. And Lipworth (below), now Chairman of the UK Monopolies and Mergers Commission, proposing the toast on that occasion.

Loyalties live long at Liberty Life. Lily Cane, virtually the company's first employee, emerged from retirement to attend the opening of the Liberty Life Centre in September 1982. Her son, Joel, is now a deputy general manager of Liberty Holdings.

Julius Feinstein, to whom the young Gordon was articled directly after matriculating, is now senior partner of Liberty Life's auditors, Kessel Feinstein. Feinstein was Gordon's mentor and one of the few who had faith enough to back him with hard cash in the very early days of Liberty Life.

Bob Miller appointed Donald Gordon as a part-time agent for the Prudential before Liberty Life was started. Miller and the North City Group, which he created, later formed an important part of the Liberty Life sales arm.

Louis Miller, Bob Miller's younger brother, was Liberty Life's sales supremo until his tragic and untimely death in an air-crash near London in 1972.

Peter Greenfield, an actuary and an executive director of Guardian Royal Exchange, now retired from the Board of GRE, but still a director of Liberty Life and Trans-Atlantic, has been one of Gordon's staunchest allies since the early Guardian Assurance days before the merger with Royal Exchange in 1968.

Ted Roy took over as Chairman of Liberty Life after Guardian bought control in 1964, and remained as such until Gordon reassumed the Chair in 1972. Roy became one of Gordon's greatest supporters and closest friends until his death in 1984.

Peter Dugdale became chief executive of Guardian Royal Exchange when Ernest Bigland reached mandatory retirement age in 1978. A close relationship developed when he became a director of Liberty Life. He regularly travels to South Africa for Board meetings of Liberty Life and Guardian National Insurance Company, a listed short-term insurance subsidiary of GRE in which Liberty Holdings has a 44 per cent interest.

Tim Collins, Chairman of Guardian Royal Exchange at the time of the 'buy-back' of control of Liberty Life by Gordon, Rapp and the Standard Bank Investment Corporation in 1978. His predecessor, Colonel (Kit) Dawnay, invited Gordon to join the London GRE Board in October 1971.

Charles Hambro, Chairman of Hambros Bank, became Chairman of the Guardian Royal Exchange in May 1988 and is the only director who outranks Gordon in length of service on the GRE Board.

The Earl of Inchcape, probably the one director of the Guardian Royal Exchange with the most vivid recollections of the young Gordon's first GRE Board meeting! He retired in 1988.

Ernest Bigland and Donald Gordon photographed together in the original Guardian Liberty Centre in the early seventies, in the middle years of a truly remarkable business relationship.

Derek Keys, now Chairman of General Mining Union Corporation, and a director of TransAtlantic, was one of only three students who, with Mark Weinberg and Donald Gordon, 'stood out as being of really exceptional ability' according to Tommy Cairns, Professor of Accountancy at the University of the Witwatersrand in Gordon's student days.

Professor Fred du Plessis, Chairman of Liberty Life's great rival, Sanlam, regarded Donald Gordon as one of the sharpest business brains in the country. 'Professor Fred' died tragically in a motor accident early in 1989 and was a great loss to South Africa.

The Lubner brothers, Bertie (left) and Ronnie (right) were childhood friends of Donald Gordon, and are among the many who turned down the opportunity of investing in the fledgeling Liberty Life at inception. The Liberty Group is today the largest shareholder in the multi-national Placor/ Plate Glass Group, of which they are the joint Chairmen.

Pandemonium on the floor of the Johannesburg Stock Exchange when trading in the shares of Guardian Assurance Holdings, now renamed Liberty Holdings, opened in December 1968 after a record oversubscription of the public issue of 6 million shares at 150 cents per share. In July 1989 these shares were trading at 4 000 cents each.

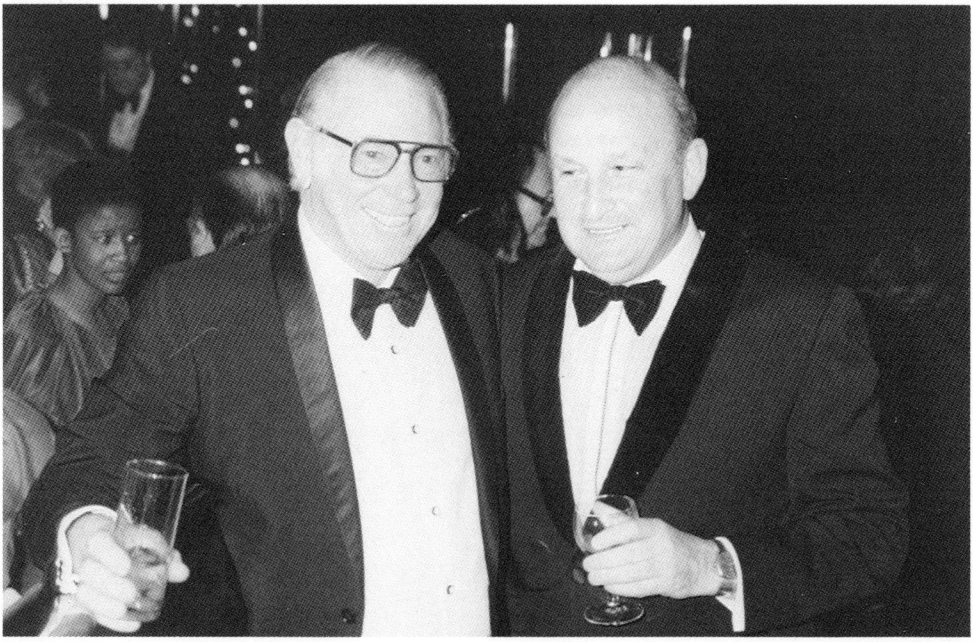

At Gordon's 50th Birthday party – Harry Brews, three years Gordon's senior and Vice Head Prefect at King Edward VII School in Johannesburg. Brews is now a deputy general manager of Liberty Life. He is due to retire in 1989.

# LIBERTY LIFE ASSOCIATION OF AFRICA LIMITED

*(INCORPORATED IN THE REPUBLIC OF SOUTH AFRICA)*

## PRE-LISTING STATEMENT IN TERMS OF THE REQUIREMENTS OF THE JOHANNESBURG STOCK EXCHANGE

This pre-listing statement is not an invitation to the public to subscribe for shares, but is issued in compliance with the Rules, ›gulations and Requirements of the Johannesburg Stock Exchange, for the purpose of giving information to the public with regard to ›e Company. The Directors collectively and individually accept full responsibility for the accuracy of the information given and certify ›at to the best of their knowledge and belief, there are no other facts, the omission of which would make any statement in this pre-›sting statement misleading, and that they have made all reasonable enquiries to ascertain such facts.

Application for a primary listing of the whole of the issued capital of the Company, consisting of 100,000 ordinary shares of R2 ›ch, will be made forthwith to the Committee of the Johannesburg Stock Exchange.

## DIRECTORS

ONALD GORDON, Chartered Accountant (S.A.), (Chairman)
4 Goudvis Road,
Melrose North,
Johannesburg. Managing Director of the Company.

AURICE SYDNEY LIPSCHITZ,
836 Innes Chambers,
Pritchard Street,
Johannesburg. Advocate.

UGH RUBIN, B.Com.,
15 Atherstone Road,
Illovo,
Johannesburg. Executive Director of the Company.

ONTY SCHAPIRO,
106 7th Avenue,
Highlands North,
Johannesburg.
Managing Director of S. A. May (Pty.) Ltd., Insurance Brokers.

YME LOUIS SHILL, B.Com., Chartered Accountant (S.A.)
2 Montgomery Avenue,
Witbank,
Transvaal. Director of Companies.

RIAN PHILIP YOUNG, B.Sc. (Med.), Chartered Accountant (S.A.)
11 16th Street,
Orange Grove,
Johannesburg. Executive Director of the Company.

## SECRETARY

EDWARD McDONALD ROBERTS
43 6th Avenue,
Parktown North,
Johannesburg.

## LONDON MANAGER

ARK AUBREY WEINBERG, B.Com., LL.B. (Rand), LL.M. (London)
Oakhill House,
Oakhill Way,
Hampstead,
London, N.W.3.

## BANKERS

BARCLAYS BANK D.C.O.
Kerk and Harrison Streets
Johannesbug.
STANDARD BANK OF SOUTH AFRICA LIMITED
Fox Street,
Johannesburg.

## CONSULTING ACTUARIES

SHEPLEY & FITCHETT,
Reinsurance House,
Commissioner Street,
Johannesburg.

## SPONSORING STOCKBROKERS

MAX POLLAK & FREEMANTLE
(Members of Johannesburg Stock Exchange)
French House,
Marshall and Ferreira Streets
Johannesburg.

Lincoln House,
76 St. Georges Street,
Cape Town.

7 Stability Buildings,
310 Smith Street,
Durban.

## SOLICITORS

EDWARD NATHAN, FRIEDLAND, MANSELL & LEWIS
Innes Chambers,
Pritchard Street,
Johannesburg.

## AUDITORS

ISAACS, KESSEL, FEINSTEIN & COMPANY,
Chartered Accountants (S.A.),
Annan House,
Commissioner Street,
Johannesburg.

## HEAD OFFICE AND SHARE TRANSFER OFFICE

4th Floor,
Loveday House,
Cor. Loveday and Marshall Streets,
Johannesburg.

## REGISTERED OFFICE

2nd Floor,
Annan House,
Commissioner Street,
Johannesburg.

## UNITED KINGDOM REGISTERED OFFICE

158 Fenchurch Street,
London, E.C.3.

## HISTORY AND PROSPECTS

The Company was registered in the Republic of South Africa as public company on the 10th September 1957, with the principal ›bject of carrying on life assurance business. On 22nd August 1958, › received a certificate of registration in terms of section 4 (3) of ›he Insurance Act of 1943, as amended, authorising it to carry on ›ng term insurance business. Active business operations were ›ommenced on the 1st October 1958.

The premium income of the Company has increased considerably ›ach year since inception and the amount arising from new business ›as each year exceeded that of the previous year. For the year ›nded 31st December 1961, the premium income in respect of new ›usiness written amounted to approximately R142,500. Business ›as continued to expand during the four months ended 30th April ›962, the premium income in respect of new business written during ›he period amounting to approximately R57,500 (compared with ›32,500 for the corresponding period in 1961).

The Company's agency network has increased steadily since ›s inception and business placed with the Company through insur-›nce brokers has risen significantly over the past year. The ›ompany has pioneered certain progressive forms of insurance, ›otably in the field of pensions for self-employed persons, which ›ave been well received by the public. The Company is in a position, ›y virtue of its well-trained personnel and aggressive sales policy, ›o make available to the South African public the latest and most ›dvanced technical developments in life insurance from the leading ›ountries in the world in this field.

The Company's ability to contain its expense ratio at an excep-›ionally low level and the favourable investment climate in South ›frica in regard to gilt-edged and other conservative investments, ›hould enable it to continue to compete on favourable terms in the ›nsurance market.

The Company has adopted a conservative investment policy and spreads its investable funds over the complete range of orthodox investment categories. In determining the apportionment amongst these categories, the prime consideration is security of capital. Within each category of investment, a policy of wide diversification and spread is applied. Some hedge against the effects of inflation is provided by the investment of a limited proportion of the investable funds in leading South African growth stocks.

It is the Company's policy to reassure to a substantial degree its obligations to the public in respect of death and disability claims, to the extent that it retains only a small portion of the risk. Satisfactory treaties are in existence with two leading international reinsurance groups, which adequately protect the Company against adverse claims experience.

A life assurance company's surpluses arise not only from the small profit factor included in its premium rates but also, and indeed primarily, from the effect of improving mortality and selection criteria, investment income earned at a rate in excess of that assumed in its premium calculations, lapses, surrenders and savings flowing from a low expense ratio. It is characteristic of a life assurance company that, particularly because of the conservative manner in which it is required to compute its liabilities towards policyholders, the surpluses generated by the above factors tend to be deferred for some years, until the cumulative effect of the increasing premium and investment income is sufficient to overtake the heavy early cost of business procuration. In the case of this Company, such a surplus arose in the actuarial valuation at 31st December 1961 and it is anticipated that this surplus will tend to rise cumulatively in the normal manner.

These surpluses can be expected, after providing for fully competitive bonuses on policies participating in the surplus of the Company, to contribute, again cumulatively, to the funds which, together with investment income referable to shareholders' capital, are applicable to the shareholders' interests.

The Directors anticipate that the Company will commence paying dividends after the end of the current financial year.

## CAPITAL

The authorised and issued capital of the Company is R200,000, divided into 100,000 Shares of R2 each. All the shares are ordinary shares of one class, which rank pari passu in all respects including voting, dividends and return of capital. All issues of shares have been for cash.

During September to December 1959, 10,000 Shares were issued for cash at R2.25 per Share to seventeen persons and these allotments were confirmed at the succeeding Annual General Meeting.

In September 1961, 10,000 Shares were issued for cash at R2.40 per share to Alherma Investments Limited, an English investment subsidiary of a Reinsurance Group, in connection with reinsurance arrangements made by the Company and the financing of its branch in the United Kingdom.

On 28th April 1962, an option granted in 1957 to Donald Gordon, the founder of the Company, to take up 8,000 shares at R2 per Share not later than 26th November 1969, was exercised and the 8,000 Shares were issued at his direction to Liberty Trust (Proprietary) Limited against cash at R2 per Share.

Although the Directors considered that the capital of the Company was already adequate for its business requirements, it was decided to increase the issued and paid-up capital to the full authorised capital of R200,000 in order to comply with the requirements of the Johannesburg Stock Exchange for a primary listing of shares. Accordingly, in May 1962 22,000 Shares were offered to and taken up by existing shareholders for cash at R2.50 per share, by way of a one-for-four rights issue and applications for excess shares; excess shares were issued to applicants pro rata (as far as practicable) to their existing shareholdings.

The Company's issued capital history may be summarised as follows:

| | Issue Price | Nominal Value | Share Premium (after deduction of issue expenses) |
|---|---|---|---|
| 50,000 Shares, prior to commencement of insurance business .. | R2.00 | R100,000 | — |
| 10,000 Shares, in September to December 1959 .. .. | R2.25 | R20,000 | R2,450 |
| 10,000 Shares, in September 1961 .. | R2.40 | R20,000 | R3,125 |
| 8,000 Shares, in April 1962 .. .. (founder's option) | R2.00 | R16,000 | — |
| 22,000 Shares, in May 1962 .. .. | R2.50 | R44,000 | R11,000 |
| Issued Share Capital | | R200,000 | R16,575 |
| Add Share Premium Account | | R16,575 | |
| Share Capital and Capital Reserve | | R216,575 | |

No capital is under option or agreed conditionally or unconditionally to be put under option. The Company has no loan capital and has not agreed to issue any loan capital.

## REPORT OF THE CONSULTING ACTUARIES

The following report dated 11th May 1962, has been received from Messrs. Shepley & Fitchett, the Consulting Actuaries to the Company, who have consented in writing (and have not withdrawn that consent) to its inclusion in this Pre-listing Statement, in the form and context in which it appears:

"The Directors, 11th May, 1962
Liberty Life Association of Africa Limited,
Johannesburg.

Gentlemen,

We have acted as Consulting Actuaries to your Company since the beginning of 1959, and report that the Company has been operated in an efficient and conservative manner and in conformity with basic actuarial principles.

We deal hereunder with certain matters relative to your affairs which we consider significant.

LIFE ASSURANCE FUND

The Life Assurance Fund is required to cover the actuarial liability under unmatured policies and includes any surplus. The actuarial liability is the amount which, together with future premiums and interest earnings, will provide for the future payment of death claims, maturity values and annuity payments, as they fall due, as well as the expenses of operating the Company.

In South Africa, a relatively stringent minimum basis of computing actuarial liabilities is obligatory under the Insurance Act of 1943 (as amended): the assurance company is required to assume that the net rate of interest earned by it will be limited to 3½% and that the mortality amongst its policyholders will be in accordance with the A1924-1929 ultimate mortality table, which was drawn up on the basis of mortality experience amongst assured lives in Britain during those years. Moreover, the Insurance Act does not permit the company in calculating its actuarial liabilities to take full allowance for the high procuration and new business costs which are general: these costs are allowed for in the premium rates charged and are recouped by the company from the payment of future premiums under each policy. The effect of the stringent statutory requirements and the restrictions on the allowance in respect of new business expenses is that a new life assurance company is invariably expected to draw on its capital for a period of from seven to ten years after its establishment in order to cover its actuarial liabilities on the basis required by the Insurance Act.

In this connection we report that, at the last valuation of the Company's actuarial liabilities which was conducted by us on the basis laid down by the Insurance Act, for the year ended 31st December 1961, only 3¼ years after the commencement of life assurance business, a surplus of R33,066 was disclosed as having arisen during the year. This surplus was sufficient not only to enable the Company to absorb entirely the extent to which establishment and procuration costs from inception had required financing out of shareholders' funds in order to meet the statutory actuarial requirements, but also to strengthen free reserves by the transfer of R7,000 to investment reserve and to leave the Life Assurance Fund as reflected in the balance sheet in excess of statutory requirements. The effect is that the Life Assurance Fund of R269,930 in the Balance Sheet at 31st December, 1961, fully covered the Company's actuarial liabilities to policyholders, calculated on the statutory basis, leaving its capital and shareholders' reserves of R164,805 entirely unimpaired. We understand that the capital and capital reserve have subsequently been increased by further issues of shares, to raise total capital and shareholders' reserves to R235,805.

The adoption of a more realistic basis of valuation, consistent with current interest rates and mortality experience, would have resulted in a substantially greater surplus, but the adoption of the statutory basis has the effect of strengthening the Life Assurance Fund and of deferring to the future surpluses which would otherwise have been reflected at this stage.

The fact that capital and shareholders' reserves remain intact after meeting the statutory actuarial requirements after only 3¼ years of assurance business, is, in our view, an exceptional achievement, reflecting the Company's efficient management and strict economy in administration, and the high class of business written by it.

On the basis of our experience in regard to insurance companies developing on conservative bases and given continuation of the experience to date, future actuarial valuations should disclose growing surpluses in the years to come, which should after the provision of competitive bonuses to participating policyholders, make an increasing contribution to the funds available for distribution to shareholders.

INVESTMENTS

The most important factor in the computation of premium rates and the production of surpluses (on the assumption of the adoption of a conservative mortality table) is the rate of interest earned on investments. In this regard, although a net rate of interest of 3½% per annum has been assumed by us in calculating the Actuarial Liabilities, the actual average rate earned on the mean Life Assurance Fund for the three years ended 31st December, 1961, has been 6.14% per annum before taxation, resulting in a net (after taxation) rate of 5.75% per annum. These figures compare very favourably with those shown in the revenue accounts of the leading life offices operating in South Africa over the same period.

We have examined the investment portfolio of your Company at 31st December, 1961, and report that it held gilt edged stocks and other approved assets substantially in excess of statutory requirements and its other major assets are conservatively invested and diversified in leading South African securities.

We also report that the redemption value of the government, public utility and municipal stocks and the market value of the other quoted securities was at that date in the aggregate in excess of the cost to the Company, and this position was further strengthened by an investment reserve of R10,000.

NEW BUSINESS

The business written by your Company has been of good quality. This is no doubt attributable to the fact that your Company has prospected for business predominantly in the higher income brackets. That the selection has been conservative is evidenced by the very low claims experience.

The new business premium income has risen each year. The following figures, showing the new business premium income for each financial year since inception, have been extracted from the Company's records.

Quarter ended 31st December, 1958: R26,366
Year ended 31st December, 1959: R74,747
Year ended 31st December, 1960: R139,094
Year ended 31st December, 1961: R142,527
4 Months ended 30th April, 1962: R57,500
(compared with R32,500 for the corresponding period of 1961)

The new business expense ratio of the Company is lower than the general average applicable to life assurance companies operating in South Africa.

REASSURANCE

We have examined your Company's reassurance arrangements, which are on an automatic treaty basis with leading international reinsurance groups, and we are satisfied that these arrangements are so devised that your Company's finances would not be seriously affected in the event of adverse claims experience.

Yours faithfully,
SHEPLEY & FITCHETT."

## REPORT OF THE AUDITORS

The following report has been received from the Company's Auditors, Messrs. Isaacs, Kessel, Feinstein and Company, who have consented in writing (and have not withdrawn that consent) to its inclusion in this Pre-listing Statement in the form and context in which it appears.

"The Directors,
Liberty Life Association of Africa Limited,
Loveday House,
Marshall Street,
Johannesburg.

Gentlemen,

We have been auditors to your Company since its incorporation on 10th September 1957. Life Assurance business commenced on the 1st October 1958. The Company has no subsidiaries.

1. PROFITS
We report that the following information has been extracted from the audited accounts of the Company. No adjustments to the figures appearing in those accounts have been considered necessary for the purpose of this Pre-listing Statement.

LIFE REVENUE ACCOUNTS SINCE THE COMMENCEMENT OF LIFE ASSURANCE BUSINESS

| | Period ended 31.12.1958 R | Year ended 31.12.1959 R | Year ended 31.12.1960 R | Year ended 31.12.1961 R |
|---|---|---|---|---|
| Amount of Life Assurance Fund at beginning of period .. | — | 5,478 | 29,544 | 111,392 |
| Premium income less re-assurances .. | 26,368 | 95,492 | 188,946 | 250,839 |
| Income on investments (less tax) .. | 262 | 956 | 4,038 | 10,558 |
| Net surplus on realisation of investments .. | — | — | — | 7,297 |
| | R26,630 | R101,926 | R222,528 | R380,086 |
| Death and disability claims .. | — | — | 12,000 | 6,420 |
| Less recovered from re-assurers .. | — | — | 8,930 | 4,787 |
| | — | — | 3,070 | 1,633 |
| Surrenders .. | — | — | — | 168 |
| Commissions and agency expenses, less commissions received .. | 12,342 | 45,488 | 62,948 | 53,227 |
| Management expenses .. | 6,972 | 26,894 | 45,118 | 48,128 |
| Establishment expenses (prior to commencement of business) .. | 1,838 | — | — | — |
| Transfer to Investment Reserve .. | — | — | — | 7,000 |
| Amount of Life Assurance Fund at end of period | 5,478 | 29,544 | 111,392 | 269,930 |
| | R26,630 | R101,926 | R222,528 | R380,086 |

PROFIT AND LOSS ACCOUNTS SINCE THE INCORPORATION OF THE COMPANY

| | Period ended 31.12.1958 | Year ended 31.12.1959 | Year ended 31.12.1960 | Year ended 31.12.1961 |
|---|---|---|---|---|
| Credit Balance at beginning of period .. | — | 1,258 | 4,350 | 5,434 |
| Income on investments .. | 2,948 | 4,858 | 4,478 | 5,259 |
| Less attributable expenses .. | 400 | 1,200 | 1,200 | 1,200 |
| | 2,548 | 3,658 | 3,278 | 4,059 |
| Net surplus on realisation of investments .. | 12 | — | 938 | — |
| | R2,560 | R4,916 | R8,566 | R9,493 |
| Taxation (not applicable to Life Revenue Account) | — | 566 | 132 | 263 |
| Preliminary and share issue expenses written off | 1,302 | — | — | — |
| Transfer to Investment Reserve .. | — | — | 3,000 | — |
| Credit Balance at end of period .. | 1,258 | 4,350 | 5,434 | 9,230 |
| | R2,560 | R4,916 | R8,566 | R9,493 |

Notes
(a) The profit figures shown in the Profit and Loss Accounts reflect only the net income from the investment of part of the shareholders' funds and net surpluses on realisation of certain of those investments. No transfers have been made to or from the Life Revenue Account. At 31st December 1961, the Life Fund exceeded the actuarial liability as computed on the basis laid down by the Insurance Act of 1943, as amended. (Refer Actuaries' Report, paragraphs headed "Life Assurance Fund.")
(b) No dividends have been declared or paid by the Company.
(c) The expenses of the Company in respect of its activities from its incorporation on 10th September 1957 to the commencement of life assurance business on 1st October 1958, amounted to R3,140, of which R1,838 was establishment expenses written off in the Life Revenue Account for the period ended 31st December 1958 and the balance of R1,302 was preliminary and share issue expenses written off in the Profit and Loss Account for the same period.

2. WRITING UP OF THE BOOK VALUE OF ASSETS
There has been no writing up of the book value of any assets of the Company during the three years prior to 31st December 1961.

3. ASSETS AND LIABILITIES
The assets and liabilities of the Company at the dates set out below, based on the audited Balance Sheets at those dates, were as follows:

| ASSETS | R 31.12.1958 | R 31.12.1959 | R 31.12.1960 | R 31.12.1961 |
|---|---|---|---|---|
| INVESTMENTS at cost (see Note (a)) | | | | |
| Government Stocks .. | 21,142 | 21,142 | 21,142 | 51,188 |
| Public Utility Stocks .. | 15,832 | 19,372 | 23,272 | 51,025 |
| Municipal stocks .. .. | 6,356 | 8,356 | 16,156 | 34,993 |
| Quoted Debenture stocks | — | — | — | 2,600 |
| Quoted Preference shares | 13,968 | 24,110 | 31,434 | 45,874 |
| Quoted Ordinary shares | — | 2,350 | 45,422 | 67,128 |
| Mortgage Loans .. .. | 11,000 | 23,000 | 22,986 | 20,780 |
| Policy Loans .. .. | — | — | — | 590 |
| Fixed Deposits with Building Societies | — | — | — | 42,000 |
| | 68,298 | 98,330 | 160,412 | 316,178 |
| FIXED ASSETS | | | | |
| Office Furniture and motor vehicle | | | | |
| At Cost .. .. | 2,110 | 6,666 | 7,298 | 6,138 |
| Less aggregate depreciation .. .. | 282 | 904 | 1,974 | 1,945 |
| | 1,828 | 5,762 | 5,324 | 4,193 |
| CURRENT ASSETS | | | | |
| Net deferred and outstanding premiums, agents and miscellaneous debtors, less provisions .. | 17,486 | 45,078 | 78,040 | 114,896 |
| Balances with bankers, deposits with financial institutions and cash on hand .. | 39,234 | 30,926 | 28,034 | 44,416 |
| | R56,720 | R76,004 | R106,074 | R159,312 |
| | R126,846 | R180,096 | R271,810 | R479,683 |
| SHARE CAPITAL (Authorised R200,000) Issued and fully paid in shares of R2 each .. .. | 100,000 | 120,000 | 120,000 | 140,000 |
| CAPITAL RESERVE | | | | |
| Share Premium Account (subject to Section 86 quat of the Companies Act), less share issue expenses .. | — | 2,450 | 2,450 | 5,575 |
| REVENUE RESERVES | | | | |
| Investment Reserve .. | — | — | 3,000 | 10,000 |
| Profit and Loss Account | 1,258 | 4,350 | 5,434 | 9,230 |
| | 1,258 | 4,350 | 8,434 | 19,230 |
| TOTAL SHAREHOLDERS' INTEREST | 101,258 | 126,800 | 130,884 | 164,805 |
| LIFE ASSURANCE FUND (See Note (b)) .. | 5,478 | 29,544 | 111,392 | 269,930 |
| CURRENT LIABILITIES | | | | |
| Balance of purchase price of investments acquired .. | 7,144 | 3,950 | 6,198 | 10,903 |
| Agents' balances and miscellaneous creditors | 12,966 | 9,448 | 12,762 | 14,494 |
| Amount due to reassurers | — | 9,694 | 10,042 | 18,201 |
| Taxation .. | — | 660 | 572 | 1,350 |
| | 20,110 | 23,725 | 29,534 | 44,948 |
| | R126,846 | R180,096 | R271,810 | R479,683 |

NOTES RELATING TO THE ASSETS AND LIABILITIES AT 31st DECEMBER 1961

(a) (i) South African Government Stocks at a cost of R21,144 are lodged with the South African Treasury in terms of the requirements of the Insurance Act of 1943, as amended.

(ii) The redemption value of the Company's Government, Municipal and Public Utility Stocks and the market value of its other quoted securities is, in the aggregate, in excess of the cost to the Company as follows:

| | Cost R | Redemption Value R |
|---|---|---|
| Government Stocks .. .. | 51,188 | 54,000 |
| Public Utility Stocks .. .. | 51,025 | 54,000 |
| Municipal Stocks .. .. .. | 34,993 | 38,400 |
| | R137,206 | R146,400 |

| | Cost | Market Value |
|---|---|---|
| Debentures .. .. .. .. | 2,600 | 2,847 |
| Preference Shares .. .. .. | 45,874 | 44,785 |
| Ordinary Shares .. .. .. | 67,128 | 71,330 |
| | R115,602 | R118,962 |

(b) The Life Fund is in excess of the actuarial liability computed on the basis laid down by the Insurance Act of 1943, as amended.
(c) Assets in the United Kingdom and the Federation of Rhodesia and Nyasaland have been converted into South African Currency at the rate of £1 = R2.
(d) In terms of resolutions of shareholders:
(i) An option was granted until 26th November 1969, to take up a maximum of 8,000 shares of R2 each in the Company at R2 per share. (Such option was exercised after the 31st December 1961).
(ii) The unissued capital of the Company was under the unrestricted control of the Directors subject to (i) above. (All unissued shares were issued after the 31st December 1961.)

4. MATERIAL CHANGES SINCE 31st DECEMBER 1961
The books of your Company have not been audited since 31st December 1961. The issued capital of the Company has been increased since that date, by the issue for cash of 8,000 Shares at R2 per share on the 28th April 1962 and of 22,000 Shares at R2.50 per share on the 9th May 1962. A summarised Balance Sheet at 31st December 1961, adjusted to reflect the effect of these increases of capital, would read as follows:

| | R | | R | R |
|---|---|---|---|---|
| Share Capital .. .. | 200,000 | Investments .. .. .. | | 316,178 |
| Capital Reserve .. .. | 16,575 | Fixed Assets .. .. .. | | 4,193 |
| Revenue Reserve .. .. | 19,230 | Net Deferred and outstanding premiums, agents and miscellaneous debtors, less provisions .. .. | | 114,896 |
| Total Shareholders' Interest .. .. | 235,805 | Cash resources— | | |
| Life Assurance Fund .. | 269,930 | As per Balance Sheet .. .. | 44,416 | |
| Current Liabilities .. | 44,948 | Proceeds of Issues .. .. | 71,000 | 115,416 |
| | R550,683 | | | R550,683 |

Except for the above issues there have, to the best of our knowledge, been no material changes in the capital structure of the Company since the 31st December 1961, nor have there been any material changes in the assets and liabilities except such changes as have resulted from the Company carrying on business in the ordinary course.

5. DEBTORS AND CREDITORS
The items "Net deferred and outstanding premiums, agents and miscellaneous debtors, less provisions" and "Agents' balances and miscellaneous creditors" do not, to the best of our knowledge, include any accounts other than those which have arisen in the ordinary course of business. In our opinion the provision for doubtful debts is adequate.
The major portion of the asset "Net deferred and outstanding premiums, agents and miscellaneous debtors, less provisions," consists of deferred instalments of annual premiums less commission and expenses payable thereon. These premiums represent the balance of annual premiums payable in instalments, for the convenience of policyholders, which are brought to account in the year in which the premium falls due, following normal accounting practice for life assurance premiums.

6. BASIS OF VALUATION ASSETS
The assets of the Company at 31st December 1961, have been valued as follows:
(a) Investments—at cost.
(b) Office Furniture and Motor Vehicle—at cost less depreciation.
At the 31st December 1961, the redemption value of the Company's Government, Public Utility and Municipal stocks exceeded book value by R9,194 and the market value of the Company's quoted shares and debentures exceeded book value by R3,360.

7. INVESTMENT PORTFOLIO AT 9th MAY 1962
At your request, we have analysed the investments and cash resources shown in the Company's books as at 9th May 1962. The cost of these assets amounted at that date to R478,741, and may be summarised as follows:

| | Cost R | Percentage of total |
|---|---|---|
| South African and British Government Stock .. (Redemption Value R56,000) | 53,673 | 11.21% |
| Stocks of Ea... Rand Water Board and Industrial Development Corporation .. .. (Redemption Value R76,500) | 73,131 | 15.28% |
| Stocks of South African Municipalities .. (Redemption Value R76,900) | 71,725 | 14.98% |
| Mortgage Loans .. .. .. | 18,667 | 3.90% |
| Mortgage Debenture Stock .. .. (Redemption Value R22,600) | 22,600 | 4.72% |
| Quoted Preference Shares (see Note) .. .. (Market Value R51,218) | 50,458 | 10.54% |
| Quoted Ordinary Shares (see Note) .. .. (Market Value R67,121) | 59,221 | 12.37% |
| Fixed Deposits with United Building Society and Allied Building Society .. | 42,000 | 8.77% |
| Balances with Bankers and Cash on Hand (Inclusive of R55,000 in respect of share issue on 9th May, 1962) .. .. | 74,896 | 15.65% |
| Other Investments .. .. | 12,370 | 2.58% |
| | R478,741 | 100.00% |

NOTE. The Quoted Preference Shares are held in 39 companies, all of which are quoted on the Johannesburg Stock Exchange; no holding in any one company exceeds R5,400. The Quoted Ordinary Shares are held in 32 companies, all of which are quoted on the Johannesburg Stock Exchange, no holding in any one company exceeds R5,200. We are informed that the detailed schedule of Quoted Preference and Ordinary Shares is available for inspection at the Head Office of the Company.

Yours faithfully,
ISAACS, KESSEL, FEINSTEIN & CO.

Johannesburg.
11th May, 1962."

## TAX STATUS

In terms of Section 33 (2) (e) ( The Income Tax Act of 1941 (ɪ amended), all insurance com panies are automatically recog nised as public companies fc taxation purposes.

## DIRECTORS ANI BORROWING POWERS

The Articles of Association o the Company include the follow ing provisions:

(a) Until otherwise determined by general meeting, a Director i required to hold 1,000 Share as a qualification.

(b) The remuneration of th Directors as such and of the Chairman is determined by the Directors, subject to con firmation at the Annua General Meeting and is pay able only after such confirma tion. The remuneration of a Director in respect of his employment by the Company must be determined by a dis interested quorum of Direc tors.

(c) The aggregate amount at any time owing by the Company and its subsidiary companies (exclusive of inter-company borrowing) may not, except with the consent of the Com pany in general meeting exceed the nominal amount of the issued and paid-up capita for the time being of the Com pany. The borrowing powers of the Company are further restricted by the provisions of Section 20 (2)(a) of the Insurance Act of 1943, as amended.

No assets have been acquired nor are any other assets proposed to be acquired by, or in the pro motion of, the Company, in which any Director had any direct or indirect interest.

There are no contracts existing or about to be entered into either written or verbal, relating to Directors' and/or Manageria remuneration.

## GENERAL

No material contracts, whethe verbal or written, have been entered into during the last three years, other than in the ordinary course of the business carried on by the Company.

No assets have been purchased or acquired by the Company since its incorporation, other than in the ordinary course of business. The Company has no commit ments in respect of capita expenditure.

No loans have been made to the Company and, except for mortgag loans and other investments in the ordinary course of business and non-material advances made to agents against commissions, no loans have been made by the Com pany since its incorporation.

No commissions, discounts, brokerages, or other special term have been granted during the pas two years in connection with the issue or sale of any shares in the capital of the Company.

The expenses relating to the issue of Shares on the 9th Ma 1962 and the application for the primary listing of the Shares on the Johannesburg Stock Exchang are estimated to be R2,500 an are payable by the Company.

The following documents may b inspected at the Head Office, 4t Floor, Loveday House, cor. Loveda and Marshall Streets, Johanne burg, during business hours at an time between the date of publica tion of this pre-listing statemen and the 18th June, 1962:

The Memorandum and Articles of Association; the original of the Consulting Actuaries Report set out above, and the written con sent of the Consulting Actua ries referred to; the original of the Auditors' Report set out above and the written consent referred to; copies of the Life Revenue and Profit and Loss Accounts of the Company for the periods referred to in the Auditors' Report and the Balance Sheets since incor poration; the detailed sche dule of Quoted Preference and Ordinary Shares held by the Company at 9th May 1962.

Signed: D. Gordon
M. S. Lipschitz
H. Rubin
M. Schapiro
H. L. Shill
B. P. Young

16th May, 1962.

Reprinted from Sunday Times, June 3, 1962, by S.A.A.N.

The one-page pre-listing statement of Liberty Life Association of Africa Limited as published prior to the listing of the company's shares on the Johannesburg Stock Exchange on 4 June 1962. This document was drawn up by Donald Gordon and Mark Weinberg immediately prior to Weinberg leaving for the UK to start Abbey Life.

An artist's impression of the famous Royal Exchange, the London Head Office of the world-wide Guardian Royal Exchange Group, which stands in the very heart of the City of London adjacent to the Bank of England and the London Stock Exchange. In 1989 a major restoration and refurbishment was being undertaken on this historic building – the birthplace of modern insurance.

innovation to South African assurance. Other life offices may well be forced to follow suit. Whatever happens, congratulations must go to Mr Donald Gordon and his enterprising team at Liberty Life for another pioneering venture."

The response was, in fact, very considerable, so much so that within less than a year it would begin to pose problems. The background, of course, was that Guardian's Ernest Bigland had never been more than lukewarm about either the mutual fund itself or the equity-linked scheme. After all, the two had nearly cost him Gordon's services during the traumatic in-fighting before Sage Fund's launch.

As far back as 20 November 1964, Bigland had written: "I think, in fact, we have probably been viewing the start of the fund from slightly different angles. From our side we have looked on it as being rather a useful addition to your life side which we would like to see started in a modest and conservative way." That was long before the launch, of course. On 16 November 1965, however, he would write: "I am pleased to hear that your Sage Growth Assurance Plan is in fact doing well despite the set-back in the market and it is indeed good news that it has not affected the orthodox business."

There was doubtless a fair amount of telephone traffic before the issue again emerged in the correspondence, but by 11 August 1966 Bigland had concrete – and, to him, worrying – statistics.

"You will remember when we agreed to start the Sage Growth Assurance Plan that I did say I was rather concerned that if it went well inevitably it would become a large part of your business and would in some ways prevent us from selling as much genuine life assurance. This position seems to have arisen rather earlier than I anticipated and I thought you might like to see a note our people produced for me which sets the figures out very clearly.

"Item A – New Business Production (from managing director's report to be submitted at Board meeting 18 August 1966).

| New Annual Premium Income: | 1966 | 1965 |
|---|---|---|
| | R | R |
| 1st Quarter | 243 000 | 281 000 |
| 2nd Quarter | 301 000 | 165 000 |
| | 544 000 | 446 000 |

| | | |
|---|---|---|
| Sage Growth Assurance Plan | | |
| (1966 35 per cent) | 190 000 | Nil |
| Other New Life Premiums | 354 000 | 446 000 |

"The figure for the first quarter 1965 is high and may have included a special item but the new Life Premium Income, excluding SGAP, for the first six months of 1966 is lower by R91 000 than for corresponding period in 1965. SGAP was launched late in 1965 and sales could be increasing rapidly quarter by quarter. I suggest, therefore, that the Liberty Life should show in their monthly and quarterly New Business Returns the split between SGAP income and other new Life Premium Income for 1966 and 1965.

"I note that you say methods are being investigated of keeping a properly balanced account and I should be interested to have your views as it does seem to be working out exactly as I predicted and it would be a pity if we allowed it to become a preponderant part of your business."

The issue was raised at the next Liberty Life Board meeting. Under the heading: "Development of Mutual Fund Linked Insurance Contracts", the minute read:

"Mr Gordon tabled a letter received from Mr Bigland expressing certain reservations at the very rapid rate at which mutual fund linked business was now being written, particularly in view of the increasing trend in that direction. Mr Gordon confirmed that, in fact, this upward trend had shown markedly during June and July and, although he agreed that it was most desirable for the portfolio to be kept in balance, he did not completely share Mr Bigland's concern in this connection. He outlined to the Board in some detail many aspects of the problem and, in particular, that viewed against the overall portfolio in force, it would still take some considerable time before unit-linked contracts would constitute anything like a major percentage of the overall business. He added that in fairness this situation had been anticipated at the time that the company embarked on the project and that public acceptance of the new concepts had been as anticipated. Mr Gordon completely reassured the Board on this matter and explained that he would be discussing the whole situation with Mr Bigland shortly. He indicated that certain solutions were available to the company, including a 'blended contract' which would consist of an orthodox insurance policy and a mutual fund linked policy in equal parts.

"Finally, Mr Gordon told the Board that to his knowledge most companies were substantially down on their 1965 figures and the fact that Liberty had been so successful in increasing its production from the very high level achieved in the previous year was undoubtedly attributable to the impact of the mutual fund linked contracts."

Gordon went over to London in September and Item 6 on his agenda was: "Development of the company's mutual fund linked policies – competitive position – 'blended policy' – new business production and strain". In view of the air of "I told you so" in Bigland's earlier letter, and Gordon's "What is he worrying about – we're doing fine" stance at the Board meeting, the discussions must have been quite interesting. Indeed, Gordon recalls that they were "lively, very lively indeed".

Anyway, Gordon and his wife Peggy flew on from London to Canada and the United States for a working holiday which was to set up some useful life insurance contacts for Liberty Life. An expurgated version of their talks formed paragraph six of a letter from Bigland dated 16 September 1966.

"We talked at some length, and I think you also raised this with the company secretary, about the problem of an increasing proportion of your business coming from your linked contracts. I did say that I hoped you would take steps to limit this trend. You talked about a new scheme you had in mind where any proposer had to take half his contract in normal whole life or endowment and only half in a linked contract, and I think this would be helpful. I know your problem that Liberty Life and Sage Fund are so closely associated but I think we would both agree that it would be wrong for the Sage contract ever to become a predominant influence in the progress of Liberty Life. This may mean a certain conflict of interests but I am sure that with a little goodwill on either side it can be resolved even if in the long run it might mean Sage possibly linking up with another life company and selling a different kind of linked contract. I am sure you will keep me up-to-date on this matter and we can, I hope, resolve it together."

Gordon's reply, on his return to South Africa, was dated 19 October 1966. "In London I indicated to you that I had some definite ideas to reduce the proportion of linked insurance we are writing. During my absence our actuaries have developed these ideas some way and it would seem that a compromise solution is definitely feasible. I have certainly refined some of my thinking in this regard with particular reference to some of the ideas I picked up in America. To some extent revision of our approach is necessary insofar as we are encountering powerful competition in the mutual fund linked assurance field. In fact, there is no doubt at this stage that our rates are well out of the market, which reinforces my contention of their substantial profitability; certainly the most profitable 'line' in our portfolio at the moment. I am sure Mr Tucker will confirm this as when I last spoke to him in 1965 he did indicate to me that we should press the linked policy as hard as possible on account of its inherent profitability. It is interesting to note that at the end of September, on a premium income basis our new business for the year was equally divided between orthodox and linked assurance.

"Finally, I would like to reassure you that there is no question of any conflict of interest as far as the Sage Fund is concerned. The interests of Liberty Life are absolutely paramount and this has been made clear at all times to our Sage Fund directors and to Mr Shill."

While Gordon's assurance that there was no conflict of interest was doubtless accepted by Bigland, there is equally no gainsaying the fact that the potential for one was present. Liberty Life directly owned 25 per cent of Investors Mutual Funds, the management company of Sage Fund; since Guardian owned 75 per cent of Liberty Life, it had an indirect 18 ¾ per cent interest in the prosperity of the new venture. Institutional Investments also owned 25 per cent of Investors Mutual Funds, and four Liberty Life directors – Gordon, Shill, Rubin and Young – between them held 95 per cent of Institutional, and therefore had a much larger, and a much more immediate, stake in its success.

So the debate raged on. The 17 November 1966 Board meeting minuted: "Following on the discussions at the previous Board meeting, Mr Gordon had discussed the problem of balancing the portfolio in terms of orthodox and unit-linked business in detail with Mr Bigland and the London actuaries. As at 30 September 1966 the balance had been maintained insofar as unit-linked business on a premium income basis had accounted for approximately 50 per cent of the total new business for the year to that date. However, the trend towards a higher proportion of unit-linked business had continued through October and November and it was clear that early constructive action was indicated to restore a reasonable balance. Since Mr Gordon's return from the United States he had actively explored all the possibilities with a view to the early introduction of a so-called 'blended contract'. The problem had been somewhat aggravated by the appearance of powerful competition in this field and the indication of similar plans being introduced shortly by some of the other leading companies in South Africa. The competition had been of a particularly aggressive nature and to some extent the company had temporarily lost the initiative in this field, as its natural promotional efforts had been somewhat stultified by its constant preoccupation with the balancing of the portfolio. Many different approaches had been tried and it now appeared that any competitive plan would require to be no less than 60 per cent linked (the other 40 per cent consisting of an orthodox policy). The matter was discussed at great length by the Board and all the various possibilities and approaches analysed. After considering all the permutations to give the company the necessary edge in competition, it was felt that a 'blended contract' consisting of 66 ⅔ per cent 'linked' and 33 ⅓ per cent on a with-profit endowment basis would be required to regain its position. An additional reason for choosing this ratio was that it had been selected by the competition and, in terms of the basic elements of the contract, it had the merit of being a relatively rational approach.

"The aspects of the overall balancing of the portfolio were examined and, on a realistic assumption of the volume of business to be done in each of the various classes of business, it was clear that if a similar pattern developed as in the past, that the desirable objective of a 50 per cent target for orthodox business in total would be achieved.

"It was resolved that, subject to the comments of the Guardian, the management should proceed to the introduction of a modified form of contract as soon as practicable."

That was all very well – or it might have been, for the "Frankenstein" of linked contracts was showing signs of getting out of control – as far as Liberty Life and the Guardian were concerned, but it was by no means what Louis Shill wanted for Investors Mutual Funds.

Although he remained on the Board of Liberty Life as a non-executive director, he was fully committed to Investors Mutual Funds, and to the consortium behind it. His duty, as he saw it, was to IMF and, although as a co-founder he felt great loyalty to Liberty Life, he was being pulled strongly away from it. After he gave up his executive duties at Liberty Life, he had sold his 8 000 shares in that company (indeed, Gordon had prevailed on Bigland, not without considerable difficulty, to give his old friend Shill a special price) and had invested the proceeds in increasing his stake in Institutional Investors, in which he was now the largest shareholder after Gordon himself.

His primary concern, therefore, was to sell Sage Fund units. The problems of balancing Liberty Life's insurance portfolio, and keeping Bigland happy, touched him only as a non-executive member of the Liberty Life Board, not in his role as chief executive of Investors Mutual Funds – although there were other problems there in that his friend and colleague, Donald Gordon, was Chairman of that company. But Sage Fund units, nevertheless, had to be sold, and if Liberty Life was planning deliberately to restrict its linked policy sales, and hence its unit purchases, Shill would have to seek other institutional buyers.

Gordon's problems, on the other hand, were twofold. One was that of portfolio balance, and of meeting the Guardian's requirements in this direction while, at the same time, remaining competitive. The other was that, although the sale of linked policies was good and profitable business in the sales and insurance sense, it had a large, in-built negative. This was that the investment of those linked policy premiums was, by definition, taken out of the hands of Liberty Life and put into those of Sage Fund.

This, in turn, led to two more issues. First, if Liberty Life was not itself investing the funds generated by linked policies, additional and unnecessary investment charges would be incurred. It was to the benefits of investment expertise that Gordon had looked as one of the potential attractions from his earliest flirtation with a new life insurance company, back in 1958.

Second, the investment objectives of an insurance company and those of a mutual fund were not necessarily the same – and could, in fact, be diametrically opposed. A life assurer is essentially a long-term investor, with long-term objectives to show good results twenty to twenty-five years down the line, where his commitments lie as long-term policies mature. A mutual fund, on the other hand, operating in a highly competitive field and working in an investment "goldfish bowl", with quarterly performance being compared by the press with that of the opposition, could be seen to be operating under short-term imperatives. That may not necessarily have been so, of course, but it was an obvious perception. This issue of the conflict of investment objectives, which was indeed a very real issue, was in fact given publicly as the main reason for the break between Liberty Life and Sage, when it eventually came.

Louis Shill's perspective was: "Conflicts were developing, particularly with regard to the investment policy which would suit the Sage Growth Assurance Plan. This policy relied on high income investments to suit Liberty Life's needs, while such investments were not ideal for the general body of unitholders. Our Board and the consortium had to primarily concern themselves with the needs of the mutual fund business. Since Donny was quite prepared to 'put out a contract on me' if I would not submit to investment control by Liberty Life, I certainly was left with very little option."

In a letter to Bigland dated 15 December 1966, Liberty Life Chairman Ted Roy summed up the issues: "These developments [the rapid growth of linked business] have produced a problem which Donald has frequently discussed with me of late and that is Liberty Life's ultimate position *vis-à-vis* the Sage Fund. Our cheque for units was around R100 000 in November so that we are investing in this manner over one million rand per annum. It needs little imagination to see how this will snowball if the present impetus is maintained.

"It also needs little imagination to see that Liberty Life is now substantially the main contributor to the growth of that Fund and that as time goes on a substantial proportion of Liberty Life's funds could be invested in Sage units. We have both come to the conclusion that the circumstances warrant a change in our approach to the running of the Sage Fund, ie that Liberty Life should now have the say in investment policy and that some other basis must be found to make due recognition of the Liberty Life contribution to growth. As you may know the service charge of ½ per cent of the capital value of the Fund is where the real profit arises in the future of the management company. Donald is adamant about these requirements and, as he puts it, the Fund has temperamentally got away from its original and close association with Liberty Life.

"Accordingly it would be our intention to put this picture squarely to the other members of the consortium in the management company, Investors Mutual Funds Limited. It might be stated that Liberty Life took its 25 per cent share 'for better or worse' but this principle of having a say in investment policy is too important to be ignored. I feel that these matters can be resolved with fairness all round, but if need be we have the alternative of working our own equity unit plan with life insurance. In the light of these changed circumstances I don't regard our proposed approach as going back on a bargain."

Bigland replied to Roy on 30 December: "I have already I think accepted in correspondence with Donald that Liberty Life should press ahead with its unit-linked scheme, and if you have agreed at your Board a new linked scheme with two-thirds of the contract linked to units and one-third ordinary life assurance, I fully accept this arrangement, and will be most interested in any new scheme Donald has in mind. I am sure he will let me have details as soon as he is ready.

"As you rightly say, the rapid sale of these contracts presents a problem on the investment side, although it is one I have fully anticipated and I think discussed with you and Donald. We have found the same position here where we already have some millions invested in funds not controlled by Guardian but in which we hold very substantial interests.

"I think the simple answer to your problem is that I would completely support your starting your own fund if you could not come to suitable arrangements with IMF for you to have far greater control of investments and I would think an increasing share in the equity of IMF. Liberty Life's share should really be increased in proportion to its contribution to IMF growth in the years ahead."

Gordon was already exploring the merits of internal linkage should the relationship with Sage go badly awry, as the rapid deterioration of his personal relationship with Shill was indicating, despite all the attempts at reconciliation made by their mutual colleagues. By now, confrontation was looming strongly on the horizon.

Something, or someone, had to give. Gordon thought that, with Liberty Life's direct 25 per cent and his own dominant position in Institutional with its 25 per cent, and also given that he was Chairman, then Investors Mutual Funds should toe the Liberty Life line.

Proposals to this end were put forward, and Shill, rather unsurprisingly, was getting increasingly concerned and agitated. A memorandum on Liberty Life proposals for Investors Mutual Funds Limited addressed the issues:

"The following proposals have recently been put forward by Liberty Life:

"A. Liberty Life should have stronger control of the investment policy of the Fund. To this end it should have a casting vote or a right of veto at investment meetings.

"B. Liberty Life should have a closer say in administrative matters.

"C. In view of its strong support of the Fund, Liberty Life should be entitled to a larger participation in the company, and in this regard other shareholders are requested to consider each disposing of one-fifth of their present shareholding to Liberty Life. The outcome of such a decision would be a revision of the Board of directors and investment sub-committee in terms of the original consortium agreement, extracts of which are attached herewith. It would also then be in the interests of Liberty Life to bid for the control of Institutional Investments Limited through its strong connections in that company so that between the holdings of Institutional and Liberty Life absolute control of the company would be gained.

"D. In view of their recent attitude, Liberty Life have indicated that they are not prepared to agree to the conclusion of negotiations with the Federated Employers' Insurance Company in terms of the proposals outlined in the letter from the manager of that company. In particular, they now refuse to allow an additional consortium partner and also maintain that the Fund has no right to enter into marketing activities with any insurance company other than Liberty Life.

"Management's view:

"A. Although having committed itself previously to this course, Liberty Life has the right to refuse to allow a further participation in the company. It does not, however, have the right to determine the marketing policy of the company and management believes that it has the duty and the right to attempt to conclude the negotiations with the Employers' Mutual on the basis of the proposals other than the participation and the Board membership. Negotiations will be severely prejudiced because of the necessity to deny participation to the Federated, but it is hoped that negotiations may be concluded if firm *pari passu* marketing facilities are offered.

"B. Many matters of principle have now been raised and it is necessary to finally determine management authority and independent investment policy.

"C. A firm decision must be taken on these matters in order to create clear precedents for future policy.

"Points considered by the management:

"A. The broad principle at the time of establishing the company was to develop an independent institution suitably supported by the various consortium members. In this regard each one of the consortium members have played their part in the development of the company, and more particularly have lent their name and become involved in the future of the company. Is it, therefore, correct to allow this company to become subject to the interests of one of the consortium members? Are we then carrying out our primary duty, viz, the management of the interests of the general body of unitholders and not a specific section of unitholders?

"B. In attempting to broaden the consortium for business purposes, the management has acted well within its mandate and decisions taken at various Board meetings over the last twenty months. Extracts of Board minutes during that period are attached for convenience. It will be realised that at one stage the suggestion was made that a new issue of shares should be considered in order to allow the participation of several other institutions. In order to avoid the impression of hawking our shares it was decided to authorise management to approach institutions individually and on a confidential basis.

"C. At a meeting held between the Registrar, the Chairman and the managing director it was indicated clearly that we would consider broadening the consortium in order to assist the Registrar in being able to restrain further applications to register funds.

"D. It is of the utmost importance to be independent and to have a public independent institutional image in the mutual fund industry.

"Many other countries and, in particular, Australia have been examples of the failure of mutual funds which have been tied to the interests of other institutions.

"It is impossible to act independently when a company becomes subject to cumulative insurance premium sales from one sole quarter. Under such circumstances the following must necessarily come about:

"i) Conflict of management.

"ii) Dictating of business terms such as a reduction in management charges (already requested by Liberty Life).

"iii) Investment control.

"iv) Administration control.

"From many points of view it is difficult to manage a company which has the image of being a subsidiary organisation. For example, the present impression in the Registrar's office where officials have been led to believe that Investors Mutual Funds Limited is a Liberty Life administered company.

"E. The movement by insurance companies to offer linked policies is fast gaining ground. Our public association with another insurance company will assist us to enter this vast market. At present we are losing access to these companies and their valuable support. National Growth Fund and soon Union Acceptances can approach these companies relatively independently. In the case of Sage thc approach must necessarily be made with the disadvantage of being considered part of the Liberty Life group. To this end the managing director has considered that, in future, in order to carry out these negotiations, it will be necessary for him to resign from the Board of Liberty Life.

"F. In our negotiations with other insurance companies we must be able to prove our bona fides. For this reason it was originally decided that we should possibly allow such companies to participate nominally and that marketing facilities should undoubtedly be offered.

"G. It has been considered that it might be in the interests of the company to entirely avoid offering linked plans and so have a more independent relationship with each of the insurance companies, including Liberty Life, who invest in our units. Such an action would have a serious and detrimental effect on the company for the following reasons:

"i) The other mutual funds are able to offer their marketing facilities as an inducement.

"ii) We are inevitably associated with the linked plan and a large measure of our promotional campaign and expenses are involved in promoting linked plans as one of the investment mediums offered. The public and agencies are unable to distinguish between the two sources of the linked plan and we are constantly and inevitably drawn into the marketing of this product.

"iii) This is a very attractive and sound way of marketing units which we should participate in as much as possible. The high commission element in the policy is a means of attracting our sales personnel and agencies and, in fact, it would be impossible to finance the early development period of our sales personnel without the inducement of such commissions.

"iv) In order to compete with other mutual funds in recruiting agencies we must be able to offer linked plans and their advantages.

"H. There are no firm undertakings at present from Liberty Life. At any time they can cease offering linked policies. At present they have in fact offered a new policy which has a reduced content of unit investment. It is even a moot point at present to know whether there is any obligation at all under the new policy for Liberty Life to purchase units as the proceeds of the policies are merely *deemed* linked to Sage units. It is also a new development in the UK to link policies to separate portfolios administered by the insurance companies themselves. This is a development at present being strongly considered by Liberty Life and conceivably by other insurance companies. In this regard it must be noted that the Federated commits itself to link exclusively to Sage Fund units.

"I. There are distinct differences in marketing approaches between Liberty Life and Sage Fund. In offering the linked plans we are bound to form part of their approach as no alternative is available. Typically the promotion in this field has been distinctly limited because of a lack of reasonable advertising or the provision of explanatory brochures.

"J. There is a distinct limitation to the extent of business which a young life company such as Liberty Life can absorb in any one year. This had adverse effects on the fund last year when Liberty Life was obliged to curtail its promotional activities in view of technical strains caused by the flow of new linked business.

"K. Other insurance companies would provide us with new sales outlets. These would probably be in spheres not covered by Liberty Life. Federated, as an example, has twelve branch offices throughout the country.

"L. If we are to refuse access to other insurance companies, our company in effect becomes a sole selling organisation for Liberty Life linked plans.

"M. It is difficult to know whether Liberty Life is diverting part of its investments away from units, but it must be recorded that on 1 January, 100 000 units were purchased by that company, whereas the purchase on 1 February had dropped to 80 000. This is very contrary to the normal cumulative effect which one would have expected.

"N. The activities of Sage Fund were severely curtailed during its initial period while under the administration of Liberty Life. Although this was the early development period the negative promotional effort undoubtedly resulted in the early failure of the company. In contrast while acting reasonably independently during the last year, the company has achieved satisfactory results in the face of many limitations.

"O. It is not the intention of the company under any circumstances to detrimentally affect the interests of Liberty Life. In actual fact, management is convinced that the active promotion of the fund in an independent fashion has, and will continue, to assist the Liberty Life promotion. The success of the Liberty Life linked plans during 1966 must be largely attributed to the Sage Fund promotional effort. Management also proposes the following:

"i) The investment policy should be fully entrenched so that the Liberty Life policyholders are protected. This would merely involve a firm undertaking of investment intention as in any case the investment policies of Sage Fund and the needs of Liberty Life are identical.

"ii) Management will attempt, to the best of their ability, to cooperate with Liberty Life and their managing director as Chairman of this company as long as the interests of our company are protected in the first instance.

"iii) Wherever possible in the marketing, Liberty Life's interests, as a member of the consortium, will be protected."

It is very clear from the above, which is quoted at length because all the many differences – of both principle and opinion – are so clearly spelt out, that matters must soon come to a head.

In February 1967, Bigland flew out to Johannesburg. A memorandum of "Points discussed with Mr Gordon and Mr Roy during visit 12 February 1967" reads: "Policy relating to IMF: It was agreed that the present linking arrangements between Liberty Life and Sage units must be preserved and maintained and that whilst Liberty Life would have no objection to Sage selling their units to other insurance companies there must be no question of the staff of IMF selling linked contracts for other insurance companies and certainly not on preferential terms.

"It was agreed that discussions would take place between the principal partners in IMF – Liberty Life, Netherlands Bank and London & Dominion Trust – at which agreement would have to be reached as to the future operations of IMF and what each of the partners expected to achieve by this association (at all stages Liberty

Life's interests to be preserved). When agreement had been reached (and if it could not be reached then consideration to be given to Liberty Life buying out some of the other interests) any new arrangements would be put to Mr Gordon and Mr Shill, as Chairman and managing director respectively, as the basis on which IMF would be continued, and their full agreement to the terms of operation to be given."

In his covering letter, dated 22 February, with the above memorandum, Bigland said: "I am sorry that I could not stay long enough to help you solve your main problem, which is the future relationship between Liberty Life and IMF, but I hope that the formula I suggested for resolving the difficulties is in fact the right one and will work. I know you and I and Ted Roy are all agreed that Liberty Life cannot alter the relationship and that we must therefore persuade the others that something on the present lines must continue in the future."

Bigland followed this up on 23 February with: "You left with me a copy of the accounts for Institutional Investments so that we could consider the value of the shares and the price you might have to pay if you were compelled to buy a few more shares to protect your position in relation to IMF.

"Our investment department have now analysed the accounts as far as they can and they consider the break-up price as being about R1,60 against the figure you gave me of about R1,80. I realise that you may have to pay rather over this figure but I hope that it will not be necessary for you to buy many shares, or any at all.

"The company secretary raised the point of whether it was legally right for Liberty Life to take up a shareholding in Institutional Investments when in fact the biggest Institutional Investments holding is in Liberty Life. You may have views on this point. If it was necessary for Guardian South Africa to take up some of the shareholding I should like to be consulted before this was done . . ."

While it is clear from the above that the Liberty Life side had made considerable concessions in agreeing that Sage units could, under certain conditions, be sold to insurance companies other than Liberty Life, Shill still felt uneasy. There had been stormy meetings within the consortium, and particularly with Gordon, with considerable support from the "outside" members for his, Shill's, resistance to Liberty Life's demands on the investment front, but the situation was fluid. Shill also doubtless recalled Gordon's earlier volte-face, when he had agreed to stay with Liberty Life instead of going with Shill to IMF. Whatever the reasons, Shill was taking steps to protect his own position, and drastic steps they were.

The key to the situation was twofold. The four-way, 25 per cent consortium ownership meant that he must first persuade one or other of the two "outside" partners – Netherlands Bank or London & Dominion Trust – to support him, and then secure personal control of Institutional Investments, which could be done by buying the 20 per cent interests held by both Young and Rubin, which, added to his own 20 per cent, would outgun Gordon. With personal control of Institutional, plus the support of one of the "outsiders", Shill would then muster 50 per cent of the votes in IMF, thus nullifying Liberty Life's 25 per cent, provided that the other "outsider" remained at least neutral with its 25 per cent.

The battles within the consortium over Liberty Life's demands had convinced Shill that he would find an ally in Netherlands Bank's Dr Bernard Holsboer, and in this he was correct, particularly as Holsboer and Gordon had never established much of a rapport. Reluctant as he was to get into any sort of a tangle with Liberty Life, Holsboer assured Shill of the bank's support – but only in the event that Shill had control of Institutional.

In order to secure that, Shill needed backing. That was a major problem, for, almost inevitably, any organisation that provided him with the wherewithal to buy the shares that he needed in Institutional Investments would run the risk of incurring – to put it at its very mildest – the severe displeasure of Donald Gordon. And that was a business risk not to be lightly taken, even in 1967.

After due consideration, Shill came, somewhat reluctantly, to the conclusion that he probably had only one option: to go to the Schlesinger Organisation, to Mandy Moross. The reluctance sprang from the fact that Shill knew only too well, from first-hand experience of the brief "Schlesinger era" at Liberty Life, that Moross was not exactly an easy partner. Yet it was really Hobson's Choice. Moross was big enough not to be overly concerned at offending Gordon; and Moross was small enough to be delighted to be given the chance of getting his own back for the slight of being forced, by Gordon, to sell Schlesinger's 23 per cent stake in Liberty Life to Guardian in 1964. To Moross, the prospect of retaliation must have been irresistable, for there was no love lost between himself and Gordon.

Gordon underlines this with an amusing story of a dinner party at which Moross was also a guest. "It was about a week before the flotation of Schlesinger Institutional Investments (SII), the holding company of the Schlesinger interests, of which Moross, of course, was the driving force. We arrived a little late at the dinner, and Moross was already pontificating, surrounded by a dozen sycophants clinging avidly to the great man's every word. As soon as he saw me, he called me over and turned on me viciously, accusing me of saying that the SII shares were worth only 50 cents compared with their issue price of R2. I denied this accusation vehemently, but Moross drove on, insisting that he had heard the story from all and sundry, including my great friend Max Borkum. I again rejected his allegations, and said mildly: 'Mandy, you've been totally misinformed. I have never said to anybody that SII shares are worth 50 cents. All I have said is that they weren't worth 50 cents.'

"Moross thereupon left the party in a fury, and I spent an embarrassing evening explaining to our hosts how I had spoilt their dinner party. In time, however, my prediction of the SII share price turned out to be generous, as my friends at Anglo American, who would finally buy SII some years later, were yet to find out."

There was another, strictly business, attraction from Moross's standpoint; African Life had no mutual fund with which to offer linked policies, and was losing out competitively. A deal with Shill would redress this imbalance. Shill maintains that the other motives cited above are "totally inaccurate. I went to Moross purely because his group represented the ideal institutional clients for our mutual fund units and, indeed, they signed a comprehensive agreement with us which to this day leaves that company (now Southern Life) as an important Sage Fund investor. It certainly is wrong to even vaguely suggest that I chose Moross as he might have wanted to get one over on Gordon."

In the event, Shill's judgement proved correct, and he got his backing. This led, early in March, to a dramatic exchange of telexes between Johannesburg and London.

"Urgent message for Mr Bigland from Mr Gordon. Could you please call Mr Gordon. Rubin and Young have just informed me that Shill and associates have made an offer for their holding in Institutional at R4,50 a share. Think Schapiro is linked in the offer. This block of approximately 104 000 shares excluding Schapiro would give Shill effective control of Institutional. Offer expires at 1 pm South

African time. Rubin and Young have indicated will accept offer from Liberty Life or Guardian at same price. My valuation Institutional shares maximum R2, hence goodwill to be paid would be of the order of R250 000 for Rubin and Young's shares. After which Guardian would still only have slightly less than 25 per cent of capital of Institutional and Gordon would have further approximately 25 per cent. But control would be secured. Have discussed matter with Roy and wish your immediate advice on advisability of matching offer to Young and Rubin and possibly Schapiro. Since dictating this I have discussed matter further with Mr Roy and we now firmly feel that we should not attempt to match the offer and that we can only really consolidate our position by negotiation with Netherlands Bank in the IMF situation."

Bigland's reply read: "Your telex received. Have since spoken to you on telephone. Fully agree cannot be forced into auction for Institutional shares. Agree you inform parties accordingly. Our object must be now to isolate Institutional and concentrate on other two partners IMF. If we three agree future of IMF and management then Institutional in very weak position. Suggest you tell Netherlands all facts including this attempt at control. Sorry about your position Institutional but if you are left with less than 25 per cent would support your view you also offer to sell. Would not think if you called extraordinary meeting other shareholders would like to know of price offered to selected shareholders and not to them and also that you who started it intend to sell out and link with Liblife-IMF weakened. All these strong points. Just because Institutional control may change this not important if we still control IMF with partners. This is still the key. Confirm your action about holding up purchase of units but must only be temporary. Good luck."

Gordon and Bigland seem to have completely misread the position regarding the two outside partners, for Gordon would write to Bigland on 8 March: "I understand Mr Roy has been keeping you informed of developments in regard to the Investors Mutual Fund problems. You are no doubt fully aware that the company effectively has been taken outside the orbit of Liberty Life by the passing of the control of Institutional Investments to Mr Shill and his associates. In this way, it would appear that the African Life and/or the Schlesinger Organisation will be gaining an indirect entrée into the Sage Fund. As you can well imagine, the whole situation as we now face it is regrettable indeed. It would appear to me that some sort of conspiracy was afoot as at yesterday's Board meeting and in our previous meeting on Friday, it was made clear to us that Netherlands Bank, London & Dominion Group and Institutional Investments were acting as one in a total disregard to the interests of Liberty Life. However, they also accept the complete right of Liberty Life to act in a completely independent way. How this situation is to benefit either the Sage Fund or ourselves we are at a complete loss to appreciate. In protest of the breach of trust shown by our co-consortium members, and with a degree of lack of option in this matter, I have resigned my position as Chairman of the company and reserved my position as to whether I should stay on the Board at all."

Shill, not surprisingly, objects to that "breach of trust" remark. He notes: "This simply was not so. In the end the break was due to a combination of factors but predominantly caused by Liberty Life's overwhelming desire to call the tune in every respect and especially in investment matters in a company which was, in fact, never controlled by Liberty Life and which had long-term objectives not necessarily at all times according with those of Liberty Life. Liberty Life should be big enough to acknowledge that Sage and Shill were purely protecting their interests and not breaching any form of trust with them."

Gordon concedes that this was technically so. "However, the Sage Fund was undoubtedly a Liberty Life initiative and 50 per cent of the shares were owned by Liberty Life and its directors. In addition, I was Chairman in recognition of the role I played in its formation, and Louis's active executive role in the company came somewhat later, after Robert Button relinquished his chief executive role."

Looking back more than twenty years later, Gerry Muller, the present deputy chairman of Nedbank, is still clearly embarrassed over the whole imbroglio. "I was only a newly appointed general manager then but if I remember it correctly, we didn't want to have to take sides as between Donny and Louis; we would have much preferred to be in a happy relationship with both sides. We had no wish to fall foul of either of them, and we certainly didn't want a parting of the ways between Sage and Liberty Life. But we had to take sides in the end. It was not that we wanted to choose between Donny and Louis, but eventually we had to look at it purely from the investment and business angle. The consortium was a good deal that we were very happy to be involved in, but our main object in going in was that we wanted to be in mutual funds – life assurance was not our target. And it looked to us that the mutual fund side would, one way or another, become Louis's side. So there it was; we joined forces with Louis."

London & Dominion's Eric Tenderini, remembering those dramatic days, says there was no question at all of any conspiracy, and expresses surprise that no direct approach was made by the Liberty Life camp, before that fateful – and somewhat noisy – IMF Board meeting that Gordon refers to in his 8 March letter, to either himself or anyone else in London & Dominion to try to get the investment company "onside".

"We had always been neutral, tending if anything towards Liberty Life because of past connections with Gordon", he recalls, "but certainly in the early days there was no need to take sides. We always regarded Louis Shill and Donald Gordon as being effectively one and the same. It was their operation; they had conceived it and they had started it. We regarded ourselves very much as junior partners, and my recollection is that Netherlands Bank felt much the same. Later on, there were a few problems, mostly little niggling things and raised more from the bank's side, to the effect that Donny as Chairman was maybe running the thing a bit more independently than they liked. Then, when the strains started to show over Louis's desire to expand in ways that Donny clearly did not want, it seemed to me that Dr Holsboer more often than not would side with Louis. So, when the crunch came and Netherlands Bank went with Louis, we had little option. It was all very unpleasant, and most unfortunate."

Unpleasant and unfortunate it indeed was, with Gordon feeling that Shill and, though to a lesser extent, Young and Rubin also, had stabbed him in the back. And Shill feeling that he had had no option, in the interests of Investors Mutual Funds as well as his own but to do what he had done. Schapiro, however, asserts that he refused the offer at the time. But the repercussions on all the members of the consortium over the next twenty years would be of far greater consequence than anyone at the time could possibly have imagined.

The next sorry step was minuted at the Liberty Life Board meeting on 16 March 1967. "Resignation of Mr H L Shill. The Chairman informed the meeting that he had received a letter of resignation from the Board (and from other Liberty Life boards) from Mr H L Shill on the 28 February 1967 and that, in view of the circumstances, he had accepted Mr Shill's resignation. This was confirmed and the Board authorised the payment of directors' fees for the period 1 January 1967 to 28 February 1967."

That there was not even a coldly formal vote of thanks to one of the "most driving co-founders" is a very sad confirmation of the depths of feeling that prevailed at the time. The Annual Report for 1966 did, however, pay Shill a graceful tribute. "At the beginning of 1966, Mr H L Shill, one of the original founder-directors of Liberty Life, resigned from his executive duties to become managing director of Investors Mutual Funds Limited. Due to pressure of work, he now feels he is unable to devote the necessary time to the affairs of this company and has reluctantly decided to withdraw from the Board of directors. It is with regret that we accepted his resignation and we wish to record our appreciation of his long standing service to the company."

Gordon recalls that the last word on this sad matter actually came from Mavis Shill, Louis's wife. "We met at a party, some little while later. She expressed regret at the split, but said to me: 'You do know that Louis will play second fiddle to nobody, don't you?' The message came through loud and clear."

Young and Rubin were to resign, with less haste, as from 31 December 1967, after Bigland had interceded on their behalf. On 22 March 1967 he wrote: "I do not think they have been really disloyal as they did offer you the first option on their shares, but of course you will know much more than I do about the background and whether they are more in your camp or the other one."

Whatever the rights and wrongs, it was quite a few years before relationships between the "Four Musketeers" were restored. Young and Rubin, in particular, lost the opportunity of mega-fortunes by cashing up their gains too early. Gordon was uncompromising in his view that they should not have been tempted to sell, at any price.

In time, the personal relationships between all four men would be reinstated, but the rift between them was a sorry ending to the partnership which had provided many a good time in those strenuous early days when they were pulling so hard together to build Liberty Life.

The break with Sage caused a redoubling of efforts to achieve a credible alternative to a life insurance linkage to mutual funds, and again Liberty Life's innovative flair came to the fore. Early in 1967, Liberty Life announced the introduction of the VIP principle and the

VIP series of policies, which were perhaps Liberty Life's most important single innovation, particularly as the principle would in 1970 be extended to linkage to real estate.

This unique method of linking policyholder benefits to the results of the internal investments of the life insurer made it possible to achieve investment results by a cost effective method without the disadvantages that so clearly emerged as part of the Sage conflict. VIP stood for "Variable Investment Participation", which incidentally also had excellent connotations for marketing purposes.

It was the VIP approach which in time effectively phased out the use of mutual funds for linkage purposes in South Africa, as the advantages of controlling their own investment policy were far more appealing to the life insurance industry. In due course, Liberty Life was able to phase out most of its business linked to Sage Fund and to replace the linkages with the VIP linkage mechanism.

In Liberty Life's eleventh Annual Report, that for the year to 31 December 1968, shareholders were told: "Equity linked policies have continued to make a significant contribution to the increase in new business. The inherent advantage of the company's Variable Investment Participation (VIP) linkage technique has reaffirmed the company's position in the forefront of the equity linked assurance field. The VIP indices on which the benefits to policyholders are based produced superior performance results during 1968 to any other South African investment medium utilised for linkage purposes."

As the trauma and the emotion generated by the row over Sage subsided, Liberty Life began to regard the whole affair as having been something of a pyrrhic victory for Sage, the Netherlands Bank and London & Dominion. However, the introduction of African Life and Mandy Moross was hurtful, and the rupture of the business relationship with his great friends and colleagues, Louis Shill, Brian Young and Hugh Rubin was without question the saddest personal event in Donald Gordon's business life to that time; he never really got over it.

The relationship with Netherlands Bank and London & Dominion Trust was never the same again either. Gordon often reflects on what might have been had the rift with Shill not occurred, and how Michael Rapp would in due course have fitted into what would have been a quite remarkable triumvirate.

On 28 August 1968, Gordon sent a telex to London. "Kindly

convey to Mr Bigland that IMF shareholding has been disposed of to members of the consortium for R1 500 000, resulting in a capital surplus of R1 335 000. We here are delighted at the outcome of the negotiations."

When, less than a year later, Sage Holdings, as Investors Mutual Funds was to become, was listed on the Johannesburg Stock Exchange, it was apparent that a potential profit, albeit a "paper" profit, of R25 million had been missed. This was sixteen times the effective price received by Liberty Life for its 25 per cent interest. This embarrassment was really the last straw. Commenting on this to the *Financial Mail* in 1978, more than ten years later, Gordon said: "Another mistake, perhaps, was going out of Sage about a year too early. I think we could have stayed with our shareholding indefinitely. There was no pressure for us to sell. From this, we learnt the lesson that there is never any sense in being emotional in business, particularly where large sums of money are involved."

Having founded the South African mutual fund industry with the launch of Sage Fund in 1965, it is fitting that one of the Liberty Life Group's first major diversifications marked its return to this field. In *The Star* of 18 December 1969, Don Wilkinson, then the financial editor, marked the occasion with a banner headline: "Guardbank – The Mutual With New Approach".

"Details of the long-awaited mutual fund with Barclays Bank DCO [now First National Bank] and Guardian Assurance Holdings [now Liberty Holdings] as principal shareholders are now available and show that it will start life on 5 January 1970, the selling price being geared to the R1 level.

"Guardian Bankers Growth Fund (Guardbank) is the name chosen for the enterprise, which will be managed by Guardbank Management Corporation whose issued equity is R1 million in R1 shares. The sponsoring shareholders are Barclays (35 per cent), Guardian (35 per cent), Liberty Life (25 per cent) and Victory Enterprises (5 per cent). [The only shareholder in Victory Enterprises was Donald Gordon.]

"The fund has certain praiseworthy features which to some extent at least reflect the lessons learned by the movement since the stock market set-back in 1970.

"Thus, as Chairman, Mr Donald Gordon says, the management company 'intends to adopt a low-key promotional policy and the major effort will be directed towards over-the-counter sales, using

Barclays branches as the principal sales centres.' The units, however, will also be available at the offices of Guardian, Liberty Life and through other selected dealers.

"Management is also keeping the initial charges low – 3 1/4 per cent on deals up to R50 000, falling to 1 per cent and less by negotiation over the R300 000 mark.

"Mr Gordon hopes lower charges 'may have the side effect of reducing the high pressure salesmanship for which the mutual fund industry has been severely criticised'. I share his hopes.

"Arrangements have been made for units to be sold at the ruling daily price at any Barclays branch throughout the country free of bank exchange, an important benefit for 'country' as distinct from 'city' investors.

"These refinements in marketing the units are aimed, of course, at the competition between the various mutuals for the public's money, but perhaps the most significant aspect of Guardbank is its investment philosophy. This differs noticeably from its competitors in many ways.

"As outlined by the Chairman, Guardbank believes 'that in the long term companies backed by hard assets, solid earnings, and sound management are superior investments in most conditions to those whose prospects are based more on glamour and unrealistic expectations'.

"The aim is to ensure 'maximum protection' of the public's money coupled with 'reasonable growth of capital and income without taking undue investment risks'.

"It is fairly clear also that the fund is not going to invest over the whole stock market spectrum, but rather to specialise, including the seeking out of special situations. This latter is not, according to the Chairman, an intention to perform any kind of 'go-go' role, but rather to look for the company undervalued on strict investment merits."

The Liberty Life Group's return to the mutual fund field was soon accompanied by another world first. The *Sunday Times* of 26 July 1970 carried the banner headline: "Guaranteed 'no loss' scheme launched" and said:

"A massive vote of confidence in the long-term future of the South African economy and the stock market, coupled with trust in its own expertise, has been shown by the Guardbank mutual fund in launching a guaranteed 'no loss' investment scheme.

"This is probably the first time in the world whereby an investor in mutual fund units can, for a small price, guarantee himself against loss. In other words, an investor makes all the profit but takes none of the loss."

Ernest Bigland was far less enthusiastic. On 3 July 1970, he wrote: "I said I would look into the question of Guardbank issuing a contract with a capital guarantee although in principle I am not in favour."

Under pressure from Gordon, however, he unbent. A letter from Bigland on 16 July 1970: "Thank you for your letter of 9 July enclosing memorandum on the Guardbank Guarantee. Sorry that I have taken a little time to reply but we have been looking into this in some detail and there has been a lack of enthusiasm for the reassurance of this risk in the fidelity department. However, I am pleased to advise you that in principle we are willing to go ahead."

So the press release of 25 July 1970 was able to announce another breakthrough. Some extracts: "Guardbank Management Corporation has pleasure in announcing that arrangements have been concluded in principle with companies in the international Guardian Royal Exchange Group for the introduction into the Republic of South Africa of a revolutionary new financial service which will guarantee unitholders in Guardian Bankers Growth Fund (Guardbank) against financial loss by reason of a fall in the price of Guardbank units. The guarantee will make Guardbank units a gilt-edged growth investment in the fullest sense, giving the public for the first time the possibility of risk-free growth investment in mutual funds, which under certain conditions are susceptible to loss through share price fluctuation.

"The Guardian Investment Guarantee will be incorporated in a master policy to be issued by Guardian Assurance Company South Africa indemnifying Guardbank unitholders who elect to participate in the scheme (which participation will be optional) against there being any shortfall between the repurchase price of Guardbank units on the maturity date and the original purchase price of the relevant units. In terms of the Scheme, the maturity date will be the earlier of:

"(a) the exact tenth anniversary of the date on which the relevant Guardbank units were acquired (the entry date);

"or (b) under certain conditions, the date of the death of the unitholder, if a natural person.

"In effect, the Scheme ensures that participating unitholders will be guaranteed the actual capital investment (including initial charges) in Guardbank units. Thus, the guarantee covers the unitholder against any costs inherent in the initial charge as well as any depreciation arising by virtue of any adverse price fluctuations in Guardbank units.

"The cost of participating in this Scheme will be a nominal half-annual premium of approximately 1/2 per cent of the capital investment based on the current Guardbank unit price and will be deducted from participating unitholders' dividends at the same time as the half-annual dividend is paid.

"The Guardian Investment Guarantee is expected to stimulate sales of Guardbank mutual fund units. Indirectly the Scheme may have a profound impact on the economic growth of the Republic and on the investment and savings habits of the nation. In the long run, it might well restore the image of the mutual fund industry in South Africa."

Thus the new mutual fund was launched, and with a flourish, although the much-vaunted Investment Guarantee scheme was destined not to come up to expectations. Reporting to Liberty Life's Thirteenth Annual General Meeting in April 1971, the Directors' Report for the year ended 31 December 1970 noted: "Guardian Bankers Growth Fund, which is managed by Guardbank Management Corporation Limited, in which Liberty Life has a 25 per cent interest, performed exceedingly well during the difficult conditions prevailing in the equity market in 1970. The management company made a net profit after tax of R31 000 for the past financial year and the indications are that, once conditions in the equity market return to normal, your company will enjoy substantial benefits as a result of this investment, which to date has not yielded any dividend."

In August 1984, the shareholdings in Guardbank Management Corporation were restructured, increasing Barclays National Bank's stake from 35 per cent to 50 per cent, with the remaining 50 per cent being held by Liberty Holdings. In that year, the net taxed profits of Guardbank Management were R674 000, compared with R496 000 in 1983.

With the Group interest in Guardbank Management reduced to 50 per cent, it has not warranted separate mention in Liberty Holdings' annual reports since that of 1984, but Guardbank continues to flourish and, under the investment management of Roy McAlpine, the canny Scottish investment head of the Liberty Life Group, is widely regarded as one of the leading South African mutual funds. The bottom line is that its performance over the two decades of its history is second to none. And performance, in mutual funds, is the name of the game. The University of Pretoria's Graduate School of Management produces the most authoritative South African survey of unit trust performance; its 1989 Unit Trusts Survey ranked Guardbank tops in four out of seven categories – and second in the remainder, for an almost incredible showing.

Further developments came in 1987, when the Chairman's Statement devoted considerable attention to Guardbank. "Guardbank Management Corporation is jointly owned by Liberty Holdings and The First National Banking Group. As the management company of the Guardbank Growth Fund, it had its most successful year to date in 1987. In order to provide the South African public with alternative opportunities for investment in the unit trust industry and to widen the suite of funds offered, two new unit trusts were launched during the year. Guardbank Resources Fund was established to provide unitholders with a method for investing into the mineral wealth and natural resources of South Africa and the Guardbank Income Fund was formed to provide unitholders with a high level of current income, while substantially protecting the capital value of their investments.

"During 1987 the aggregate net inflow to the above funds amounted to R148 million. At 31 December 1987 the total size of Guardbank Growth Fund and the aforementioned new funds amounted to approximately R435 million."

Fittingly, Guardbank Growth Fund, now with assets of almost R700 million, was in 1988 again the best performer in the industry – and on this occasion by the widest margin ever. And Guardbank Management Corporation, now having achieved its maturity, continues to place its faith in the highest calibre equities available in the South African market.

# 8 The Fast Lane

Having in August 1965 committed himself firmly to Liberty Life, and to the greater Guardian Group, Donald Gordon in the December of that year received an accolade to which he still refers with pride. He was named Businessman of the Year by the *Financial Mail*. Outside South Africa, newspaper "awards" of this nature are not of any particular moment, but the *FM*, although itself less than seven years old at that time, was the country's only financial journal, and had established a considerable reputation. "Businessman of the Year" was, and still is, its most prized award. That it should go to the managing director of a company barely eight years old was remarkable.

Much of the article that appeared on 17 December 1965 is apposite to the present time; on occasion, quite remarkably so.

"Baldly stated, one business success story is often much like another. The lean years, the big break, the pay-off – it is not the milestones but the speed and vicissitudes of the journey which so frequently distinguish one brilliant career from the next.

"However, Donald Gordon, the 35-year-old founder and managing director of Liberty Life Association, earns this year's Businessman of the Year award not just for a specially fast and skilful climb to the top. He has been chosen for bringing to South African insurance a significantly wider and more sophisticated range of services and – most important – for introducing, this year, the Republic's first mutual fund and its first life insurance-mutual fund package deal. SA Growth Equities Fund (its promoters call it Sage Fund, not Sagef) began with the formation of a management company, Investors Mutual Funds, late last year and marketed its first units in June. That this is certain to be the start of something very big on the South African investment scene can be gauged from the fact that a competing open-end trust – National Growth Fund – is already on the market while two or three more are in the offing.

"A run-down of Donny Gordon's principal achievements shows that in a short eight years as insurance entrepreneur he has:

* launched Liberty Life, pushing boldly into the preserve of long-established insurance giants;

* established Liberty Life as a successful operation within six months (instead of the usual 8 to 10 years) of its formation;

* initiated the underwriting of retirement annuities by insurance companies in South Africa;

* put this country's first life insurance stock on the Johannesburg Stock Exchange;

* negotiated a profitable takeover for Liberty Life by the worldwide Guardian Group; and

* started the local mutual fund movement.

"There is nothing of the swaggering tycoon about Mr Gordon. Far from breathing fire, he seems at first meeting restrained, even withdrawn. Only on closer acquaintance does one sense the steely will and unrelenting determination underneath. Undemonstrative, he is the archetype of the ambitious conservative, backing big ideas with painstaking research and infinite care in their implementation. He believes a sound accounting background is the finest entrée to business: 'One needs the right mixture of conservatism and progressive thinking. Complete single-mindedness is more important than brilliance.'

"He has surrounded himself with men of like background, 'who give great attention to detail while still keeping sight of broader perspectives, are not in the game for quick fortunes and can work as a team in the long follow-through on early planning.'

"It has been a success story from the start: 'We have hardly had to alter our original goals at all – most have been achieved faster than even we expected. We have throughout managed to keep costs very low. In fact our expense ratio – at 8 per cent – is the lowest in the field and about half that for some of the larger companies.'

"How did it all start? 'Well, when I finished school (King Edward VII, three distinctions) I thought I might be a scientist. Nuclear physics and astronomy fascinated me, and I still dream of entering atomic or space research, although it now seems impossible.

"'But there wasn't enough money for that, so I started articles in accountancy, qualifying as a CA in 1951. In March 1953 I and about a dozen friends started Cloud (now Institutional) Investments Pty with R1 900. It became quite a force in Liberty Life and is now one of the consortium of four controlling Investors Mutual Funds.

"'I stayed in accountancy until 1957, mainly in finance, company and insurance work, by which time I felt I was sufficiently informed about insurance to succeed on my own. I had developed a great interest in life assurance – its wide scope in all phases of higher finance and actuarial work was an irresistible challenge. The competition was clearly tremendous, but I thought we could offer a fresh approach, especially in assurance for the professional man. As it turned out, the firm I was with offered me a partnership and I had a crucial 48 hours to decide one way or the other. A year later (having got married) I wouldn't have done it, but I decided (aged 27) that it was now or never, and went capital hunting to form my own company.'

"In January 1958 Liberty Life was born 'on the smell of an oil rag', with Cloud Investments as an important shareholder. In its first year all the incorporation and legal work was done by Board members (all of whom were professional men) and the small, carefully selected staff had to share modest offices with another company. Once the initial establishment was complete, however, LL rushed to offer a full range of services. Selling as it did predominantly to higher income buyers – and with negligible costs – premium income exceeded expenses and actuarial liabilities were covered within a few months.

"By early 1960 the company was leading the field in innovation. Following the introduction of the necessary legislation, it was the first insurer to underwrite retirement annuities, a logical development from its earlier 'life with disability benefits' policies.

"Then in June 1962, to raise capital and 'take the mysticism out of life insurance', the public was offered shares. 'This was really the turning point in our fortunes', says Gordon, progress thereafter being spectacular.

"In 1963 Mr John Schlesinger's R75m African Life paid R300 000 for a 23 per cent interest in LL, getting shares at R10 each. Less than a year later they were sold to Guardian Assurance for R19 apiece. 'When Guardian (with assets of R1 200m) acquired a controlling interest, we acquired the security and experience of their world-wide ramifications,' explains Gordon.

"The Republic's first mutual fund, conceived by Gordon and his team even before Liberty Life's incorporation, began in November 1964 with the formation of the management company, with Gordon as Chairman. 'We came upon mutual funds while looking for protection against inflation for insurance funds', he says. 'It also seemed a way to protect the man in the street from his own investment folly.'

"Since the Guardian deal, Liberty Life has experienced a tremendous surge in life policy sales. More business has been written in 1965 than in the company's first 5¼ years of operation. Says Gordon: 'The speed of LL's development has in fact been unequalled in post-war years by any life assurance company in the world.'

"The price of Sage Fund units – reflecting a spread of investments over more than 70 companies – has held remarkably steady since the fund came on the market. In view of the general stock market drop, Gordon feels this supports his confidence in Sage. 'We are not perturbed by the thought of four or five other mutual funds sharing the market', he adds. 'We enjoy a challenge, and in any case I do not see the movement being oversold in the near future.'

"Now living comfortably (with wife and three children) in a ranch-style house high on Craighall Park ridge, Gordon admits he has had time for little except LL in the past eight years. 'But I am rather keen on yoga. I find it the best cure for tension.' That is important for a man who seldom lets up.

"'He survives on astonishingly little sleep,' says one of his friends, 'and often gets up in the middle of the night for a few hours' homework before dawn.'

"'The fact that he has become financially secure (and even wealthy) is unimportant,' remarks one of LL's directors. 'He lives for his work – the money is incidental. He's a difficult man to keep up with.'

"In manner Gordon is assured though diffident. Fidgeting with papers or suddenly lighting a cigarette, he betrays an inner restlessness. He seems a man constantly pushing himself: 'his will, amounting occasionally almost to obstinacy, can be indomitable', says one friend. 'Even today he likes to see everything right down to the most trifling *aide mémoire*. Perhaps for his own sake he should learn to let go a little.'

"The last word comes from another associate. 'Donny Gordon is Liberty Life and vice versa. I simply cannot imagine him leaving.

He's the living example of how it's still possible for one man with virtually no capital to go out and have his own large, private, financial adventure.'"

While much of what the *Financial Mail* wrote twenty-four years ago is still valid to-day, as Donald Gordon's "large, private, financial adventure" continues to unfold, the publication was guilty of one or two minor flights of fancy. There is no doubt that having Guardian as Big Brother and being able to boast "A Member of the Guardian Assurance Group" on Liberty Life literature was good, indeed very good, for business, but there was nevertheless an element of hyperbole in the *FM*'s assertion that "More business was written in 1965 than in the company's first 5 1/4 years of operation."

When Liberty Life's Annual Report for the year ended 31 December 1965 appeared, dated 10 March 1966, the Board was able to report: "Significant progress has been made during the year in building up our agency network and the company's new business connection has been significantly increased. The gross premium income per annum (excluding single premiums and considerations for annuities) in respect of new policy contracts effected during the year under review, amounts to the total of R847 534, compared with R608 352 for 1964, which constitutes an increase of approximately 39 per cent and which can be considered satisfactory in view of the ever-increasing competition encountered on the South African market."

That 39 per cent gain was indeed a satisfactory increase, and under the impetus of the changed circumstances new business premium income would almost double to R1 651 527 in the following year, a performance which the Board would then consider "highly satisfactory", but the impact of the Guardian was not quite as dramatic as the *FM* had maintained.

It is a moot point, of course, whether that extraordinary 95 per cent jump in new business premium income owed most to the newly acquired Guardian cachet or to the new linked policies; it was much more likely the latter, especially in view of the strains and problems they were provoking. The Board noted, in the Ninth Annual Report, that for the year to 31 December 1966, that: "The advent of mutual fund linked policies made a significant contribution to the increase in new business.

"As previously reported, Liberty Life introduced the Sage Growth Assurance Plan on 1 October 1965. This plan was the first mutual fund linked assurance policy to be introduced in South Africa. During March 1966, the principles applicable to the Sage Growth Assurance Plan were extended to the funding of retirement annuity fund contracts similarly linked to the units of a mutual fund. This particular concept has been extremely well accepted by the South African public and has resulted in our lead being followed by a number of leading life assurance companies operating in the Republic.

"It can already be claimed that the concept of linking life policies to mutual funds is firmly established in the minds of the sophisticated sector of the South African insurance public. Variations have already been introduced, particularly in the area of partially linked policies, which combine the elements of orthodox and linked assurance in appropriate blending. The advent of mutual fund linked assurance, however, in no way alters our conviction of the important economic and sociological necessity for the orthodox forms of life assurance."

Growth continued apace in 1967, with both the Life Fund, at R10 366 906, and total assets, at R13 125 800, exceeding the R10 million mark for the first time, and new business premium income putting on a very respectable 43 per cent to reach R2 364 329. These new business figures of two decades ago are dwarfed by the achievements in this area of 1988, by which time new business premium income had increased more than one-hundredfold to no less than R247 million.

To mark the tenth anniversary of the company, the Report and Accounts took on a new, foolscap-sized format, and made use of photographs (two, one each of Roy and Gordon) and colour (a full page artist's impression of the Group's first own, purpose-built head office, then under construction in Johannesburg's rapidly growing Braamfontein district) for the first time. From now on, the Liberty Group annual reports would steadily grow in stature and importance, adding, over the years, a new dimension to institutional corporate reporting. And winning, in 1987, 1988 and 1989, the Investment Analysts' Society's Award for the Best Chairman's Review for the year. This is another, if little recognised, area in which Liberty Life has been a pace-setter in South Africa. It is an area, also, in which Gordon has always taken a keen personal interest – to the extent, indeed, of sparking a major row in the Guardian Royal Exchange Boardroom on one occasion when he was asked to comment on that august institution's own Report. Comment, of course, he did, rather more than somewhat critically!

Another major Liberty Life innovation in 1967 was the introduction of a totally original linked scheme – a world first – in which the linkage was to Liberty Life's own equity portfolio, not to an external (or internal, for that matter) mutual fund.

The directors reported, quite calmly: "The development by the company of Variable Investment Participation (VIP) during the year under review was perhaps the most significant development in the South African insurance industry in 1967. The VIP technique, to the best of our knowledge, is unique in the world and provides a solution to the basic problem of maintaining policyholder equity which has concerned the insurance industry for many decades. We consider the technique a major breakthrough in life insurance thinking in South Africa and an important advance in the sphere of equity linked policies which have the objective of hedging policy benefits against the erosion of monetary values due to inflation.

"Variable Investment Participation has the advantage of making the policyholder a direct participant with the company in the fortunes of its own investment portfolio. In addition, a very efficient linking mechanism is secured and the charges of mutual funds are substantially reduced. Investment policy, being the responsibility of the insurer, can be more closely geared to the requirements of long-term insurance contracts, which objectives may differ from the investment aims of an outside investment medium."

The *Financial Mail*, on 24 November 1967, waxed lyrical. Under the banner headline: "Great Insurance Breakthrough?" (although the query mark did detract slightly from the impact) it trumpeted:

"Liberty Life has done it again. In 1965, it pioneered mutual funds in South Africa and linked policyholders' benefits to the performance of their units in the same year.

"Now Liberty Life has developed a technique that has eluded experts in insurance the world over ever since policies were first written; how to calculate, for each individual policyholder, the capital appreciation and income attributable to him from the investment of his premium payments.

"This is a breakthrough which may well revolutionise the life insurance industry. Not only that; it will also have direct relevance to pension funds.

"What started Donald Gordon, managing director of Liberty Life

– the new technique is his brainchild – on the trail was realisation of various weaknesses inherent in policies whose premiums are partly and automatically invested in mutual fund units:

"(i) insurers abdicate control over, and responsibility for, the investment of a large portion of premium income (usually two-thirds) to mutual fund management companies;

"(ii) there is no guarantee that the investment policies of mutual fund managers will always suit the particular needs of long-term policyholders – and could conceivably run directly counter to them;

"(iii) in addition to the provisions an insured must make as a result of prudence and to accord with statutory requirements, benefits to policyholders from this form of equity hedge are, in practice, also diluted by:

"(a) the reduction in the amount invested by deduction of mutual fund charges.

"(b) the idle cash balances held by mutual funds (say 5c out of every 100c received for investment) and

"(c) the absence of growth in that part of a mutual fund portfolio comprising the statutory holding in gilts which duplicate that of the insurer.

"The result is that only about 85c out of every 100c of that part of the premium going to mutual funds actually gets into equities.

"So, some months ago, Gordon and his colleagues set themselves the task of finding a way to enable policyholders to enjoy in practice the full capital growth which should accrue to them in theory from life and endowment policies (a problem posed *inter alia* by the impossibility of frequently revaluing an insurance company's assets in order to calculate its day-to-day operating surplus for individual groups of with-profits policyholders).

"Their solution: the formulation of two indexes – the Growth Index and the Composite Index – which respectively measure the growth in value of Liberty Life's own equity portfolio without, and with, dividend income reinvestment.

"Labelled Variable Investment Participation, the VIP principle will be applied in the first instance to a major segment of Liberty Life's business: retirement annuity funds.

"Policyholders can choose one of two alternatives:

"(i) a policy part of whose premiums are linked to a "Growth Index" which enables the full benefit of capital appreciation to be passed on to the policyholder. Dividend income accrues to Liberty

Life and emerges as bonuses reflecting the policyholder's share in the profits of Liberty Life itself, or,

"(ii) a "Composite Index" linked policy in which income from the equity portfolio is deemed to be continuously reinvested pro rata for the benefit of this class of policyholder, but in which there is no subsequent participation in Liberty Life's profits as such.

"In other words, under (i) the policyholder ties his fortunes to Liberty Life's skill as both an investor and an insurer; under (ii) his benefits are geared only to Liberty Life's success as investor.

"What gives a tremendous boost to benefits is, of course, the regular investment of a full 100c of each equity rand of premium: 'The value of the saving in mutual fund charges alone', Mr Gordon explained to the *FM*, 'is boosted tremendously by the operation of compound interest.'

"In addition, under the VIP contract, Liberty Life guarantees a minimum benefit at a pre-determined level related to the basic sum assured, irrespective of any adverse fluctuation in its equity portfolio.

"Liberty Life believes this spells capital growth plus security. It may well have a policy package that few insurers will find it hard not to try to emulate."

It is quite fascinating to compare the above with a background memorandum that Ernest Bigland had prepared for his Chairman, Colonel Dawnay, on 14 September. The view from London was once again from a very different perspective:

"Our Liberty Life company in South Africa was the first company there to introduce a life policy linked with a unit trust. When we purchased Liberty Life there were no unit trusts in South Africa, but in fact Liberty Life sponsored and started the first unit trust there, known as the Sage Trust, the management company being called IMF and being run through Liberty Life. The four partners were Liberty Life, Netherlands Bank, London & Dominion Trust and Donald Gordon's personal interest.

"This arrangement has worked well up to date but due to friction in the management, Gordon's assistant, Shill, was given the position of full-time manager of IMF and we allowed it to be run completely separately. Further difficulties have arisen in that whilst we originally had virtual control of IMF through our Liberty Life interest and Gordon's personal interest, the position has now changed, with the shareholding previously held by Gordon having altered. We now have to make a decision either to continue our full-time arrangement with Sage (Mr Roy, our Chairman, and Gordon are directors of the management company) or to make new arrangements.

"There are two further reasons for considering a change:

"1. It has always been felt that the life company was relinquishing control of much of its investment responsibility by passing this over to the unit trust and unless we had management control the investment interests could easily conflict.

"2. Expenses and other margins of mutual funds in South Africa are normally higher than necessary.

"For all these reasons we have approached the Registrar of Insurance (who so far has authorised only six mutual funds and is not likely to authorise any further new funds) for approval to treat the whole of Liberty Life's equity portfolio as a mutual fund for the purpose of calculating a monthly unit or share index. The equity portfolio could be valued each month on very similar lines to a unit trust in this country and the unit price or index will automatically reflect the movement in the value of the underlying securities. These proposals have been accepted by the Registrar and it is therefore Liberty Life's intention to offer new life contracts on this basis, that is to say, a life policy tied to these internal units. Any life premium in rands will be converted into units and at maturity the total of the units will be converted back into rands, using the then current life fund index. This scheme will effect a reduction in margins, a saving in expenses and will leave the control of investment policy entirely in the hands of Liberty Life.

"We will be writing to Liberty Life laying down certain rules for the operation of the scheme, but it does seem in the circumstances the best proposal and also it will avoid a major clash of interests with Sage and probably undesirable publicity."

While Liberty Life's growth rate was earning it, and its founder, the by then accustomed plaudits from the press, the share price, in the Johannesburg Stock Exchange's bull run that was to peak in 1969, was skyrocketing.

On 1 March 1968, under the headline "A non-stop share?", the *Financial Mail* remarked: "One of life's minor mysteries, recently, has been the spectacular share price performance of Liberty Life Association of Africa. It was partially solved this week when this outstanding company announced its results for the year to 31 December 1967.

"At 5 500 cents now the yield on the projected 1968 minimum dividend is an ultra-modest 0,54 per cent (it was down to 0,32 per cent at 4 600 cents on the old dividend) and the price:earnings ratio is 77:1 (it was 122:1 at its peak).

"I asked managing director Donald Gordon how he felt about this sort of valuation. His view is that, while present price levels undoubtedly discount growth well into the future, they are not wholly unjustified by the company's performance and promise."

And a few weeks later, on 19 April 1968, the *FM* looked at "That share again". "When I discussed the meteoric share price performance of Liberty Life, as recently as 1 March, the share had risen from 2 800 cents, at the beginning of the year, to 5 000 cents. Now it is up to 9 000 cents, having touched 9 500 cents at the beginning of this week."

The market conditions, and his own natural entrepreneurial flair, were now leading Gordon to his next major leap forward; the consolidation and flotation on the JSE of all of Guardian's South African interests. That he first broached the subject to Bigland at a time when almost all of the latter's considerable mental energies were bound up in consummating a long-cherished ambition – the merger of Guardian with the much older and even more prestigious Royal Exchange – was fortuitous.

Master of timing though he is, not even Gordon could have got this one quite so right. Although the matter had already been raised in broad, general terms, he had assumed (with good reason) that his proposals would be less than warmly welcomed by Bigland, if only because they could possibly result in Guardian's overall control of its South African interests dropping below 75 per cent ("Don't ask me why," says Gordon, "but Ernest had a mania, almost a fixation, about 75 per cent control. Maybe it was his lucky number!").

Surely it would not have been possible even for Gordon's hard-working top team to have prepared a five-page memorandum on the proposed consolidation, dated 8 March 1968, within four days of the receipt of the telex below from Bigland. But then maybe they did achieve just that – the timing was too good to be a mere coincidence!

The telex was dated 4 March: "You will have seen announcement of negotiations between Guardian and Royal Exchange. I think you know my views. These moves will not affect in any way our relations or Liberty Life but if as hope all goes well should much strengthen our joint position. This reason could not confirm date visit April although still hope to come."

Gordon's reply underlined his concern: "Your telex of this morning. Have no knowledge whatsoever of any announcement of negotiations Guardian and Royal Exchange. Would appreciate any information you can give me."

Bigland came back immediately. "Your telex. So far only formal announcement Guardian and RE having negotiations with view to merger. Barings acting for us, Morgan Grenfell for RE. Obviously cannot say more at this stage but if you in any way worried don't hesitate to telephone me."

The telephone talk did not wholly reassure Gordon, as an aside in a letter to Bigland dated 7 March confirms: "As may be expected, I am a little concerned about the outcome of negotiations with the Royal Exchange – in particular as to how they will affect the future of Liberty Life, and I would appreciate, as far as possible, your keeping me abreast of the situation." But he nevertheless moved rapidly ahead with his own consolidation plans, in the full knowledge that when merger discussions between two great institutions are announced publicly in London, inevitably they will be consummated. And this, in fact, took place before the year-end.

A covering letter dated 8 March 1968 enclosed a precise, detailed and very perceptive memorandum. "You mentioned that you had had approaches from Philip Hill in regard to a possible flotation of the Guardian Group interests in South Africa. As it happens, Ted Roy and I have for the last few days been discussing this possibility between us and had proposed discussing it with you in detail when you come out to South Africa in April. In view of the fact that the matter has already been raised with you, I have taken the liberty of sending on to you a memorandum covering our first thoughts on the possibility of consolidating and rationalising the Group interests in South Africa and with a view to a possible flotation of these. We appreciate fully that you are involved in negotiations with the Royal Exchange, but it had occurred to us that our thinking here might well have a bearing on these negotiations. I would like to stress that the market climate in South Africa is now ideal for an operation of this type and both Ted and I commend this for your urgent consideration. We feel that, if our recommendations meet with your approval, we should move on it as soon as possible – certainly if this is practicable, before the end of June."

The memorandum was headed: "Suggested plan for the rationalisation and consolidation of the South African interests of the Guardian Assurance Company."

"A. Introduction

"In view of the political and economic factors and the investment climate now prevailing in South Africa, it is considered desirable that the South African interests of the Guardian Group be consolidated and rationalised by means of the formation of a Stock Exchange quoted holding company.

"It is considered that great advantage will accrue to all concerned by such an arrangement and that the image of the Group as such would be immeasurably advanced by such a financial manoeuvre. In addition, the large capital appreciation on the Guardian's Liberty Life holding could be consolidated.

"It might be considered preferable for the Guardian South Africa to be separately listed on the Johannesburg Stock Exchange but, in the writer's view, substantial benefit could accrue at this stage from a consolidation of the images of Liberty Life and Guardian South Africa. If thought desirable, the listing of Guardian South Africa could be considered at a future time as a separate operation.

"B. Financial aspects

"It is proposed that a 'holding' or 'development' company be formed with a name appropriate to the circumstances, which would absorb the entire holding of the Guardian Group in Guardian Assurance Company South Africa Limited and the Liberty Life Association of Africa Limited. The proposed new company would immediately apply for a listing on the Johannesburg Stock Exchange.

"C. Capital

"It is proposed that the authorised capital of the company would be R12 000 000, divided into 12 000 000 shares of R1 each.

"For the purpose of the listing, it is considered that a total of 10 000 000 shares of R1 each should be issued at a price of R2,50 per share. It is further proposed that the Guardian Group as vendors would receive a total of 8 000 000 shares of R1 each issued at R2,50 in exchange for their entire holdings in Liberty Life and the Guardian South Africa – ie a consideration of R20 000 000. For the purpose of the exercise, the value of the Group interest in Guardian South Africa would be valued at R4 000 000, and the value of the Guardian 75 per cent interest in Liberty Life (consisting of 471 792 shares of R1 each) at R16 000 000. Although the market value of the Liberty Life holding on 8 March 1968 was approximately R33 000 000, it is considered that for purposes of the listing, a value of R16 000 000 be placed upon them.

"Prior to the listing, a total of 2 000 000 shares would be offered to the South African public (giving Group and insurance connections preferential treatment) at a price to be determined closer to the time but not less than R2,50 per share. Two million shares of R1 each would be held in reserve.

"A pro forma balance sheet of the estimated consolidated position at 31 December 1968 is attached as an annexure hereto.

"By virtue of the aforementioned, an amount of R5 000 000 will be raised which it is proposed could be utilised for the furthering of the Group's investment interests in South Africa. Further, at the appropriate time, part of these funds could be utilised for the development of the company's Braamfontein property and for possible additional developments – real estate or otherwise – in the future. In the interim, these additional funds should yield not less than 4 per cent per annum after tax.

"In addition, it would be of substantial advantage in the long-term interest of the Group to make not less than 2 1/2 per cent of the total issued capital available for the purpose of stock options to be given to executive members of the Group staff in South Africa.

"D. Financial prospects

"In the writer's opinion, based on an issue price of R2,50, the company should be capable of being floated successfully on a 2 per cent dividend yield. The cost of servicing the capital of 10 000 000 shares will consequently be R500 000 per annum (ie a dividend of 5 per cent on the issued share capital).

"Based on a reasonable projection of the dividends payable by the Guardian South Africa and Liberty Life for the year ended 31 December 1968, this amount would be forthcoming as follows:

| | |
|---|---|
| Liberty Life | R200 000 |
| Guardian South Africa | R200 000 |
| Investment of additional funds | R200 000 |
| Total | R600 000 |

"This amount would, after charging administrative expenses, easily cover the projected R500 000 dividend payable by the holding company. In 1968, the maiden dividend would be 2 1/2 per cent (dividend income would accrue to the holding company at 31 December). This would leave adequate surplus to write off preliminary expenses in the first year.

"The consolidated earnings of the Group would be of the order of 10 cents per share, which would cover the dividend approximately twice.

"E. Preliminary expenses

"Expenses of the proposed flotation would be approximately R100 000.

"Conclusion

"It is considered that an offer of the Guardian Group interests on the aforementioned basis, particularly in view of the large content of Liberty Life shares contained, would be very favourably received by the South African public and it is the writer's view that within a year the shares could well be quoted on a 1 per cent dividend yield, ie the shares could appreciate to roughly 500 cents per share with exceptional growth prospects over the years.

"The advantages of the plan may be summarised as follows:

"1. The Guardian's South African interests would be more closely identified with the economic future of South Africa in conformity with current South African sentiment.

"2. The South African public and the company's business connections would be given a financial stake in the fortunes of the Group, with all the attendant advantages, which could be expected to reflect in terms of overall increased business.

"3. The Group would be in receipt of additional financial resources for the more active development of its investment interests in the dynamic South African economy.

"4. The Group would become one of the largest composite groups in the Republic.

"5. The financial exercise proposed would enable the Guardian's South African interests to be completely self-sufficient in terms of its future financial requirements.

"6. The Group would be facilitated for a more rapid development of its insurance interests by the availability of additional finance.

"7. A substantial unrealised capital surplus would accrue to the parent company, which it will have achieved without in any way derogating from the absolute control of its South African interests.

"8. The consolidation of the Guardian South Africa and Liberty Life through a common holding company would result in an enhancement of the overall image of both.

"9. The problem of financing the Group's property development in Braamfontein would be solved and finance would be available for further development in the property field and for following up interesting medium- and long-term investment opportunities which become available from time to time.

"10. In view of the consolidation, definite economies could be effected in administrative and investment functions, which presently are being duplicated.

"11. The executive staff of the companies concerned would be given a far greater incentive by being able to identify themselves more directly with the fortunes of the Group. The writer has in view that this would have the desirable effect of stabilising staff difficulties to which South African companies in general are susceptible.

"The one disadvantage that can be foreseen is that dividends distributed by the proposed holding company would be subject to the 15 per cent non-resident shareholders tax, whereas dividends distributed by Guardian South Africa and Liberty Life do not attract this tax. However, it is understood that any tax payable is capable of being offset against taxes payable in the United Kingdom."

It was a well-reasoned and carefully thought out proposal, as, of course, one would have expected. But Bigland's reaction, when it eventually came (after all, he was indeed preoccupied with the, to him, overridingly important Royal Exchange merger negotiations), was not encouraging.

It took the form of a counter-memorandum, dated 9 May 1968: "Memorandum on proposal to form one company to bring together the interests of Guardian and Liberty Life in South Africa".

"1. The principal point that emerges is the reduction which would arise in Guardian's holding in Liberty Life from, at present, 75 per cent in Liberty Life and 100 per cent in Guardian of South Africa, to 66 $^{2}/_{3}$ per cent of the whole. I do not think a reduction of this nature would be acceptable to our directors at the present time.

"2. I accept the point that the market value of Liberty Life must not unduly be taken into account in our consideration, but I do question whether during a period of spectacular growth this is really quite the time to sell any part of our holding.

"3. I accept the fact that the proposal would be in the interests of

South Africa and I think that ultimately this is a proposal that I accept in principle but one I would qualify on the question of time. Our own financial position in this country has had some severe ups and downs and when we make the decision I would wish to do so as one operation and not carry out part of the scheme now and then deal with a further part in the future.

"4. I accept that your stock market is hungry for shares and in this way the opportunity is good, although following the recent agreement on gold our view is that markets may well weaken over the next period and this undoubtedly will have some impact on your South African industrials.

"5. I fully accept your views about Hill Samuel. [A confusion with Philip Hill, to whom Gordon had earlier objected as proposed merchant bankers.]

"6. You suggest that great advantages will accrue to all, and whilst I can see advantages I rather question the advantages to the Guardian shareholders who really are the main people concerned. Again this comes back to timing.

"7. I think you know my view that the Guardian of South Africa has far too short a record of profits to contemplate a quotation at the moment. This position still applies and when you are considering bringing together a Life Fund (Liberty Life) and a General Fund (Guardian of South Africa) it must be kept in mind that our operations, although called a company, are in fact only part of our world-wide operations and inevitably would be affected by world-wide reinsurance arrangements to take one example. In other words, Guardian of South Africa could not possibly write the lines of business that it accepts without the support of Guardian and without proper reinsurance arrangements. For this reason their results tend to fluctuate wildly and until I have a set pattern which I can guarantee for the future I think we could come in for some severe criticism if we joined the two together and then possibly had two or three years of bad results on the general insurance side.

"You have given some figures of valuation of the Guardian of South Africa but it is difficult to agree these without further information. Also we do rather question the tax position which I think is overstated in our favour. There too is the question of whether any sale would be subject to capital gains tax. If this was the case it would make any scheme at the moment very unattractive from Guardian's point of view.

"8. When you suggest the fixing of a price for the 2m shares to be placed among our friends I think this would be an extremely difficult operation at the moment as any figure would be considerably distorted by the predominance of Liberty Life.

"9. I am by no means certain that any real economies would be achieved as I should have thought that at present there is very little duplication. All we would be doing would be bringing together the units (as we intend to do) in our new building and the only overlapping (if any) would be possibly one or two seniors.

"10. Considering your proposal from the point of view of the recent purchase of Liberty Life shares I would hardly think that the suggestion would be very attractive, as instead of having an interest in a dynamic life company we would be asked to change into a company with a composite portfolio, the results on the general side of which could well fluctuate widely. As you know, our investment in Liberty Life is held in our Life Fund and there could well be difficulties from our point of view in merging the interests of the Life Fund and General Fund. These problems are not insuperable but are genuine difficulties.

"11. You make a plea for the introduction of a staff profit scheme for executives. For many years here we had a staff share scheme which subsequently became a staff bonus scheme tied to the dividend. Due to our expansion and to inflation the scheme eventually had to be abandoned, and although I considered every possible alternative scheme of this kind offered in this country I came to the conclusion that none of them provided a satisfactory answer in an inflationary era. I am firmly of the opinion that the only way properly to reward staff is to pay them the correct salary and give them an adequate pension scheme. I know your pension scheme is not as good as the Guardian one but I am sure over a period we can bring it up and I would much prefer to follow this pattern.

"I am sorry that you may find the views I have expressed in many respects do not coincide with those held in South Africa, but I think they are so fundamental that I would not wish to recommend to our directors the formation of a new company to bring our interests together at the present time. I do not rule this out for the future but I think that the disadvantages at the moment outweigh the advantages, even taking into account the possible difficulty of raising the appropriate funds to deal with the Braamfontein property."

Given the very wide divergence of the views expressed in these two memoranda, it seemed that a major clash was inevitable. And in view of the very large area of disagreement, it is, in fact, little short of amazing that Guardian Assurance Holdings, as the new corporate vehicle was to be named, was actually listed on the Johannesburg Stock Exchange as early as 11 December 1968, just seven months later.

The listing was not achieved without drama, and plenty of it. The telex and the telephone between London and Johannesburg fairly buzzed; Bigland flew out to South Africa in May, and Gordon went to London in July. Most of the arm-twisting went on in these face-to-face encounters which, Gordon recalls, "were stormy, very stormy indeed. But I sensed that the Johannesburg bull market did not have all that far to run, and I was insistent that we go for 1968. After all, we were here on the spot; London, I was convinced, could not read our share market."

Since so much was done in person and by telephone the correspondence is patchy, but absorbingly interesting.

Gordon to Bigland, 14 May 1968, on receipt of the counter-memo. "Thank you for your memorandum on the proposals to bring the interests of the Guardian and Liberty Life together. As we will shortly see each other, I think it may be advisable to hold my comments until you are here."

Gordon clearly impressed his views strongly on Bigland when the latter was in Johannesburg from 25 May to 2 June, and he made considerable progress. He used every possible argument, including threats that his personal motivation was at issue, as is clear from Bigland's letter of 13 June, written after his return to London.

"We had our Annual General Meeting yesterday. I am glad to say everything went quite smoothly and we had no awkward questions.

"This has allowed me today to give a little more thought to your affairs and the ideas for the future. I have talked to the Chairman about the idea of a holding company and I have today dictated a memorandum on the subject. As I told you, I will give you a decision within the next month or two (I hope earlier). I also hope it will be a favourable one although I much appreciate your saying that if for technical reasons, ie taxation or otherwise, this could not be done at the present time you would understand and that your loyalty is, as it has always been, to Liberty Life which you would continue to build up as you have so ably done in the past."

A good deal more progress was made when Gordon was in

London from 7 to 10 July, but, even so, no firm decision had been taken when Lady Luck decided to join the party. One of Liberty Life's great rivals, South African Eagle Insurance (and coincidentally also the South African arm of a British insurer, Eagle Star – itself a keen United Kingdom competitor of Guardian) announced its plans to go public with a Johannesburg Stock Exchange listing. This greatly strengthened DG's hand.

Gordon to Bigland, 19 July. "I enclose for your information photostats of press cuttings relating to the proposed flotation of the SA Eagle Insurance Company – our major competitor in the South African market. I do hope they have not stolen a march on us!

"As I mentioned to you in London, we shall have to decide in regard to our own plans fairly shortly if we wish to proceed this calendar year. Otherwise, as I see it, we might well have to hold it over until the 1968 accounts are complete. My particular problem is that of pre-incorporation profits, which might adversely affect the picture."

Gordon was now winning. Bigland, 23 July: "I have not overlooked the urgency of making a decision about our future organisation in South Africa and if I can agree one with the Chairman within the next week or two I hope we can go ahead before the end of the year. If not, I do not think we will lose a great deal by leaving it until early 1969."

But Gordon kept up the pressure. On 27 July: "In regard to the second paragraph of your letter concerning the future organisation in South Africa, I feel that provided we take a decision by not later than the end of August, we could get the operation off the ground this year. Failing this, I am afraid it will be rather difficult in the early part of 1969 and, as I see it, the earliest date possible will be June 1969 (almost a year from now). My reasoning behind this is that the Stock Exchange will not allow us to publish accounts more than a year out of date in any prospectus or pre-listing statement."

And again, on 2 August: "Regarding the proposals for the formation of a holding company for the Guardian interests, I thought I should let you know that I have ascertained that the name 'Guardian Assurance Development Corporation Limited' is acceptable as far as the authorities in Pretoria are concerned. I am also convinced, taking all factors into account, that all interests would be best served if the operation was initiated this year and I believe that we should do everything possible to secure this position. I was slightly concerned about the problem of pre-incorporation profits but I believe that this problem can be easily overcome insofar as I have available an ideal vehicle for the operation – being a company which I formed in February this year for a completely different purpose. The company is completely clean and has not been utilised at all. All that would be required to be done would be:

"1. To change the name.

"2. To convert it to a public company and to adopt a new Memorandum and Articles.

"3. To increase the authorised share capital to the required level (the existing authorised and issued share capital of the company is R300 000 – the shares have been allotted to me against cash – consequently the entire assets of the company consist of R300 000 in cash).

"I do look forward to your views in this matter at the earliest possible time."

Having that "ideal vehicle" available was probably one of the most astute moves of Donald Gordon's remarkable career. Investors Equity Trust Limited had been incorporated as a "private investment company" on 28 February 1968 and, whilst one must accept that he formed it for a "completely different purpose", the timing was felicitous indeed. By the time of the flotation of Guardian Assurance Holdings, Gordon's shares in Investors Equity Trust had been transmuted into 1,2 million GAH shares – which proved to be a very substantial plank of his personal fortune.

But Bigland still had not given way. On 8 August: "I have now had an opportunity of talking to the Chairman about our exchange of letters in connection with the proposed new holding company in South Africa, particularly your last letter of 19 July pointing out that the South African Eagle are going ahead rather rapidly. Personally I would not be too concerned about what the Eagle are doing as our operations and yours are far more soundly based. [Amusingly, Bigland is now 'knocking' SA Eagle, which Gordon had, more than somewhat flatteringly, described as 'our major competitor'.] I am sure it is better to make the right decisions even if it may take just a little longer.

"I am pleased to tell you, although I think at this stage you should keep it confidential between yourself and Ted Roy, that when our Chairman spoke to the Chairman of RE about our proposals the RE's immediate reaction was that they were thinking of floating in

South Africa (knowing their size this seems a little out of keeping). It therefore seems that by next year there is every probability that we will be able to bring them in to any new unit we propose to form, and obviously this will make it even larger and more important.

"For this reason, and also for the fact that, as you rightly point out, so much of the year has now passed that we would have to produce a new set of accounts, I think we would be wiser to hold over the proposition until early next year. If we can get your accounts and those of Guardian of South Africa and RE out early I see no reason why we should not consider the new holding company concept by, say, the end of March. I trust the market will still be as strong at that time and I am sure in fact it will."

The "red herring" of Royal Exchange's South African interests was like a red rag to a bull as far as Gordon was concerned, and he came out fighting. His letter of 15 August 1968 was prefaced by the coldly formal "Dear Mr Bigland", instead of the by now long-customary "Dear Ernest":

"Thank you for your letter dated 8 August 1968 suggesting that we defer our plans for the formation of a South African holding company until early next year. I have discussed the matter at some length with Mr Roy and although we fully appreciate the validity of the reasons for the deferment of the project, we nonetheless feel that it is of considerable importance to implement the operation at the earliest time and, if possible, during the current financial year.

"Our views are to a large extent influenced by the serious threat to our position brought about by the proposed flotation of the South African Eagle. In a nutshell, the problem is that, in terms of their flotation arrangements, they have set aside 630 000 shares for their brokers and agents and that they are offering substantial blocks around the market, particularly to connections they have not previously been able to penetrate, on the understanding of future business support. In this way, most of our senior connections have been contacted. They are exploiting this aspect with considerable skill to cement existing arrangements and to entice brokers to support them where they have been unsuccessful before. This operation has been facilitated by outstanding press publicity. You will agree that this type of tactic is virtually impossible to counter by orthodox means and really amounts to exactly what we had in mind for Liberty Life and Guardian South Africa.

"The position is further aggravated by various other companies, such as The Guarantee Life and SA Metropolitan, indicating that their companies will soon be going for a public listing and that brokers' support will be compensated by the allocation of substantial lines of shares at a future stage (undefined).

"In view of Liberty Life's substantial success over the past few years, it is becoming increasingly clear that many other companies are making determined efforts to break into areas of influence which have previously been our preserve.

"To summarise the position, I believe it is fair to say that unless we act shortly, we could well find ourselves dislodged from our pre-eminent position in this market – a position which has been so hardly won. There is no doubt that for the time being the South African Eagle have wrested the initiative from us and we are now in very much a defensive position with, at best, an opportunity of neutralising their advantage. These problems are already reflecting themselves in a noticeable decline in our new business production – a position which admittedly may be coincidental, but which nonetheless exists. The reorganisation scheme originally formulated has now changed its nature from being a desirable manoeuvre to one of fundamental necessity.

"I am normally happy to accept that our opposition are entitled to the fruits of their initiative but in this particular instance, they have been able to get ahead purely on the basis of our procrastination. Notwithstanding the Royal Exchange merger, I am somewhat at a loss to understand why the Guardian has delayed a proposition of such obvious merit and which could result in great benefit to its interests in South Africa.

"I have redrafted the original memorandum setting out the scheme, which I enclose herewith. The document outlines my proposals, including the suggestion to overcome the problem of pre-acquisition profits by the utilisation of a shell company, which incidentally also enables the implementation of certain other ideas regarding my personal position, etc. I estimate the entire operation would take approximately two to two-and-a-half months from the date of your firm agreement, which would enable us to have the new company listed by the end of November 1968, provided we get the final green light by not later than early September. I am of the opinion that an early press announcement indicating our intentions would to some extent serve to neutralise the impact of the SA Eagle.

"If the matter is held over to 1969, it would not be possible to complete this operation before June 1969 at the earliest. At that time, we cannot be at all certain that market conditions will be as favourable as they are now, particularly having regard to the fluidity of the international political and currency situation. It is my opinion that the optimum time might have already passed. [It is of interest to recall that the Johannesburg Stock Exchange's 1966/1969 bull market peaked in May 1969; Gordon's market sense was almost uncanny, as it would again be in the Crash of 1987.] Nonetheless, if immediate action is taken, and the current economic climate continues reasonably unchanged and on reconsideration of my memorandum of 14 August 1968, I feel that we could possibly pitch the issue price at a dividend yield of 1 1/2 per cent, ie at 200 cents per share.

"I do hope that I have been able to put the nature of the problems to you in this letter and that you will see your way clear to reconsidering your decision. I cannot stress strongly enough the importance of moving expeditiously in this matter."

The revised memorandum that Gordon enclosed was very much along the lines of his original document, except that he now proposed the issue of 20 000 000 shares, at a price "of, say, R1,50 per share". He also spelt out that the issued capital of the shell company should "be retained beneficially by the writer or his nominees", and it was noted that this would represent "3 per cent of the proposed issued capital of the company".

By this time it was August and, of course, the City of London, and with it Ernest Bigland, were on holiday, so the above letter and the memorandum had been addressed to Peter Greenfield, then Guardian's company secretary, with the request that they be forwarded to Bigland.

Greenfield wrote on 14 August, seemingly to underline Gordon's temerity in questioning a decision that had been handed down, as it were, from on high. "I refer to your telephone conversation yesterday and understand that you are now replying to Mr Bigland's letter of 8 August as you are anxious that the proposals relating to the new holding company are implemented this year rather than deferred until next. I think you will appreciate from the managing director's letter of 8 August that careful consideration has been given to the proposals and the timing of their implementation, both by Mr Bigland and by Col Dawnay. It would, therefore, be necessary to put forward any representations you make to the managing director and the Chairman, both of whom are at present on holiday, the former until 4 September and the latter until 6 September."

Even if it was not quite the way things were normally done in the City, especially during those precious summer holidays, Gordon's tough letter turned the tide in his favour. Bigland's holiday in Scotland (where else? – it was grouse time) was interrupted and on 29 August he telexed: "Your letter 15th received. Am sure you realise that whilst your proposals have my full support in principle I still have to carry with me Board who have not been so closely connected our joint affairs as you and I and most important persuade our new partners support us at all stages. Fully intended talk other Chairman next week and hope settle either join us now or we go ahead on our own. Would have thought that an announcement our intentions sufficient stabilise our position and complete if agreement obtained by say November. Honestly not really impressed SA Eagle proposals. Number of shares available will only provide minimum allocation and in long run brokers and clients will always support best company irrespective any small investment.

"We both in general agreement terms except that whilst my Chairman agrees some personal holding yourself feels your proposals rather high. Sure we can settle these final details. To summarise will do utmost to obtain agreement from Boards if obtained will approve general announcement hope can then complete by end year. In view of importance whole operation will have to agree with you all details. Do not be too worried some slight tactical advantage is not a battle won."

Bigland's final reference was, of course, to the inroads that Gordon had said the SA Eagle was making. But Gordon took it to heart, and decided to press his own hard-won "tactical advantage" as toughly as possible by going over to London and finishing off the job in person.

His telexed reply, also on 29 August. "Please convey to Mr Bigland receipt of his telex. Content has been discussed with Mr Roy. Pleased to know have full support in principle. In view of the circumstances and urgency of the matter believe it imperative for me to be in London next week prior to the discussion with the Group Chairman. There are so many aspects, permutations and possibilities which could have bearing on ultimate decision that it is highly desirable for preliminary discussion prior to proposals being put formally to Board. As time is now very short also essential to settle much of the detail. Kindly advise if my arrival Thursday morning would be convenient."

In London, from 5 to 10 September, Gordon's formidable negotiating skills prevailed. It was, of course, not easy, but he eventually won the day after what he remembers as "some of the toughest talking of my life. The clincher came at the Bath Club, but this time it was Ernest who felt the heat in the sauna."

The following announcement was made on 18 September: "The Guardian Assurance Company Limited of London ('Guardian London') announces that, subject to the consent of the Bank of England and the South African Exchange Control Authorities and the completion of all other necessary formalities, it has been agreed in principle to consolidate and expand its South African interests by means of a holding company whose shares it is proposed will be listed on the Johannesburg Stock Exchange before the end of 1968.

"To achieve these objectives, Guardian London proposes to transfer to the holding company its 75,6 per cent interest in Liberty Life Association of Africa Limited (consisting of 707 688 shares of R1 each) and its 100 per cent interest in Guardian Assurance Company South Africa Limited (consisting of 1 000 000 shares of R1 each). The value of the interests to be transferred is currently in excess of R50 000 000, in exchange for which Guardian London will receive approximately 80 per cent of the issued share capital of the holding company. Not less than 15 per cent of the proposed issued share capital of the holding company will be made available for subscription by the South African public on terms to be announced later, but preference on a basis still to be determined will be given to business connections of the Guardian Assurance Company South Africa Limited and Liberty Life Association of Africa Limited.

"The new capital to be raised by the public issue will be utilised to further the Guardian Group's insurance interests and its investment penetration in South Africa, for the formation of a new investment and issue house which it is proposed will be established in due course, and to finance the Group's proposed new headquarters to be erected in Braamfontein, Johannesburg.

"Mr E J G Roy will be the Chairman of the proposed new holding company and Mr D Gordon the deputy chairman. The full composition of the Board of the holding company will be announced later."

So Gordon, to the subsequent very considerable benefit of all concerned, had carried the day. Bigland also agreed to be deputy chairman, and at 5.30 pm that day Gordon sent him this happy telex: "Announcement in terms of your telex made at 3.30 pm South African time today. Delighted at your decision to appear as deputy chairman. Best wishes to Guardian from us all for the success of the venture."

All now went smoothly and, by dint of an incredible effort on the part of Liberty Life's senior management, the public offer of 6 000 000 shares of 25 cents each in Guardian Assurance Holdings at 150 cents a share opened on 5 November 1968, a bare seven weeks from the green light. For a major issue, this is probably still a record, and it was a highly commendable achievement.

The issue was an astounding success, even at a time when new issues, in the rampant bull market then raging, were all pulling in large oversubscriptions. On 23 November, the following triumphant announcement was made:

"The Board of directors of Guardian Assurance Holdings (South Africa) Limited wishes to announce that in respect of the recent offer to the public of 6 000 000 shares of 25 cents each at R1,50 per share, a total of more than R275 000 000 has been subscribed, representing an approximate 30 times oversubscription of the shares offered. Taking into account that 3 000 000 shares were reserved for brokers, agents and other business connections of the company, the issue was oversubscribed 60 times by other members of the general public.

"The amount subscribed for the Guardian issue constitutes an all time record for any share offer in South African financial history. It is also a record in respect of the number of applications received.

"The Board is extremely gratified at the magnificent public response to the offer, particularly in view of the fact that the offer ran concurrently with three other public issues and that more public placings are probably currently in process than ever before."

Bigland telexed: "Warmest personal congratulations on wonderful success of offer. This completes first phase of saga which I mentioned my speech tenth anniversary. Every confidence in future of new company. Please accept yourself and convey my sincere thanks all concerned."

The final amount subscribed was R285 000 000 and, as Gordon noted in a letter to Bigland on 27 November, this massive sum produced a large windfall profit. "As I indicated to you on the phone the other day, the interest factor is really enormous and my estimate is that it will exceed R400 000 – which will more than take care of the total issue expenses." In the event, the interest factor turned out to be in excess of R600 000.

It is almost unbelievable that, with all the other matters that he had to contend with at the time, Gordon foresaw the possibility of this profit, and took extraordinary steps to maximise it. Throughout the two weeks' currency of the offer – although, of course, the bulk of the money came in over the last two days – Gordon had arranged that application cheques would be flown, each day, by private courier, from Johannesburg to centres such as Cape Town and Durban to be banked as soon as possible; every single day's interest was going to add to the totality of the "calculated windfall", not to mention the savings on bank charges, which would alone have been in excess of R100 000, due to the banking custom in those days of charging a fee for the clearance of "out-of-town" cheques.

And later, when the Receiver of Revenue sought to tax the windfall as a gross revenue profit, Gordon was to make South African tax law by taking the issue to appeal – and winning.

Dealings in the newly listed company's shares were due to commence on Wednesday 11 December 1968. As might well have been anticipated after that massive oversubscription, the market's response was rapturous. By 11.50 that morning, Gordon was able to send this telex: "Message for Mr Bigland. Price Guardian Holdings after High Change 435 cents. Approximate volume 250 000 shares."

By the year's end they were 500 cents, and they peaked with the market on 9 May 1969, at 655 cents. By October that year Guardian Assurance Holdings had fallen 72 per cent from that high to 185 cents – an interesting contrast to what would happen to share prices in the Crash of 1987, then still light-years away!

In June 1978, less than a decade after the most successful public offer in South African financial history up to that time, Donald Gordon and Michael Rapp were to buy back control of the Liberty Life group with the purchase of 21,5 million shares in Guardian Assurance from Guardian Royal Exchange in London – for 125 cents per share. By early 1989, a further decade after that momentous event, these same shares had appreciated by some thirty times to reach a level of 3 800 cents per share and a total value of over R800 million. The dividend for 1988 of 116 cents broadly matched the net exit price of 125 cents paid ten years earlier.

Such is the excitement and opportunity of big business in the financial stratosphere. It is heartening to record that GRE remained all these years with 4,7 million shares in Guardian Holdings (now Liberty Holdings), with a current worth of R180 million; this, of course, is in addition to the R27 million the GRE received on the sale of those 21,5 million shares in 1978. These sums should be compared to Guardian's total original entry cost into Liberty Life in 1964 of around £900 000.

So honour was preserved by all; and all profited mightily, to a greater or a lesser degree.

# 9 Onto the Board

Donald Gordon tells an amusing story, part of it told to him many years after the events by Ernest Bigland, concerning the Boardroom machinations in Guardian Royal Exchange in 1969, when Bigland became joint managing director of the merged GRE. Prior to the merger between Guardian Assurance and the Royal Exchange in 1968, Ernest Bigland was managing director of Guardian and Martin Wilkinson was managing director of Royal Exchange. Each was quite determined that he, and his company, should emerge top dog.

Recalls Gordon: "Ernest was very shrewd and at times perhaps somewhat devious, but he managed to see that the Guardian came first – that the new merged company's title was Guardian Royal Exchange, and not Royal Exchange Guardian, as the Board of Royal Exchange and Wilkinson would have expected. It was almost unbelievable, given that Guardian was marginally the smaller of the two companies as well as being nearly 100 years younger than Royal Exchange, but Bigland got his way even though it almost wrecked the whole deal. But the cost to Bigland personally was considerable; to get his own way on the corporate title, he had to accept that a Royal Exchange director, Lord Kindersley, would be the first Chairman of the merged group and that he and Wilkinson would be named joint managing directors of the new entity. This was a bitter pill for Ernest, but he swallowed it, particularly as it was also agreed that Colonel Kit Dawnay, the then Chairman of the Guardian, would succeed Kindersley on his retirement only a few years away.

"Even so, he was determined that the position regarding Wilkinson and himself wouldn't stay that way for long. His opportunity came soon afterwards, when he came out to Johannesburg to celebrate with us the launch on the Johannesburg Stock Exchange of Guardian Assurance Holdings in December 1968. The launch was enormously successful and Guardian Assurance shares were quoted at around R5. Ernest and I were having a drink that evening, and he was grumbling again to me about his 'joint' situation. I said: 'Ernest, I have the solution. At the present Guardian Holdings share price, our market capitalisation in Johannesburg is actually greater than that of GRE in London. Hence, although you control Guardian Holdings, it is actually technically possible for us to change roles and for Guardian Holdings to make a takeover bid for Guardian Royal Exchange – and then I will give you the top job!' We had a good laugh, but technically such a reverse takeover bid was perfectly feasible at that time.

"Soon after that, Bigland had a policy dispute – one of many – with Wilkinson and in frustration went to the Chairman, Kindersley, and said: 'Look sir, this is quite ridiculous, this joint MD thing is just not working. When I was in Johannesburg recently, I was talking to Donald Gordon and he explained to me just how it would be possible for him to make a takeover bid for the GRE, and I'm convinced he can do it. If I don't get the top job here and now, I'll do my level best to see that Gordon does take us over. And, mark my words, he probably will succeed.'

"Well, Bigland got the top job and Wilkinson retired as joint managing director. And I got a reputation in London that created all sorts of difficulties for me in the years to come. Apparently, old Lord Kindersley was a nervous sort of character, and he actually took the threat seriously; he nearly had a heart attack at the thought of a South African takeover of the great Guardian Royal Exchange. Anyway, that's how I won my spurs in the City of London."

Meanwhile, important domestic events were in train. By the end of 1970, the South African interests of the greater Guardian Royal Exchange Group, that is Guardian Holdings and Liberty Life, were beginning to assume a meaningful role in the London Group's world-wide affairs. At 31 December 1970, GRE's assets world-wide exceeded £1 000 million, to which Liberty Life's contribution was R42,6 million; GRE's net premium income was over £250 million and Liberty Life's was R10 million. Not large in proportion, of course, but the growth had been dramatic. On a stock market valuation basis, however, Guardian Holdings was proportionately far more important. And Gordon was beginning to feel, very strongly, that South Africa's contribution to the greater GRE Group's overall fortunes should be accorded tangible recognition.

In February 1971 Ernest Bigland paid one of his regular visits to South Africa. On the "Agenda for the visit of Mr E F Bigland to

South Africa during the week beginning 22 February 1971" was an innocuous looking Item 7, which read, very simply: "DG – position re managing director of GAH and GRE." And a somewhat ambiguous Item 8: "New management structure GRE (UK) in relationship to South African affairs."

Discussions under these heads were obviously wide-ranging, and were not confined to the seemingly simple issues. Pressing the matter really seriously probably for the very first time, although it had been raised a number of times before, Gordon suggested to Bigland that he, Gordon, should be strongly considered for membership of the main London Board of Guardian Royal Exchange in recognition not just of his own contribution, but of the South African Group's rapidly increasing importance in the affairs of GRE on a world-wide basis.

It was customary, in the dealings between the two men, that Bigland would briefly confirm by letter, after his return to London, the main issues that had been discussed. His reference to that important Item 7, in his letter to Gordon of 16 March 1971, rather skated over the big issue. "As far as your position is concerned in relation to the GRE Group world-wide, and particularly to London, we agreed that your principal contacts would be through me as they have been in the past."

He was no more forthcoming in his comment on the discussion of Item 8. "Your agenda raised the relationship in the new Guardian Royal Exchange management structure as far as South African affairs are concerned and I think this is answered in 7 above."

Having formally raised the issue and made his point, Gordon now let the matter rest, and there was no further reference to it in the correspondence for the next couple of months. Anyway, he planned to be in London in May, and face-to-face discussions with Bigland and the Chairman had invariably, in the past, proved more fruitful than letters.

And indeed, once again, they were. Gordon's "Agenda for Discussion with Mr Bigland During Trip to London – May 1971", contained, at Item 27, the one word: "Personal". Against it, very clearly written, after the meetings, in Gordon's own hand, is the notation: "Directorship GRE within a year."

Even so, the matter was far from resolved, for the two principals were not wholly in agreement as to what had passed between them.

Gordon to Bigland, 14 June 1971: "I think it is now common cause between those who are aware of the ramifications that the importance and contribution of the South African Guardian Group fully justifies representation on the main London Board. As you know, I have advocated this policy for some years now and personally I believe that a development of this nature is of fundamental importance if the GRE Group is to become a truly leading international operation in the difficult years ahead.

"Now that the 1971 Annual General Meeting is out of the way, I find it somewhat disconcerting that this basic decision is to be further deferred and I hope this is not an indication of reluctance on the part of certain interests to take this progressive step. Personally, I am of the view that matters have developed to the point where it would almost be inconceivable for the South African end of the Guardian Group to be overlooked in any contemplated Board structuring.

"I think you are fully aware of my reasoning on this so I do not propose to repeat my arguments here. I had hoped to have a frank discussion on this matter with the Chairman during my recent trip to London but, unfortunately, as you know, he was away. Perhaps a note from Colonel Dawnay generally setting out objectives and views would be useful at this juncture. I am sure you will accept my remarks in the context of the very frank dialogue we have always had between us."

Bigland replied on 22 June. "I must admit I was somewhat concerned to receive your letter of 14 June. As you know, I telephoned you on Friday evening to say that I was sorry you seemed so concerned about matters which we had very fully discussed when you were here only recently and on which I thought we had reached agreement.

"Let me take your personal position. You will know that I and the Chairman and certainly the directors of the old Guardian are very conscious of your achievements on behalf of the Group in South Africa and for some time have had in mind ways in which you might become more closely concerned with our overall operations. The position might well have altered very much earlier if we had stayed as Guardian, but three years ago we became Guardian Royal Exchange. As you know, for the first eighteen months very little integration was achieved. In the last eighteen months a great deal more has been done, but this inevitably meant a large number of directors leaving the Board of the Group. As I explained to you in some detail, it could have caused us some considerable embarrassment if at the time we were making these changes we had made other appointments which were not directly related to the changes being made.

"I must be honest and say that your letter clearly conveys to me that when you were in London recently someone else must have given you a completely different idea of what might be done. I personally have never changed my views, nor have I conveyed to you any opinion other than that your name was very high on the list and that it should not be long before a decision was made. In fact, even since you returned to South Africa I have told you that the Chairman had raised the question himself and that it is only a matter of a week or so before further talks will be held.

"To summarise. I talked to the Chairman again yesterday and, as I have already told you, he is suggesting talks about the future constitution of the Board. He rightly says that there are a few names on his list, of which yours is an important one, and he feels that he must deal with them together and not in isolation. He expects to make a decision in the fairly near future after discussing the matter with the deputy chairman and others. His timing would probably be about September. He would like to see you and discuss the position with you before any appointment is made.

"I appreciate your final paragraph in which you rightly say that we have always been completely honest with each other, and I would be very sorry if this ever altered. However, the present exchange of letters and our conversations over the telephone have made me a little concerned and I do hope we will be able to bring our affairs back to the happy basis they have always been on in the past."

Gordon clearly felt he was winning, and sought to cool the issues in a letter on 2 July. "I am afraid at times our personal relationship of complete frankness and honesty, particularly when this is committed to writing, sometimes gets misconstrued. I believe this is certainly the case with my problems which have been the subject of certain correspondence and telephone discussions. You will appreciate that our approach is sometimes very much different and that at times, being the sort of man I am, I do suffer certain frustrations which are very much aggravated by our not being able to talk things over on a day-to-day basis.

"I am perfectly happy with your assurances concerning the future constitution of the Board and I believe that it is desirable that before anything is done, I have a full and frank discussion with the

Chairman. This is an important matter to me and, as I have indicated before, I will not take on anything which I cannot see through and make some contribution. Looked at from my point of view, you will appreciate that we first began discussing this matter more than three years ago. I fully accept all the reasons but nonetheless I do not think you can completely blame me for allowing some of my frustrations to show through. I was extremely pleased at the progressive step of the Board in appointing three executive directors last year. However, taking all factors into consideration, in particular the important contribution I have made to the GRE Group, I am sure you can understand my disappointment at being overlooked on that occasion.

"I again hope you will accept what I have said in the right spirit and, for my part, the matter is now closed; certainly I am sure the matter should stand over until we next meet as I am sure the written word was never the most appropriate for this type of debate."

Bigland accepted the proffered olive branch, and replied on 5 July. "Many thanks for your letter of 2 July. I fully agree with you that it is never easy to reconcile business matters and those concerning business which are also personal. I am sure that much of the misunderstanding about your own position has arisen for this reason. In the past we have always been able to solve our differences when we have met and I am quite sure we will always be able to do so in the future.

"In relation to your own position, I am afraid things here develop slightly differently from the way similar situations would develop in South Africa, but at no time has your very great value and contribution to the Group been overlooked. I am confident it will continue to be fully recognised in the future changes that are made."

That was very nearly that. Gordon went over to London in July, completely rebuilt his bridges with Bigland, and had some very "full and frank discussions" with the Chairman, Colonel Kit Dawnay.

There followed, on 13 September 1971, a letter from Dawnay to Gordon. "I am pleased to let you know that at a recent meeting the directors agreed to invite you to accept nomination to the Board. Would you let me know whether you will be willing to accept such an invitation, before I put a formal proposal to the Board which I propose to do at the next meeting on 22 September. If you accept, the appointment would date from 1 October.

"As you already hold an important executive position in the

Group, your election to the Board would be on the same terms as the other executives, namely that if and when you cease to hold your position in the Group, on retirement or otherwise, you would automatically offer your resignation from the main Board. I am sure you will agree that a similar arrangement should apply in your case. Would you let me know that you agree?

"We have all been very pleased with the growth and success of our business in South Africa, and I am sure your appointment will further strengthen the links between us here and you in South Africa."

Gordon, having now won his three-year battle, replied happily on 21 September. "I was extremely pleased to receive your letter of the 13 September 1971 inviting me to accept nomination to the main London Board of the Guardian Royal Exchange Assurance Group. I regard this gesture by you and your colleagues as a great honour and the culminating point of eight very successful years as a member of the Group.

"In accepting the invitation, I would like to express the hope that, in spite of the geographical disadvantages, I will be able to make some real contribution to future developments. For me, the appointment represents a great challenge and I only hope I will justify the confidence you have shown in me.

"I fully understand that on retirement I would automatically offer my resignation from the Board but I hope that this will not occur for many years to come.

"My personal relationship with the London end of the Group at all levels has always been an extremely pleasant one and I am sure that this has added much to the growth and stature of our business in South Africa."

He also sent a note to Bigland. "I have replied to the Chairman's invitation to join the main GRE Board and by the time you receive this note, the date of confirmation of my appointment will have passed. I did however confirm the matter on the telephone so my acceptance was purely a formality in any event.

"I do think it is appropriate at this point to thank you most sincerely for the tremendous measure of co-operation and understanding that has existed between us over the past eight years. I must say that neither you nor I could have visualised the long way we have come from the very small and meagre beginnings of our relationship in 1964.

"I am not very adept at this kind of communication but I am sure you will understand what I am trying to say and how much our personal relationship has contributed to this very important highlight in my career."

"Highlight" it certainly was, and a very richly deserved honour. Only those with a fairly intimate knowledge of the inner workings of the City of London in general, and of its close-knit core of top financial institutions in particular, can fully appreciate the achievement of an "outsider", and a foreign outsider at that, in breaking into the magic "inner circle". Bigland had been – with Gordon's very considerable help – the first "employee" to make that breakthrough a few years earlier, but that had been merely to the Board of a relatively "young" institution, the Guardian. For Gordon to make it to the main Board after the added snootiness of the even older-established Royal Exchange had put several extra hurdles into his path, was a magnificent, almost incredible, achievement.

Looking back nearly two decades later, Gordon recalls: "One of my proudest moments was in October 1971, when I was invited to join the main London Board of GRE, as the first 'foreigner' ever to be accorded that honour, and certainly the first South African ever to be elevated to the Board of a major British composite insurer, and perhaps the only one to this day. I had, and still have, a very high regard and emotional involvement with GRE, and all its historic connotations, and for my colleagues on its Board. The respect was an attitude almost of awe, which always permeated my very being the moment I entered the portals of the historic Royal Exchange building. I always found it easier to operate in my own office, in an atmosphere and environment with which I was more familiar and comfortable. The GRE Boardroom, even after many years of familiarity, always intimidated me.

"Only Prince Wittgenstein, a West German industrialist and erstwhile Chairman of GRE's successful German subsidiary, Albingia, was also accorded the honour of being a non-British director, when he joined the GRE Board in 1974, a few years after me. We served side by side, both literally and figuratively, until he retired at the mandatory age of seventy in 1987. My appointment being senior in time to his, his Board seat was always immediately to the right of mine. As the men seated to our left retired one by one, the Prince and I made our slow progress clockwise round the famous oval GRE Boardroom table.

"We, the two foreigners on the Board, became firm friends, and with Bigland we formed a triumvirate which often discussed our concerns and aspirations about the future of GRE, and indeed the world, over many a quiet and enjoyable West End dinner."

On 22 September 1971, Guardian Holdings issued a press statement in Johannesburg. "The Board of directors of Guardian Royal Exchange Assurance Limited has announced in London that, with effect from 1 October 1971, Mr Donald Gordon of Johannesburg will be joining the main London Board as a non-executive director.

"Mr Gordon is currently the managing director of Guardian Assurance Holdings (South Africa) Limited and Liberty Life Association of Africa Limited and the new appointment will not affect his executive responsibilities in relationship to the aforementioned companies.

"The Guardian Royal Exchange Assurance Limited is a major international insurance group with assets in excess of £1 000 million and at 31 December 1970, controlled a net premium income of over £250 million per annum.

"Guardian Royal Exchange Assurance Limited was formed as a result of the merger in 1968 of the Guardian Assurance Company Limited and the Royal Exchange Assurance, and the Guardian Royal Exchange Group now operates in 35 countries through over 40 principal insurance subsidiaries and has been continuously engaged in the insurance field for over 250 years since the Royal Exchange Assurance was first incorporated by Royal Charter on 24 June 1720.

"Mr Gordon has been associated with the Group since 1964, when the Guardian Assurance Company Limited acquired a 76 per cent controlling interest in Liberty Life Association of Africa Limited, which he founded in 1958."

The final courtesy in this saga was paid by the Liberty Life Board at its meeting on 18 November. The minute reads: "Appointment of Mr D Gordon to the Board of Guardian Royal Exchange Assurance Company Limited. The Board congratulated Mr Gordon on his appointment to the Board of Guardian Royal Exchange Assurance Company Limited."

Despite all the many trials and tribulations that would follow, the biggest of which would be the very severe strain on personal relationships occasioned by Gordon's (and Rapp's) uncompromising approach to the 1978 buy-back of control of Liberty Life, Gordon remains a highly respected member of the Board of directors of the Guardian Royal Exchange Assurance Limited, of London. Now in 1989, after eighteen years of Board service, he is one of the most senior and undoubtedly the most widely experienced insurance man of the non-executive directors.

We have already mentioned the rather nice tradition regarding seating at GRE's oval Boardroom table. A new director is seated furthest from the Chairman, anti-clockwise around the table, and on a death or retirement everyone moves up one place. DG now sits two places to the right of the new Chairman, Charles Hambro, who took office in May 1988, and immediately next to the deputy chairman, Julian Sheffield. It is a wonderful vantage position facing the executive directors and one from which all the Board members and the secretariat are clearly visible.

For all his present eminence, however, Donald Gordon remains a modest man, and he still has a vivid recollection of his very first GRE Board meeting, way back in 1971.

"I didn't say a word; I was totally overawed by the whole event. The GRE Boardroom, with its magnificent panelling, its ten-foot high grandfather's clock, the enormous oval table and the overall ambience were enough totally to overwhelm an unsophisticated lad from Johannesburg, Transvaal. The Chairman, then Colonel Kit Dawnay, went through the Board papers like a meteor, and I soon found myself battling to keep up – ten pages behind! It was many, many months before I dared open my mouth and then it was only when I was asked to speak.

"At the end of the meeting, all the directors stood up and gathered in small groups in the four corners of the Boardroom, and I quickly realised that this was where all the major decisions of the company were actually made. As nobody included me in their group I rather sheepishly drifted out into the anteroom where pre-lunch drinks were to be served. The guests of the day had already arrived; I think they were from Allied Breweries, a major client of GRE.

"I called over a man standing at one end of the room whom I took to be the major-domo and asked him to pour drinks for the guests. He obligingly, and very efficiently, did so, as the rest of the directors drifted in. At the lunch, as it was my first Board meeting, I was given the place of honour on the right of the Chairman. Halfway through the meal, and feeling very much more relaxed, I was glancing round the table when I suddenly saw the man who had poured the drinks sitting at the end of the table. To my consternation, on enquiring of the Chairman as to the man's identity, I was told he was the Earl of Inchcape, a director of GRE who, having missed the Board meeting, had nevertheless come in for lunch. I mumbled embarrassedly to the Chairman that I had met him earlier in the day.

"And so ended my first GRE Board meeting, and I am sure that Kenneth Inchcape never forgot his first meeting with that brash young man from Johannesburg; but he was always polite and friendly, as only a true British aristocrat can be in such circumstances."

# 10 Mutual Mergers

While Liberty Life had succeeded, albeit not without some difficulty, in reversing the unsatisfactory new business trend of 1968 and 1969, and while the new property bonds would greatly help to stabilise the situation, Donald Gordon's fertile mind was constantly seeking new angles. One such was provided by a South African government commission of inquiry report published in March 1971. After having had the "very voluminous" report "digested and summarised" DG wrote a lengthy, prescient and very far-reaching memorandum which, over the next three years, was totally to transform Liberty Life. He sent it, with a covering letter, to Ernest Bigland on 23 June 1971. It was, if ever the description was justified, a truly seminal document.

"Memorandum on the Rationalisation of the South African Life Assurance Industry.

"1. Introduction

"The Third Report of the Franzsen Commission of Inquiry into fiscal and monetary policy in South Africa was published in March 1971 and insofar as it affected the life assurance industry, highlighted certain problems which pointed strongly towards the desirability of rationalising certain aspects of that industry.

"It is common cause that South Africa is served by more insurance companies relative to its potential insurance market than any other country in the world and it is the writer's view that the total available business is insufficient to economically sustain the number of companies operating in the Republic. This undesirable situation has now reached the point where, in order to survive, certain companies are resorting to practices which are not only undesirable but, in the end result, could do considerable harm to the industry and ultimately the public interest.

"There are innumerable companies, including many of the well-established organisations, which for some years have shown little progress and certainly are producing minimal profits out of all proportion to the size, effort and scope of their operations. This is particularly so in relation to certain overseas companies who are suffering from the added disadvantage brought about by decentralised management inasmuch as they are attempting to cope with excessive competition without having complete South African autonomy. Many of these organisations are now faced with the Franzsen Commission recommendations of compulsory domestication and ultimately the spreading of their shares.

"It occurs to the writer that the merger of certain of these interests, which would facilitate autonomy and effect important economies, could establish a larger unit which would be far more viable than its integral parts.

"2. Motivation for Merger

"The factors which would motivate a merger, particularly of the overseas companies operating in South Africa, may be summarised as follows:

"(a) The government's declared policy both to domesticate foreign companies and to increase South African participation, as is clearly evidenced by the Franzsen Commission's Third Report, has been more clearly indicated by innumerable pronouncements of senior government ministers and officials.

"(b) The South African public, being a relatively small economic community, is very susceptible to size and success in its support of financial institutions and in this particular aspect, the largest companies – ie the Cape based SA Mutual and Sanlam – have an undue advantage.

"(c) In an atmosphere of severe competition, a company operating with its effective management control abroad is at a severe disadvantage as compared with those companies operating under local control.

"(d) South Africa suffers from a chronic shortage of trained manpower particularly in the highly technical area of insurance and the plethora of medium sized companies results in a wastage of available human resources, which in any event are insufficient to meet requirements. Hence, efficiency in the life insurance industry in South Africa is dropping at an alarming rate, fundamentally on account of staff instability and lack of motivation.

"(e) The large number of medium sized units militates strongly against many of them really becoming viable units in terms of their return to shareholders (or their head offices as the case may be) and reduces their ability to produce meaningful bonus rates which are vital in the excessively competitive conditions.

"(f) Should the recommendations of the Franzsen Commission be implemented, the aforementioned factors will be aggravated by domestication of foreign interests which will require the local operation to be backed by substantial capital resources on which only a minimal return can be expected.

"(g) Should it be possible to create a really large insurance grouping in the Transvaal this could result in the epicentre of the insurance industry being transferred to Johannesburg, which is the logical geographical location inasmuch as the bulk of the South African market is situated in or around the Witwatersrand.

"(h) In view of the rapidly increasing complexity of the South African market, the utilisation of sophisticated computer installations is becoming essential. This would create an unduly heavy burden on the medium sized companies which could be greatly alleviated by the combined use of one system and a single large computer installation by a number of medium sized operations.

"3. Advantages of Merger

"As an alternative to the process of individual companies domesticating by the creation of separate South African registered companies, it would appear desirable for a number of these companies to consider the merging of their interests in one major operation. This would be a gradual process but if the trend could be initiated by two or three of the larger medium sized operations, particularly where their method of operation was complementary to one another, very considerable advantages could result.

"(a) The creation of a unit of proportions large enough to compete with the large Cape mutuals could well diminish the significance of the Cape as the insurance centre of South Africa.

"(b) A more rational concentration of manpower and the utilisation in key posts of the most efficient of the personnel available as a result of the merger.

"(c) The conversion of a number of non-viable operations into one highly flexible and economic unit.

"(d) Concentration of investment power in terms of more efficient investment management and opportunity.

"(e) Specialisation and improvement in efficiency and the gradual elimination of non-productive endeavour in areas currently uneconomic on account of duplication.

"(f) Increase in aggregate reinsurance limits and development of viable sub-standard facilities resulting in improvement in general service to combat the Franzsen criticism of inadequate capacity of the South African market.

"(g) Considerable expense savings, particularly in the following areas:

- (i) investment department;
- (ii) branch operations;
- (iii) computer;
- (iv) executive management and secretarial services;
- (v) staff arrangements and amenities;
- (vi) administration;
- (vii) actuarial department;
- (viii) new business processing.

"(h) The aggregate benefits of market penetration would be considerably more effective on the marginal cost principle.

"(i) Substantial psychological boost stemming from market leadership and pure size.

"(j) Improvement in staff recruiting possibilities.

"(k) Access to combined expertise of a number of leading international companies.

"(l) The merger of a number of overseas interests would probably meet the Franzsen Commission's objectives as it would reduce the number of international companies operating in this market and would have the beneficial result of achieving the spreading of shares and to this extent the adverse implications of foreign control discussed in the Franzsen Report will be somewhat alleviated.

"(m) Based on the creation of a really viable unit, quotation of the shares on international stock exchanges would create interesting possibilities.

"(n) Access to a more strongly constituted South African Board in so far as currently the best available people are spread very thinly over the number of companies operating in South Africa.

"(o) Each of the companies which would be suitable for participation in the proposed merger produce business in different ways; some relying on agency forces while others are more broker-orientated. A merger of these companies could well result in our achieving optimum market penetration from both direct and indirect selling methods.

"4. Mechanics of Merger

"It is considered that Guardian Holdings/Liberty Life Group could be ideally suited to act as the vehicle for any proposed merger which could come about for the following reasons:

"(a) Liberty Life in particular over the past decade has proved itself to be the most dynamic and successful of the foreign controlled companies operating in South Africa and is still making substantial progress in terms of the rapid expansion and profit growth of this relatively young organisation, in spite of the competitive background.

"(b) Liberty Life has been the major innovator in the South African market over the past decade and has acquired a public image of progressive dynamism tempered by the accepted conservative background of its London holding company.

"(c) Both Liberty Life and Guardian Holdings are already established public companies with an excellent stock market image and a very substantial spread of shareholders. Guardian Holdings in fact has the largest number of shareholders of any South African company (over 30 000)

"(d) Guardian Holdings has made substantial inroads into related financial operations which are now considered to be essential adjuncts to the development of life assurance (which is but one aspect of the savings industry). This follows the world-wide trend which has been particularly marked in South Africa. The Guardian Group diversifications in question have involved the creation of a well-established issue house operation (Guardian Liberty Investment Corporation Limited), a mutual fund in partnership with Barclays Bank DCO (Guardbank Management Corporation Limited, managers of Guardian Bankers Growth Fund), and the development of an important property development organisation (Guardian Real Estate Corporation).

"(e) Guardian Holdings is well situated in so far as it has a large and well-established short-term insurance business which is regarded as an essential aspect in creating an overall insurance-savings service.

"5. The Position of Foreign Mutual Companies

"In the Franzsen Commission recommendations, it is contemplated that branch offices of foreign mutual companies should be incorporated and domesticated. It is the writer's opinion that foreign mutual companies would not necessarily be precluded from participation in the overall plan of rationalisation in so far as it is contemplated that their policyholders' interests would be far better served on the basis of economies effected by the proposed merger in terms of their accepting (say) a 90 per cent participation in profits rather than a 100 per cent participation in profits implied by being a mutual company. It is the writer's view that a very strong case could be made out for this concept in view of local circumstances.

"6. Conclusion

"It will be clear from the aforegoing that a very powerful case could be made for a rationalisation of the South African life assurance industry, particularly in terms of merging certain of the medium sized units into a much larger and more viable operation.

"The writer believes that the interests of all, including the economic aspirations of the Republic, policyholders and shareholders, would be greatly enhanced by a well-ordered rationalisation of the life assurance industry along the aforegoing lines."

Anybody in the insurance industry could have seen the potential implications of the Franzsen Report, particularly in so far as the foreign controlled mutual companies were concerned. Perhaps some others did, but it is a tribute to Donald Gordon's outstanding entrepreneurial acumen that it was he, and he alone, who actually took action. Others did emulate Liberty Life's example in this strategy, but only many years later, when the best prospects had already long since disappeared, mostly into Liberty Life.

Within three years, the South African operations of two of the most important of those foreign controlled companies – Manufacturers Life of Canada and Sun Life of Canada – had been swallowed by Liberty Life. And within seven years, Liberty Life itself was to be "domesticated" – an event clearly foreshadowed in the memorandum recorded above. And finally, in 1986, the most desirable of all, the Prudential Assurance Company of South Africa, the listed subsidiary of the Prudential of London, was also absorbed into Liberty Life.

Bigland's initial response to Gordon's far-seeing paper on the possibility of merging with foreign controlled mutual insurers was, characteristically, less than enthusiastic. His normal response to anything new was a bucket or two of cold water, and this knee-jerk reaction was reinforced by his inordinate concern for the magic number "75". Control, to Bigland, had to be 75 per cent, and if equity were to be issued in any upcoming merger, GRE's holding in Guardian Assurance Holdings could possibly fall below this figure.

His first response was a brief telex on 29 June. "Yours 23 June received. Memo read with interest and will write with any comments."

Uncharacteristically, he did not in fact do so, and all the discussions took place over the phone and during two visits by Gordon to London, in July and October 1971. It was a particularly busy time in the affairs of both men and other matters were taking priority.

The issue of Gordon's appointment to the Guardian Royal Exchange Board was generating a good deal of heat and taking up a lot of correspondence time. Another important matter was the Liberty Life convertible preference share rights issue that Gordon was pressing for; it took a considerable amount of time, and much of Gordon's patience, to overcome Bigland's objections – most of which again concerned percentage control.

A note prepared by GRE's investment department and dated 29 June illustrates this concern. Headed "Liberty Life", it reads:

"Guardian Assurance Holdings (GAH) currently owns 76,3 per cent of Liberty Life: a 1 for 1 rights issue reduces this to 68,7 per cent, while a 3 for 5 rights issue reduces this to 71,3 per cent. Since GAH does not have the money to take up its entitlement the percentage ownership of LL will fall as shown.

"GRE owns 83 per cent of GAH and thus indirectly 62,75 per cent of LL. If none of the rights were exercised this would fall to 57,0 per cent with a 1 for 1 issue, or 59,2 per cent with a 3 for 5 issue."

(A three for five rights offer of 3 369 600 7 per cent convertible redeemable cumulative preference shares of R1 each at par was eventually announced in a circular to shareholders dated 30 July 1971.)

Another contemporaneous matter was a mooted takeover by Liberty Life of Hill Samuel Group (South Africa), concerning which Gordon had prepared a detailed seven-page memorandum in June. He was not overly keen on this one, and so was quite relieved when it fell through, with a frosty, if amusing, exchange of notes, in August.

Sir Kenneth Keith, Chairman of Hill Samuel, UK, to Ernest Bigland, dated 9 August 1971: "Many thanks for your letter of 21 July, which I found awaiting me on my return from the United States. The terms as set out in the memorandum attached to your letter of 6 July had some attraction for us, but I regret to say that the revised terms, as amended in your letter of 21 July, have none. I suggest we forget it."

Bigland's reply, dated 12 August: "Thank you for your letter of 9 August and I apologise again for the error in my memorandum setting out the proposed terms. Obviously in the figures quoted there is an area for negotiation, but I felt the memorandum reasonably set out the present relationship from the figures available. I note you think we should drop the whole matter and I will file the papers. I hope that if at a later date there seems some benefit in our having further talks you will be agreeable to doing so."

Neither letter actually spelt out what had gone wrong. It was simply that Bigland had made a monumental error in his memorandum of 6 July. He offered five GAH shares for every three Hill Samuel SA, when he was supposed to have offered only three GAH for every five Hill Samuel. Small wonder that the "revised terms" had no attraction for Sir Kenneth!

Gordon had his own way over the first two issues, and was content with the upshot of the third. And, at the same time, he battled, in intense and sometimes heated discussions and correspondence with Bigland and Peter Greenfield, to convince them of the logic of a deal with Manufacturers Life. It appeared on the agenda for his London visit in July as Item 6 – "L & G and Manufacturers Life", L & G being Legal & General, whose South African operations were regarded as another interesting potential takeover target at the time.

Bigland's customary written confirmation of matters discussed seems to indicate that he was still far from sold on the issue. However, against Item 6, on 11 August 1971, he wrote: "We discussed the progress of our talks with other life companies in the light of the Franzsen Report. We still both consider that the company here [meaning Legal & General] is the most suitable and are confident this will develop satisfactorily. In the meantime I see no objection to your continuing your talks with your Canadian friends."

He was still less than lukewarm when, on 15 September, he finally got around to commenting on Gordon's June memorandum. "I have not written to you in reply to your letter of 23 June with which you enclosed a memorandum which you had written about the South African life insurance industry. We had, however, a chance of talking about it on your last visit and I said that basically I agreed with all you said. My only comment was that I would have suggested some slight change of emphasis in parts of the document. However, as I understood you had already issued it I think probably it should stand as originally written unless you particularly want me to make any comments. I imagine that if the matter comes up again you may write a second memorandum, in which case we could consider any changes at that time."

This somewhat condescending approach was soon overtaken by events as Gordon, fed up with all the procrastination from London, moved ahead on his own. On 21 September he wrote to Bigland: "You will recall the other day that I mentioned to you I had received a very positive reaction from The Manufacturers Life Insurance Company of Canada in regard to our rationalisation proposals. I have had some very preliminary discussions with their chief executive in South Africa and also their executive vice president, Mr E S (Sid) Jackson, who has telephoned me from Canada.

"In order to keep you completely informed as to the magnitude of the proposition, I have pleasure in sending you herewith a copy of the annual return of The Manufacturers Life to the Registrar of Insurance of the Republic of South Africa under the Insurance Act of 1943. You will notice that the return gives a fairly full breakdown of their affairs in South Africa and I am sure you will agree that this particular concern would mesh into our operations admirably. Perhaps it would be beneficial for one of your senior actuaries to examine the figures in some depth as it will obviously be necessary for us to determine a value in terms of Liberty Life shares at some point in the future. I must say, to my knowledge, the quality of The Manufacturers Life business in South Africa is probably only second to the quality of our own at Liberty Life. There is also the added advantage that they operate mainly through a direct agency force in contradistinction to our method of operation being mainly through the brokers.

"I very much look forward to any comments or advice you might have. Should this matter develop further, it is our preliminary proposal to meet with the Manufacturers Life people in London – possibly the first week in November, which obviously will enable us to take the matter as far as practicable at this stage."

Bigland now began to take the Manufacturers Life matter seriously, but not unduly so, as his letter of 24 September 1971 indicates: "Thank you for your letter of 21 September letting me have some figures for the Manufacturers Life. These are really only their published figures which, whilst useful, merely confirm the size and spread of their operations. I think what we are really mainly concerned with is the price we would have to pay if we did a deal.

"If you could give me some idea of what you have in mind or anything that may have been mentioned this would be helpful. I am perfectly prepared to meet them in London later in the year, say, November, but I always believe, as you know, in narrowing the field of negotiation so that we are very clear on both sides whether we are likely to come close enough together to do a deal or not before we meet."

Gordon immediately pressed for action and after a lengthy telephone conversation with Bigland it was agreed that Gordon would visit London in October, with "Manufacturers Life Insurance" as Item 2 on his agenda.

He confirmed this on 1 October 1971: "Thank you for your letter of 24 September acknowledging the figures I sent you concerning the Manufacturers Life. I also refer to our telephonic conversation of yesterday where we decided to try and co-ordinate my visit to London to fit in with the Board meeting on 20 October.

"I have consequently made arrangements to arrive in London on Tuesday morning, 19 October, returning to Johannesburg on the evening of Tuesday 26 October. This will give me the opportunity of dealing with the Manufacturers Life matter, attending my first Board meeting [of Guardian Royal Exchange] and of sorting out a few of the outstanding matters between us.

"I have been in telephonic communication with Sid Jackson, of the Manufacturers Life, who will be in London during the week beginning 18 October. This will give us the opportunity of carrying through our preliminary discussions. In my communications with Jackson, I have indicated our preliminary thoughts that the acquisition of the Manufacturers Life South African portfolio, based on the information we have available, would be something of the order of 1 million Liberty Life shares. My personal feeling, without having analysed the figures in depth, is that to acquire this particular portfolio at anything up to 2 million shares would give our Liberty Life business a tremendous boost in this market. I think Jackson certainly has a clear view of our thinking and, clearly, the matter can only be resolved by across the table negotiations. In my last talk with him he did comment that, although we had suggested the proposition by way of a 'merger', it did look very clearly as if we really had a take-over in view. In point of fact, I suppose this would really be the effect of the exercise.

"It is probably very difficult at a distance of 10 000 miles to narrow this particular matter any further, but I certainly feel that the prospect of adding this plum to our business would be well worth the special effort involved."

Various tactical manoeuvres then took place, with telexes and telephone calls flying between London, Toronto and Johannesburg as meetings were arranged, and re-arranged. Bigland set the scene in a letter dated 7 October: "We had a telephone call from Mr Gale of Manufacturers Life yesterday suggesting a meeting on Sunday 24 October but I intend to ring back to say I have no intention whatever of dealing with this matter on a Sunday afternoon.

"I well remember our discussions at the Bath Club when you first came here but I think the present position is quite different. I am sure it would be far better for us to have an opening meeting with probably Mr Greenfield and myself when we go over the principles of the transaction to find out that we are in general basic agreement. I think we could then break up into more or less a committee in which you could deal with the details. I think Mr Greenfield would like to be very much involved in these. This could take place on 21 or 22 October. We could then, I trust, meet again possibly for an hour in the following week to see whether the principles and the details have been reconciled.

"A little stage-managing in this particular case is important. I am sure you will be agreeable to my taking the Chair at the first meeting which we can have in one of our Committee Rooms to establish the right atmosphere. You can then carry on from there, coming back again to a more or less formal meeting early in the following week.

"I note your suggestion about the number of shares we may have to give. You know my view that I would not be prepared to drop our holding in Liberty Life below 50 per cent and I think we agreed that it might be necessary to give them mainly Liberty Life but possibly some GAH shares or, if they wished, some other kind of deal – preference shares, or debentures, or even some cash.

"I am glad Mr Jackson has raised at an early stage the question of a merger or take-over, as quite clearly we intend this to be a take-over. I think we can probably in our talks use the words 'amalgamate our two businesses'. I really do not see how we can have a merger when we will very obviously be the predominant partner and will be running the business in the future."

The carefully stage-managed talks with the Canadians were tough, but fruitful. It would take another five months to get all the complex issues finalised, and there were a number of slips along the way. Gordon would return to London for tense talks in January, but the issues were finally settled when the Canadians flew into Johannesburg in March 1972. It is interesting to note that the final price in Liberty Life shares was 1 267 000 ordinaries, showing that Gordon's early "feel" for the right price was pretty close. However, after months of tough negotiations, he did achieve a result closer to the lower end of the parameters he had contemplated for the Manufacturers Life deal.

Looking back at the deal in an interview many years later, Gordon tended to simplify the issues. Asked if the takeovers of Manufacturers Life and Sun Life were not "fortuitous to a degree in that, because of the Franzsen Report, these companies felt they had to get out of South Africa", he responded: "No. In both cases we made the first moves. We had developed a strategy, probably around 1969, that in order to gain size, and as there were so many companies just plodding along and not making any major impact, it would make sense to rationalise the industry and eliminate some of these middle size companies and make one substantial proprietary company." It was this strategy that he had set out so forcibly in his June 1971 memorandum to Bigland.

Gordon continued: "I think it was the concept which we put to them which appealed, and I think it worked very strongly in their favour. There is no other way they could have achieved the results they did.

"When we came into the life insurance industry, Sun Life and Manufacturers Life were standing very high in the market. With the changes we made in the whole market philosophy and in product design, they were finding the going very tough. They were both losing ground hand over fist, although basically very strong companies.

"When the opportunity came for us to speak to Manufacturers Life, we made a very powerful case as to why they should sell to us. But I don't think they had any illusions about the fact that they couldn't really get on, and our approach obviously offered an excellent solution to their problems."

Back to 1972, when the issue emerged in Liberty Life's minutes for the first time at the Board meeting on 16 March as "Proposed merger with the Manufacturers Life Company of Toronto, Canada."

"Mr Gordon informed the meeting that discussions had taken place with a view to merging the South African life insurance operations of Manufacturers Life with those of Liberty Life. Mr Gordon proceeded and outlined the benefits that such a merger would produce for both shareholders and policyholders of the company.

"It was agreed that Mr Gordon be authorised to proceed with this matter and to keep the Board informed of future developments."

Future developments came swiftly indeed, and a Board meeting on 27 March 1972, to which Peter Greenfield had flown post-haste from London, minuted: "Merger with Manufacturers Life Insurance Company of Toronto, Canada. Mr Gordon tabled the proposed Heads of Agreement to be entered into between the company, Guardian Assurance Holdings South Africa Limited and Manufacturers Life (a copy of which was tabled and initialled by the Chairman for purposes of identification) which set forth the terms and conditions relating to the merger of the life business in South Africa of Manufacturers Life with the life business of Liberty Life. The proposed agreement would be subject to the necessary formalities being completed and the various approvals being obtained from the South African and Canadian authorities, the South African Supreme Court and the shareholders of Liberty Life in Extraordinary General Meeting approving this transaction and increasing the authorised share capital of the company.

"In consideration of the acquisition by the company of the business, personnel, agency connections and goodwill as well as the South African assets and liabilities of Manufacturers Life with effect from 1 January 1972, 1 000 000 new ordinary shares of R1 each and 2 000 000 7 per cent convertible redeemable cumulative preference shares of R1 each [equivalent on conversion to 400 000 Liberty Life ordinary shares] will be allotted to Manufacturers Life which will rank *pari passu* with the existing classes of shares in issue save that they would not participate in any dividend declared in respect of the financial year ended 31 December 1971.

"After discussion, the Heads of Agreement were approved and confirmed and Mr Donald Gordon, the managing director of the company, was authorised to sign the Heads of Agreement on behalf of the company and further empowered to do all such things and execute any documents necessary to give effect to this Agreement.

"After discussion, it was resolved that pending the finalisation of the above merger and in order to restrict speculation in the company's shares, which are quoted on the Johannesburg Stock Exchange, Mr Donald Gordon, the managing director of the company, be authorised on behalf of the Board to approach the president of the committee of the Johannesburg Stock Exchange to request a temporary suspension of the listing of the company's shares (both ordinary and preference) for Monday 27 and Tuesday 28 March 1972 and that he be authorised and empowered to sign any documents necessary to give effect thereto.

"It was noted that an announcement in regard to the aforementioned merger would be made to the Johannesburg Stock Exchange, shareholders and the press on Tuesday evening 28 March 1972."

At the next Board meeting, on 25 May 1972, it was recorded that: "Mr Gordon informed the meeting that the merger of the Manufacturers Life with the company was proceeding satisfactorily. There were still many problems of a technical nature to be overcome, many of which he expected to clear up in Canada during his proposed visit in July.

"It was necessary at a suitable time to convene an Extraordinary General Meeting to approve the Manufacturers Life merger and to increase the authorised share capital to R15 million – R9 million in ordinary shares of R1 each and R6 million in 7 per cent convertible redeemable cumulative preference shares of R1 each."

Finally, the Board was told on 17 August 1972 that the whole transaction had been finally consummated during that July visit to Toronto. "Mr Gordon informed the meeting that following his visit to Canada, the terms of the merger between the company and Manufacturers Life had been amended. Previously the company was to allot to Manufacturers Life 1 000 000 ordinary shares of R1 each and 2 000 000 7 per cent convertible redeemable cumulative preference shares of R1 each. In addition, a R2 000 000 fund was to be created for ten years for the purpose of guaranteeing that the Manufacturers Life's participating policyholder dividends would be maintained at not less than the current level, the guarantee fund, to the extent that it was not required for this purpose, being refundable to Manufacturers Life, together with interest at 7 per cent per annum.

"It has now been agreed that in lieu of the above arrangement, the company would allot to Manufacturers Life a total of 1 267 000 ordinary shares of R1 each and that whilst the aforementioned guarantee fund would still be created for the aforesaid purpose, it would no longer be refundable to Manufacturers Life.

"After discussion, the variation of the merger terms was approved and confirmed and Mr Gordon, or failing him Mr Roy, was authorised to sign the final agreement and any other related documents on behalf of the company.

"Mr Gordon then tabled a draft circular to shareholders setting out the revised terms and conditions of the proposed merger. Mr Gordon also tabled a notice convening an Extraordinary General Meeting of shareholders of the company to increase the authorised share capital to R12 000 000, divided into 8 000 000 ordinary shares of R1 each and 4 000 000 7 per cent convertible redeemable cumulative preference shares of R1 each."

The transaction was signed in Johannesburg by Donald Gordon for Liberty Life and by Sid Jackson for Manufacturers Life. Following this, Jackson was welcomed to the Board of Liberty Life.

The deal was greeted with acclaim by the press. The *Rand Daily Mail* of 29 March carried a banner headline: "Liberty's Major Coup"; the *Sunday Times*, 2 April: "Gordon's master-stroke – Liberty Leaps 4 Years into Future". The *Financial Mail*, on 30 March 1972, gave a thoughtful appreciation under the headline "Liberty's Leap Forward":

"In many respects, Liberty Life's take-over of the South African life assurance operations of the giant Canadian Manufacturers Life must be regarded as a major coup.

"In one fell swoop Donald Gordon has virtually doubled the size of his life operation, at a cost, in Liberty Life paper, of only R12 million; he has set yet another precedent on the SA assurance scene by being the first to 'cash in' on the Franzsen Commission's recommendations on foreign ownership; he has set new standards of takeover security for investors; and he has blazed a trail, in terms of the suspension of sharedealings in takeover situations, that others are bound to follow.

"Taking these points in turn:

"1. For 1 million Liberty Life ordinaries (940c pre-suspension) and 2 million convertible prefs (120c), a pre-announcement paper total of just under R12 million, Liberty Life gains Manufacturers Life's total assets in SA of over R50 million and its annual income (net premium and investment income) of about R10 million to add to its own R70 million assets and R25 million income.

"2. Franzsen's recommendation that "foreign mutual companies should also be required to operate under the same conditions (mainly concerning incorporation in SA) through local companies" makes life potentially difficult for them.

"In the tricky nine-month long negotiations that preceded this week's announcement I have no doubt that the thought that this Franzsen recommendation might be implemented played some part.

"From this it follows that other foreign owned mutual life concerns (they include, among the Top 20, Colonial Mutual, Sun Life of Canada and National Mutual) might also seek local bed-fellows (Liberty Life again?) in the months ahead.

"3. On security and suspension, this deal is in a class of its own. Early Monday morning, Gordon asked the JSE to suspend dealings in Liberty and its parent, Guardian, "pending the outcome of important merger negotiations".

"From then until the promised official statement, late on Tuesday, the favourite guessing game in Hollard Street and newspaper offices was "spot the victim" (favoured targets, who may or may not be flattered, included Barclays National Bank, Commercial Union, Hill Samuel and the National Growth Fund management company, National Fund Investments). So far as I know, Manufacturers Life was never mentioned.

"And the lead given by the request for suspension itself is of vital importance. On New York and in London, it's common, even normal, to have dealings suspended while takeover negotiations are being finalised; here, hitherto, "suspension" almost always meant trouble.

"It needed a major company like Liberty Life to blaze the trail. Now, I hope, thanks to the example that has been set this week, this type of suspension will become the norm here as well.

"If it does, then Gordon will have earned the gratitude of the general body of investors, quite apart from those in Liberty Life and Guardian.

"But how grateful should these latter two be? When dealings recommenced on Wednesday, Liberty Life shot from the pre-suspension 940c to 1 150c, and Guardian from 153c to 180c; so the market gave its clear endorsement.

"Even so, I've certain reservations.

"For Liberty Life, increasing its equity capital by 1 million shares to 6,6 million, or nearly doubling its life base at a cost, after conversion, of only about 16 per cent of its equity, the deal certainly looks good.

"But, of course, in life assurance, it's the quality of the business written that matters. Liberty Life, in existence only 10 years or so, enjoys high-quality, high-profit business; Manufacturers has been trading here since 1903; its "life book" must be far less profitable.

"That this must be so is acknowledged in the official statement: 'There should be no dilution of earnings attributable to Liberty Life's ordinary shareholders on account of the merger', although 'it should ultimately produce considerable benefits'.

"The full picture will only become clear when the detailed particulars are published 'in due course'. But this must mean that, initially, the profit contribution from Manufacturers Life is expected merely to service the shares issued for its acquisition.

"Most important, to my mind, is the potential change in Liberty Life's 'image'. Until now and, I think, deservedly, it has enjoyed an exceptional market rating; largely because of its fantastic growth and its low cost structure – and the latter has been, in large measure, because of the tight head office organisation and its broker orientation.

"The new 'Manufacturers/Liberty Life' will, it seems, inherit a lot of run-of-the-mill life business, although its general quality is high (until the life fund of the 'old' Manufacturers is closed, 'the products of both companies' will continue to be marketed, although, I understand, only for the next nine months or so) and the marketing approach will diversify as 'the existing career agent structure of Manufacturers Life' is added to 'the broker orientated promotional approach of Liberty Life'.

"So there may be a short-term penalty to pay (in terms of a change in the 'go-go' image) for those 'considerable benefits' that rationalisation of the two companies should bring. And, while 'image' perhaps shouldn't really be a factor in market price, I think it has long been so in the case of Liberty Life.

"Then there's the load to be carried by Donald Gordon himself. In the context of the South African – perhaps even the world – insurance industry, he's a genius; but he is only one man. He has built up a team in Guardian and Liberty Life which, he feels, gives the group the best 'management in depth' it has ever had, but (with the added pressures of this deal) a lot still devolves on him.

"With top policy-making responsibility for a merchant bank, a mutual fund, a property empire, a major short-term insurer and now two very different life assurers, the strain must be enormous.

"So whether the profits that will flow from Manufacturers Life will compensate Guardian/Liberty Life shareholders for having a yet more thinly spread top management remains to be seen."

Results quickly showed that none of the above fears were justified. Reporting to shareholders in April 1973 on the results for the year to 31 December 1972, the directors stated:

"The operating and surplus account reflects a substantially higher operating surplus which has enabled the company to continue its impressive record of consistently increasing rates of bonuses to participating policyholders whilst at the same time increasing its dividend distribution to ordinary shareholders.

"Augmented by the absorption of Manufacturers Life, the company's total income before taxation was R37 918 000, compared to R21 891 000 in 1971. The net premium income inclusive of single premiums increased to R25 893 000 from R16 048 000 in the previous year. Investment income, facilitated by the acquisition of the Manufacturers Life investment portfolio, rose to R8 514 000, an increase of 153 per cent."

And, under the heading "New Business":

"The merger with Manufacturers Life has not only provided Liberty Life with a greatly expanded asset base and increased investment strength but has also provided improved potential for market penetration.

"The gross annualised new business premium income (excluding considerations for annuities and single premiums) in respect of new policy contracts effected during the year under review increased by 68 per cent to a new record level of R5 376 000 compared with the previous record of R3 209 000 achieved in 1971. The contribution from the career agency force of Manufacturers Life to the aforementioned new business production was relatively small in view of the fact that the impact of Liberty Life's broader policy range was only felt in the closing months of 1972."

The following year, with the merger successfully consummated in a period of less than two years, the directors were able to report even more substantial growth. "Liberty Life's total income from life assurance operations before taxation was R50 567 000 in 1973, compared to R37 918 000 in 1972. The net premium income after reassurances inclusive of single premiums increased by 47 per cent from R25 983 000 in 1972 to R38 206 000 for the year under review. Investment income applicable to the Life Fund before taxation rose to R10 319 000, an increase of 21 per cent over the previous year.

And: "The gross annualised new business premium income ... increased by 53 per cent to a new record level of R8 241 000, compared with the previous record of R5 376 000 attained in 1972. Gross new sums assured in 1973 were over R460 000 000, compared to the previous record level of approximately R300 000 000 achieved in 1972."

One major point of interest arising from Liberty Life's takeover of the South African life operations of Manufacturers Life and, subsequently, those of Sun Life of Canada, was that the takeovers raised a novel principle. This was that a mutual company was being taken over by a proprietary company, something that, to the knowledge of all concerned, had never been done anywhere in the world before that time. That this aspect aroused no press comment is surprising, but perhaps not all that so, in view of the general lack of knowledge of the issues involved.

These were simple in concept, but complex of resolution. A proprietary life insurance company, of which Liberty Life is South Africa's prime example, has both policyholders and shareholders, and the latter, of course, are the owners of the business. In mutual life insurance companies, on the other hand, as were both Manufacturers Life and Sun Life, there are no shareholders and the policyholders, theoretically, are the owners of the company.

The word "theoretically" is used advisedly, for when the Canadian mutuals' operations were taken over by Liberty Life, their owners, the policyholders, received no cash compensation, such as shareholders in a similar position would have expected – although their rights as policyholders were fully and comprehensively protected. The answer to this seeming illogicality is that it was merely the South African branch assets of the two Canadian companies that were taken over, and that compensation was indeed paid, in the shape of Liberty Life shares, to the true owners – the Canadian parent companies – and thus indirectly to their owners, the world-wide policyholders of the two Canadian mutual life companies.

Another aspect – that perhaps some slight stigma might attach to "demutualisation" – was raised by Bigland during the course of the negotiations. In a telex to Gordon in October 1971, he said: "On consideration feel that onus to demutualise must be put firmly on other side. As a continuing and leading entity in life field we could not be involved in any actions to limit rights of policyholders. If other side anxious to consider withdrawal and prepared take necessary steps talks may be useful but must be that basis." Bigland's fears were clearly groundless, but the fact that he raised the issue indicates that even he, a top City of London insurance man (probably even the top man at that time) had no clear conception as to how the problem of linking the unlinkable – a mutual and a proprietary – might be solved.

But Gordon and his team had done their homework well. Early in 1972, when negotiations with Manufacturers Life were well advanced, they went to Pretoria to see the Registrar of Insurance, Wynand Louw. Louw had taken over the post in March 1970 from his predecessor, Rudolph de Villiers, who had been so helpful to Gordon in Liberty Life's fledgeling days.

Louw recalls: "Mr Gordon – Donny – came into my office and simply said, 'Look, I want to take over one of the Canadian mutual life insurance companies in South Africa.' There were two at the time, Manufacturers Life and Sun Life of Canada. And he just came out with this quite unheard of thing: 'We want to take over one of those mutuals, Manufacturers Life.' It really was most unusual because in the minds of everybody at that time it was just an unheard of suggestion for an equity company to take over a mutual company: the two were like chalk and cheese – they just don't mix. Basically, it just seemed impossible.

"But we listened to him, and he and his people had it all worked out. In the end, it all came down to protecting the policyholders, especially the participating policyholders, to making absolutely certain that they would not – indeed could not, because solid safeguards had to be built in – be even a tiny bit worse off over the years. Well, we listened, and eventually I said to him: 'Well, maybe it will work, but there will be some very difficult hurdles to cross, and the most difficult one will come at the very end – the Supreme Court.'"

In the event, all worked out well so far as the South African authorities were concerned. It was the Canadian Superintendent of

Insurance who proved the more difficult to convince, and his consents were the last to be granted.

By the end of 1973, the welding of the agency field force of Manufacturers Life onto the broker base of Liberty Life was a *fait accompli*, a remarkable achievement in less than eighteen months. And things were going quite well on the administrative side, although there were problems, which would continue for several years, occasioned mainly by the fact that the South African operations had indeed been treated as "branch" operations – all policy records were held in Toronto!

Donald Gordon was now ready for his next move. Sun Life of Canada, an even bigger fish than Manufacturers Life had been, and in many ways a more important one in terms of prestige, was the next target. The Liberty Life team had been working on this one for some months, although there is, surprisingly, no mention of it in the London correspondence (perhaps because, during this period, Bigland was pressing Gordon to take over GRE'S "small" life operation in Rhodesia. Gordon steadfastly refused to do this – pleading, among other things, that his senior staff was fully stretched, even over-stretched, with absorbing Manufacturers Life). However, "Sun Life of Canada" did appear on the agenda for Gordon's London trip on 27 May 1973, and "SL" on the agenda for Bigland's visit to Johannesburg in November. The Board minutes for 16 January 1974 record: "Sun Life Assurance Company of Canada. Mr Gordon reported on the visit he had made to London on 12 and 13 December 1973 to discuss a possible merger between Liberty Life Association of Africa Limited and the South African operations of the Sun Life Assurance Company of Canada.

"Mr Gordon stated that certain understandings had been reached and that it was desirable that disclosures be made at the earliest time to the shareholders of Guardian Assurance Holdings (South Africa) Limited and the company informing them that negotiations between the companies are taking place."

An announcement of the negotiations was duly made the next day, 17 January, and was received with acclamation by the press.

Clearly, Gordon had made very considerable progress indeed in his London December talks with Tom Galt, the president of Sun Life of Canada. In a letter dated 2 January 1974, Galt wrote: "We have been getting ahead with the preliminary steps. Our executive officers are in agreement. The executive committee of the Board gave its approval last month and the full Board will consider the matter on 8 January. The Superintendent of Insurance gave his approval verbally and we have applied formally to the Minister of Finance and hope to have his approval soon. We have made arrangements for some of the valuations and calculations to be done by a leading firm of actuarial consultants in the United States who have had experience with mergers.

"Our general manager for South Africa, Peter Mathewson, will be here for the week commencing 7 January. At that time we will be able to have detailed discussions with him as to the best way to handle an announcement in South Africa that we are holding discussions. I hope that I will have heard from you by mid-January that you have received the necessary preliminary approvals from your executives, boards of directors, and the Registrar. If that is the case, it is my present thinking that our vice-president, administration, Mr J T Bradbury, might return with Peter Mathewson to give him support in connection with the announcement. It may be that the staff will feel more insecure than the agency force initially, and Mr Bradbury and Mr Mathewson would no doubt hold discussions with you on how best to reassure them."

Bigland was on holiday, which from Gordon's viewpoint eased matters considerably! On 9 January, he wrote to Peter Greenfield, who was in charge at GRE. "I have just received a letter from Tom Galt, a copy of which I enclose for your information. I take it that you are perfectly happy to indicate the preliminary approval of our Board and major shareholders as is visualised in Tom Galt's letter. I am sure that on the terms discussed in London, there is no doubt that a special effort should be made to bring the proposals to fruition." A postscript added: "Since writing, I have spoken to Tom Galt on the telephone and he tells me that the proposals have passed their full Board and although Peter Mathewson was rather shocked initially, he has indicated his full acceptance of the situation and his co-operation to see it through to finality."

Unlike the Manufacturers Life deal, matters now moved fast, very fast. Gordon to Greenfield, 30 January: "I must say since last communicating with you, things here have been unbelievably hectic. I have had two Sun Life vice-presidents descend on me unexpectedly but this has enabled us to move things along somewhat faster than we had hoped. As you can imagine, the problems presented by Sun Life are entirely different from those of Manufacturers Life. First, we are dealing with a much larger staff complement and sales force – who are unbelievably pro-Sun Life – and in addition, the emotional and human problems presented by the very powerful Sun Life indoctrination have created considerable problems. Nonetheless, by dint of great effort and endless talking, we seem to be carrying the day. Even some of the most die-hard Sun Life people appear to be moving towards us. Nonetheless, this particular aspect has presented some unexpected difficulties. Taylor Bradbury, the vice-president administration of Sun Life, has facilitated the task and things have settled down to such a degree that he has now left for home. The early problems have been overcome to such a degree that the entire Sun Life sales force have now been allowed to sell Liberty Life products without any restriction.

"The technical aspects are moving ahead well and the vice-president, general counsel of Sun Life, Graham McCracken, has been with us since last Thursday. The whole attitude and business approach of these people differs so radically from that of Manufacturers Life that it is almost inconceivable that they both operate out of the same country.

"You will have gauged from the aforementioned that Sun Life are driving hard to complete this matter at the earliest possible time. With this in view, it is now proposed that Tom Galt and his team should be in South Africa soon after Easter to conclude the terms. It was initially envisaged that this should take place in the middle of May but I am sure you will go along with our desire to conclude as soon as possible. There are innumerable influences at work to try to upset the deal and the sooner it becomes unconditional, the better. The intentions are that Tom Galt will be here with a powerful support team and for this reason, I think it is important for you to be with us at the time."

Bigland, back from his holiday, and having approved the developments in a long telephone conversation, wrote on 4 February: "I can well understand that the Sun Life staff were not too pleased about the announcement, as apart from anything else they must see the possibility that the Manufacturers Life having already joined Liberty Life, their staff may well have been appointed to the best jobs. They can obviously see some difficulty and competition in the new merger which is now in hand. You must have done extremely well to have pacified them and already have them working partly in the Liberty Life Group."

Matters went smoothly, apart from certain problems with some agents, and on 13 March 1974 the Board minutes recorded: "Mr Gordon informed the Board of his discussions on the proposed merger between the company and Sun Life, and advised the Board of certain basic parameters which had been laid down as the basis for the merger. He continued that since his discussions with Sun Life in London certain vice presidents of Sun Life had visited South Africa for discussions, and that Mr Galt, the president of Sun Life would, together with certain senior executives, be visiting South Africa in April to finalise negotiations. Mr Greenfield had agreed to be in South Africa during the same period.

"Mr Hilkowitz informed the Board that attempts had been made by certain outside parties to entice the Sun Life agency field force away from Sun Life, but it seemed that these problems had been overcome and he was reasonably confident that the integration of the sales force would proceed satisfactorily. Mr Hilkowitz stated that Sun Life had permitted their agents to sell Liberty Life products, and at the date of the meeting about 60 per cent of the total Sun Life sales were Liberty Life products."

Monty Hilkowitz, whose name appeared in the Liberty Life Board minutes for the very first time on this occasion, was a somewhat brash young actuary recruited from the Swiss South Africa Reinsurance to Liberty Life just prior to the launch of the property bond series of policies in 1970. He was immediately thrust into this project which quickly acclimatised him into the workings of Liberty Life and its innovative marketing culture. Hilkowitz matured and developed rapidly, and soon asserted himself as the undisputed head of the promotional division with the title of general manager (promotions). He emerged rapidly as the most forceful and dominant of the general managers, and quickly assumed the role of senior general manager in 1978.

Following Gordon's reassumption of the chairmanship, Hilkowitz was appointed managing director of Liberty Life in March 1982, the first man other than Gordon himself to hold this position. At the same time, Mark Winterton and Stephen Handler, two long-standing stalwarts of the company, were also appointed executive directors. When Hilkowitz left Liberty Life to go to Australia in 1986, Winterton, who had been seconded by GRE to Liberty Life in 1970, immediately assumed the mantle of managing director, which title he now shares jointly with Dorian Wharton-Hood, who came into the

Liberty Life fold with the acquisition of the Prudential of South Africa in 1986.

Back in 1974, the meetings over the Easter period were some of the toughest that Gordon can recall. "They sent out an expert team, including the president, Tom Galt, and five vice-presidents, who between them were specialists in every conceivable area of life insurance; they really knew their stuff and we had to be on our toes to cope with them."

The six Sun Life heavyweights faced Gordon day after day across the Liberty Life Boardroom table, where he sat supported by his senior men, Hilkowitz, Winterton and Handler. Basically, however, Gordon conducted the whole negotiation alone, as he was the only one who fully understood all the aspects of life insurance which were relevant to the issues under discussion. The individual Sun Life men were far too specialised to appreciate all the implications, and it was on this basis that Gordon won the day in the end.

"One indication of the rigour of the bargaining was that the Sun Life people started out at a price of R37 million – which was ridiculously high, of course – and after a week of extremely tough negotiations, which all but broke down on at least three separate occasions, we eventually beat them down to R8,7 million." That achieved, a formal joint announcement was made on 16 May:

"The Boards of directors of Guardian Assurance Holdings South Africa Limited, Liberty Life Association of Africa Limited and Sun Life Assurance Company of Canada have pleasure in announcing that their negotiations for the merging of the South African life assurance operations of Sun Life with Liberty Life have been brought to a successful conclusion.

"As previously indicated, Liberty Life will be the vehicle for the proposed merger in view of its incorporation in the Republic of South Africa, its substantial shareholder participation (both through itself and through Guardian Assurance Holdings) and its quotation on the Johannesburg Stock Exchange. Guardian Assurance Holdings, the 67 per cent controlling company of Liberty Life – which is itself controlled by Guardian Royal Exchange Assurance Limited, London – will continue to control Liberty Life after the proposed merger is completed.

"Subject to certain adjustments of a technical nature, the net South African assets of Sun Life represented by the indebtedness of the Sun Life South African branch to its head office in Canada, is to be settled by the allotment by Liberty Life of approximately 8 million 7 per cent convertible redeemable cumulative preference shares of R1 each at par. These preference shares will rank *pari passu* with the existing convertible preference shares of Liberty Life already in issue, which may be converted into ordinary shares of Liberty Life on 1 July 1975, 1976 or 1977 at R10 per share. Sun Life will undertake to convert into ordinary shares not less than 50 per cent of such preference shares in due course (that would be 400 000 ordinary shares).

"In the negotiations, the Boards of both Liberty Life and Sun Life have fully affirmed their intention to safeguard the interests of Sun Life policyholders in South Africa and South West Africa and special arrangements have been made to entrench their interests."

Shareholders had been informed of the coming merger in March, when the Report and Accounts for the year to 31 December 1973 had been issued. The directors then noted that: "At 31 December 1973, Sun Life, which has operated in the Republic of South Africa since 1913, had South African assets exceeding R87 000 000 and an annual income of approximately R19 000 000, inclusive of R5 500 000 from investments."

Comparable figures for the combined Liberty Life/Manufacturers Life at 31 December 1973 were total assets of over R207 000 000 (which included the Life Fund at R144 000 000), and an annual income of over R50 000 000, inclusive of R10 300 000 from investments.

Looking back to Liberty Life pre-Manufacturers, that is to 31 December 1971, the comparable figures were total assets of just under R60 000 000, and annual income of R21 700 000, inclusive of R3 300 000 from investments, but this comparison is rendered invalid by the fact that two years of Liberty Life's own dynamic growth are included in the 1973 figures. Even so, these two major acquisitions virtually tripled Liberty Life in size, in a period of only three years.

Final confirmation of the Sun Life deal was given by the Liberty Life Board on 24 June 1974. "Mr Gordon reported to the Board on his recent visit to Montreal in connection with the finalisation of the terms of the merger of the South African life assurance operations of the Sun Life Assurance Company of Canada with the company, and tabled the Agreement and Scheme of Amalgamation and Transfer between Sun Life Assurance Company of Canada and the company. After discussion it was resolved that the Agreement and the Scheme relating to the transfer to the company with effect from 1 January 1974 of the South African life assurance operations of the Sun Life Assurance Company of Canada be and are hereby approved and confirmed."

Those final Montreal talks, incidentally, were among the toughest of the whole difficult series of negotiations, and Gordon and his team were just about exhausted at their conclusion. Hilkowitz remembers that, despite this, "the guys were all having a bit of a party in Donny's suite. But Donny and Peter Dugdale [of GRE] were catching an early evening plane back to London, and wanted a bit of a rest. So they finished up lying on the bed together while the rest of us carried on partying around them. Fortunately, it was a double bed."

On the legal front, however, the Sun Life deal gave rise to high drama. Michael Katz, Liberty Life's Johannesburg solicitor, tells the story: "Liberty Life acquired the South African operations of Sun Life with effect from 1 January 1974, and the deal was subject to a whole string of conditions precedent, which had to be fulfilled by 31 December 1974; if they were not fulfilled by that date, the whole deal would lapse.

"So it was of fundamental importance that we got everything through by the end of December. It was really a very complex deal and had to be done in compliance with the South African legislation, primarily the Insurance Act of 1943, as well as the relevant Canadian Act. There were numerous South African authorities that had to approve the transaction – the Registrar of Insurance, the Minister of Finance, the Exchange Control authorities and, naturally, the Supreme Court of South Africa. So, too, the deal needed many approvals on the Canadian side. With all these consents and approvals to be obtained, time was pressing, and the time-table that we drew up to implement the transaction was very finely tuned. We had to advertise in South African and Canadian publications, with specific time periods laid down by law. With all the constraints, it transpired that the only day that our application to the Supreme Court could be made was 26 November 1974. That was a Tuesday, and it was the last week of the Term of the Court; so if the application did not succeed, the deal would be off.

"We had enough problems with the time-table as it was, but a major complication occurred when a group of twenty-six Sun Life agents, who described themselves in the court papers as 'The Sun

Life South African non-White Life Agents,' started making objections and claiming racial discrimination, among other things. First to the Registrar of Insurance and to the Minister of Finance in South Africa, and then to the Canadian Superintendent of Insurance and the Canadian Minister of Finance. In every case we persuaded the authorities that the agents' objections were invalid, and we got the go-ahead; but all the while time was pressing. [There are many, within Liberty Life, who felt sure that the dissident agents were encouraged, and indeed funded, by a rival life insurance company, but Katz will not be drawn on this.]

"We were then informed that the agents were opposing our application to Court; so not only was this going to be a very complex application, but now it was going to be opposed.

"The application opened on the morning of Tuesday 26 November. Our case was briefly put; it took barely two hours. Then the opponents' advocate started the attack. With all due respect to him, I must point out that a case which ought to have taken perhaps a day at the most to argue was drawn out until the Friday – the last day of Term. He kept arguing and reading books page by page instead of just handing them in.

"Well, eventually he came to an end, and at 3.40 on that Friday afternoon Judge Boshoff gave an order sanctioning the transaction. But then came further excitement. I was terrified that when we got Judgement, they would immediately lodge an appeal – and the effect of that would be as bad as losing, for an appeal could only be heard in the following year, and bang would go our conditions precedent. Fortunately, however, no lodge of appeal was ever served."

By March 1975, when the directors reported to the Seventeenth Annual General Meeting on the results for the year ended 31 December 1974, the full impact of the double merger was clearly apparent. Total assets of R335 000 000 (including the Life Fund at R260 000 000) were five-and-a-half times those of three years previously, and total income was R88 000 000, a better than fourfold advance. The directors noted: "The most momentous development during the year under review was the successful merging of the South African life assurance operations of Sun Life Assurance Company of Canada with Liberty Life. This merger, which followed within two years of the successful absorption of the South African operations of Manufacturers Life, has substantially increased the scale and scope of operations of Liberty Life. The acquisition of the Sun Life business will, in the next few years, result in substantial benefits for Liberty Life by reason of the expected economies of scale, increased market penetration and the augmented financial strength and resources of the company."

Despite all the courtroom histrionics, those cruel early jibes, which had emanated mostly from representatives of Manufacturers Life, Sun Life and Prudential SA, about "Liberty Life of Doornfontein" and "Liberty Life of Witbank" had rebounded with a vengeance, and now looked very silly indeed.

With the advent of Tom Galt to the Liberty Life Board, it was a remarkable fact that the Boardroom was now graced with the heads of five insurance companies, including three major international offices. They were Ernest Bigland, of Guardian Royal Exchange; Sid Jackson, Manufacturers Life of Canada; Tom Galt, Sun Life of Canada, and Hayton Watson, Guardian Assurance South Africa, as well as Donald Gordon himself. Additionally, the new Chairman of GRE, Tim Collins, was also on the Liberty Life Board; one can hardly conceive of a more prestigous group of Board members in any insurance company anywhere.

# 11 The Property Factor

For a company that would in two decades become one of the major property investors in the Western world, underscoring Donald Gordon and Michael Rapp's faith in bricks and mortar as the soundest of long-term investments, Liberty Life got off to a relatively slow start on the property front. This division of the investment portfolio only really took off after the advent of Michael Rapp into the Liberty Life camp.

The Sixth Annual Report, that for the year to 31 December 1963, records an investment portfolio totalling R1,7 million, of which the "property" content consisted solely of mortgage loans of R16 818, and these were internal loans concerning senior staff housing. The very first mention of property, in the investment sense, came in the Board minutes for 14 November 1963:

"Property Investment. Mr Shill notified the meeting that he had investigated a number of propositions in regard to the acquisition of suitable premises for the company. He reported that one proposition in Braamfontein, Johannesburg, had considerable merit and he was asked to proceed with further investigations and to report to the Board once he had completed these."

He did so, and a Board minute for 30 January 1964 reads: "Mr Shill reported on the progress he had made in the aforementioned matter, and after discussion the meeting approved his actions and authorised him to proceed with the purchase of a prime site, corner Wolmarans and Rissik Streets on the Braamfontein ridge, just below the Johannesburg Civic Centre, at a total consideration of R40 000, and the options and first rights of refusal he had negotiated in relation to the two adjacent sites."

Then, at the Board meeting on 23 March 1964, that first tentative investment was quadrupled, and Liberty Life's lasting involvement with property was really launched.

"Courtieston House (Pty) Limited. A letter from the Northern

Trust Company Limited dated 13 March 1964 was tabled, informing the company that the offer made to shareholders of Courtieston House on 28 February 1964 had been accepted by all the shareholders of the latter company." Courtieston House owned two further sites in the same block as the site originally acquired, and was used step by step to assemble the entire block, ultimately including the area then occupied by the Standard Bank. Courtieston House was also the first vehicle for holding property in Liberty Life's great drive into real estate world-wide over the next quarter of a century. It certainly whetted Gordon's appetite for this form of investment.

"It was resolved that the company acquire 35 000 shares of R2 each in Courtieston House (Pty) Limited for a consideration of approximately R147 500. As this acquisition would constitute 100 per cent of the shares of Courtieston House, the latter company will become a wholly owned subsidiary of Liberty Life." Not only was Liberty Life now truly into property, but it had also made the first of what would prove to be a very long string of acquisitions!

In the meantime, Guardian Assurance of London had entered the picture, taking control of Liberty Life in March 1964, and its Chairman, Lord Blackford, had joined the Liberty Life Board.

At the Board meeting on 2 February 1965: "A lengthy discussion then ensued on the advisability of developing the site as the future head office of the company. Lord Blackford, having made independent enquiries and having examined the site in great detail, was strongly of the view that it would constitute an ideal and prestige location for the head office of Liberty Life, as, in his view, the city is definitely developing towards Braamfontein. It was felt that the proposition should not necessarily be considered on pure investment criteria and that provided a reasonable return of not less than, say, 6 per cent could be obtained, steps should be taken to develop the proposition as soon as possible. On a full consideration of the situation, it was felt that in spite of the obvious economy of a full block development it might be desirable, particularly in view of the lesser capital expenditure involved, to develop the initial L-shaped site for the company's own purposes, the design to take into account the possibility of absorbing the Standard Bank and the remaining corner site at a later stage."

These sites were acquired in due course, and on completion of the building Standard Bank returned as a tenant and established a new branch on the site. Eventually, that site would house the Group's first self-owned headquarters. But hardly "in the reasonably near future", for it was to be six years down the line, and after many vicissitudes, that all head office staff moved into Guardian Liberty Centre during 1973. Then shareholders were proudly told, in the 1973 Annual Report: "Guardian Liberty Centre stands as a symbol for the dynamic business philosophy of partnership between shareholders and policyholders which has revolutionised the insurance industry and brought major benefits to the South African public. The building is a milestone of achievement and a foundation for further successful enterprise in the interests of the South African public."

As an aside, it is quite amusing to note that while Guardian Liberty Centre was indeed to stand as a "symbol" as noted above, it also stood very tall, as if to emphasise that Donny Gordon was no longer, in any sense whatsoever, Mandy Moross's "boy". Their relationship, as has already been chronicled, was a stormy one during the short period when the Schlesinger Organisation was a large shareholder in Liberty Life; it finally soured when Gordon "persuaded" Moross to sell out to Guardian; and it deteriorated further when, in 1967, Moross provided Louis Shill with the cash backing he needed to remove control of Investors Mutual Funds from Liberty Life.

So Moross must almost have had apoplexy when he opened his Johannesburg *Sunday Times* on 14 April 1968. Guardian Liberty Centre was to be built on a block just an intersection away from, and diagonally opposite, Moross's own pride and joy, the Schlesinger Centre, which towered high above all it surveyed on Braamfontein Ridge. The *Sunday Times Business Times*, under the headline "Liberty Life to build HQ near Civic Centre" carried a big picture of the area, with an artist's impression of Liberty Life's new building superimposed on it.

The caption read: "Above is an artist's view of the proposed R4 million building of the Liberty Life Association of Africa and Guardian Assurance Company superimposed on a photograph of the area of Johannesburg in which it will rise. The 320-ft 22-storey office tower will be 30 ft higher than its tallest neighbour, the Schlesinger Centre to the east."

A very fine piece of one-upmanship indeed, and an incident that tends to confirm that there is far more to business, even big institutional business, than the mere making of money.

The new building was not to serve Liberty Life's fast-growing needs for very long, and as early as 8 March 1976 – barely two-and-a-half years after the Group had moved in – the following minute appears: "Guardian Liberty Centre. After Mr Gordon and Dr Conradie had disclosed their interests as directors of United Building Society, Mr Gordon explained that UBS had approached the company to establish whether it would be interested in selling Guardian Liberty Centre to UBS for purposes of their new head office.

"Mr Gordon explained that the building had been designed before there had been any intention to merge with the South African operations of Manufacturers Life and Sun Life, and as a result of these mergers together with the rapid expansion of the company's operations the building had certain drawbacks. He continued that whilst it was not immediately necessary to seek alternative accommodation, long-term plans should be developed with this as an objective.

"After a full discussion it was agreed that the company's approach be communicated to the UBS which organisation could then decide whether they are prepared to make an offer for the building. Notwithstanding the UBS attitude it was agreed to commence investigations into the advisability of developing a new head office complex for the group."

In the event, nothing would come of the UBS approach, but the "investigations into the advisability" would lead to the development of the Group's present magnificent R30 million head office complex, also in Braamfontein, the site of which would be acquired, after intensive search and investigation, in 1980. The new head office, Liberty Life Centre, was officially opened by Dr Anton Rupert – Chairman of the Rembrandt Group and another of South Africa's great entrepreneurs – on 8 September 1982. This date coincided almost exactly with Liberty Life's twenty-fifth anniversary. The event was celebrated by a glittering banquet in the magnificent atrium of the new building which was attended by many of the business establishment of South Africa and a number of dignitaries from abroad.

Within six short years, Liberty Life Centre was already bursting at the seams, and a major extension was announced in May 1988, notwithstanding the fact that Liberty Life had also developed Libridge, a 35 000 square metre development on a site immediately adjacent to and to the east of Liberty Life Centre. Libridge to-day is partially occupied by certain Liberty Life divisions and by the head office of Guardian National Insurance Company, now an associate company of Liberty Life by virtue of the 44 per cent equity stake owned by Liberty Holdings. The 51 per cent control of Guardian National is, of course, owned by GRE, of London.

"This major new extension will enable Liberty Life to maintain the necessary cohesion of staff involved in centralised head office functions, which has become increasingly difficult since the merger with the Prudential," said Mark Winterton, Liberty Life's joint managing director. It would be ready for occupation in 1990, he added. Site work commenced in August 1988. An additional 10 500 square metres of open-plan office space will be provided, bringing the total area at Liberty Life Centre to about 27 450 square metres. The extra accommodation, together with the space available for Group needs in Libridge, will ensure that the Liberty Life Group will have adequate space for its requirements into the twenty-first century. It is intended to connect Liberty Life Centre to Libridge by way of an overhead bridge over Melle Street, the road between the two buildings, in order to achieve the maximum benefit to the Group from linking the two high-quality office buildings to form a much-enlarged head office complex.

Going back to earlier times, it is interesting to note that the Report and Accounts for the year ended 31 December 1967 – the tenth anniversary Accounts – were the first to use colour and photographs. And the very first illustration used was an artist's impression of Guardian Liberty Centre.

Another point worth noting from the earlier Annual Reports is the way they illustrate another Liberty Life speciality: the gradual acquisition of shareholdings in potential "target" companies over, if need be, a very long period of years. A case in point is the Real Estate Corporation of South Africa, in which Liberty Life took eight years before it had acquired sufficient shares to back a successful approach for control. This excellent listed property company was eventually swallowed in 1972 in an opposed takeover against stiff competition from other predators.

Rapp & Maister first emerged as being within the Liberty Life orbit when it was listed on the Johannesburg Stock Exchange in June 1968. The *Sunday Times* of 26 May 1968, in a preview of the listing under the banner headline: "R25m Property Venture Launched" carried, among others, a picture of Donald Gordon, who was to be a director of the new company. Earlier dealings with Rapp & Maister, which was Liberty Life's landlord at the pre-Guardian Liberty Centre head office in downtown Johannesburg, had included debenture financing for Sandton City, but it would not be until 1975 that Rapp & Maister, too, would be absorbed into Liberty Life.

The next property milestone was the formation of Guardian Real Estate Corporation Limited (Grecor). From the 1969 Directors' Report: "As a consequence of the Guardian Group's intention to play a larger role in real estate development in South Africa, Guardian Real Estate Corporation Limited (Grecor) was incorporated as a subsidiary of Guardian Holdings during July 1969.

"On 1 October 1969, the 50 per cent interest of the company, together with the 50 per cent interest of Guardian Assurance Company Limited, London, in the share capital of Courtieston House [Guardian Assurance had temporarily put up 50 per cent of the capital for the enlarged development] was transferred to Guardian Real Estate Corporation on the basis of a sworn appraisal which valued the Braamfontein site at R1 620 000. In exchange for the company's interest in Courtieston House, Liberty Life was allotted 686 047 deferred shares in Grecor issued at R1 per share, which shares will rank for dividend as from 1 January 1973 to coincide with the planned completion of the Courtieston House development. In addition, loans made by the company to Courtieston House have been exchanged for convertible loan stock carrying a conversion right into further shares in Grecor. As a result of these transactions, an extraneous capital surplus of R446 000 accrued to Liberty Life, which has been transferred to investment reserve."

This was Liberty Life's very first profit from property – a precursor of far greater things to come.

"In addition to the Courtieston House development, Grecor has acquired a 75 per cent interest in a further major site in the south-west financial district of Johannesburg, on which an eighteen-storey air-conditioned office block is in the course of erection at a total estimated cost of R5 800 000. Further propositions in the real estate field are currently being considered by Grecor and Liberty Life has, by its participation, acquired a major foothold in real estate development in the Republic."

In the 1970 Report and Accounts, the frontispiece of which was a photograph of the completed core of Guardian Liberty Centre towering proudly above Braamfontein, with other property photographs at the rear, the launch of the Liberty property-linked concept of life insurance was announced to shareholders.

The cover of the 1971 Report was graced with a dramatic photograph, taken through the Miners' Monument in front of Johannesburg's Civic Centre, of the growing Guardian Liberty Centre, showing the building completed to halfway up the core. With property development now in the capable hands of Grecor, in which Rapp & Maister had an interest, shareholders were merely told that: "Grecor, a fellow subsidiary of Guardian Assurance Holdings in which Liberty Life has a substantial interest, expanded its property investments."

One such expansion, introduced quietly in a Liberty Property Bonds feature at the rear of the Report, would eventually become the biggest suburban retail, office and hotel complex in the southern hemisphere, let alone the Republic of South Africa. The picture of a very early stage of construction is modestly captioned: "Sandton City complex under construction to the north of Johannesburg."

The growing property interests of the greater Guardian Group required a degree of rationalisation, and this was formally noted at a Board meeting on 25 August 1972: "Reorganisation of the Group property interests. Mr Gordon informed the Board that negotiations had taken place with Real Estate Corporation of South Africa Limited (REC), Rapp & Maister Holdings Limited (R&M) and the Guardian Holdings Group regarding their respective property interests." It took some months to complete this major property package, and it was not until 7 December 1972 that the five companies concerned were ready to put out a joint announcement:

"On 26 August 1972 it was announced that agreement in principle had been reached between Guardian Assurance Holdings (South Africa) Limited (GAH); Guardian Real Estate Corporation Limited (Grecor); Liberty Life Association of Africa Limited (Liberty Life); Rapp & Maister Holdings Limited (R&M) and Real Estate Corporation of South Africa Limited (REC) in terms of which REC would make an offer to acquire the entire issued share capital of Grecor (the property-owning subsidiary of GAH) on the basis of 16 new REC shares for every 100 Grecor shares to be acquired.

"Subsequent to the aforementioned date, Grecor increased its capital resources from approximately R5 100 000 to approximately R7 000 000 by way of a one-for-four rights issue at R1,10 per share to facilitate the financing of its property investments and to increase its working capital. As a consequence of the adjustment in the net asset value of Grecor on account of the aforementioned rights issue, it has now been agreed that the acquisition of Grecor by REC will be settled by the issue of 15 new REC shares for every 100 Grecor shares acquired. The net asset value of each Grecor share to be acquired by REC will be not less than R1,50 per share on the basis of valuing Grecor's property investments on an agreed basis. Thereafter REC will make an offer on the same terms to acquire the remaining shares in Grecor held by the other shareholders.

"Prior to the effective date, Grecor will increase its 60 per cent interest in the Corner House (Proprietary ) Limited – which owns the Corner House Building – by the acquisition of a further 20 per cent interest in the share capital of and the loan accounts against the Corner House (Proprietary) Limited from Liberty Life and will also acquire the remaining 25 per cent interest in the share capital of and the loan account of R&M against Verson Investments (Proprietary) Limited which owns 20 Anderson Street.

"The consideration payable for these acquisitions will be settled by the issue of new Grecor shares to be allotted at a price of R1,50 per share. The underlying assets of Grecor on the effective date will, as a result of such acquisitions, consist *inter alia* of the following major property developments:

"1. Guardian Liberty Centre, the 21-storey air-conditioned office building being erected on the corner of Rissik, Wolmarans, Loveday and Smit Streets, Braamfontein, Johannesburg, which will, on completion in 1973, become the head office of the South African Guardian Assurance Group.

"2. 20, Anderson Street, a major 19-storey air-conditioned office block under construction in the financial district of Johannesburg, due to be completed in 1973.

"3. An 80 per cent interest in the Corner House, a modern prestige 17-storey air-conditioned office building located in the heart of the financial district of Johannesburg.

"4. A 25 per cent interest in Westaline Properties (Proprietary) Limited which is owned jointly with R&M, Johannesburg Consolidated Investment Company Limited and Downtown Real Estate Corporation Limited. Westaline Properties owns the "Durban City" property which is a major 9 000 square metre site located between West, Aliwal and Pine Streets in the central business district of

Durban, upon which a shopping and office complex will, in due course, be erected.

"In addition, on the effective date, REC will acquire from R&M the entire issued share capital of and loan accounts against Cumberland Mansions (Proprietary) Limited which owns National Board House, a 17-storey air-conditioned office and shopping complex situated in the central business district of Johannesburg opposite the Supreme Court. The purchase consideration based on an agreed valuation will be settled by the issue of REC shares at R10 per share.

"The present issued share capital of REC consists of 1 074 800 shares of 50 cents each and as a result of the aforegoing acquisitions, it is contemplated that approximately 2 000 000 new shares in REC will be issued. Guardian Holdings, together with its subsidiary Liberty Life, will effectively control the reconstituted Real Estate Corporation.

"The merging of the property interests of Real Estate Corporation, which primarily consist of established central city retail shopping and office premises together with the new major prestige office developments of Grecor and the proposed acquisition by REC of National Board House, will result in the creation of an extremely powerful property development group with total assets amounting to approximately R60 000 000. The financial backing of Guardian Holdings and Liberty Life, and the development expertise of Rapp & Maister, which is to acquire a significant 18 per cent stake in Real Estate Corporation, will enable the reconstituted group to participate in major property developments and to undertake the redevelopment of certain of its prime central city sites, which development hitherto has not been practical."

The press greeted the new development with the enthusiasm that seemed to be reserved for the Liberty Life Group's moves. Bernard Nackan, in the *Rand Daily Mail* of 29 August 1972: "New R50m property giant. The interlocking of the investments and expertise of the three groups that will be affected by the reverse takeover of Real Estate Corporation by Grecor will create a powerful new force on the property scene and in Hollard Street.

"Yesterday's announcement of the proposed deal between REC, Guardian, Liberty, Grecor and Rapp & Maister will, I understand, result in a company whose property portfolio will exceed R50 million – compared with the present Real Estate portfolio of about R18 million.

"In a nutshell what is happening is this – the Guardian/Liberty Life group will acquire control, and Rapp & Maister will get a substantial minority holding in a vastly enlarged REC."

In April 1973, in the Report and Accounts for the year ended 31 December 1972, the implications were spelt out to shareholders. "As a consequence of this arrangement [the sale of Liberty's 20 per cent stake in Corner House for 587 005 REC shares] and the undertaking to convert the company's Grecor convertible loans into 300 000 Real Estate Corporation shares on or before 1 January 1978, the company's interest in Real Estate Corporation will amount to 28 per cent. As a result of the aforementioned, Liberty Life, together with its holding company, Guardian Assurance Holdings, has acquired effective control of the reconstituted Real Estate Corporation, the total assets of which at 1 April 1973 exceeded R50 million, consisting mainly of prime central city properties."

Meanwhile, back at the ranch, Ernest Bigland was looking somewhat askance at all these rapid advances into property. He was far from being a keen property man himself, and the correspondence reveals many relatively minor skirmishes over the topic. Gordon himself recalls that the biggest upset he ever had with Bigland (he refers to it as "the only real row", but that should be taken with the proverbial pinch or two of salt) was over a property deal that Michael Rapp wanted to do in New York.

It is a fascinating story, and the background to it is that in 1975, in New York, one Natie Kirsh, a prominent South African entrepreneur, was trying to put together a property deal that would, had it succeeded, have been the biggest deal of his life. Kirsh recalls: "It required $20 million, of which I could find $5 million myself. That deal today (1987) must be worth a profit of at least $3 000 million.

"The transaction involved about 11 million square feet of real estate in ten buildings in New York, including the head office of J C Penny, next to the Hilton Hotel, the head office of IT&T on Park Avenue, and 55 Water Street. It also included Kinney Parking, the biggest parking company in New York, and National Cleaning, the biggest office cleaning operation in America, with 20 000 employees. Those two companies alone had a net annual cash flow of $7 million. Each building was a separate corporate entity and individually financed with excellent long-term low rate mortgages and there were no cross-holdings. The reason I couldn't raise the money was the atmosphere at that time – it was the time when New York City itself was going bust. The price wasn't actually $20 million, it was $50 million for the package. But I had persuaded the sellers, Warner Communications, to give me five years to pay off the additional $30 million, and they would hold the scrip as security until this was done. There was cash flow aplenty in the company to do that. All I had to do was to put $20 million down – and the upside was just unbelievable. But I had only $5 million available. That's when I asked Michael Rapp to come to New York: we talked it over from all angles, and he said he'd recommend, through Liberty Life, that GRE should guarantee the other $15 million. He'd put it to DG, and – 'don't worry, Donny will agree'."

Let Gordon take over the tale. "Michael had been over in New York, where he'd met up with Kirsh. He was away a few days longer than expected, which didn't please me as we were, as usual, under a lot of pressure. He told me he had been looking into a rather interesting real estate transaction. 'Warner Communications want to dispose of their real estate interests and there's a whole portfolio of New York properties available. I've spent a day or two looking at the numbers, and the cash flows are fantastic, and the buildings are outstanding. Warner Communications believes that its rating on the New York Stock Exchange is prejudiced by its owning the real estate company, whose very cheap mortgage financing is then consolidated into Warner's balance sheet. Without the property company, Warner would show $100 million cash on its balance sheet and no borrowings. So they want to sell – and Natie Kirsh has an option. All we have to do is put up a guarantee for $15 million and it's on.'

"I spent a day or two going through the figures with Michael and came to the conclusion that it did look an outstanding deal. But we couldn't do it without the intervention of Guardian Royal Exchange because of exchange control constraints, so I phoned Ernest Bigland and said I would like GRE to provide the $15 million to enable the group to participate in acquiring a real estate portfolio in New York which we thought was such an excellent portfolio. He said he'd look at it and come back to me the next day.

"The very next day, he did indeed come back. He was very, very critical and somewhat sarcastic – very unlike Ernest, who was always incredibly diplomatic and gentlemanly in our relationship. He said to me: 'Donald, for the first time in our association, I actually question your judgement. I have checked on this proposition that you talked about; it's been offered around the entire world, everybody has had a go at it – it's total rubbish. And I refuse to lose $15 million of our money, or your money or anybody's money. I just cannot believe that you could have had such a rush of blood to the head.'"

Gordon was totally mortified and extremely embarrassed. "As you can imagine, I didn't relish being spoken to like that. I was furious and he was very angry because he thought I'd made a fool of him. I was extremely upset, to put it mildly. I called Michael Rapp into my office and I really blasted him. 'How dare you get me into such an embarrassing situation, getting me involved in such a ridiculous proposition. If the whole world knows about it, and has rejected it, it must be complete and total rubbish. They must be desperate to have to find a South African, to have to find Kirsh to get themselves out of their mess. It's probably not worth anything, and we can only lose our shirts on it. You are a very smart property operator in South Africa, but don't think you can take on those New York sharks, they'll have your guts for garters.' Michael walked out with his tail between his legs and that was that. I mended my bridges with Ernest and proceeded to forget about the whole affair as soon as possible.

"A few years later, Michael Rapp and I were in Toronto and we had an appointment with a certain Paul Reichmann, a very well-known and successful real estate entrepreneur in Canada, today probably regarded as the top property man in the world. I remember our impressions of the magnificence of his key building, Number One Canada Place. Totally magnificent, a building of a quality the like of which we had never seen. The size of the lifts – four times the size of any lift I had ever been in. It was a Sunday morning – Paul Reichmann is a very orthodox Jew – he used to walk around the office with his yamulka on and he never worked on Saturdays, but he did work on Sundays. We went to discuss a number of things with him, including the possible acquisition of his United Kingdom property company, called English Properties, and we touched on many areas of mutual interest. It was an incredibly fascinating and wide-ranging discussion, lasting from about nine in the morning until one.

"In the course of our talks, he mentioned to us the real estate deal that had made him. He had done that very same New York deal a month or two after we'd been forced to turn it down. He told us that the portfolio was then worth four billion Canadian dollars; that he had sold off half of it to realise about two billion, and that he still held the rest to nothing. It occurred to me that perhaps we – with the assistance of Ernest Bigland – had missed the greatest real estate deal of all time. And Michael Rapp has never allowed me to forget it. But that is the rub of the green."

The true magnitude of that miss is underlined, if any emphasis is needed, by an article in *Time* magazine of 18 April 1988. "Two miles from the Bank of England, in a section of London's East End once inhabited by Cockney stevedores, the largest commercial development in Europe is slowly taking shape. By 1995, a spacious retail and office complex known as Canary Wharf is slated to rise on seventy-one acres of former docklands.

"When Canary Wharf is completed – at a cost somewhere between $5,4 billion and $7,2 billion – a gleaming minicity will burnish London's skyline. It will be a sizeable addition: twenty-four buildings with twelve million square feet of space, including three office towers, two 400-room hotels and dozens of shops and restaurants. One edifice will be Britain's first significant skyscraper: a fifty-storey obelisk some 200 feet taller than any other building in London.

"The megadevelopment involves spectacular risks for the businessmen with sole responsibility for the project: the Toronto-based Reichmann brothers. Few people can make property judgments with the authority of the Reichmann brothers – Albert, 59, Paul, 57 and Ralph, 54. In little more than a decade, they have emerged as the world's biggest private urban developers. In the process, the intensely private family has put together a powerful conglomerate of real estate, natural resources and industrial concerns worth more than $20 billion.

"The Reichmanns have steely nerves. In 1977, when New York City was perilously close to bankruptcy, the brothers spent $320 million on eight Manhattan office buildings. The properties, two of which have since been sold, are now worth $3 billion."

That was the start of the Reichmann fortune – and that is the one that got away.

A further disagreement – albeit only a paper one – arose with Bigland over the developing Real Estate acquisition. The reverse takeover resulted in REC's Chairman, Sir Ian Gwynne-Evans, being invited to join the Liberty Life Board. Bigland, somewhat incautiously, used the circumstances surrounding this appointment to vent his displeasure over the whole property issue.

Bigland to Gordon, 2 March 1973. "I must say I was very much concerned when reading the Real Estate papers last night to find the back letter to Sir Ian Gwynne-Evans as we knew nothing about it here and I see it was dated 7 December 1972. I fully realise the difficulties you had in negotiating this rather complicated deal, and from what you told me this morning I accept that it is not an absolutely binding agreement on the part of Real Estate. As you pointed out, at the stage the letter was written we did not, and still do not, control a majority shareholding, so that technically I also accept that it does not affect the public quotation position, although I am sure we both agree it does really make a binding moral contract.

"Sir Ian is, as you say, 64. You mentioned that he would go at 65 but this is only at his discretion, and under Clause 3 (a) on page 2 he has a firm right to stay as an executive director until age 70. However, this is now all in the past, and I only trust neither you nor I have to negotiate such a troublesome personal arrangement again."

Gordon took the opportunity to explode into righteous indignation: on 6 March 1973 he wrote, "I must say I was most unhappy at the completely unreasonable criticism of my handling of Sir Ian Gwynne-Evans's position in connection with the reverse takeover of REC. You say you knew nothing about the letter of 7 December which quite frankly, in a deal of this size I considered to be a matter of minor detail and completely within my authority to handle, particularly as you and I had previously agreed to Sir Ian continuing as Chairman for a number of years. In addition, all the draft circulars we sent to London contained full details of the breakdown of the directorate, which in my view gave fair weight to the interests involved.

"On the moral side, I undoubtedly agree we have a commitment – and rightly so. REC has been the life's work of Sir Ian and quite frankly there was little reason for him to have changed the status quo at this stage. He has not in any sense sold out (in fact, to my knowledge, he has not disposed of any shares at all) and has nonetheless agreed to pass effective control to us on very favourable terms in the face of a cash offer of over R13 per share from a third party [the ill-fated Slater Walker group]. I would have thought it perfectly reasonable for a normal man in these circumstances to ask us for a formalisation of his position in REC and to ensure his being able to remain on the Board to protect his interests and those of his backers, during the declining years of his life. In addition, his advisers insisted on this quite forcibly as a condition of agreeing to the deal. I cannot believe that you would have lost the deal on this account and I am completely convinced that I acted in the best interests of all concerned.

"As far as disclosure is concerned, I think you must bear in mind that the deal was done in South Africa and, as such, South African practice should apply. In addition, the REC circular is the prime responsibility of the REC Board and by no stretch of the imagination does any responsibility for its issue devolve on the Guardian Group. Finally, the back letter was written by Guardian Assurance Holdings, Rapp & Maister and Liberty Life in their capacity as potential future shareholders of REC and the propriety of this was completely cleared by all attorneys and merchant bankers at this end.

"I appreciate it is very difficult to be sitting six thousand miles away and to have the atmosphere surrounding a deal of this magnitude but I do not think, in the circumstances, it is difficult for you to leave decisions of this nature to people on the spot. I cannot remember letting you down too often."

In the face of this unambiguously expressed and, indeed, fully warranted wrath, Bigland backed off. After a conciliatory telephone call, he wrote on 12 March: "I felt I should acknowledge your letter of 6 March and put everything right for the record. I telephoned on Friday to say that I was extremely sorry if you felt my approach to your handling of Real Estate was unreasonable. I certainly did not mean it to be construed in this way and I do apologise if you thought I was criticising your very able handling of the deal.

"As I said in my earlier letter, I very clearly appreciate the problems you faced and the higher offer that had been made. My reaction was purely a temporary one based on reading, wrongly, from the letters and the papers that we might be locked into a difficult position. I should have accepted, as I readily do now, that when these things are settled any decisions must be, as they are, fully supported. I am glad we agreed on the telephone that we can look on the matter as closed."

This important victory behind him, Gordon now moved swiftly to consolidate on the property front. First, control of Real Estate Corporation was shifted from joint Guardian/Liberty Life to Liberty Life on its own. The 1973 Annual Report: "Acquisition of control of Real Estate Corporation of South Africa Limited. Shareholders will recall that in 1972 an agreement was concluded whereby your company acquired a 26 per cent holding in Real Estate Corporation which, together with the holding of Guardian Assurance Holdings, gave effective control of Real Estate Corporation to the Guardian Liberty Life Group. On 9 May 1973 it was announced that an agreement had been entered into in terms of which Liberty Life transferred its holding of 867 118 ordinary shares in Rapp & Maister Holdings to Real Estate Corporation in exchange for the allotment and issue to the company of an additional 182 095 shares in Real Estate Corporation. In November 1973 an agreement was concluded whereby with effect from 1 April 1973 Liberty Life acquired the 652 838 shares in Real Estate Corporation held by Guardian Assurance Holdings in exchange for the allotment and issue to Guardian Assurance Holdings of 718 122 Liberty Life ordinary shares.

"These transactions were concluded not only to rationalise the property interests of the Guardian Liberty Life Group but also to establish a more direct relationship between Liberty Life and the Real Estate Corporation in view of the implications arising from the substantial growth of the company's property orientated life assurance business, which in your directors' view requires control of the underlying property investments to be vested in the insurer.

"After conversion of certain partly convertible development loans made by the company to Guardian Real Estate Corporation (now a wholly owned subsidiary of Real Estate Corporation) which Liberty Life has duly undertaken to convert by not later than 1 January 1978, the company will own more than 52 per cent of the issued share capital of Real Estate Corporation against the holding of 48 per cent held at the year end."

As a consequence of the assumption of control of REC, the consolidated accounts for the year to 31 December 1973 showed, for the first time, the true extent of Liberty Life's growing property involvement. "Freehold property" of R53 000 000 figured in total assets of R197 000 000, so that the "property exposure" was almost 27 per cent.

But 52 per cent of Real Estate was but a stepping stone along the way. On 10 November 1974, a Board meeting was held at Gordon's home in Hyde Park, Johannesburg – at 6.15 on a Sunday evening. "Proposed Scheme of Arrangement with Real Estate Corporation of South Africa. It was resolved that application be made with immediate effect to the Johannesburg Stock Exchange for the temporary suspension of the listing of the issued ordinary and 7 per cent convertible preference share capital of the company pending the outcome of negotiations pursuant to which the company, which holds approximately 52 per cent of the issued share capital of Real Estate Corporation, intends by Scheme of Arrangement to acquire the entire issued share capital of REC."

The Directors' Report for the year ended 31 December 1974 told shareholders: "In November 1974 it was announced that Liberty Life proposed to acquire the 48 per cent minority shareholders' interest in its subsidiary, Real Estate Corporation, with effect from 1 January 1975, by way of a Scheme of Arrangement. If the Scheme is approved and implemented, shareholders of Real Estate Corporation (other than Liberty Life) will receive for every 100 shares in that company: 50 ordinary shares of R1 each in Liberty Life and 500 7 per cent convertible preference shares of R1 each in Liberty Life.

"On the assumption that all the holders of the existing and new preference shares exercise their conversion rights, Guardian Assurance Holdings, which company controls Liberty Life, will continue to do so with a shareholding of approximately 51 per cent of Liberty Life's then issued ordinary share capital.

"The acquisition of the shares in Real Estate Corporation not already held by the company is in accordance with Liberty Life's policy of acquiring tangible underlying assets, particularly immovable property, to immunise long-term policyholders against the erosion of capital values brought about by continuing inflation. This transaction will further increase Liberty Life's capital base to approximately R50 million, making it the most powerfully capitalised life assurance company in the Republic."

The next step was to be the acquisition of Rapp & Maister, and with it, of Michael Rapp himself, who would become Gordon's right-hand man, and almost sole business confidant, for the next ten years – a decade that would see further dramatic growth in Liberty Life's fortunes, not to mention those of the two men most closely concerned. They had been growing personally closer in the seven years that Gordon had been on the R & M Board, and had come to hold each other's quite diverse abilities in high regard. Gerald Stein, the Rapp family lawyer, recalls participating in serious takeover talks two years earlier, in 1973, but says that: "Michael was then not ready to surrender his independence. He loved running his own ship, and wanted to go on steering it himself for as long as he possibly could."

But the inexorable build-up of Liberty Life's shareholding in Rapp & Maister, which had begun in 1968, continued. At the Liberty Life Board meeting on 17 September 1975, it was noted that: "After Mr Gordon and Mr Rapp had specifically drawn attention to their disclosures of interest relating to the Rapp & Maister Group of companies, the acquisition of 810 000 additional Rapp & Maister shares acquired at 145 cents per share was confirmed." This brought the Liberty Life stake in Rapp & Maister to 4,3 million shares, or 26 per cent. The end of Rapp & Maister's, and of Michael Rapp's, independence was in sight.

But, by now, it was by no means completely unwelcome. By 1975, the property boom had run its course, and all of South Africa's hitherto highflying property developers were finding the going tough. Wolf Cesman, who has run Rapp & Maister since Rapp translocated to London in 1986 to take charge of the Liberty Life Group's burgeoning property interests in the United Kingdom, was, in 1975, contemplating an offer from Rapp for him to join R&M.

"I looked at it, thought about it very carefully and I really saw two benefits going that route as opposed to going into business on my own. The first was that I foresaw that one day, and probably quite soon, Rapp & Maister would actually be taken over by the Liberty Life Group. I knew that they had close connections, because when I was with Summit, we'd worked with Rapp and Gordon on Eastgate. I knew that one day every property company had to end up in the hands of a large insurance company – or maybe go bust – and many of them had gone bust already. That was one reason, and the other was that I thought I'd end up with some options in R&M which one day would make some money for me. The takeover came before I commenced at R&M and before I got my options, but I decided, anyway, to give it a try." Cesman has not regretted that decision.

Rapp was thinking very much along similar lines and very soon another emergency Sunday Board meeting was called at Gordon's home, this time at 11.45 on the morning of 23 November 1975.

"Proposed acquisition of control of Rapp & Maister Holdings.

"The Chairman tabled a memorandum in regard to the proposed acquisition of control of Rapp & Maister Holdings Limited and explained that discussions had taken place between the company, Guardian Assurance Holdings and R&M with a view, by means of a Scheme of Arrangement, to the acquisition by the Guardian Liberty

Life Group of the entire issued share capital of R&M not already owned by the Group.

"The advantages to Liberty Life and Guardian Assurance Holdings of the proposed Scheme of Arrangement would, *inter alia*, be:

"1. All future building contracts entered into by Liberty Life and Rapp & Maister would be done at cost;

"2. The acquisition of a major and prestigious real estate portfolio at a substantial discount on net asset value;

"3. The minimal dilution of overall earnings of Liberty Life;

"4. The rationalisation benefits of the property interests of Liberty Life;

"5. The acquisition of an outstanding property construction enterprise at no goodwill;

"6. The acquisition of a first-class property management organisation;

"7. The elimination of conflicts of interest between R&M and Liberty Life;

"8. The substantial savings on development costs in respect of propositions being undertaken currently and in the future;

"9. The assumption of existing fixed low interest-bearing long-term finance already raised in respect of existing R&M projects, and

"10. The acquisition of outstanding expertise in the property field."

Shareholders were told of the deal in the 1975 Report and Accounts. "In December 1975, it was announced that Liberty Life, in conjunction with its holding company, Guardian Assurance Holdings, proposed to acquire the entire issued share capital of Rapp & Maister Holdings, with effect from 1 January 1976, by way of a Scheme of Arrangement. Rapp & Maister is a leading listed South African property owning and development company which has been closely associated with Liberty Life for many years by way of important shareholding and financial inter-relationships and as a consequence of numerous building developments which have been undertaken on a joint basis. This transaction will increase the company's property interests to approximately R125 million and total assets are expected to increase to nearly R500 million by the end of 1976. As a consequence of these arrangements, the shareholders' funds of Liberty Life will increase still further to over R60 million compared to R9,6 million at the end of 1970 and less than R1 million ten years ago."

The terms of the deal were complicated by the cross-holdings between the two companies (R&M had, over the years, acquired 303 115 Liberty Life ordinaries and 3 031 150 of the 7 per cent convertible prefs) and by the ever-present need – in Bigland's eyes, at the very least – to dilute the stake of Guardian Royal Exchange in its growing South African empire by as low a percentage as was possible and practical. So each R&M share was to be exchanged for one share in Guardian Assurance Holdings and 65 cents in cash to be paid by Liberty Life. Liberty Life issued 1 150 000 new ordinaries to GAH in exchange for its R&M shares, and the shares held by R&M in Liberty Life were also transferred to Guardian Holdings.

The net result was that, while the interest of Guardian Holdings in Liberty Life rose from approximately 52 per cent to 62 per cent on receipt of the new Liberty Life shares, the interest of Guardian Royal Exchange in GAH fell from approximately 83 per cent to approximately 65 per cent as the latter issued new shares to the erstwhile R&M shareholders. It had taken a very major effort indeed on the part of Gordon to persuade Bigland that the R&M deal was of such pressing importance that GRE's stake should be permitted to fall below the "magic" 75 per cent.

Another interesting aspect of the R&M takeover is that it was the first major corporate deal to be done in South Africa by a Scheme of Arrangement, a method which was subsequently to become increasingly popular. Michael Katz, Liberty Life's solicitor, recalls: "It was one of the first deals where we had to be concerned about separate classes of shareholders for the purposes of the Companies Act. So what we did was that Liberty Life undertook to the Rapp family that Liberty Life would propose a Scheme of Arrangement which would affect all the shareholders of R&M equally. And the Rapp family undertook to vote in favour of that Scheme in respect of their shares.

"The simple issue was that Liberty Life wanted to buy the shares of the Rapp family, and the Rapp family wanted to sell their shares to Liberty Life, so both parties wanted to be committed. But if Liberty Life had bought the Rapp shares, then the Rapp family could not have featured as part of the 75 per cent acceptances required by the Act. So it was fundamental that they should not constitute a separate class of shareholder, otherwise we would have had to obtain acceptances by 75 per cent of the minority – that is, all other shareholders excluding the Rapps, which would have been undesirable, and difficult.

"The issues – at that time at any rate – were fairly complex, and there appeared to be a risk that the Court, for whatever reason, could refuse to sanction the Scheme, when the objectives of both major parties, namely the acquisition by Liberty Life of the Rapp shares, would have been frustrated. So we said that in that eventuality Liberty Life would propose an offer in terms of Section 314 of the Act – that's just an offer to acquire shares, not by way of a Scheme of Arrangement – and the Rapps would then be bound to accept that offer just as any other minority shareholder would be entitled to do.

"In the event, the Court accepted the Scheme, and in subsequent judicial decisions the structure that we pioneered has been upheld.

"One last point I would like to make regarding the Rapp & Maister deal was that it represented the first major tie between a long-term insurance company and a property development company. This showed considerable foresight on the part of both parties, because it became clear after the deal that we were in a new era where property companies without access to institutional funding could not succeed. So there was a clear benefit to Rapp & Maister in being tied to Liberty Life, but on the other hand there was the benefit to Liberty Life that they acquired considerable property expertise. The synergy of that deal was of vast benefit to both parties."

Thanks to that synergy, property would from then on take up an ever-increasing proportion of each successive Annual Report, and property illustrations would proliferate as the Annual Reports grew more elaborate. For 1976, the Directors' Report: "As a result of the Scheme of Arrangement sanctioned by the Supreme Court on 15 June 1976, and with effect from 1 January 1976, Rapp & Maister Holdings became a wholly-owned subsidiary of Real Estate Corporation of South Africa, Liberty Life's major property owning subsidiary. The acquisition of Rapp & Maister Holdings has resulted in substantial rationalisation of Liberty Life's property operations and should achieve considerable benefit for both the company and its policyholders. A total of R55 million of prime and strategically located fixed property was added to Liberty Life's portfolio as a result of the absorption of R&M, at a substantial discount on both market and replacement values, thereby widening Liberty Life's tangible asset base and improving the inherent strength and diversification of our property holdings.

"During 1976, a start was made on the R40 million Eastgate project straddling the Bedfordview/Johannesburg boundary on the Jan Smuts Airport freeway, in which Liberty Life has a 50 per cent undivided interest. Although only scheduled for completion at the end of 1978, Eastgate's near 100 000 square metres of shopping are already 57 per cent let on favourable terms, primarily to four of South Africa's leading retail groups – namely Edgars, Greatermans, OK Bazaars and Woolworths."

Eastgate would prove to be one of R&M's most successful regional shopping complexes, comparable only to Sandton City, also a massive 100 000 square metre shopping complex, but with a hotel and office towers in addition, set right in the centre of Johannesburg's prosperous northern suburbs.

The Eastgate regional shopping centre was originally a joint venture between Liberty Life and Summit Construction. The latter company, now defunct, got into severe financial difficulties, as did many of its contempories, and the Summit 50 per cent of Eastgate finally finished up in the hands of one of its major creditors, Union Acceptances Limited, a Nedbank subsidiary which was desperately keen to rid itself of this "albatross".

At the same time, Nedbank was anxious to acquire one of Liberty Life's buildings, the Bank of Lisbon building in Sauer Street, Johannesburg, as a future Nedbank head office. Gerry Muller, then deputy chairman of Nedbank, suggested to Donald Gordon at a dinner party that a straight swop – Bank of Lisbon building for Nedbank's 50 per cent of Eastgate – could well be of interest to Nedbank.

Gordon immediately grasped the potential of such a deal, and a meeting was arranged. It was in DG's office and was attended by Michael Rapp, Rob Abrahamsen (then Nedbank's managing director, since departed), and Johan Nel (then managing director of UAL, since retired). The ground rules were set by agreement between Gordon and Muller: the two transactions were to be dealt with individually but would encompass the principle that the price of the two transactions would be equal but would not depend on each other. And it was agreed that Eastgate would be dealt with first.

A price of R27 million for 50 per cent of the vast shopping complex was agreed within two minutes, with Gordon making that offer on behalf of Liberty Life. It was now Nedbank's turn to make an offer for the Bank of Lisbon building. Abrahamsen offered R20 million. Muller reminded him of the rules of the game and the offer was increased to R23 million, and above this Abrahamsen refused to go. So Muller's carefully thought out swop transaction was aborted, much to the amazement of all, as Abrahamsen stubbornly stuck to his guns.

So the Nedbank 50 per cent interest in Eastgate was sold to Liberty Life for a mere R27 million, while the Bank of Lisbon building remained firmly in Liberty Life's pocket. Neither Gordon nor Rapp could believe their luck – or the degree of misjudgement of Abrahamsen and Nedbank's negotiating team.

Only a year later, Liberty Life turned down an offer of R35 million from Nedbank for the Bank of Lisbon building. The full extent of Nedbank's error can be gauged from the fact that Eastgate (all 100 per cent of it) was valued at R300 million in Liberty Life's 1988 property valuation.

Another interesting anecdote from the seventies concerns Raymond Ackerman and Pick n Pay. Ackerman, who had built up the Checkers supermarket chain for Greatermans in the sixties, had begun again in the early seventies with six small stores in the Cape, and that was the beginning of Pick n Pay, a major success story in its own right. But it only really began to take off when it invaded the Transvaal, and the real spur to its growth came with the expansion of its hypermarket chain. That was when Liberty Life entered the picture. Wolf Cesman takes up the tale:

"In 1976 and 1977 the country was deep in the property doldrums and Raymond Ackerman, of whom we knew very little, approached us. He had secured a site in Norwood, a suburb to the north-east of Johannesburg, and highly accessible, and was looking for finance to build his second hypermarket. It would cost some R6 million, a lot of money in those times, especially for property development. But, thanks to our link with Liberty Life, money was less of a constraint to Rapp & Maister than it was to almost all our rival developers. Anyway, Rapp and I quite liked the look of the proposition – and we badly needed the construction work.

"So we presented the deal to Donald Gordon. He was horrified; he perceived the whole hypermarket concept to be an enormous risk, and 'who was this man Ackerman, anyway?' Even so, we set up a meeting, and I remember DG saying to Ackerman: 'I don't know how you'll ever make this thing pay – it's going to be a R6 million white elephant.' And Ackerman riposted: 'Don't worry, I know what I'm doing, and it will pay.'

"Then we looked at his balance sheet, and it showed a lot of money in the bank. DG immediately said: 'But that's not your money, you owe almost the whole lot to your creditors, your suppliers.' Ackerman explained that that was the way he ran his business – the goods came in, were turned into cash, and then the creditors were paid. At that time, of course, the net worth of Pick n Pay was nowhere near what it is today, and Gordon remained sceptical about the Norwood hypermarket deal.

"But Rapp & Maister needed that construction work badly, and Rapp and I came up with an ingenious plan. What about a R6 million insurance policy on Ackerman's life, ceded to us? DG relented – after all, it was a big fat policy for Liberty Life. So we went ahead with the R6 million project, and a R6 million 22-year endowment policy on Ackerman's life was taken out with Liberty Life, and ceded back to Liberty Life as security."

So the Norwood hypermarket was built and Pick n Pay did a great deal more business with Liberty Life over the years, "before they got smart and started funding some of their shopping developments themselves". Gordon freely concedes that Liberty Life missed a great opportunity by not backing Pick n Pay and Raymond Ackerman more whole-heartedly from the beginning.

The Annual Report for the year ended 31 December 1977, which marked the Group's twentieth anniversary, was noteworthy for the fact that it contained Liberty Life's very first "Chairman's Review". Hitherto, the "Directors' Report" had embraced both the statutory and general aspects of communication with shareholders. From 1977 onwards, the "Chairman's Review" would grow more and more wide-ranging and authoritative. From 1977's modest 4-page start, it would burgeon to 13 pages by 1988, by when it had become a document that annually attracted considerable press attention, both in South Africa and overseas.

The Annual Report for the year ended 31 December 1979 was the first to note property interests above R200 million. Gordon had said in 1970 that Liberty Life's objective was to have R100 million invested in property by the end of that decade. Inflation, of course, played its insidious role in the doubling of that target. "Freehold property, leasebacks and other property interests" totalled R227,6 million, out of total investments of R940,3 million, or a property exposure of 24,2 per cent of the whole. The Report also carried an architect's illustration of the new Group Headquarters that was soon to rise in Braamfontein. "The dramatic expansion of the Company in recent years has given rise to the need for functionally designed corporate headquarters. Planning has been preceded by detailed research into the long-term requirements of a major life insurance group, and in-depth studies of developments overseas. The buildings are being specifically designed to cater for the special functional requirements of the Liberty Life Group with all levels of management being involved in the planning process."

Around this time, the once-proud first Liberty Life Group head office – the building that was taller than Mandy Moross's – was sold to South African Airways for a capital gain of almost R20 million. For technical reasons, this transaction was completed by way of expropriation.

The balance sheet for the year ended 31 December 1980 showed property investments up to R360 million out of an investment portfolio totalling just over R1 305 million, or a property exposure of 27,6 per cent. Some financial commentators regarded this as being on the high side, and Gordon in his "Group Chairman's Statement for 1981" took up their challenge: "The past year has been highlighted by the complete vindication of Liberty Life's long-standing faith in real estate, which has been reflected by an uplift in underlying value, including surpluses realised, of over R100 million in 1981 as disclosed in the annual open market valuation of Liberty Life's property interests conducted at 31 December 1981. This escalation in value has resulted in substantial benefits to shareholders and to policyholders who have property-related life policies with Liberty Life or who participate in managed funds which are also importantly geared to Liberty Life's property portfolio. The uplift in property values, together with the surplus arising from the expropriation by the South African Airways of Guardian Liberty Centre and Shell House, both of which are situated close to the Railways' Headquarters in Braamfontein, Johannesburg, has been the major single factor accounting for the significant increase in non-distributable reserves. In addition, the R49 million increase in investment surpluses, development and other reserves included in the Life Fund arose to a large extent as a result of property revaluations and at the year end, these reserves aggregated nearly R190 million."

In September 1982 Liberty Life celebrated its Silver Anniversary by taking up occupation of its outstanding new R30 million head office building in Braamfontein, "designed to satisfy the growth requirements of the Group well into the twenty-first century". Well, perhaps, but that was written a few years before the takeover of the Prudential of South Africa – and this, as we have noted, led to a major expansion of Liberty Life Centre in 1988.

Property investments continued to grow, particularly as they reflected the Group's rapidly growing United Kingdom interests, and at 31 December 1982 they totalled R630 million out of an overall portfolio of R2 227 million, or 28,3 per cent.

In his "Group Chairman's Statement for 1983" Gordon proudly listed the major current property developments: "In real estate, the second phase expansion programme for Sandton City, north of Johannesburg, was virtually complete by year-end and the synergy of the component parts of this massive development can be expected to result in a significantly enhanced contribution to the Group's income in the coming year. Among the project's major features is the new R55 million Sandton Sun Hotel that was opened in February 1984. With its innovative design and high quality construction, I predict that the Sandton Sun is destined to become one of South Africa's great hotels, and one that will measure up to the highest standards found anywhere in the world. We are proud to be associated with the Southern Sun Hotel group in this exciting venture.

"A number of other projects will be completed in 1984, including the R33 million Libridge office complex in Braamfontein, and the R25 million Liberty Life Building in Pretoria. The group's real estate interests also include an indirect stake in Capital & Counties plc, a major London property investment company, and this brings the total value of our property interests to well over R1 billion."

Sandton City – the jewel in Liberty Life's property crown – was originally planned by Rapp & Maister in the late sixties as an up-market residential development in the suburb of Sandown, north of Johannesburg.

With the proclamation of the new municipality of Sandton, incorporating both Sandown and the adjacent suburb of Bryanston, in 1969, the plans were changed dramatically as Michael Rapp rapidly grasped the importance of the site he had assembled on land adjoining the new town's city centre. Despite objections, noisy public hearings and all possible obstruction by the – mostly rich and influential – residents of the area (one of whom, the late Ian MacPherson, was a director of Liberty Life) consents for the office and shop development, as opposed to the original residential-only zoning, were granted in 1973 – the actual Promulgation was on 30 May of that year.

By then, with Rapp & Maister cannily taking advantage of the business rights earlier granted over a relatively small portion of the site assembled (much of the remainder was first utilised for parking, pending rezoning) the first stage of Sandton City was nearing completion. It opened on 11 September 1973. Although its original 30 000 square metres would later be temporarily dwarfed by Eastgate's 100 000 square metres, Sandton City was in fact the first big regional shopping centre in the southern hemisphere, and great credit for its conception must go to Michael Rapp – now pioneering similar complexes in the United Kingdom for the Group's UK property company, Capital & Counties.

"Sandton City phase two", recalls Cesman, "began in 1982 when Rapp started to become concerned about the extent of retail competition in the northern suburbs. Rosebank had been developed into an important centre and Rapp was worried at the growth of various other smaller centres around our catchment area. He took the view that if we didn't expand Sandton to make it a really dominant centre, then we would have trouble with the competition.

"So the concept was to treble the centre's size from 30 000 square metres to 100 000 square metres, to build additional offices in the form of the Twin Towers, to incorporate an international-class hotel and to add more parking. Although world-wide there are now bigger centres – there's one in Edmonton, Canada, which is 400 000 square metres, and our own Capital & Counties Lakeside development just outside London will be 120 000 square metres – I don't believe there is, anywhere in the world, an integrated centre with a hotel, three office towers, acres of parking, plus 100 000 square metres of shopping. Sandton City is unique.

"It was all very well to triple the shopping space, however, but we believed that, to be successful, the centre would need Woolworths as a major tenant. We regarded Woolworths as the premier store operator at the time, and a major drawcard; I still do, in fact. But the snag, and it was a very large snag, was that Woolworths had only recently opened a large new store in Rosebank, barely four kilometres away. I talked to Woolworths' property director, Ernst

Loebenberg, and he advised me that the Woolworths Board was split – some said they should come into Sandton City, others that since they had already opened in Rosebank, there was no point opening in Sandton. They felt that the two stores would be serving the same traffic, and that there would not be enough custom for both.

"We tried our damnedest to convince them they were wrong, because we were sure in our own minds that we really needed Woolworths. My friend Loebenberg came up with a wonderful expression which he got from his Chairman, David Susman: 'We are only prepared to open in Sandton provided we don't have to eat our own entrails.' Well, we were still anxious to have Woolworths, and at last we came up with an unusual idea. As far as I'm concerned, the deal we struck with Woolworths was the most unusual property transaction we have ever done.

"Normally, an anchor at that time would pay a minimum rental of perhaps R6 or R7 per square metre per month, or a turnover rental, whichever was the greater. To persuade Woolworths to come into Sandton City with a store of about 4 000 square metres, we offered them an abnormally low basic rental of R100 000 a year, or a normal turnover rental, whichever was the greater. But, and this was the very big but, for as long as their turnover at Rosebank fell below the level of R12 million a year, or R1 million a month, which they were doing at the time, then the new Sandton store would pay us only that token R100 000 a year, and its turnover clause would not operate, irrespective of the magnitude of the turnover generated in Sandton City. So, if we were wrong, we could be saddled for years with a derisory rental from the Sandton anchor – it was probably the biggest property gamble we have ever taken.

"Before signing the lease, we agreed on two refinements. The first was that we would work on a moving twelve-month average period rather than a fixed financial year. Second, they accepted that if Rosebank did not drop below its R12 million in the twelve months, then the turnover rent at Sandton would operate as from day one.

"Well, you can imagine that I was more than a little interested in how things were going at Woolworths, Rosebank. I told my wife to shop there, and to tell all her friends to, as well: I even contemplated hiring a bus to ferry shoppers from Sandton City to Rosebank! I wasn't a bit concerned as to how Woolworths were faring in Sandton, though they did exceptionally well right from the start. I telephoned the Rosebank manager every single week for his turnover figures, and I kept a piece of paper on my desk on which I recorded his moving turnover total. Rosebank hit the magic figure of R12 million within nine months of Sandton City's opening, and so the whole exercise turned out to be academic. And the Sandton City Woolworths paid full turnover rental from the day it opened.

"It may have turned out in the end to have been merely an academic exercise," Cesman concludes, "but it was also a very exciting one – and one which typifies the entrepreneurial spirit that permeates the whole Liberty Life group."

Liberty Life is justifiably proud of Sandton City. Gordon sees it as typical of Liberty Life's attitude. "Part of our approach has been to try to identify our policyholders with our real estate developments. We want a policyholder to feel able to go into Sandton City and say, proudly: 'I actually own a chunk of this amazing complex.' We have put this sort of approach over as best we can in our advertising and in our marketing, and we know that our policyholders are proud of what their savings have helped to create."

In the 1983 balance sheet, which of course, reflected only part of Capital & Counties' portfolio, property investments figured at R892 million in a total portfolio of R3 197 million, or 27,9 per cent. By 31 December 1984, however, property holdings had indeed hit the rand billion mark, the balance sheet at that date recording R1 047 million out of a total of R3 978 million, down slightly to 26,3 per cent.

In his 1985 "Group Chairman's Statement", Gordon reported: "The Liberty Life Group's total assets increased by almost 60 per cent to reach R6,87 billion at 31 December 1985 (31 December 1984: R4,31 billion) having doubled over the past two years from R3,46 billion at 31 December 1983. The substantial increase in 1985 arose primarily as a result of consolidating Capital & Counties plc for the first time. This quality United Kingdom property company became a subsidiary of Liberty Life in July 1985." One important effect of the consolidation of Capital & Counties was that the balance sheet showed property investments more than doubled to R2,27 billion, representing 36,3 per cent of the portfolio total of R6,25 billion. Much of this, however, related directly to the minority shareholders of both Capital & Counties and TransAtlantic Holdings plc, Liberty Life's UK associate.

In the following year, however, Liberty Life's holding in TransAtlantic Holdings, of which Capital & Counties is a major subsidiary, was reduced following a rights issue to below 50 per cent, and the Group's United Kingdom interests were de-consolidated. The Liberty Life balance sheet at 31 December 1986 showed property investments sharply lower at R1,36 billion which, out of a total portfolio slightly higher at R7,27 billion, represented a virtually halved "property exposure" of a relatively modest 18,7 per cent.

This figure, of course, now represents only the South African property interests of the Liberty Life Group. That these have risen from that first ultra-modest R40 000 in 1964 to over R2 billion in 1988 does indeed emphasise Liberty Life's abiding faith in the investment virtues of bricks and mortar. And this figure excludes, of course, the property portfolio of Capital & Counties, which exceeds R3 billion in value in its own right.

From this point on, however, the major focus of the Group's real estate development is more likely to move into the United Kingdom and the international arena. Thus another fascinating era is opening up for Liberty Life in the sophisticated world of real estate, and Liberty Life's vast experience in this field internationally adequately qualifies it to take on this challenge.

# 12 The Battle for Edgars Stores

On Wednesday 3 February 1982 the newspaper headlines trumpeted: "Liberty, Press keep Edgars". Behind that cryptic comment lay an enthralling story of business foresight and naked ambition. And, when the dust had finally settled, the stage would be set for Liberty Life's next great industrial leap forward – to joint control of Premier Milling and through it a dominant position in South African Breweries.

The "Press" of that headline was Sydney Press, founder of South Africa's leading clothing retail group, Edgars Stores, and, with his family trusts, the major shareholder in the Edgars' controlling pyramid, Edgars Consolidated Investments (Edcon). Control of Edcon, with its 50 per cent stake in Edgars, carried with it effective control of Edgars; hence Edcon was the prime, the cheapest, and the simplest route for acquiring control of the mammoth stores group, which in 1982 had 387 stores across the nation.

But first, it is necessary to paint in the background. Although Press had originally formed Edcon to protect his control of Edgars, as was fashionable in the post-war years in corporate South Africa, such control was not watertight in this case, particularly as the family trusts had needed, from time to time, to sell parcels of shares. Some six years previously he had invited Donald Gordon to join the Edcon Board. Says Gordon: "It was in 1976 that, quite out of the blue, I received an invitation from Sydney, whom I barely knew." Perhaps Press was being far-sighted, looking ahead to the day he would need a powerful big brother.

In the event, the two men, both entrepreneurs extraordinary, got on well. "It was a pleasant, if not very exciting Board," muses Gordon, "and over the years we did a few deals and handled one or two debenture issues for Edgars. It was a very easy, convivial, appointment."

And, as the family interests from time to time sold small parcels of shares, the Liberty Life investment department, in common with many another institution, was a willing buyer in the market. Thus by early 1982 Liberty held some 10 per cent of Edcon, not all that important a holding in itself, and of considerably less moment, in terms of what was to come, than the rapport that had built itself up between the two men. And the Press family stake was down to 28 per cent – enough for effective day-to-day control but by no means a cast-iron position should predators be on the prowl.

Another event of importance to this story had occurred in 1978, when Press had appointed, as managing director of Edgars, one Adrian Bellamy, a bright, brash, ambitious and very efficient young man. He proved an outstanding appointment. Says Press: "Following his appointment, Bellamy soared like an eagle. Totally committed to the task ahead, he worked phenomenally hard and with a mind which must be likened to a computer."

And just as well, because Press' health soon began to falter, and early in 1981 he underwent serious open heart surgery. "While I was recovering, Bellamy sought to acquire Russells Furniture, which would have been a disaster. Fortunately for us, Natie Kirsh pipped him to the post." A large line of Russells' shares was, ironically, provided by Liberty Life, who were completely oblivious of Edgars' interest.

Press recovered, but Bellamy's takeover appetite had been whetted, and he now turned his attentions towards Greatermans, a big retail conglomerate (Checkers supermarkets and Greatermans and Ackermans departmental stores) that had had a more than somewhat chequered career in recent years.

Gordon takes up the story: "Bellamy was very much in control at Edgars and towards the end of 1981 a proposal kept on coming up to the Edcon Board that Edgars and/or Edcon should acquire the Greatermans group. From time to time Sydney seemed somewhat receptive to the idea, and then he would turn against it. He appeared to me to be always conscious of the right opportunity and the right price. A lot of discussion went on and I watched mainly from the sidelines."

Press recollects: "Initially, I was positive about the acquisition, but later turned firmly against it – a consequence of two steps taken: Firstly, I called on Natie Werksman, who had long served on the Greatermans Board and, in response to the penetrating question, would the customary month suffice to check into that group, or should we request three months before exercising our option, got an eloquent grimace plus the terse observation: 'Rather three months . . .' That significant reply gave me pause.

"Additionally, I sought the opinion of Herb Seegal – former president of Macy's (nation-wide) in the United States – whom I had engaged, post-retirement, as consultant to Edgars. Seegal, a redoubtable retailer with an unusually analytic cast of mind, pointed out that Edgars' merchandise range comprised circa 45 000 SKUs (stock-keeping units) whereas Greatermans department stores would extend across some 120 000 – including classifications such as crockery and glassware, cutlery, appliances, refrigerators, washing machines, etc, about which Edgars knew nothing. Years would be needed to identify and develop the necessary merchandise managers."

Gordon continues: "I had certain reservations about the acquisition. I remember going down one weekend to Max Borkum's (senior partner of stockbrokers Davis, Borkum, Hare, and a highly trusted friend and associate of Gordon) farm in the Eastern Transvaal with Bellamy to talk about it all with Isaac Kaye (then joint controller of Greatermans). We spent the whole day drinking wine under the doringboom (thorn tree); all sorts of ideas were kicked backwards and forwards, but nothing concrete came of it all. Even so, it was a most enjoyable day, although we were badly shaken by flying through an electric storm on the flight back to Lanseria Airport.

"Time went on, and Bellamy was getting more and more excited at the prospect of acquiring Greatermans, which he regarded as a very enticing proposition. My reservations, however, became more acute – I began to have severe doubts about Greatermans, its viability and its management. The matter became more and more a topic for the Edcon Board – as the controlling Board – and I think there must have been disagreements between Press and Bellamy, as Bellamy was pressing harder and harder.

"By early 1982, Sydney Press was seriously ill again, and during January, when I was in London, I received a call from him to tell me that he had to go to the Cleveland Clinic, in Ohio, for a re-do of his earlier quadruple by-pass surgery, and to ask whether I would act as Chairman of Edcon in his absence. And he specifically conveyed to me that under no circumstances was I to be pushed by Bellamy into the Greatermans deal."

Here, one should perhaps digress to look at the composition of the

An artist's impression of Liberty Life's first self-owned Head Office building in Braamfontein, Johannesburg. The original Guardian Liberty Centre was occupied by the Group until the move in 1982 to Liberty Life Centre, a few blocks to the north west, close to the University of the Witwatersrand and adjacent to the South African Breweries head office at the crest of Jan Smuts Avenue.

Standing outside the original Guardian Liberty Centre after its 1973 opening are Gordon with three of his senior executives, all subsequently appointed to the Liberty Life Board. From left are Mark Winterton (who was appointed to the Board in November 1974 and is now joint managing director), Donald Gordon, Monty Hilkowitz (the managing director from 1981 to 1986 when he relocated to Australia) and Steve Handler (the executive director in charge of individual life administration who was appointed to the Board in February 1979).

Farrell Sher, who was appointed an executive director of Liberty Holdings in July 1981, has been with the Group since completing his law degree at the University of the Witwatersrand in 1968. Sher, a close confidant of Gordon, has been heavily involved in virtually all of the Liberty Life Group's corporate transactions over the last two decades. He is also responsible for the management of the Group holding company, Liberty Holdings.

Roy McAlpine, who was appointed to the Board of Liberty Holdings in July 1981, is a Scottish trained chartered accountant, and has, for the past 15 years, been in charge of the Group's investment operations other than its real estate. McAlpine is managing director of Liberty Asset Management and is responsible for the GuardBank Management Corporation, the management company of the Group's successful mutual fund operations.

Wolf Cesman, who is also a chartered accountant, was appointed to the Board of Liberty Holdings in July 1981, and assumed the position of managing director of Rapp & Maister Real Estate following Michael Rapp's relocation to the UK. Cesman has full responsibility for, inter alia, the Group's South African R2 billion real estate operations.

Lewis Neuburger, who is a civil engineer, has been the managing director of Rapp & Maister Construction since 1977 and has been responsible for the construction of virtually all of the Group's real estate developments in South Africa from that date. Neuburger was appointed to the Board of Liberty Holdings in July 1981.

Extensions to the Head Office of the Group – Liberty Life Centre in Braamfontein, Johannesburg – to be linked by way of an overhead bridge over Melle Street to Libridge, another major Liberty Life property development immediately to the east of the Head Office.

Sandton City to the north of Johannesburg – the first and phenomenally successful regional shopping centre developed for Liberty Life in South Africa, includes 3 office towers, a 'five star' hotel and 100,000 square metres of shopping.

Eastgate, another highly successful Liberty Life owned regional shopping complex on the main road to Jan Smuts International Airport, also provides about 100,000 square metres of shopping facilities to the residents of the conurbation which has grown rapidly to the east of Johannesburg.

Wynand Louw was an outstanding incumbent of the important office of Registrar of Financial Institutions from 1972 to 1980 and later joined the Boards of both Prudential SA and the United Building Society, of which Gordon was deputy chairman.

Professor Michael Katz, one of South Africa's leading corporate lawyers, played a vital role in most of Liberty Life's major corporate transactions during the past two decades.

Donald Gordon and E S (Sid) Jackson, President of the Manufacturers Life Insurance Company of Toronto, Canada, sign the historic 1972 agreement which marked the first merger of a 'mutual' with a 'proprietary' life insurance company in South Africa. Sid Jackson later assumed the Chairmanship of Manufacturers Life.

In 1974 Sun Life of Canada joined the Liberty Life family. After Sun Life's Chairman, Tom Galt, joined its Board, Liberty Life had a unique directorate which included (from left) Tim Collins – Chairman of the Guardian Royal Exchange, Donald Gordon – Chairman of Liberty Life, Tom Galt – Chairman of Sun Life of Canada, Sid Jackson – President (later Chairman) of the Manufacturers Life, and Ernest Bigland – managing director (later deputy chairman) of the GRE.

Donald Gordon and Sir Ian Gwynne-Evans signing the agreement to acquire the Real Estate Corporation of South Africa – a move which culminated in Liberty Life's emergence as one of the leading property owners in South Africa, with real estate at year end 1988 valued at over R2 billion, excluding some R3 billion of real estate owned by associate company Capital & Counties in the UK.

One of South Africa's foremost entrepreneurs, Dr Anton Rupert – Chairman of the giant Rembrandt Group and a close associate and personal friend of Donald Gordon – officially opening the Liberty Life Centre in 1982. Liberty Life is a substantial shareholder in the Rembrandt Group and the international offshoot, Richemont Securities.

Ernest Bigland marks the occasion of the opening of the Liberty Life Centre with a speech to an illustrious gathering of leading business luminaries and other connections at a sparkling banquet held in September 1982, in the atrium of the new Head Office building.

Gerry Muller, retired managing director of Nedbank which was Liberty Life's first banker. Muller has been a long time supporter of Liberty Life and personal friend of Gordon, albeit a reluctant erstwhile partner in Eastgate! He was an early director of Investors Mutual Funds which launched Sage Fund in 1965. Liberty Life disposed of its interest in IMF in 1968 following a dispute with Shill over the policy of the company.

After the opening ceremony Peggy and Donald Gordon commenced the dancing and were joined on the floor by Cyraine and Peter Dugdale. GRE's managing director and his wife specially flew to Johannesburg for the opening of the Liberty Life Centre in September 1982.

The Board of Edgars at the time of the 1982 battle for control prior to the acquisition of the group by South African Breweries shortly thereafter. Front row, from left: Adrian Bellamy; Sydney Press and Sydney Chatfield. Back row, from left: Dudley Preston; Ken Whyte; Gerald Browne; Bill de la Harpe Beck; Bill Wilson and Archie Aaron.

Edgars' founder, Sydney Press (left), and his protégé, Adrian Bellamy, whom Press said was 'totally committed to the task ahead. He worked phenomenally hard and with a mind which must be likened to a computer.' Bellamy was later appointed as a director of South African Breweries until he relocated abroad.

Dick Goss, Chairman of Sun International. Goss was the chief executive of South African Breweries for many years and a major participant in the takeover of the Edgars Group. He resigned from the SAB Board in 1983 following the tumultous events involving the acquisition of a 35 per cent interest in SAB by the Premier Group.

Archie Aaron, longstanding director of Edgars, a leading corporate lawyer and a senior partner of the legal firm, Werksmans, was a major player in the acquisition of Edgars by the South African Breweries.

Max Borkum, senior partner of Davis Borkum Hare Inc, doyen of the Johannesburg Stock Exchange, and close confidant and friend of Gordon. Borkum's strategies initially frustrated the South African Breweries in their acquiring control of the Edgars Group by a well timed 'dawn raid' on Tuesday, 2 February 1982. He has been involved in most of the Liberty Life Group's corporate transactions over a quarter of a century.

# STRUCTURE OF THE LIBERTY LI

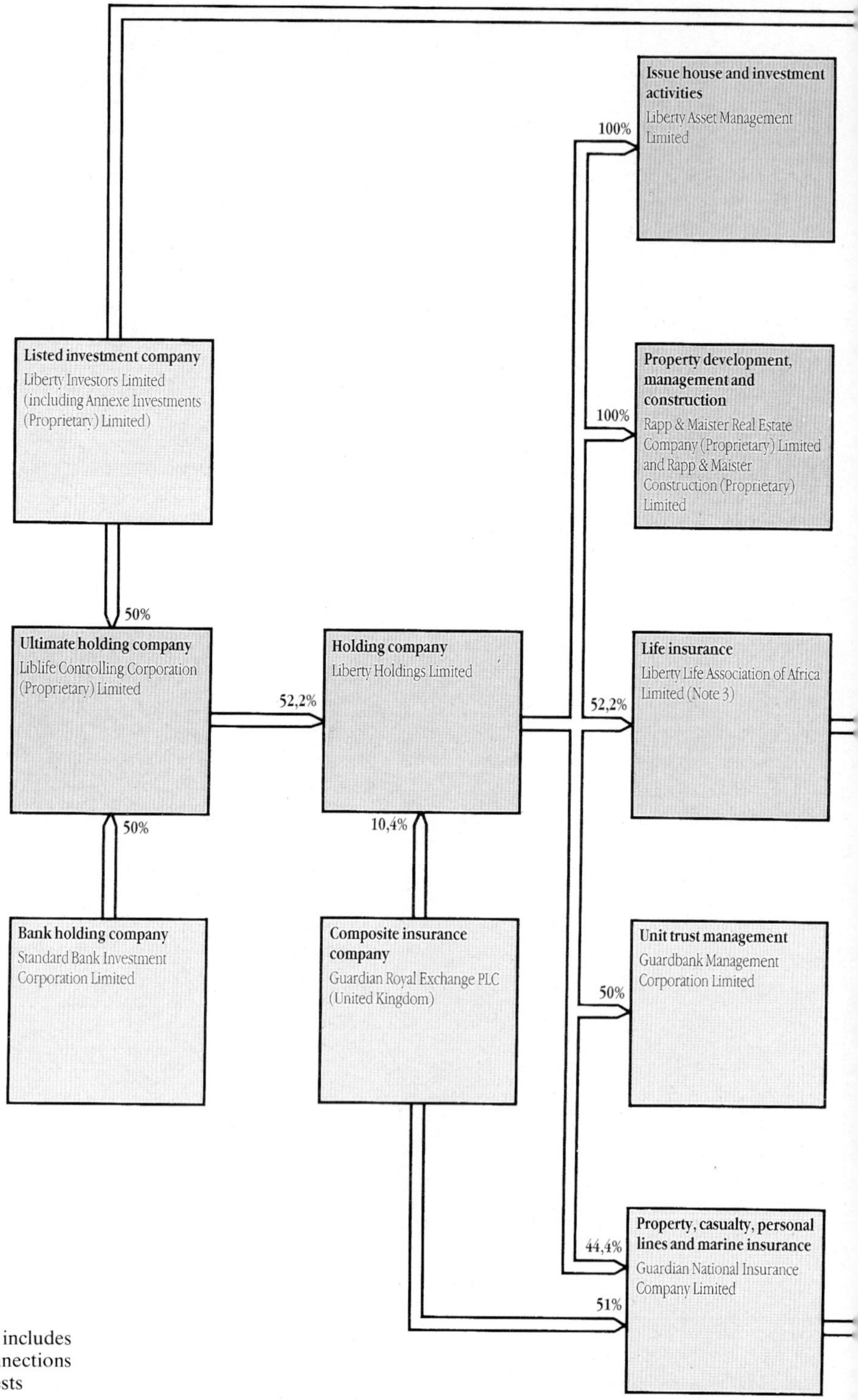

Issue house and investment activities
Liberty Asset Management Limited
100%
Listed investment company
Liberty Investors Limited (including Annexe Investments (Proprietary) Limited)
Property development, management and construction
Rapp & Maister Real Estate Company (Proprietary) Limited and Rapp & Maister Construction (Proprietary) Limited
100%
50%
Ultimate holding company
Liblife Controlling Corporation (Proprietary) Limited
52,2%
Holding company
Liberty Holdings Limited
52,2%
Life insurance
Liberty Life Association of Africa Limited (Note 3)
50%
10,4%
Bank holding company
Standard Bank Investment Corporation Limited
Composite insurance company
Guardian Royal Exchange PLC (United Kingdom)
Unit trust management
Guardbank Management Corporation Limited
50%
Property, casualty, personal lines and marine insurance
Guardian National Insurance Company Limited
44,4%
51%

This table includes major connections and interests

# ROUP AT 31 DECEMBER 1988

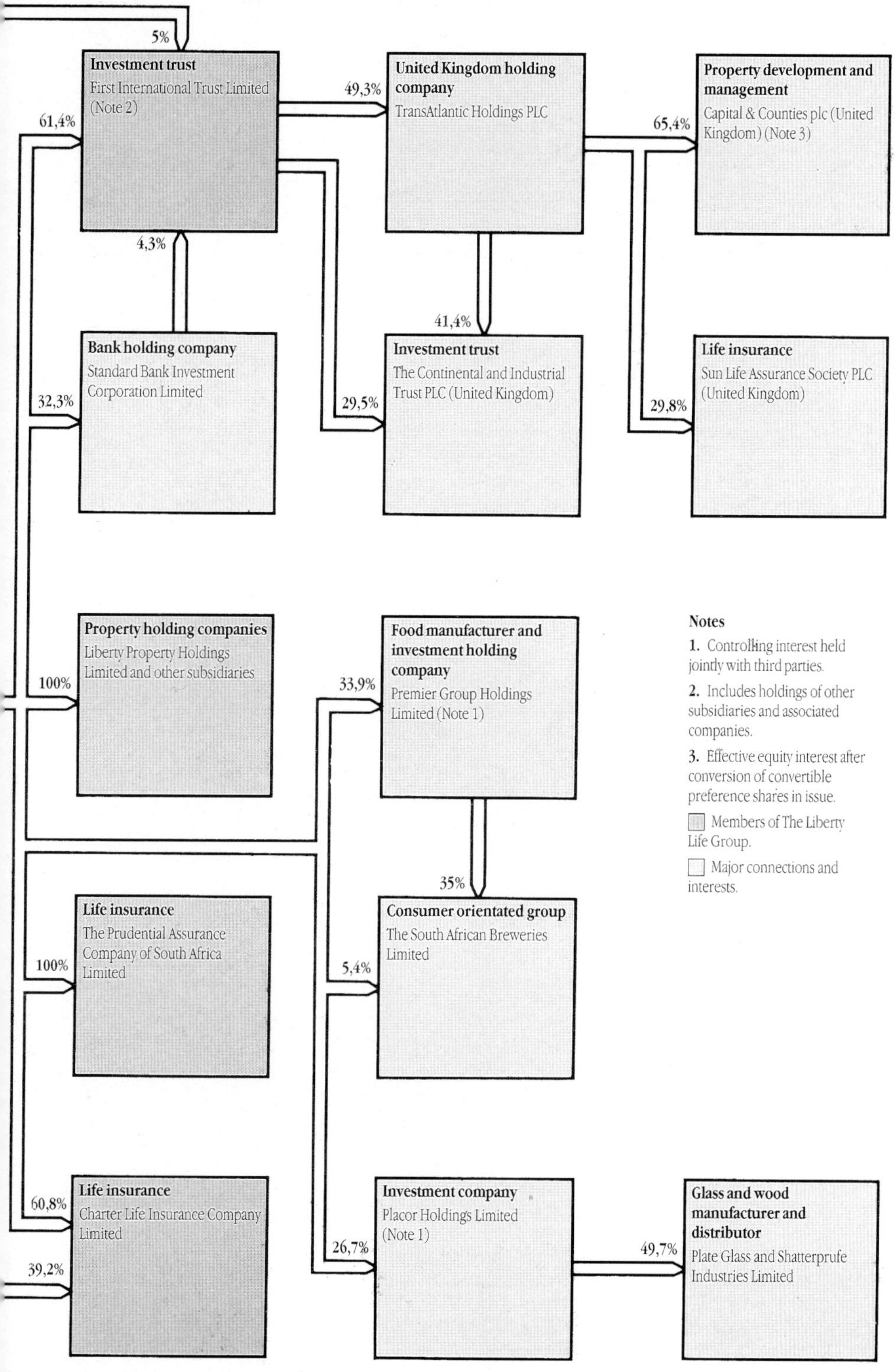


**Notes**

1. Controlling interest held jointly with third parties.
2. Includes holdings of other subsidiaries and associated companies.
3. Effective equity interest after conversion of convertible preference shares in issue.

▒ Members of The Liberty Life Group.

☐ Major connections and interests.

South African Breweries executives before the big imbroglio in 1983. From left: F Mc D Moodie; Laurie van der Watt; Ken Williams; Meyer Kahn; Sol Kerzner; Dick Goss; Craig Waigel; Selwyn MacFarlane; Adrian Bellamy; R S Cohen and T J Olivier.

Tony Bloom (left) was Chairman of the Premier Group at the time of the 1983 South African Breweries clash. He was also, at that time, a director of Liberty Life. On his retirement from the Chair of Premier in 1988 he was succeeded by Peter Wrighton, who had previously served as deputy chairman. Bloom was the fourth generation of his family to head up this food and milling empire.

Gavin Relly was appointed Chairman of the mighty Anglo American Corporation in 1983 on Harry Oppenheimer's retirement. Relly was, early in his reign, confronted with problems arising from the drama of the South African Breweries clash. Liberty Life is a significant shareholder in Anglo American and the wider Anglo American/De Beers Group.

Gordon Waddell, Chairman of Johannesburg Consolidated Investment Company at the time of the South African Breweries drama, played a major role with Gordon and Bloom in the acquisition of the Premier Group from Associated British Foods and in the linking of the shareholdings in SAB of Liberty Life, JCI and Anglo American under the control of the Premier Group.

Meyer Kahn, who became group managing director of South African Breweries in 1983 after Goss's resignation, was previously deputy managing director and prior to that managing director of OK Bazaars. In 1983 Kahn joined the Boards of both the Liberty Life Group and JCI. SAB has seen unprecedented growth under Kahn's leadership, with taxed earnings exceeding R500 million in 1989.

Sol Kerzner, who also resigned from the Board of South African Breweries in 1983 after the Premier/SAB clash, initially acquired 51 per cent of the casino interests of its hotel subsidiary, Southern Sun Hotels, separating them from the core hotel business. Kerzner formed Sun International and was joined by Goss.

Frans Cronje was Chairman of South African Breweries until he retired in 1984. He was also Chairman, for a very long period, of Nedbank and was a director of Investors Mutual Funds for many years. Cronje presided over the traumatic 1983 SAB Board meetings following the structuring of the Premier/SAB transaction.

Jan van der Horst, Chairman of the South African Mutual, South Africa's largest life insurer. He was a director of South African Breweries for many years and of Anglo American Corporation from whose Board he resigned in protest following the announcement of the 1983 Premier/SAB transaction. Notwithstanding clashes between Liberty Life and Old Mutual over the years, Donald Gordon has the highest admiration for van der Horst and his achievements, particularly at the Old Mutual.

Max Borkum, Donald Gordon and Meyer Kahn at a celebratory luncheon in November 1988 following the launch of First International Trust as the international investment vehicle of the Liberty Life Group.

Alan Romanis, a Scottish trained chartered accountant, joined Liberty Life in 1975 and was appointed to the Liberty Life Board in August 1986. He is now the financial director of Liberty Life.

James Inglis joined Liberty Life's investment department in 1974 and was appointed to the Board of Liberty Holdings in August 1986. He plays an important role in administering the burgeoning investment interests of the Liberty Life Group and is responsible for the fund Management services rendered by Liberty Asset management, of which he is also a director.

Dorian Wharton-Hood was appointed joint managing director of Liberty Life in April 1987 following the acquisition of Prudential Assurance Company of South Africa in 1986. He was previously managing director of Prudential SA and played a major role in the negotiations leading up to the acquisition of this subsidiary by Liberty Life.

Yves D'Halluin joined the company in 1972 following the acquisition of Manufacturers Life. He has gradually moved up through the ranks and his great success in the promotional field was rewarded by his appointment to the Board of Liberty Life in March 1989. He has responsibility for the marketing operations of Liberty Life.

Henri de Villiers, Chairman of Standard Bank since 1985 and now also deputy Chairman of both Liberty Life and Liberty Holdings, was appointed to the Boards of both these companies in February 1979 following the major role he played in the reacquisition of control of Liberty Life from GRE by Liblife Controlling Corporation in 1978, when Standard Bank became a 25 per cent shareholder of the latter company. He was also heavily involved in increasing the Standard Bank Group participation in Liblife Controlling to 50 per cent in 1983. De Villiers, in conjunction with Ian Mackenzie, strongly promoted Liberty Life's acquisition of the largest shareholding in the Standard Bank Group, to the maximum statutory level.

Ian Mackenzie was Chairman of Standard Bank Investment Corporation throughout the period from when Liberty Life first became associated with the Standard Bank Group until his retirement in 1985. He was a staunch and enthusiastic supporter of Donald Gordon and the close association between the Standard Bank Group and Liberty Life. Mackenzie went to great lengths to persuade Standard Chartered Bank to accept the powerful linkage between the two institutions.

Conrad Strauss, the group managing director and chief executive of Standard Bank Investment Corporation, joined the Boards of Liberty Life and Liberty Holdings in November 1983. He has played a major role in strengthening and extending the existing links between the two institutions.

The new administration building in Johannesburg for the Standard Bank Group, in which Liberty Life has a substantial equity interest. Liberty Life also has a financial participation in the building, which was erected by Rapp & Maister Construction.

Quality is a cornerstone of the Liberty Life philosophy. This dedication to excellence is highlighted by this striking modern office block in Fifth Street, Sandton.

Dennis Marler was the managing director of Capital & Counties when TransAtlantic acquired its first 29,6 per cent interest in that company in 1981. He had taken the Chair of Capital & Counties prior to the acquisition of full control by TransAtlantic in 1985 and was strongly supportive of, and a catalyst for, the formation of the excellent relationship that developed.

Robin Baillie, as managing director of Standard Chartered Merchant Bank, was one of TransAtlantic's early advisors in the UK. He still is a non-executive director of Standard Chartered Bank following his retirement from executive duties at the merchant bank and late in 1988 he joined the Board of TransAtlantic.

David Fischel, a chartered accountant trained at Touche Ross, a leading London accounting firm, joined TransAtlantic in 1986. He became finance director of TransAtlantic in April 1988 following the resignation of Michael Middlemas. Fischel additionally assumed the position of financial director of Capital & Counties in December 1988 when he was appointed to the Board of that company.

Julian Benson was for many years a partner of the London stockbroking firm of Laing & Cruickshank and looked after the affairs of Liberty Life following its London listing in 1981. He was appointed to TransAtlantic's Board in 1980 and negotiated the acquisition of the initial stake in Sun Life from the Kuwait Investment Office. He has been deeply involved in building up TransAtlantic's interest in Sun Life to its current 29,8 per cent level.

Sir Brian Corby, the managing director of the Prudential Corporation of the UK has a long-standing relationship with Liberty Life and Donald Gordon. He was personally responsible for negotiating the disposal of Prudential's South African subsidiary to Liberty Life in 1986. Corby was knighted in June 1989 and will become Chairman of Prudential, the UK's largest life assurer, in 1990.

The Marquess of Douro joined the Board of TransAtlantic in December 1983 and was nominated by TransAtlantic as one of its two representative directors on the Board of Sun Life following the September 1988 EGM when Sun Life's controversial proposals to issue 18,2 per cent of its enlarged capital to French insurer UAPI and to dilute TransAtlantic's holding were defeated.

Peter Grant, formerly deputy chairman of the London merchant bankers, Lazard Brothers, was appointed Chairman of Sun Life in December 1982. Since his appointment he has been Donald Gordon's constant adversary in TransAtlantic's objective to achieve an accommodation with the Sun Life Board. Since September 1988, however, a more conciliatory relationship has developed.

Richard Zamboni (right), was, until early 1989, managing director of Sun Life. Contact between him and TransAtlantic was restricted to a minimum by his Chairman, Peter Grant. Zamboni was succeeded by John Reeve (left) who had joined Sun Life the previous year.

Peggy and Donald Gordon and Henri de Villiers entertaining some members of the TransAtlantic Board at leisure in Plettenberg Bay during a visit to South Africa in February 1989. From left: Robin Baillie; Gail Benjamin (DG's secretary); Henri de Villiers; Peter Greenfield; Lord Newall; Donald Gordon; Ivan Gray; the Hon Sir Angus Ogilvy; Peggy Gordon; David Fischel and Julian Benson.

Donald Gordon with his current secretary and aide, Gail Benjamin, who joined him in June 1982. She is an exceptional secretary, dynamic, efficient and a true professional. Gail is enormously supportive of the requirements of Gordon's demanding business life.

The ubiquitous and loyal Isaac More, Gordon's chauffeur, has now been with Liberty Life for over two decades and despite his advancing years is determined to stay on in the company's service, until Gordon retires.

Farrell Sher, Donald Gordon and Roy McAlpine pictured on the floor of the Johannesburg Stock Exchange at the commencement of the listing of Liberty Investors Limited in November 1986. Libvest is the public company through which Gordon and his executives hold their interests in the Liberty Holdings Group, through Liblife Controlling Corporation. Libvest and Standard Bank Investment Corporation have effective joint control of the Liberty Life Group.

Peggy and Donald Gordon after 32 years of marriage and teamwork, do not appear to be showing too much of the stress and pressure inherent in the lifestyle involved in having brought Liberty Life to its current point of eminence and success. Peggy is a director of Liberty Investors Limited.

Boards of Edcon and Edgars. Edcon had Press as Chairman, Gordon, Harold Morony, Owen Sherry and Bill Wilson. On Edgars were Press as Chairman and Bellamy as managing director, with Sydney Chatfield, Archie Aaron, Bill de la Harpe Beck, Gerald Browne, Sir Jan Lewando, Ken Whyte and Bill Wilson. Only two directors sat on both Boards – Press himself, and Wilson, the retired Anglo American managing director and a personal friend of Press. The Edgars Board was the "working" Board, and Bellamy, as managing director on that Board and very much in control at the coal face at that time, bitterly resented his exclusion from the "top" Board. Harold Morony, retired managing director of Barclays Bank, puts that even more strongly: "Bellamy was the type of chap who could not brook control, and he resented the very existence of Edcon, the company that had 50 per cent of Edgars."

Gordon returned to Johannesburg and to his office on Thursday 28 January 1982. Barely had he sat down at his desk when there was a phone call from Bellamy. Could he come urgently to see Gordon – the Greatermans deal was on! Bellamy arrived, together with Archie Aaron (a senior partner in Werksmans, a leading firm of attorneys, and, as noted above, a director of Edgars). They told Gordon that they were very close to a deal with Greatermans and they were both highly enthusiastic about it. Time was pressing, however, as Edgars' option on Greatermans expired on Monday, 1 February, and a potential rival, Natie Kirsh, had – and was thought likely to take up – the second option. There was to be a meeting at Edgars that evening to finalise the deal and Gordon was invited to it as an observer, representing Edcon.

Gordon went to the meeting, attended by the full Edgars Board with the exception of Press, of course, but the proceedings were tape recorded for his benefit. "We started at 5 pm and Bellamy made a detailed presentation. I listened – the proposal was to reverse Edgars into Greatermans, and the theme was developed in great detail by Bellamy. The Board enthusiastically supported the project, everyone, apart from Bill Wilson, even Sydney's overseas advisor Sir Jan Lewando, a retired director of Marks & Spencer, who sat on the Edgars Board at Press's special invitation. I was very concerned as I previously had severe doubts about Greatermans and the idea of reversing Edgars, itself a first-class operation, into that controversial group disturbed me enormously. So I indicated that the deal could not be done without Press's approval, and the approval of the Edcon

Board. Even so, the Edgars Board approved the transaction in principle as the option from Kaye would expire on the Monday."

Press's recollection is based, of course, on the tape recording and on what he was told after his return from Cleveland: "I was opposed to Greatermans and yet the Edgars Board, in my absence, were prepared to go ahead with the deal. It was Bill Wilson and only Bill Wilson who had the gumption and the loyalty to oppose the acquisition of Greatermans. Astonishingly, men of good judgement like Bill Beck and Jan Lewando went along with the deal. So I thank goodness for the Edcon Board, who unanimously supported to me."

Later that same evening, Gordon called an emergency Edcon Board meeting at his Hyde Park home. His colleagues agreed with him that they could not allow Edgars to go ahead with the deal, particularly in view of Gordon's brief from the absent Press, and the fact that Gordon himself was very uncomfortable about the transaction in any event. But it was a tricky situation in view of the Edgars Board's almost unanimous decision, and the very strong feelings being expressed by an emotionally charged Bellamy, who claimed also to be expressing the views of Edgars' top management. Hence it was arranged that there would be an in-depth presentation to the Edcon Board at Gordon's house the next day, Friday 29 January.

Says Gordon: "All the directors of Edcon were present throughout this presentation. The more we went into it and the more we questioned Bellamy and Aaron the more unhappy and uncomfortable I became. I soon decided that there was no way I could be a party to such a transaction and that Edgars were paying a ridiculous price for this acquisition in terms of the effect of the reverse takeover. However, in view of all the sensitivities, I made myself have the patience to sit through the whole two-day presentation – right through Friday and right through Saturday. By then I knew I was absolutely correct and the more we probed Bellamy more and more skeletons came tumbling out of the cupboard and the worms came out of the woodwork. In the end, about 6 pm that Saturday evening, I called a separate meeting of the Edcon directors to decide on tactics; in fact, that separate meeting took place in the adjacent lounge of my home. Our view was unanimous and unequivocal. We then called Bellamy and Aaron into the lounge and I said to them: 'I have to tell you there is no way I can give you the approval of the Edcon Board for this transaction with Greatermans short of a thorough and detailed investigation of Greatermans, and of its finances – a real due diligence auditors' check out.'"

"That's impossible," Bellamy screamed, "the option expires on Monday night at 6 pm, and the sort of investigation you're demanding will take months. And Natie Kirsh has got the second option – if we give up he's going to snap it up."

"Well, so be it," responded Gordon, "if you can't get the option extended, I cannot do anything more about it." The meeting then became very emotional, tempers flared and voices were raised. Says Gordon: "Archie Aaron – I shall never forget this – turned to me and said: 'Do you realise that if you stop this transaction now, Donny, you could be faced with the entire management of Edgars walking out on Monday morning?' I replied: 'I understand that fully, Archie, but nothing is going to force me into accepting this proposition; it is just not a starter.'"

As was to be expected, Gordon firmly stood his ground, and the meeting ended, certainly not on a happy note. Gordon phoned Press in Cleveland, where he was being prepared for serious surgery on the Tuesday. He briefed him on the unhappy situation, got Press's warm gratitude and fullest support – and the news that his doctors wanted no more phone calls – total rest was required ahead of the operation, and probably for several weeks afterwards. So Gordon was left holding the baby, and to his own judgement relative to Sydney Press's life's work, an awful responsibility and a classic no win situation.

An interesting digression here is that, on the Sunday morning, Gordon telephoned Natie Kirsh and had a long conversation. Gordon's recollection is that he asked Kirsh if he was serious about taking up his second option on Greatermans. Kirsh's reply was: "If you don't take it, we're going to buy it." Says Gordon: "I spent an hour and a half with him on the phone trying to persuade him not to go ahead. I said please don't think this is sour grapes, but I must tell you this will be your undoing if you buy Greatermans. The worms in the whole thing are quite, quite horrific; in fact, it is nothing but a can of worms. Do yourself a favour and walk away from it." Said Kirsh, ruefully, four years after the event and shortly after Sanlam had swallowed his Kirsh Trading Group retailing empire, partly (some analysts say almost entirely) as a consequence of his ill-fated takeover of Greatermans: "I just wish he had been that much more persuasive."

That is how financial history is made: that single telephone call could have had a very major impact on the whole future pattern of retailing in South Africa.

Of greater importance to our story is the fact that Bellamy, piqued, disgruntled and bitterly disappointed, went straight to Dick Goss, managing director of South African Breweries. The two men had met previously, at Archie Aaron's house, some weeks earlier. As Aaron remembers it: "I had a call from Dick Goss. We [Werksmans] act for Breweries, and he knew that I was on the Edgars Board. We met, and he said he wanted to make a bid for Edgars; he knew that Press was the major shareholder, and he wanted my advice as to whether he should talk in the first instance to Press or to Bellamy. He made it quite clear that he would not do a deal unless Bellamy remained with the company."

It is interesting to note here that Breweries, which had been rapidly diversifying under Goss's management, had long targeted Edgars as a desirable acquisition. "This was not an opportunistic decision," says a senior Breweries man, "Edgars, and hence Edcon, had been high on our acquisition list for at least four years, and we had been quietly buying shares as and when they became available. Edgars fitted ideally into our concept of Breweries as a mass consumer marketing group."

Aaron continues: "I took the view that there was no point in bothering Press, a sick man, if Bellamy wouldn't go along with a deal, and advised Goss accordingly. He then asked me to arrange a meeting with Bellamy, which I did, at my house. Goss put a broad proposal to Bellamy, who said he wanted to think about it for a couple of days. There were a few more meetings, and eventually Bellamy gave Goss a commitment that if Breweries got control of Edgars, he, Bellamy, would stay on and run it."

Press regards Bellamy's actions at this time in a critical light. "Bellamy had no business talking to Breweries at all. Indeed, it eventually emerged that, eleven days before I left South Africa for Cleveland, Bellamy, without a word to his Chairman or other members of the Board, pursued negotiations with Dick Goss."

Goss recalls the situation only in general terms: "Well, there were lots of rumours floating about concerning both Edgars and Greatermans, but the one that really had me bothered was the prospect of another bidder coming in for Edcon – a major Afrikaans house was rumoured to be interested. The situation was fluid, and everyone gets jittery in a situation like that. I reckon I've done as many deals as most people, and one thing I have always realised is that it's no good having recriminations afterwards; in these situations you should shoot, and you shoot first time, because if you fiddle around wondering what to do it's going to be too late. In this Edcon/Edgars thing, which we had anyway wanted for some time, it seemed to me that more than a few straws in the wind showed that somebody else was lurking around and perhaps getting something together. In that case, I thought I might as well do something right away rather than wait till it was too late."

Whatever really did transpire on Sunday 31 January 1982, it most certainly was not a day of rest. Late that afternoon, Gordon had a telephone call from Goss. It was a matter of urgency – could they meet?

Gordon: "I had a very good business and social relationship with Dick at that time. We used to play tennis together and we would talk about our futures and about our frustrations in business. He'd spent twenty-five years in his business and so had I in mine, and we both thought it was getting a bit much. Anyway, we had a very good, friendly, relationship at family level.

"He came to see me and he said that he believed Edcon was on the point of buying Greatermans. I assured him that he was incorrect and that as far as I was concerned Edcon had not the least intention of buying Greatermans. He persisted, saying that he had it on very good authority, and I again assured him that we were not buying Greatermans. Again he riposted, saying that if we did buy Greatermans, he would immediately launch a bid for Edcon. Obviously, that was the bottom line, so I said: 'Dick, I give you my solemn word of honour that we are not going to buy Greatermans, and I want from you, as Sydney Press is going on the operating table on Tuesday in Cleveland, your promise that you will not make a bid for Edcon until he is back.'"

Gordon further assured Goss that in the unlikely event of a change of mind on Greatermans, he undertook that Goss would be informed immediately. They shook hands, and that's how Gordon thought the matter rested on the afternoon of Sunday 31 January.

Goss, for his part, totally denies having given any kind of undertaking to Gordon, and his overriding concern, it seems, was his strong feeling that a rival bidder – possibly Sanlam – was lurking in the wings. His impression was that Gordon shared his concern that

Edcon was vulnerable to a predator, and if that predator were indeed to be a big life insurance rival, Gordon might even be supportive of Goss.

Whatever the merits of the situation – and in the cut and thrust of big business, a contested takeover is one in which the Queensberry rules are frequently disregarded – there are those who regard that Sunday visit of Goss to Gordon as something of a smokescreen. For the fact of the matter was that Breweries, on the Monday, was buying Edcon shares, heavily. And buying them outside the Johannesburg Stock Exchange, by direct approach to Edcon's many institutional shareholders, who were being offered R12,50 a share, a premium of over 50 per cent above the previous Friday's closing price of R8. Naturally, the institutions were accepting in droves.

Gordon takes up the story again: "Late that Monday, about 5 pm, the head of our investment division, Roy McAlpine, told me that UAL (Union Acceptances Limited – the merchant bank acting for Breweries) had approached us to bid for our Edcon shares. For very sensible and obvious reasons, we were the last institution to be approached. My investment people came to see me and their view was that the offer, more than 50 per cent better than Friday's close, was very attractive, and that unless I had any serious objections they proposed to sell our Edcon shares to Breweries. In a large life insurance office, the investment division must act totally in the interests of the company and its policyholders, irrespective of the fact that their actions might clash with the personal wishes of their directors. Another point was that Breweries were saying that, if they ever raised their offer, even if we had already sold to them, they would give us the benefit of the higher price. This made the offer even more attractive, although in the event it turned out to be Breweries' cardinal error. Incidentally, such an offer would probably have been illegal on the London Stock Exchange. Anyway, the Liberty Life executives were keen to sell, and for the first time in my life I found myself at the wrong end of a takeover bid. I was quite upset, the more so in view of the fact that Sydney would be undergoing surgery the next day, and I felt I was under a personal obligation to him. Anyway, I told the Liberty Life investment division to stall UAL, and called an Edcon Board meeting for that night at my home. The Edcon Board certainly worked hard for their fees during that brief but dramatic period.

"We discussed the matter at length, but there obviously wasn't very much that we could do in the circumstances, especially as even my own people wanted to sell our Edcon shares at the offered price. I was very depressed, and in the end we decided there was nothing we could do; it was very sad and it looked like it was the end for Edcon, and for Edgars. Breweries had obviously been round all the large shareholders, and it seemed most unlikely that they had not taken up the offer. It looked like a dead duck, particularly as, even if I wished to do so, it was very difficult to stop Liberty Life's investment division from selling, as they had their clear fiduciary duties to consider. Anyway, at midnight we broke up the Edcon meeting, and as we parted someone said that this was the wake for a lovely company that was about to be swallowed up by SA Breweries.

"I went to bed, but woke about 4 am, feeling very agitated, and rather depressed and unhappy. I didn't like the situation one little bit, and felt very uncomfortable – almost defiled. I'd been left in the position of custodian of the company by Sydney, who was completely out of touch, and I thought that I just had to try to do something. So, about 5 am, I phoned our stockbroker, Max Borkum, and a few of my senior colleagues, and called them to a meeting at my house at 6 am.

"We took a fresh look at the situation, and tried to find a possible strategy to redress the position. In the dawn light it was clearly an uneasy position; the Press family had about 28 per cent of Edcon, and Liberty Life had some 10 per cent, a combined stake of maybe 38 per cent. The Breweries' institutional foray had probably carried them to nearly 50 per cent already. So Edcon was in fact doomed. But then someone – it may have been Max – spotted what turned out to be the Breweries' Achilles' heel, that undertaking to give any seller the retrospective benefit of any subsequent higher price paid. That meant that we could go to those institutions with a higher offer, and Breweries would be in a quandary at a preemptive strike delivered quickly and efficiently.

"It was a difficult decision, and of course I had no way of knowing what Sydney's attitude would be, or even whether we would have his support. And McAlpine and his team were, to put it mildly, less than happy at the prospect of spending a further R30 million or so on buying Edcon shares at a higher price than the R12,50 offer from Breweries that they in any case felt that we should accept, as they regarded the price as extremely attractive. So I had to take a view, and, somewhat reluctantly I must admit, I decided that we should go into the market, and back to the institutions, to get the 2 million or so shares needed to secure control, making the assumption that Press would go along with us. We could not by any means be sure of this, as I thought him to be somewhat unpredictable and nothing was certain, particularly in view of his poor health – that was another difficult factor in the whole equation, as heart by-pass operations were a new technology at that time and their outcome was uncertain. With great trepidation, I nonetheless gave Borkum the brief to buy 2 million Edcon at R14 a share, knowing that if anything went awry the full consequences would be on my own head."

And buy Edcon was just what Borkum did. An experienced "Dawn Raider" from Anglo American's famous London assault on Consolidated Goldfields, which he had masterminded, he set about his task with relish. Breweries had made a fatal mistake; they had not firmly tied up the institutions that had tentatively agreed to sell Edcon shares at R12,50. In this league of big money, some men's words are not necessarily their bond. After all, the institutions, and their managers, have always their "fiduciary duties" to consider, and to shelter behind, if need be. So, as Borkum went the rounds of the institutions with Edcon's share register in his hands, enough of them switched allegiance; of course, for a number there really was the matter of fiduciary duty – R14 was a better price than R12,50, so they just had to accept. (Indeed, the next issue of *Finance Week* was to describe Breweries' institutional foray that Monday as "An inept dawn raid".)

As Borkum bought, so Breweries dithered. Liberty Life was in the market, buying at R14. If Breweries were to go in as well and pay R14, they were committed to go back to all of Monday's R12,50 acceptors and also pay them R14. As Goss agonised as to what was the best thing to do, Borkum continued buying, and by the time – some time after 11 am – that Goss took the decision that Breweries should indeed enter the market, it was too late. By 11.30 that Tuesday morning, Borkum was able to tell Gordon that the combined "friendly" stake was above the critical 50 per cent mark, on the assumption, of course, that Press would be "onside" with his family's 28 per cent holding.

About midday, Gordon phoned Goss. "Look Dick, between us Press and Liberty Life now have control of Edcon." Gordon was bluffing to some extent, as he couldn't know Press's attitude for certain, but he thought it safe to assume that he would not want to lose the business that had been his life's work. "Goss said he didn't believe me, and by then of course they had started buying. So I said I was sorry that he didn't believe me, but that I thought that we should stop the bloodbath – that he was throwing good money away. Anyway, he wouldn't listen, and they went on buying until 4 pm or so, and then he phoned me and said he had 38 per cent. I said that's fine, because we have 51 per cent. He expressed the hope that Breweries would get Board representation and I retorted: 'No ways, Dick. If you couldn't get in by the front door, you're not going to come in by the back door.'"

"In the fullness of time we would have to relent on this issue", admits Gordon, "but at that moment the adrenalin and the emotions were running high."

So, almost single-handedly – and certainly only by dint of his own very strong will and determination, and his aversion to being taken over – Gordon had prevented control of Edcon going to Breweries. In effect, the decision to intervene in the market was his, and his alone. His senior colleagues were opposed to it, but in the end Gordon persuaded them because of the strategic strength of Liberty Life's potential position. Force of will and an eye to the next move, plus his stubborn determination not to be beaten by anyone, had carried the day. He gives generous credit to Borkum ("Max did a fantastic job"), but Gordon took the vital decisions, and they were not easy ones to take.

But victory brought with it problems, and major problems at that. Press was incommunicado; it was not known when, even if, he would be able to return to work, or indeed even if he would survive his operation, as complications had unfortunately set in. And Breweries, with its 38 per cent, was the largest single shareholder, with the Press family sitting on 28 per cent. Liberty Life, now with just over 22 per cent, was in the middle, in a potentially uncomfortable situation, particularly for an insurance company, with its inescapable fiduciary responsibilities to its policyholders.

To protect its own position, Liberty Life first sought to establish a watertight voting pool arrangement with the Press family interests. Gordon worked assiduously at this in order to tie up the loose ends, and the first draft of a note spelling out the conditions for setting up such a pool is dated 4 February, the Thursday after Tuesday's famous victory, a good example of how fast Liberty Life's internal corporate team, then, as now, headed by Farrell Sher, can move. Its final paragraph, numbered seven, and itself a hand-written addendum to the first two-page draft, is illuminating in the light of subsequent events. It states: "The proposals set out in this note are made without prejudice to the Liberty Life Group's rights and interests and shall not be binding upon it or upon the Press family group." It was added, as a precaution, by Gordon himself.

In the event, it proved impossible to get any positive action on the pool agreement from the Press side. Sydney's eldest son, Clifford, proved stubbornly unwilling to act, as did the non-family trustees – and Press himself was immured in the intensive care unit at the Cleveland Clinic.

As the days passed, Gordon, and his senior colleagues – some of whom were certainly thinking "I told you so," even if they were not saying it – grew increasingly uneasy. "I was feeling worried because the market was tailing off," notes Gordon. "I couldn't communicate with Sydney, but there we were, sitting on over 22 per cent of Edcon, and not knowing where we were going, or even that the Press family shares were firmly onside."

This was the uneasy situation when, on Friday 12 February, only ten days after his initial defeat, Goss returned to the fray. His new approach to Liberty Life was doubtless inspired by the knowledge that it might not, now, be wholly unwelcome, as Gordon had earlier expressed his growing discomfort with the situation in a private conversation with JCI's Chairman, Gordon Waddell. The latter, as a director of Breweries, in which JCI was vitally interested as its biggest shareholder, had doubtless passed this useful intelligence on to Goss. Indeed, it is highly likely that he was intended to do so – Gordon certainly is not given to idle gossip, particularly where business matters are concerned.

After some tough talking, Goss came up with another offer – together with an ultimatum. The new and final offer, of Breweries shares and cash plus a dividend adjustment to give an effective total of R15,38 per Edcon share, was open for acceptance only until 6 pm on Sunday 14 February. The offer was, of course, to be extended to the Press family holdings, and to minority holders. Inevitably, it was accepted, but only after strong negotiation and compromise from both sides.

The final price was nearly 25 per cent in excess of Breweries' original offer of R12,50, and almost double the market price before hostilities opened. It was a very fair premium for control and represented quite a deal for Sydney Press, whose family trust stood to collect R54 million. It was achieved by Gordon's stubbornness and courage, but would Press ever understand all the circumstances when informed of the loss of his company without his knowledge, let alone his consent?

"I felt very sorry for Press, and didn't relish the job of the person who told him the bad news," Gordon recalls. "When Press was finally told, while still in the Cleveland Clinic, he immediately despatched from New York Joe Flom, the senior partner of one of the world's greatest takeover specialists, Skadden Arps, to look into the position and report back to him.

"Flom gave everyone involved, including myself, an in-depth grilling, and he certainly left me feeling rather uncomfortable. I never knew what he finally reported back to Press, but I do know that he arranged for the Breweries shares that the Press family interests received for their Edcon shares to be placed with JCI and the Old Mutual on favourable terms. Significantly, Liberty Life was not included in that placing."

Breweries' "ultimatum", and the accompanying "threat" that if the offer "was not accepted by the stipulated time, a further offer would probably not be forthcoming for a considerable time or could be deferred indefinitely" were probably designed to help Liberty Life, and Gordon himself, to rebut the anticipated criticism that he, and they, had sold a desperately ill Sydney Press "down the river", abandoning a friend at the time of his greatest need.

In the emotional atmosphere that prevailed at the time, these totally unjustified accusations were indeed made. Liberty Life had foreseen the possibility, and at a press conference on Monday 15 February a carefully drafted two-page release marshalled all the arguments. The most telling were: (i) That after SAB had acquired its 38 per cent interest and became the largest shareholder in Edcon, control of that company would have passed to them on 2 February, "had Liberty Life not intervened". Liberty Life then, "with 22 per cent of Edcon's equity and with the traditional attitudes of a life assurance company, involuntarily found itself in the situation, together with the 28 per cent Press family interests, of being potentially an effective joint controller of a major retail chain." (ii) "It is Liberty Life's conviction that at least 60 per cent of Edcon's shares would have been acquired by SAB at R12,50 per share prior to noon on 2

February had Liberty Life not intervened. This intervention, however, had the effect of raising the price to shareholders to R14 per Edcon share immediately, and subsequently to an effective R15 plus."

The final paragraph, which had been drafted and re-drafted a number of times, spelt out the real concerns of Gordon and his colleagues. "Finally, the Liberty Life Board faced the task of taking the unenviable decision on the change in control of Edcon in the face of Mr Press's fifty years of endeavour in building a great business enterprise although it is clear that the Press family interests did not in fact constitute control. Nonetheless, the fiduciary responsibility of the Liberty Life Board to its policyholders and shareholders must remain paramount and the consideration of the interests of the general body of Edcon shareholders was the most important consideration from the viewpoint of the Edcon Board. Any delay in protecting the interests of all affected parties, particularly in the present economic climate, could not be justified."

The unfair criticism quickly died down, particularly as the arithmetic began to sink in. Liberty Life's intervention, as the *Rand Daily Mail* pointed out the next day, had cost Breweries R22,3 million, but of this, Liberty's own "profit" was only R3 million (plus, of course, the higher price obtained for its original Edcon stake) – not the sort of calculation that true corporate raiders like T Boone Pickens would like to read! The rest of that involuntary premium accrued to outside shareholders, with the Press family getting some R9 million more than they would have received had not Gordon stuck his own neck out to protect his colleague Sydney's interests.

Press still refuses to be drawn on the issue, preferring to stick to the "authorised version" as published in an article by Patric Lee in *Style* magazine in October 1983: "Contrary to assorted rumours, Donald Gordon did not act treacherously towards me in the takeover of Edcon engineered by SA Breweries. Indeed, he informed me ahead of Adrian Bellamy of what was afoot, on the eve of open heart surgery in Cleveland. Breweries' appetite for Edcon was so sharp that, eventually, a price was offered which he had a fiduciary duty to his policyholders to accept."

Even so, there can be little doubt that, at the time, Press was badly hurt. As Morony puts it: "He was terribly upset that a colleague on the Edgars Board had let him down." Gordon remembers: "I think he was a trifle bitter. When he got back, there was a farewell party for him, and in his speech he said that someone had let him down badly. People assumed he was referring to me, but he wasn't – it was to Bellamy, no question about it." Press asserts that he was referring to neither Bellamy nor Gordon, and the transcript of his farewell speech confirms this.

But the overriding importance of the Edcon affair is not the fact that Donald Gordon went to extreme lengths to protect his colleague Sydney Press, and got little immediate public credit for so doing. The vital issue was that, as Liberty Life converted its Edcon shares into shares in South African Breweries, its stake in that great company rose to just over 7 per cent, making it the third largest shareholder, behind JCI and Old Mutual. And, as part of the settlement, Gordon joined the Board of Breweries, even though his previously close personal relationship with Goss had become perhaps a little more distant.

The stage was now set for Liberty Life's next big industrial stride forward – to effective joint control of the Premier Group and, through it, to a dominant stake in South African Breweries itself.

# 13 The 1983 Breweries Clash

In 1983, South African Breweries was South Africa's mass marketing consumer giant. As the first industrial company to be listed on the Johannesburg Stock Exchange (back in 1893) it was, and was proudly regarded by its management as, the most important consumer-orientated concern in the Republic. Its highly efficient beer division had a virtual monopoly; SAB was dominant in furniture (Amrel and Afcol), in clothing (Edgars), in hotels (Southern Sun) and was, through OK Bazaars, in the top three in retailing and food distribution.

There were, for sure, some large shareholders. Johannesburg Consolidated Investment Company (JCI) dominated with 25 per cent, a stake, and a link, that dates back to SAB's founding fathers, Sammy Marks, Isaac Lewis and Barney Barnato. And, given JCI's own position squarely in the Anglo American Corporation's camp, SAB was widely regarded as being in the Anglo fold, too, although perhaps rather loosely so.

Down in Cape Town, at Mutual Park, the headquarters of what is still South Africa's largest life assurer, the Old Mutual, Chairman and chief executive Jan van der Horst was thought to consider that, with his 15 per cent holding (and a perceived "understanding" over shareholdings with JCI) it was Old Mutual that could call the shots at Breweries when the chips were down.

At the time, Gordon Waddell was securely ensconced as JCI Chairman. However, he returned to Scotland in 1987, having been Chairman of Breweries also for three years following Frans Cronje's retirement from that prestigious position in 1984.

At Liberty Life, meanwhile, Donald Gordon was sitting, perhaps a trifle uncomfortably, on the new 8 per cent holding in Breweries that Liberty Life had built up after acquiring its first big Breweries stake in the course of the controversial Edgars/Edcon battle of the previous year.

At Number Two Jan Smuts Avenue, Johannesburg, Dick Goss sat securely behind the chief executive's desk of Breweries. He was not terribly concerned about his next door neighbour and landlord, Gordon, in Liberty Life Centre at Number One Ameshof Street; or about the hopes and/or aspirations of Van der Horst, in Cape Town, or Waddell, across metropolitan Johannesburg in Consolidated Building. Goss, then fifty-five, had sat in the Breweries hot-seat for sixteen years, having taken over as a relatively young man from the near-legendary Ted Sceales, when the latter was tragically killed in a motor accident on his way from Plettenberg Bay in the eastern Cape, where Donald Gordon, Gordon Waddell, Michael Rapp and, more recently, Tony Bloom all have their holiday homes.

After qualifying as a chartered accountant, Goss had spent all of his working life with Breweries. He was Breweries, and was so regarded by his colleagues, who themselves comprised just about the most highly regarded group of business managers in the country. He himself stood almost alone as one of the most respected business managers of his generation, and had twice, in recent years, received the accolade of Businessman of the Year from two of the country's leading financial journals.

Goss, basically, was a professional manager. His shareholding in Breweries, such as it was, came from options. But as one of South Africa's top professional managers, he sat secure in his seat. He was very little concerned by the idea that some shareholders might think that their respective companies should have a say in the affairs of South African Breweries. However, as a sixteen-year occupant of that seat, he had started to look to the future. In May 1983, he had appointed his protégé, Meyer Kahn, then managing director of Breweries' OK Bazaars subsidiary, to be deputy managing director of Breweries, and hence as his heir-apparent – as and when an heir might be needed.

Even so, and for all of his oft-asserted independence, there were some who regarded Dick Goss as, essentially, an Old Mutual man. And who therefore saw Breweries as firmly in the Old Mutual camp – regardless of the relatively broad spread of shareholdings. This Goss firmly disputes. "I was always," he avers, "my own man – and every inch a Breweries man. If there were those who saw me as close to Old Mutual, this was much more a matter of personal relationships – relationships with particular people built up over a very long period of time. For example, Jan van der Horst and Mike Rosholt had been on my Board for maybe fifteen years, and so I was close to them. Much closer than with the JCI chaps, for they kept chopping and changing – except for my good friend Joe Wells. The fact that Breweries' multi-million pension fund resides with Old Mutual has nothing to do with allegiancies – it was there for many years before the events of 1983, and is still there now, despite all that has happened."

That then was the situation when, in November 1982, Goss invited Gordon to join the Board of Breweries – partly, of course, in recognition of Liberty Life's enlarged shareholding after the Edcon deal, but also to help to repair the personal bridges between the two men that had been weakened by that unhappy affair.

Goss may well have been relaxed about the control situation so far as Breweries was concerned. There was JCI with 25 per cent, Old Mutual with 15 per cent, and Liberty Life with 8 per cent – a total that would normally spell effective control, should any two of the three participants decide to work together. Goss did not expect that they would do so, and in any event he felt secure in his own unassailable position as the Boss of Breweries.

Gordon felt a little differently. He was acutely aware of the need for Liberty Life to move into an influential position in the vitally important retail and food sector, and was still smarting from Van der Horst's year-earlier sortie into Barlows, when a tough share-exchange deal involving Imperial Cold Storage and Tiger Oats put the massive Barlow Rand conglomerate firmly into the Old Mutual stable. Liberty Life had been unhappy with the deal in general, but particularly with the terms of the exchange.

So Gordon reviewed his strategic fingerholds in Breweries and in Standard Bank (in which Old Mutual also held a large position) and thought it time that he himself talked to some of the other players.

Says Gordon: "After a year or so on the Breweries Board, and basically minding my own business and listening – I think, in business, it is always important to be prepared to listen, and when necessary I do listen a lot – I came to the clear view that, despite the shareholdings, Van der Horst and the Old Mutual generally had tremendous influence over all the top men in the Breweries management – they had really got them into the situation of being very pro-Mutual. Just looking round that Boardroom as I sat there, I had the impression that Old Mutual really had control of that Board, and that at that stage Mike Rosholt, of Barlows, who was also a director of Old Mutual, had a tremendous goodwill and rapport with Goss and with the management of Breweries generally. I regarded Breweries as being very much in the Old Mutual camp.

"As I saw it, the relationship was close indeed, and I felt it proper to go informally to see Gavin Relly, then the recently appointed Chairman of Anglo American, to discuss my impressions. I said to him: 'You know, Gavin, I don't know whether it is of any importance in your life, but you could be about to lose control of Breweries. The executive there are so switched on to, and so much in tune with the Old Mutual, that though you believe you have the most important stake, you don't really. I think Van der Horst has the Breweries thing tightly wrapped up.' Then I added: 'Jan van der Horst is forcefully ambitious and has his eyes on some of the country's key companies.' Relly retorted: 'You also show some signs of that.' 'That may well be,' I replied, 'but I don't think that I'm quite at the advanced stage of Van der Horst. But Gavin, if that's your feeling, there is nothing much more I can say – I came here to warn you as a friend that you are about to lose Breweries to Van der Horst and the Old Mutual.'"

"That's not going to be all that easy," said Relly. "OK," said Gordon, "but I, for one, have no desire to sit in an in-between situation. Maybe one day I'll decide to use our 8 per cent interest, and then you could have a problem."

Next, says Gordon, having made no progress with Relly, he decided to go and confront Dick Goss, and point out to him that Liberty Life was a major shareholder, sitting uncomfortably in between Old Mutual on the one hand and JCI and Anglo American on the other.

Goss was not very receptive or forthcoming, taking the position that he, as chief executive, really couldn't get involved in wrangles between his principal shareholders. He added, however: "Donny, if you really want to move ahead, if you really want to be in the big league, then you have to go to work with the big players. In this context, that means you have to talk to the Old Mutual."

Gordon, though perhaps a trifle disappointed at failing to get Goss "onside", wasted little time. His next move was a direct approach to his arch-rival, Old Mutual's redoubtable Van der Horst. As Gordon recalls it: "I invited him, I think it was on 1 March 1983, to come first to my office for a general late afternoon chat, and then we were to go out to dinner – preferably somewhere where we wouldn't be recognised. We had a fascinating discussion that lasted two-and-a-half hours or so, and covered a large number of topics.

"In the course of it, I told him I would like to analyse for him what I saw as his business aspirations and ambitions, and I said that this analysis would centre on two areas – his company's stake in South African Breweries, and the then-dominant stake that it also held in Standard Bank of South Africa. Before I went ahead, I asked him during the build-up if I was on track, and he said: 'Go ahead, I'm listening with tremendous interest and fascination.'

"I told him that my view was that, sooner or later, Standard Chartered Bank, of the UK, was bound to sell out of its South African interests, and that would present Old Mutual, as the then largest outside shareholder, with the opportunity of taking control of Standard Bank of SA – giving him, Van der Horst, a very real chance of achieving what I perceived to be his greatest ambition, that of putting together the biggest banking group in the country by merging Standard Bank and Nedbank." (The latter, of course, was already firmly within Old Mutual's orbit.)

Then, continues Gordon: "I said, Jan, you know, at the end of the day you and I have to live together if I've put my finger on what you really do want. We've got a critical stake in Breweries and you have a critical stake in the Standard Bank. What I am prepared to do with you is simply this – I'm prepared to do a swop with you – our Breweries stake for your Standard Bank stake, with an appropriate cash adjustment, of course."

According to Gordon, Van der Horst clammed up immediately, even though Gordon assured him that the offer was a serious one. They broke up on a reasonably convivial note, but for two or three weeks there was no further contact or communication. Gordon had put the proposition into Van der Horst's court, and eagerly awaited some response from him.

After a month of waiting, Gordon phoned Van der Horst. "Jan," he said, "I put a serious proposal to you the other night. Are you interested, or aren't you interested?" The reply was abrupt, and very much to the point: "Over my dead body will I do that swop with you, Donald." Gordon, somewhat incensed, snapped back: "You might at least have had the courtesy to phone me – I've had to phone you."

That is fate, or one of the great imponderable might-have-beens of business life. Indeed, an imponderable that might well have affected the whole South African economy, had those two insurance giants come together at that time. But, as is so very well known, the moving finger writes. . . And, at that very moment, over in Newtown, a seamy and unfashionable industrial suburb of Johannesburg, a young (or youngish) man sat pondering his own fate.

Then aged forty-four, Tony Bloom was Chairman and chief executive of the Premier Group, one of South Africa's leading food producers, which had been in the Bloom family for four generations. It was his father, Joe, who had really put the company on the map, but it had also prospered and been successful under Tony's guidance.

But Joe, in the course of building up Premier, had in 1963 sold control to a powerful partner. And that partner, with 51 per cent, was an overseas concern: the UK based Associated British Foods (ABF). While Bloom was well aware that ABF's control had thus far been benevolent in the extreme ("As far as I can remember, the ABF Chairman came to South Africa to only one Premier Board meeting in sixteen years"), he was also painfully aware that, with the Bloom family shareholding down to a minuscule 6 per cent, he, and the family, were very vulnerable.

As Bloom put it: "There was always the risk that someone, without my knowledge, would approach Garry Weston of ABF. And although he and I had a good working relationship, business sense would override sentiment. And then, one day, the phone would ring and Garry would say to me: 'Sorry Tony, you've done a great job for us over the years. But we've had an offer from XYZ Corporation that I just couldn't refuse, and they will be coming to see you tomorrow. I hope it all works out well for you, and you still have a job.' "

By February 1983, matters, so far as Bloom was concerned, were coming to a head. He had a feeling that ABF could perhaps be sellers, and he thought that Fred du Plessis, boss of the second-ranking insurance giant, Sanlam, or Anton Rupert, of the Rembrandt Group, might try to do a deal. A deal with Sanlam, in particular, would have made sense as Sanlam's arch-rival, Old Mutual, already had effective control of Barlows, and with that, of Premier's main competitor, Tiger Oats. And, Bloom says: "I had been told that there had already been informal contact between Rembrandt and ABF. I also thought I saw a window through which a deal could be done. At that time South African exchange control was – for the first time for years – relatively relaxed, and capital repatriation was allowed in commercial rands. If I could find a way to raise the money, the proceeds could be freely remitted abroad. Thus a deal, at that point in time, could perhaps be made attractive to ABF. I also had a premonition that things were about to get much more difficult for South Africa from a political point of view, and that international pressures would mount against doing business with South Africa. I realised that pressures would intensify and that the chances were extremely slim that ABF would provide further capital from Britain to South Africa for the expansion and development of Premier's business; accordingly, they were not an ideal majority shareholder for the future."

Bloom then went to see his second biggest shareholder after ABF, Donald Gordon, whose Liberty Life had built up a stake of about 11 per cent in Premier. Bloom recalls "Many of their shares came from disposals from our family trust. When the trust decided to sell, I made strenuous efforts to see that the shares were put into friendly hands, ie people whom I thought would be compatible in the future. Both Liberty Life and JCI got relatively substantial blocks of shares in this way." Bloom was also on Liberty Life's Board at the time. The immediate reaction of Gordon, who had himself five years earlier bought back control of Liberty Life to South Africa, was one of considerable interest. "I immediately saw the potential implications," he says, "and told Bloom I would be prepared to try to work out a deal if we could persuade Gordon Waddell and JCI to come in and buy Premier together with them on a joint control basis."

The immediate rationale was that JCI, whose Waddell was a close personal friend of Bloom, itself held about 4 per cent of Premier. But of vastly greater importance, both to the repatriation of control of Premier and to the enormous shock waves that the whole deal was to set in train, was the fact that JCI and Liberty Life were the first and third largest shareholders in South African Breweries. In between them sat Jan van der Horst and the Old Mutual.

From Gordon's point of view, the potential of the deal went far beyond the mere repurchase of control of Premier from ABF. "As I saw it, if JCI and Liberty Life were to buy control of Premier jointly, then a condition must be, from our point of view, as we had the larger stake in Premier, and JCI the smaller, that both sides must throw their Breweries shares into Premier in exchange for the issue of new Premier shares. We put about 20 million Breweries shares into Premier, and JCI and Anglo American put in 71 million Breweries shares, and the total of 91 million shares gave us a dominant 35 per cent stake in Breweries. What actually happened was that Liberty Life bought control of Premier on a roughly equal basis with JCI, but with Anglo American purchasing a further 15 per cent of Premier, and in order to adjust the price differential, we all put our Breweries shares into Premier at an agreed price of 885 cents. Liberty Life would naturally have to top up by paying a cash adjustment, the amount depending on the outcome of the compulsory offer to outside shareholders of Premier to give them an equal opportunity to sell, as control would be changing hands in terms of the Johannesburg Stock Exchange's rules. Liberty Life would finish up with 35 per cent, and JCI and Anglo American combined with 51 per cent, in the enlarged Premier, with the public holding the balance; and Premier would have acquired that dominant 35 per cent stake in Breweries.

"An essential part of the arrangement was that Liberty Life and JCI would each contribute 25,5 per cent of the capital of Premier held by them into a voting pool, with the extra shares in Premier held by both sides, and those held by Anglo American, not being subject to the pool voting arrangement. That established a joint control position by Liberty Life and JCI in Premier. The votes of the 'extra' Premier shares in excess of those put into the voting pool held by JCI, Anglo American and Liberty Life were effectively neutralised by that bloc of 51 per cent held equally between the 'partnership' of Liberty Life and JCI.

"So the whole arrangement was to be entrenched as an equal partnership, although JCI and the Anglo American group held more shares than us outside the pool, and so could technically outvote us, they couldn't outvote the pool. The implications are fascinating, but in a strange sort of way – maybe like the threat of the atomic bomb keeps world peace – it works."

Bloom's perspective has it: "While it is perfectly true to say that it was Donald's idea to bring the issue of the control of Breweries into the Premier transaction, it was at my instigation that Premier itself was used as the vehicle. If you think about it, it was the least logical approach – a holding company which held the shares in Premier and SAB separately would have been far simpler and, of course, much easier for Breweries to accept.

"A voting agreement between Liberty Life and JCI would also have been less problematical as the issue of SAB being acquired by a smaller company would not have arisen. Another option which was considered was to have Liberty and JCI buy Premier from ABF and then inject it into SAB in return for shares, thus consolidating the control position. However this was abandoned as it was thought, with some justification, that the Mutual directors on SAB's Board would never sanction the deal.

"However, given the relatively high levels of borrowing of Premier and its future capital needs, I was very keen to get the Breweries investment into Premier itself and so dramatically change its entire balance sheet structure."

Gordon and Bloom then put the carefully thought-out proposition to Waddell, who liked the concept, and he, in turn, put it to Anglo American's chief, Gavin Relly, who gave it his blessing. Relly doubtless remembered Gordon's earlier warning about Breweries and Old Mutual, and was only too happy to seize an opportunity to entrench the Anglo American/JCI group's interests in Breweries.

And Van der Horst could well have been sorry that he had not listened more attentively to Gordon a few weeks earlier.

With the mechanics of the deal agreed, and with a clear understanding that the maximum price that they were prepared to offer was R25 a Premier share, Waddell, Gordon and Bloom proceeded to London. Gordon takes up the story: "The first meeting had been set up in Garry Weston's office over Fortnum & Mason (owned by Weston family interests) in Piccadilly. Tony introduced us, Gordon Waddell and myself, to the illustrious Garry Weston. I was delegated to develop the theme that we were the right people to deal with. Weston then took the floor and lectured us for a full hour, in the most polite and civilised manner, of course. However, I did not miss any of the nuances. His central theme was that Premier Milling was the jewel in the ABF crown; that they would never ever consider selling; and that it was a gross error for anyone – meaning us – even to think that they would ever contemplate such a thing.

"When he had finished – and it was one of the longest hours I've ever endured – I said, most politely: 'Look, Mr Weston, we hear exactly what you are saying, but, just in case you should change your mind, we would be prepared to pay R22 a share.' He went on and on about having spent an hour telling us he was not a seller. I interrupted, and said, perhaps a little less politely this time: 'No, please Mr Weston, you misunderstood me. All I'm saying is that, just in case you should change your mind, we are prepared to pay R22 a share.' At that, he took us downstairs, put us into a taxi, and said to me: 'Mr Gordon, please feel free to call on me whenever you are again in London.'"

"After that opening gambit, Tony Bloom took over the role of intermediary, backwards and forwards between ourselves and Weston's number two, Harry Bailey. He 'indicated' – not that they were sellers, of course – but that if we offered R32 a share they would be prepared, maybe, to look at it. I told Bloom I was not prepared to bargain – that our top price was R25, and we would stick to it. This went on for two or three weeks, with them coming down gradually all the time. First R30, then R29, then R28, bit by bit all down the line. Then it came down to R27, but I still stuck to our agreed R25 limit – I told Tony: 'Look, you tell these people that when I say R25 is our top price – that's precisely what I mean.'"

Bloom asserts: "I remember being substantially more than an intermediary – I had to work very hard indeed to persuade Weston that he had an almost unique opportunity to extract himself from South Africa because of a unique combination of the relaxation of exchange control, the high prices prevailing on the JSE and the presence of able and willing buyers. As a result of these efforts, which took several days, his opening bid of R32 a share was finally extracted. It was like pulling teeth!"

Gordon continues: "I stuck to my guns, and when they came back and said R27 was the lowest they would go, I told Tony to tell them that I wasn't negotiating and that I was leaving the UK the next day – and if we hadn't concluded a deal by then it was all off. Next day, I phoned Bailey from Heathrow Airport to say farewell, and asked if there was any news, and he said: 'Yes, I think we're going to do the deal.' I said: 'Fine, thank you very much,' and went off to Florida to meet with the Chairman of Lincoln National Life Insurance, who shortly after became participants with us in our TransAtlantic Holdings operation in London. That Premier negotiation on price was one of the most fascinating of my career, but I was determined not to yield as I considered R25 to be totally fair, if not on the generous side [the market price at the time was around R22]. The future would prove me correct. Michael Rapp and Tony Bloom stayed in London to sort out the details, and by the time I returned from Florida, the transaction with ABF had been fully documented and closed."

Bloom observes: "It was very much a team effort – Donald Gordon as usual a master strategist and able negotiator; Gordon

Waddell infinitely practical and skilled at negotiation; and myself actively participative as the party whose future would be most affected by the structure of any deal."

The arrangements within the consortium, as drafted by Gordon overnight in his characteristic "handprint", and after a certain amount of bickering and fine-tuning between Gordon, Waddell and Bloom, and a cursory review by Linklaters & Paines, Liberty Life's London solicitors, was signed by the parties only after intense debate on the price at which the Breweries shares would be included, a matter more critical to JCI and Anglo American than to Liberty Life. Waddell extracted 885 cents despite fierce counter-arguments by Gordon and Bloom. The Breweries shares were trading below that price, but JCI wanted a premium. Anglo American's Gavin Relly was brought into the debate, but would not agree to anything below 885 cents. Gordon capitulated and it was at this figure that the deal was finally closed.

The most sensitive aspect was how the parties could terminate the joint venture if it was shown to be unworkable. To cover this, Gordon insisted on a "Texas auction clause" regarding the 25,5 per cent stake in Premier contributed by each of Liberty Life and JCI to the voting pool. This meant that either party could, at any time, bid for the 25,5 per cent interest of the other party at any price of his choosing. The "bidee" would have the choice of either accepting the offer made, or of acquiring the bidder's shares at the stipulated price. A drastic solution, perhaps, but a fair one calculated greatly to concentrate the minds of all concerned.

Rapp and Bloom then returned to South Africa with the deal in their pockets, and with lawyer Michael Katz went off to Pretoria to clear it with the Reserve Bank and the Competition Board. All with maximum secrecy and security, of course, because, as an anonymous protagonist put it: "If Van der Horst had found out about it, he'd have done his level best to scupper the deal by any means at his disposal."

Katz's recollections are interesting. "Farrell Sher, one of Liberty Life's top executives, phoned me one Sunday morning and asked if I could attend an important meeting that afternoon, to implement a Heads of Agreement that had just been entered into in London. The essence of the transaction was that Liberty Life, Anglo American and JCI as a consortium would take over control of Premier from ABF, and they would then inject their respective holdings of

Breweries shares into Premier in exchange for new Premier shares. This would make Premier the holding company of an important strategic stake in Breweries, the end result being that approximately 35 per cent of Breweries would be in the consortium's hands, either directly or indirectly through the reconstituted Premier.

"That was on the Sunday afternoon. We looked at the deal, and immediately saw that a fundamental implication was that Competition Board consent would be essential, for we were effectively putting together Anglo American, with its large food interests through Tongaat and others, with Breweries, with its food interests through OK Bazaars, and Premier, which apart from anything else was a big supplier to OK. Apart from the concentration within the food industry, there was also the matter of a significant concentration of economic power. So the attitude of the Competition Board would be critical to the deal.

"An essential element in getting Competition Board consent to a deal is that it must involve the acquisition of a controlling interest. No controlling interest involved – end of matter. We decided we had to go to the Board on the basis that a controlling interest was involved, having regard as to how the balance of the shares in Breweries were spread. Control is *de facto* control; it is not necessarily 51 per cent, and we were arguing that 35 per cent of Breweries was *de facto* control."

The team worked through the night preparing their submissions to the Board, and presented them in Pretoria on the Tuesday. They got a provisional ruling in favour of the deal, but, in this instance, Katz was not satisfied with just a provisional ruling.

"For a totally binding ruling, one has to get the approval of the Minister of Economic Affairs. Normally, the Board's provisional ruling is adequate, but in this case I thought a binding ruling was essential because there was a foreign institution involved, and because it was likely to become a highly controversial deal, with control of Breweries effectively changing hands, or at least a new controlling interest in this major concern being established."

Anyway, the then Minister, Dawie de Villiers, agreed to see them in his office in Parliament in Cape Town at 2.15 the next afternoon. "We flew in the Premier plane – Waddell, Bloom, Rapp and myself – and went to the internationally famous Mount Nelson Hotel for lunch. We hoped not to be seen by anyone who mattered, but as we were leaving we bumped into the head of one of South Africa's leading life insurance companies, the late Professor Fred du Plessis."

By then, however, it did not matter even if Du Plessis should guess what was afoot. They saw the Minister, argued their case, "and at about 3.45 pm he said he would let us know the result as soon as possible – he would telephone me at home. And when I got home there was a message from De Villiers to say that the deal had been approved."

Everything looked fine; a major and very important deal had finally been sewn up, and all concerned, particularly Bloom, Rapp, Waddell and Gordon, were entitled to feel very pleased with themselves. From the Liberty Life side especially, it was a major coup. But, in the euphoria of the moment, two highly important details had been overlooked – and diplomacy was never one of Gordon Waddell's strong points.

The first was that Van der Horst was – and, in fact, still is – firmly convinced that he had an undertaking from Waddell that, should JCI at any time sell its shareholding in Breweries, Old Mutual would have the right of first refusal – and JCI likewise concerning Old Mutual's interest in Breweries. Waddell does not dispute that, but points out that JCI did not sell its Breweries shares, but merely put them into Premier. "I didn't sell the Breweries shares. All we did by putting the block together with Donny was to make it a much larger interest held in a different way."

One consequence of this major top-level "misunderstanding" was that Van der Horst resigned in a fury from the Board of Anglo American, something that has never happened before – or since. Gavin Relly, who had only recently taken over Anglo American's Chair from Harry Oppenheimer, was particularly upset by the row, which was not a very propitious commencement to his reign.

The second problem was that, in their natural desire to maintain complete security, nobody told Dick Goss of what was afoot. This was deliberate, however, as Bloom recalls: "The question of how Dick Goss would react to the deal was considered in London and, while we were all sure that he would not in any way welcome it, an assumption was made that we would attempt to persuade him to go along with it by structuring a position and financial package that would make it extremely attractive for Dick personally. I had negotiated a generous stock option for myself and the thought was that something similar would be offered to Dick. We did not fail to consider his position, but took the view that it was more dangerous to bring him in at that stage (due to his perceived alignment with the Old Mutual), than to advise him at the last possible moment and take the consequences of his wrath. Incidentally, with the benefit of hindsight I believe that decision to have been correct – if Dick had been advised earlier, there is no doubt in my mind that he (and the Mutual) would have blocked the deal." Another possibility was that the Old Mutual could offer its Rennies (a major conglomerate with important hotel interests) shares to Breweries for SAB shares. If the majority of the SAB Board had voted for this attractive acquisition, the main Premier/SAB deal could well have been frustrated.

When he was told, Goss was, not unsurprisingly, to put it as mildly as possible, angered and offended, and, indeed, very much enraged at what he perceived to be a dastardly act, and a number of serious consequences flowed from this.

Waddell was delegated to tell Goss about the agreement, and to offer him the generous package put together between Liberty Life and JCI. Recalls Gordon: "It was agreed between us that Goss would be offered the chairmanship of South African Breweries and assured that the full independence of Breweries would be totally respected. In addition, generous share options were contemplated to secure the futures of Breweries' top executives."

But by the time Rapp and Bloom had concluded the deal in London, Waddell had had to go to M'bulwa, the luxurious Anglo American estate in the Eastern Transvaal, to outline the agreement to Relly and his senior executives. He secured their approval and then flew back to Johannesburg in a chartered helicopter to see Goss.

What happened, according to Bloom and Waddell, was that Goss did not, at first, react to what Waddell told him. He said he wanted to give some thought to the deal, but during the meeting he certainly did not go through the roof. He obviously did so afterwards, but he did not do so at the time. Waddell then returned from his meeting and told the rest of the consortium that Goss had been calm, but wanted time to think out the implications.

Gordon, back in London from Florida, takes up the tale again. "Peggy and I went to Annabel's that night to celebrate the deal, the final details of which had been settled on the telephone, not knowing anything of the brouhaha developing in Johannesburg. But at about 2 am Relly and Waddell found me there (by a process of deduction which to this day I don't fully understand), and I spent virtually the rest of that night on the telephone, trying to calm things down, because Goss had erupted and the official announcement was due to be made first thing the next morning, a Friday. Throughout, Goss was insistent that the structure of the deal would have to be changed. He said he would never accept that Premier should control Breweries."

Despite the growing tension Bloom made what came to be regarded as a somewhat thoughtless and provocative telephone call to Goss at 9 am that fateful Friday. Bloom made this call, he now claims: "Out of a sense of courtesy and with the purest of motives. I could immediately hear that Dick was in an unbelievably emotional state as he could hardly breathe during the telephone call. He urged me to withdraw the circular at all costs and said that it was going to create the most unbelievable difficulties. I said that I could not for two reasons – firstly, because I did not have the power to do so, and secondly because even as we were speaking, the circular was being released at the Stock Exchange. That is how I can fix the time of my call with Goss with such exactitude. Again with the benefit of hindsight, I can see that Dick, in the upset and emotion of the moment, could well have misunderstood the purpose of my call."

The joint announcement was duly made, and it read: "Agreement has been reached in South Africa for the sale by a wholly-owned subsidiary of Associated British Foods Limited of 13 486 564 ordinary shares in Premier representing 52 per cent of its issued ordinary share capital to a consortium led equally by JCI and Liberty Life and including AAC ("the consortium") for a consideration of R337 164 100 equivalent to R25 per share (ex Premier's final ordinary dividend of 37 cents per share in respect of the year ended 31 March 1983).

"The members of the consortium have agreed to dispose of their present shareholdings of approximately 34 per cent of the issued ordinary share capital of The South African Breweries Limited to Premier at a price of R8,85 per ordinary share (ex SAB's final ordinary dividend of 25 cents per share in respect of the year ended 31 March 1983). The consideration for this transaction will be satisfied by Premier allotting and issuing new ordinary shares in Premier to the consortium at R25 per share. AAC's participation in Premier will not exceed 20 per cent of Premier's issued share capital.

"The transactions referred to in this announcement have the full support of the Board of directors of Premier and its senior management. Mr A H Bloom will remain as Premier's Chairman and will retain his personal shareholding in Premier. Representatives of the consortium will be invited to join Premier's Board."

"That was tough enough for the Breweries' people to swallow," Gordon recalls, "but Bloom, who was by dint of the new structure Chairman of the new holding company that was to control both Breweries and Premier, had already aggravated a tense and delicate situation by his telephone call to Goss. That really got under Goss's skin in no uncertain manner, because he, Goss, not unnaturally, regarded himself as considerably senior to Bloom in the South African business hierarchy, and thought Breweries to be at a far superior level of corporate status to Premier." The fury at Breweries was greatly intensified by the lead story in the Johannesburg *Sunday Times* of May 29. Its headline, "Got it," was a comment widely attributed to Bloom, not unnaturally, since it quoted him as being "delighted", but he denies having made it.

There is a story, probably not wholly apocryphal, which has Goss exploding: "There's no way I'll ever allow Breweries to become the equity-accounted appendage of a dog-food manufacturer."

Continues Gordon: "So it all blew up and a Breweries' Board meeting was called for the Monday morning. I was at a health farm in the UK for the weekend, and they phoned me at lunchtime and said an emergency Board meeting of Breweries had been called for 9 am the next day. I said I couldn't possibly get back in time, so they changed it to 11 am. I flew back for it, and when I went into the Boardroom straight off the airplane just before 11 that morning, everyone was there, the Chairman Frans Cronje, Goss, Rosholt, Van der Horst, Waddell, Rapp, Kerzner, Kahn, and all the executive directors. The tension was unbelievable, and the atmosphere could have been cut with a knife. Kahn (who would succeed Goss) made a major statement by way of introduction. Then Goss spoke, very emotionally and forcefully, and the climax and thrust of what he had to say was a threat that if the transaction was not stopped or restructured, he and six of his executive directors would walk out *en bloc*.

"Well, that just was not on, and on my insistence we adjourned for lunch. I had arranged for Sydney Kentridge, South Africa's most respected and able advocate, and a Senior Counsel, the equivalent of a Queen's Counsel in the UK, where Kentridge has also become well-known, and Michael Katz to join Waddell and me at Liberty

Life Centre next door to Breweries. Waddell and I returned to the meeting that afternoon to face Goss with Kentridge's firm opinion that if the Breweries' executive directors proceeded with Goss's threat of mass resignation then the company would sue them all for damages on the basis of dereliction of duty. It was all very dramatic and emotional, but eventually things temporarily calmed down and wiser counsels prevailed."

There followed two weeks of intensive and exhaustive negotiations, conducted in a glare of media publicity that was unprecedented, and highly embarrassing for many of those concerned, both directly and on the sidelines. This was particularly so in the case of Anglo American, whose public stance, so far as possible, was to stay aloof from business controversy, and for Liberty Life and Gordon, for he too preferred not to be embroiled in public fights. Anglo American was also highly embarrassed by Van der Horst's resignation and the Old Mutual's allegations against Waddell and JCI, which were not strictly valid. Michael Rapp and Gordon Waddell were cast in the role of negotiators – hatchet men, if you like, with Bloom and Gordon on the sidelines for different reasons, Bloom because in his position as Chairman of the Premier Group he was to bear the brunt of the Breweries' wrath, and Gordon because the consortium wished to defuse the situation – he was, at the time, viewed by some members of the SAB Board as the villain of the piece.

In an endeavour to find a way out of the impasse, the consortium, unbeknown to a very emotional Bloom and the Premier Board, conceived the bones of a so-called "elegant solution". This involved the original ABF holding company, called South African Food Industries, being used as a pure investment company to hold the Breweries shares on the one hand and the old Premier Group shares on the other. A new independent Chairman would be elected to lead this holding company Board and Bloom and Goss would be appointed joint deputy chairmen. This would have effectively ended the original deal and was an attempt to pacify Goss and the SAB executives.

Bloom recollects: "Strenuous efforts and pressures were put on Premier to unwind the deal by Gordon and, to a lesser but nevertheless significant extent, by Waddell. This resulted in a most unpleasant situation as I was already at odds with my new controlling shareholders. I was compelled to take independent legal advice on behalf of the Premier Board with Don Jowell of attorneys Hofmeyr, Van der Merwe. However, in an effort to achieve a compromise, I eventually said I would stand down as Chairman in favour of somebody of great esteem, such as either Harry Oppenheimer or Gavin Relly. As one can imagine, this was a considerable sacrifice as I was the fourth generation of my family to be Chairman of Premier."

So the compromise was reached. With extreme reluctance, and almost unbelievable trauma, Bloom agreed to step aside, for a period, as Chairman of Premier Holdings, the top company in the new structure, a symbolic position that Goss, in particular, found impossible to stomach. He had found himself and his senior Breweries colleagues in a juxtaposition with Bloom which he, and they, simply could not live with. Gavin Relly was now to be Chairman for a year, with Bloom and Goss as joint deputy chairmen, responsible for Premier and Breweries respectively. Throughout all this, Gordon discreetly kept himself strictly in the background, which is by no means his accustomed position, to avoid stirring things any more than was absolutely necessary.

Hence another joint announcement on 8 June 1983:

"1. On 27 May 1983 it was announced by JCI, Liberty Life and Anglo American (referred to as "the Consortium") and the Premier Group, that the members of the Consortium had agreed : (1) to acquire 52 per cent of Premier from Associated British Foods plc and (2) to dispose of their present shareholdings of approximately 34 per cent of the issued ordinary share capital of SAB to Premier.

"2. In assessing the implications arising out of the complex transaction, it is considered appropriate and beneficial for all parties concerned to amend the original structure. In particular, the Board of SAB was concerned that its largest single shareholder would be a Group actively engaged in manufacturing and trading, which, in their opinion, might have resulted in potential conflicts of interest. Furthermore, the Board was of the view that the independence of the SAB Group, which factor has been a major contributor to its past success, should not be affected.

"3. Accordingly, discussions were initiated and these finally resulted in mutually acceptable solutions being found which are considered to be in the best interests of all the companies concerned and their shareholders.

"4. It has therefore been agreed that:

"4.1 As originally announced, Premier will acquire 34 per cent of the ordinary shares of SAB from the Consortium at a price of R8,85 per ordinary share. The consideration for these SAB ordinary shares will be satisfied by Premier allotting and issuing approximately 32 million new ordinary shares in Premier to the Consortium at a price of R25 per share.

"4.2 Premier will become an investment holding company and its name will be changed to one which connotes that objective, but incorporating the name Premier.

"4.3 Premier will transfer its trading interests to a subsidiary company. In due course, the feasibility and desirability of seeking a listing for that subsidiary will be investigated.

"4.4 As a consequence of 4.2 and 4.3 the assets of Premier (as an investment holding company) will be the 34 per cent shareholding in SAB and 100 per cent of the above-mentioned subsidiary.

"4.5 The parties to this agreement have recognised that the independence of the SAB Group has been a major contributor to its past success and will continue to support that independence.

"4.6 In addition to the existing directors, the Board of Premier will be enlarged to include:

(i) Mr G W H Relly as Chairman,
(ii) Mr A H Bloom and Mr R J Goss as joint deputy chairmen.
(iii) Nominees of the Consortium.
(iv) SAB representatives will be invited to join the Board.

"4.7 The Consortium will have the right to appoint the majority of the Board.

"4.8 Mr A H Bloom will be invited to join the Board of SAB.

"5. The new structure affirms the concept of managerial independence for SAB, and removes the disadvantages of its shares being held by a trading, rather than an investment holding company. In addition, it guarantees the trading integrity of Premier's and SAB's subsidiaries in relation to their customers and suppliers throughout South Africa.

"6. The above proposals have the whole-hearted support of the companies concerned and their respective managements."

The settlement had finally been reached in dramatic fashion. It had become painfully clear to the "peacemakers", the prime movers among whom (although many more were involved) were Michael Rapp and Sol Kerzner, that Goss and Bloom had to be brought face-to-face, if anything were to be achieved. At some stage Bloom had, in fact, suggested that nothing would be lost by putting the two chief "protagonists", himself and Goss, in a room to see whether a compromise would not be possible. This had been resisted as the consortium had held the view that his presence would simply further inflame matters.

Eventually they met on a Tuesday at 5 pm. By 2.30 on the Wednesday morning, a fragile truce was declared, at the Breweries group's own Landdrost Hotel, which was the only venue where food – and, more essentially, drink – were available until that hour. The detailed recollections of one of the participants, Premier's Peter Wrighton, are: "We met at 5 pm at Werksmans' office. The Breweries team was Dick Goss, Sol Kerzner and Meyer Kahn and the Premier team Tony Bloom and myself. [It had been decided to exclude all members of the consortium.] Goss was in a highly emotional state and said very little except that he would leave no stone unturned, he would move heaven and earth to undo the problem of Premier control over SAB. He was shocked and distressed and he believed that the deal was not to SAB's advantage. Most of the talking on the SAB side was done by Kahn and Kerzner, the latter saying that he had put his fortune on the line when he had threatened to resign; that he had only gone into SAB originally as it was an independent company, and he now found the situation to be intolerable.

"After much hard bargaining, during which I pointed out that the Premier senior management now felt exactly the same as the SAB senior management should the deal be reconstructed in any way, and that they would also be de-motivated, a new "elegant solution" was agreed to. This involved leaving the deal as it was, but for Bloom to step down as Chairman of Premier in favour of Gavin Relly, as it was felt that both Bloom and Goss could respect him as Chairman. They would then become deputy chairmen and, after a year, Goss would take over the chairmanship of SAB from Frans Cronje, who was due to retire, and Bloom would resume the chairmanship of Premier.

"Relly was brought out of bed at midnight and the proposal was put to him that he should accept the chairmanship, which he somewhat unwillingly agreed to do as this appeared to be the only alternative acceptable to both managements. The lawyers were called in and, as there were no typists at that time of night, they were asked to write out the agreement by hand and to bring it across to Annabelle's Restaurant in the Landdrost Hotel, where Kerzner had laid on a spread of some considerable proportions. All the other representatives of the consortium, who had been sitting at home and waiting with bated breath for the outcome, were advised that an agreement had been reached and they were invited to Annabelle's for the signing ceremony, which took place at 2.30 am."

All concerned breathed huge sighs of relief; the hard-fought "Landdrost Accord", or "Annabelle's Agreement", would restore stability and smooth ruffled feathers. At least, that's what the joint announcement had said.

Bloom recalls that: "Paragraph 6 of the announcement stated that the above proposals had the whole-hearted support of the companies concerned and their respective managements. This was certainly true at the time, as during that night there was much joy and back-slapping. Dick Goss had achieved what he wanted – he would not be seen to be subservient to me – and I had had to back off slightly. He was to be appointed Chairman of SAB in a year. Much joy all round."

Asked later on SABC television why the problems had not been foreseen, Bloom replied: "Why didn't we foresee the unhappiness at Breweries? You have to realise that negotiations of this sort are conducted under extreme pressure, in very difficult circumstances. Quite frankly, we did foresee that there might be a problem some way or another, but it was always open to us to sit down as reasonable men and look at the structure which had been announced and see if it could be altered to nobody's prejudice. I think that's really what has to be seen to come out of this deal and we have had to restructure the nature of our company slightly, but it really, from our point of view, is not a worry."

But it was not to be; the wounds were too real, too deep. Within two months, the Accord was in tatters and Kerzner, taking Goss with him, had walked away with what many saw as the jewel in Breweries crown – Sun City, the glittering Bophuthatswana casino hotel complex of Breweries' Southern Sun hotel subsidiary, which would form the nucleus of the present Sun International Group.

There are, inevitably, a variety of versions as to what went wrong. At the time, the most general impression was that of an emotional Kerzner holding everyone to ransom, an indecisive Anglo American and an ambivalent Liberty Life surrendering with barely a whimper.

As Gordon recalls: "After Landdrost, we all thought the drama would settle down, and everyone would benefit from what was, after all, a great deal for all concerned. But no; within a few weeks, we were told that another special Board meeting of Breweries had been called. I was away, but Kerzner was there. He said he was absolutely switched off, demotivated, unhappy and miserable and he was either going to withdraw from the Board and start doing his own thing; or alternatively, he had raised the backing to buy the whole of Southern Sun; or he would like the Board to buy his Southern Sun shares from him. A whole lot of alternatives – he apparently put on a great performance."

Van der Horst and Rosholt, Goss having recused himself, seemed determined that SAB was going to sell Southern Sun to Kerzner; Liberty Life, and Bloom in particular, fought fiercely over the price – and eventually succeeded in having it raised by some 50 per cent, but it was still a ridiculous transaction – they sold off the casino complex to Kerzner for a song.

Bloom well remembers that dramatic meeting: "I was the only director who raised any objections. Remember that this was my first meeting as a SAB Board member and I was about as welcome as a frozen dead fish! I therefore did not want to stir the waters too aggressively, but felt very strongly that both the principle of the deal and the numbers were absurd. Subsequent events have certainly proved me right on the latter! I spoke out against it.

"In view of the fact that I was the only director who was voicing any objections to the deal (Michael Rapp had been instructed by Donald Gordon not to make waves), I said that I would not vote against the deal but that I wanted my objections recorded. The next day I sent a brief note of the points which I had made to Craig Waigel (the SAB company secretary) to incorporate in the minutes. I deliberately did this as I wanted the minutes to properly record my strong objections."

JCI and Anglo American took a very different view, and long after the event, in an interview in 1987, Waddell was still relaxed about it. After first observing that "it's awfully easy to indulge in Monday-morning quarter backing" – a delightful rugger-bugger's phrase for hindsight – he went on: "I'm uncomfortable with earnings coming from casinos. It may be a moral attitude, but I also suspect, especially elsewhere in the world – and I am by no means raising this suspicion here – that there has always tended to be a suggestion of a criminal element, especially in America. That's obviously not true here, but we were uncomfortable with casino earnings, and as I understand it most outside financial institutions are also uncomfortable with casino earnings. Now certainly there was a difference of opinion between Donny and Michael Rapp on the one side and myself on the other. I thought it was much better to have a clean break and to do the best deal it was possible to do with Kerzner – and then let Meyer Kahn and the management get on with it. I suspect subsequently I have been proved correct. At the time, however, I must tell you that Donny and Michael both regarded me as an extremely soft politician who was incapable of striking the appropriate deal. Both of them felt strongly that it was too good a deal for Mr Kerzner." Gordon recalls another possible factor. "At the time, there were rumours of the intervention of the President of Bophuthatswana, Chief Lucas Mangope, on behalf of Kerzner. Bophuthatswana is not only known for Sun City and the famous casino resort, but also for platinum. And, of course, JCI is synonymous with platinum."

Kerzner, obviously, still sees things differently: "As a senior Breweries executive, I'd been very upset by the deal, and particularly by the way it was handled. Nevertheless, when it came to the Landdrost Accord – to which I was a party, and maybe I played a not unimportant role in it – I was happy with it; under all the circumstances, I thought it was fair, and we could go ahead.

"I certainly had no hard feelings. But then I found, after several weeks, that my motivation no longer was the same. So, during June, I took a week off to go to Mauritius and do nothing – just lie on the beach, and try to figure out why I was feeling demotivated. I came back, went to the office every day, but I found I was totally switched off. So at the end of June, to the middle of July, I took two weeks off – one week at Wimbledon, and one week cruising in a friend's yacht in the Med. I eventually came to the conclusion that my motivation had gone, that I couldn't perform as Southern Sun deserved. So I came back, called Dick Goss, said I'm sorry, but I'm no bloody good any more so let's call it a day."

Then on to that special Board meeting, and the fight over price. Kerzner thinks he paid a fair price: "At that time, it was, I believe, a fair deal – it's all very well to look back and say, 'Hey man – look how much money Kerzner's made, what sort of deal was that?' What people forget is the size of the risk I took – the heart of the deal was Sun City, in Bophuthatswana, where the gaming rights could run out after a few years. Hell, things could have easily gone wrong."

Finally, from one last angle; that of the man who took over the hot seat from Goss, the man who physically signed the deal with Kerzner, Breweries' present chief executive, Meyer Kahn: "First, let's be clear that the Board of SAB – the whole Board – supported us in recommending that transaction. [Gordon, however, points out that he was overseas at the time.] The price was sweet, but it was willing. It turned out to be far sweeter than anyone anticipated because of the subsequent deal that Sol and Dick did with Safmarine. That's all very well, but the real question is why did we do the deal?

"First, we were a brand new management team – Dick was going, and he was our mentor and our leader; Sol was going, and he was a name known world-wide in the hotel industry; Bellamy had left. So you had the position where I was a brand new chief executive; we'd just appointed Hammond to take over Edgars from Bellamy; we had to appoint Hood to take over OK Bazaars from me; we had to find a new man to run the hotel business; four out of the seven top guys in the business were new to their jobs. So our priorities were to stabilise the business and to get rid of the rancour and put SAB on a sound managerial footing again.

"Then, remember, at that time Holiday Inns was owned by Old Mutual; so Dick and Sol, on leaving us, were obviously going to lay their hands on Holiday Inns – and the Holiday Inns casinos – as they in fact were to do. And with them the possibility of the rights to a casino in kwaNdebele, only thirty minutes from the Johannesburg and Pretoria areas. So what were we going to be left with? With a hotel chain without any management. We'd already been told by the Bophuthatswana government that when our contract for exclusive gaming rights expired in four years time, Sol was going to get gaming rights as well; so we'd be competing with him. Some prospect! Just to make certain I'd no doubts about that, I had been flown up to the Mmabatho Sun [one of the other less important casino hotels in the group] in a private plane to meet President Mangope, with Sol and Dick sitting across the table.

"So now the whole company is at risk, because of the trauma and the resignations. We've got four new chief executives including myself; we know nothing about the hotel industry, because Sol was a law unto himself, and rightly so. We're going to lose our rights in Sun City and he's going to come into kwaNdebele with a massive casino and he's going to take our management away from Southern

Sun. And remember, our real business is beer, soft drinks, selected manufacturing and retailing – and our profits for the first quarter of the year are down 35 per cent.

"We really had no option, and so we did a generous deal with the guys. But – and this is the most important thing – for every rand that Dick and Sol have made themselves, they have made a rand for Breweries as well. Looking back, the separation of the casino operations from the resort and business hotels was the only logical route to follow, and it has worked out very well indeed for both parties. Long range, that deal with Sol was the best thing I've done for Breweries."

So, with hindsight, and with the considered opinions (given years after the event to the author) of some of those intimately concerned, it is clear that the deal that led to the formation of Sun International – and which was the highly visible culmination of the whole Premier/Breweries affair – was forced upon Breweries by simple but clear commercial considerations.

The importance of this major deal, and its longer-range effects, can hardly be overstated. Rennies, Holiday Inns, Safmarine, Kersaf, Southern Sun, Sun International, quite apart from Premier and Breweries themselves, are among the companies that have emerged strengthened from, or have been submerged by, the turmoil.

But the very clear winners are Liberty Life, and Donald Gordon. Both, six years down the line, have greatly enhanced prestige and stature. Liberty Life has broadened its power base and flexed its financial muscle into areas where it was not previously represented; its influence now extends even more deeply into South Africa's retail, industrial and commercial life.

Tony Bloom has since relocated to the United Kingdom, as also have Michael Rapp and Gordon Waddell. Peter Wrighton has taken over as Chairman of Premier and only Donald Gordon and Meyer Kahn, of the main protagonists, stand firm as the heads of their respective corporations. Even Sol Kerzner and Dick Goss are now somewhat removed from the public focus.

South African Breweries and Liberty Life move inexorably from success to success, notwithstanding the increasingly hostile environment; both Gordon and Kahn sit on each other's Boards and draw strength from one another.

Because of the potentially drastic impact of the "Texas auction" clause contained in the consortium's original London agreement,

JCI was for many years unwilling to finalise the formal detailed agreement which had been envisaged.

"Of course, Liberty Life was not prepared to make any concession on this for obvious reasons," says Gordon. "So for years it looked likely that the future of this vast trading empire would rest on the London Heads, drawn up in the middle of the night by me, and also, of course, on the tremendous goodwill that exists between Liberty Life, Anglo American and JCI.

"Nobody on the Anglo American/JCI side disputed the legality and the enforceability of the clause, and certainly Gordon Waddell, who signed the Heads of Agreement in London on behalf of Anglo American and JCI, was unable to wish it away."

Donald Gordon himself was quite relaxed about the situation; indeed he was happy with it, and totally reliant on those London Heads of Agreement, which covered all the important points. And there was always complete consensus on vital aspects such as JCI's lead role in South African Breweries and Liberty Life's similar position in the Premier Group. Even so, a final, detailed agreement was worked out eventually, and was signed, most amicably, in June 1989. And, over the years of working closely together, the relationship between Anglo American, Liberty Life and JCI has improved and matured very considerably.

Finally, the South African financial press saw the three prime movers in the deal on the one side – the Three Musketeers – as Waddell, Bloom and Gordon. First, in mid-1987, Waddell announced that he was leaving South Africa. This occasioned little surprise, as his concern about the political dispensation had become clear. However, there was a good deal of consternation when Bloom announced, early in 1988, that he too was leaving South Africa for the UK. After all, he had, only a few years earlier, achieved his major ambition of returning control of Premier to South Africa. Was it, some wondered unkindly, a case of out of the frying pan and into the fire? Had Bloom not perhaps exchanged the absentee, but essentially non-interfering, control of Associated British Foods for the far heavier hands, and at much closer range, of JCI and Liberty Life? "Not so," says Bloom, who asserts that his major reason for leaving South Africa was to have a new focus and to accept a new challenge in a more exciting environment.

No matter what Bloom's real reasons, which are solely his own business, the local press began to speculate about the third of the

Three Musketeers – Donald Gordon. He, genuine patriot that he is, was justifiably irritated. "I will emigrate only in my coffin," he is reported to have snapped, very forcibly indeed.

Following Bloom's actual departure from South Africa, late in 1988, when Wrighton became Chairman as well as chief executive, there was a strong demonstration of support for him, which was also indicative of a greater involvement in Premier's affairs. That was when Donald Gordon and JCI's new Chairman, Murray Hofmeyr, representing the Anglo American/JCI interests, agreed to become joint deputy chairmen of the Premier Milling Group.

A further important development, and one which hopefully would bring this chapter to a happy ending, occurred in June 1989, just as this book was going to the printer. This involved the re-structuring of The Premier Group in a deal which effectively disengaged it from its interest in the South African Breweries. This transaction was not only calculated finally to diffuse the animosities aroused by the events of 1983, but it would also refocus The Premier Group on its core businesses, and at the same time unlock the values which would arise by the separation of the components.

The plan involved Premier divesting itself of its shareholding in SAB, which would be passed into a new holding company whose sole interest would be 93,6 million SAB shares – 33,8 per cent of the equity. The new company would be listed on the JSE in its own right, initially with exactly the same number of shares as were in issue in Premier. These shares would be passed on to existing Premier shareholders on a one-for-one basis so that each present shareholder in Premier would initially hold precisely the same number of shares in the new company as he previously held in Premier. Thus, for each Premier share owned, he would also hold one new share in the new SAB holding company. It was contemplated – quite rightly, as it turned out – that the total value of this package would exceed the value of the existing Premier share.

Prior to the separation, a R280 million rights issue would be held to reduce Premier's debt to a level more appropriate for the company on its new stand-alone basis. In this way the dominant shareholding in SAB will remain firmly ensconced in the new listed holding company, which will still be jointly controlled by JCI, Liberty Life and Anglo American, who, together with their associates, will own nearly 85 per cent of the new company's shares. In addition, the original consortium will also own a similar proportion of the shares in Premier, now to be concentrated and focused on its core businesses.

So at last the grand design was finally put in place, fully documented and agreed to the satisfaction of all concerned – the South African Breweries included.

For Liberty Life, it had secured joint control of Premier and of the new holding company, which will have a 33,8 per cent interest in SAB, thus constituting it as the dominant shareholder in SAB. Premier and its interest in SAB will now be separated from one another with surgical precision. All of this would certainly not have been possible without going through the unfortunate trauma and tension brought about by the original ungainly structure that was expediently put together in the heady days of 1983.

Premier, now to be known as The Premier Group, would thus go back to its roots and would in future stand on its own two feet under the new management team.

# 14 Standard Bank Synergy

In June 1978, when Donald Gordon approached Standard Bank's Henri de Villiers to arrange the R23 million of finance required to buy back control of the Liberty Life Group from Guardian Royal Exchange, the two men hardly knew each other. De Villiers remembered Gordon best as an adversary from the early mutual fund battles of the mid-sixties: "Gordon and Shill got in first with Sage Fund, and I recall them doing their level best with the Registrar to stymie the fund I was connected with, National Growth Fund."

Just nine years after that important first deal, in August 1987, Liberty Life raised its shareholding in Standard Bank Investment Corporation (Stanbic), the holding company of Standard Bank of South Africa (SBSA), to the legally permitted maximum of 30 per cent that insurance companies were allowed, in terms of the Banks Act, to hold in a bank. With the Insurance Act putting different constraints on the shareholdings of banking groups in insurance companies, Stanbic had, since 1985, held 50 per cent of Liberty Life's ultimate holding company, Liblife Controlling Corporation (LCC). De Villiers was deputy chairman of Liberty Life, and of its direct holding company Liberty Holdings, while Gordon was on the Board of Stanbic.

How did all this come about, and in such a brief time-span?

There are those, and Henri de Villiers himself is among them, who hold that Donald Gordon had the whole four-step progression clearly mapped out in his mind before he even took that first vast stride towards independence in 1978. "He always plans way ahead, and he sees much further than most people," says De Villiers, whose own career to the top of South Africa's biggest banking group confirms that he is himself no mean achiever. "Maybe he didn't see the whole way at first, as his immediate concern was to get the financial backing to buy back control of his 'baby', Liberty Life, but I'm quite sure that as soon as the dust had settled on that deal – and, remember, it was the biggest and most important deal of his life – then he was already looking at stage two, and beyond that."

The net effect of the 1978 deal was that Gordon himself, through his family company, DGI Holdings, owned 50 per cent of the newly formed ultimate controlling company, LCC, with Michael Rapp's family company, Annexe Investments holding 25 per cent and Stanbic the remaining 25 per cent. An agreement between DGI and Annexe gave Gordon himself a casting vote, and thus control. Stanbic paid R2 million for its equity stake, and put up R21 million of what was effectively loan capital, though it took the form of redeemable preference shares. It was this money that enabled Gordon and Rapp to acquire from Guardian Royal Exchange 21,5 million Guardian Assurance Holdings (now Liberty Holdings) shares, and these shares, together with their existing shareholdings, gave them control of Liberty Holdings – to give it its new name – and, through it, of Liberty Life.

A very important side issue was that all the senior executives in the Group – in Liberty Holdings, in Liberty Life, and in Rapp & Maister – were made participants in the control companies by being allotted shares in either DGI or Annexe. Payment for the shares was made partly from capital available to the executives concerned, or from loans made to them by Gordon and Rapp personally. Their "golden handcuffs" turned out to be greatly beneficial to all, as the loans were rapidly repaid out of the ever-increasing income flowing from the growth of the underlying Liberty Life Group, as it continued to achieve its target dividend growth of at least 20 per cent per annum.

Asked why Standard Bank so readily provided what was, only a decade or so ago, a comparatively large sum of money to a virtual business "stranger", De Villiers is emphatic. "We might not have had much in the way of business dealings with Liberty Life, but we knew and admired the company. Basically, I'm a merchant banker, not a commercial banking man, and I looked at the whole transaction as a merchant banking proposition. So long as we could get a respectable chunk of the equity, I had no problems about the loan component. And Donny didn't argue – well, not really all that much – about our having a 25 per cent stake. After all, he needed an institutional partner, and I was doing some forward thinking for myself. Early in my City Merchant Bank days I had come to the conclusion that it was valuable for a banking institution to have a meaningful stake in a life insurance company, and here I was being presented with the opportunity to get that stake in the best life insurance company in the country. And, let's face it, R2 million for 25 per cent of Liberty Life was a steal. So, for that matter, was the price Donny paid the London people for those Liberty Holdings shares."

Ian Mackenzie, at that time Chairman of Stanbic and later to become a great supporter of Gordon, and of Liberty Life, concurs. "It was a great deal for us, and there was no disagreement whatsoever on my Board. We were 100 per cent behind it." Standard Bank's present chief executive, Dr Conrad Strauss, with hindsight sees a strategic, as well as an investment, motive behind the 1978 deal. "I was then the managing director of Standard Bank and as such was not involved at all in the strategic decisions of the holding company, Stanbic, although I was informed as to what was going on. At that time, all the other major banks had some life insurance connection, some close, some loose. Barclays, through Anglo American, with Anglo Life; Volkskas and Trust with Sanlam; Nedbank with Old Mutual. We were out in the cold, and I think the Liberty Life deal came along at just the right time. Nonetheless, it was also a first-class investment for us."

Liberty Life's shareholders were told of the change of control in the Chairman's Statement with the 1978 Report and Accounts. "In July 1978, agreement was reached with Guardian Royal Exchange Assurance Limited, London (GRE) which culminated in a new South African company, Liblife Controlling Corporation Limited, acquiring 21,5 million ordinary shares in Liberty Holdings from GRE in October 1978. This acquisition, together with certain additional ordinary shares in Liberty Holdings transferred to Liblife Controlling Corporation by members of the controlling consortium, constituted that company as the holding company of Liberty Holdings and its insurance and finance-orientated subsidiaries. As part of the arrangements with GRE, the entire shareholding in Guardian Assurance Company South Africa (GASA) was transferred to GRE by Liberty Holdings in consideration for the cancellation of approximately 9,3 million ordinary shares in Liberty Holdings held by GRE.

"Following on the above transactions, the name of Guardian Assurance Holdings was changed to Liberty Holdings Limited and this name not only reflects the new South African control, but also the company's major interest, namely its 81 per cent equity shareholding in Liberty Life. Both companies, however, remain listed on the Johannesburg Stock Exchange. The symbol on the cover of this annual report is intended to depict the close nexus and relationship which exists between Liberty Life and Liberty Holdings. [It was two Liberty Life "flaming torch" symbols, side-by-side and intertwined, one in gold and one in silver.]

"The GRE has retained 4 719 978 ordinary shares, representing a 10,7 per cent equity interest, in Liberty Holdings and remains well represented on the Boards of both Liberty Life and Liberty Holdings. In addition, in terms of the arrangements, on 1 January 1979 Liberty Holdings subscribed for approximately R4,25 million of additional capital for a 25 per cent equity stake in an enlarged GASA. I continue to be the Chairman of GASA and remain on the London Board of GRE. It will be clear that although slightly loosened, the close bonds of friendship and co-operation between our Group, GRE and GASA remain very strong indeed."

It is interesting to note that, although the continuing links with the past were stressed in that Chairman's Statement (perhaps even over-stressed, for the phrase "slightly loosened" is, at the least, somewhat specious!) there is no mention at all of the vitally important new links with Stanbic and Standard Bank. The sole clue is that the name H P de Villiers appears on the Boards of both Liberty Life and Liberty Holdings, and the Directors' Reports of each state, baldly, that: "On 28 February 1979, Mr H P de Villiers, managing director of Standard Bank Investment Corporation Limited, and Mr J L S Hefer, managing director of United Building Society, were appointed to the Board."

Although the relationship with the Standard Bank Group continued to flourish, particularly at the personal level so far as Gordon, De Villiers and Mackenzie were concerned, and the Liberty Life Group prospered greatly under its new-found independence, there was still no overt acknowledgement of the existence of any "special relationship". In 1982, when De Villiers was elevated to be joint deputy chairman of Liberty Life, Gordon's Chairman's Statement merely noted that: "In view of the enlarged scope of the Group's activities, Mr H P de Villiers was appointed as an additional deputy chairman [with Ernest Bigland] of Liberty Life and Liberty Holdings with effect from 1 January 1982."

By 1983, Gordon was getting ready to move to the second stage of the Standard Bank saga, in which Stanbic would lift its shareholding in Liblife Controlling to 50 per cent. Gordon recalls: "Like all the deals I do, it was relatively simple and straightforward. I told the Bank what I wanted to do, but it was essentially so simple that I don't think anyone believed me. We began to talk, it was probably quite early in 1983, about consolidating the position. My situation was plain; I said to the Bank that I was feeling the pressure and the responsibility of controlling an institution the size of Liberty Life very much indeed. I was also concerned about the long-term future of the company; what would happen after my demise, or my retirement? 'Basically,' I said, 'I want you to have the responsibility for Liberty Life on my death. I don't see my children following me in that role, and I want to be quite sure that Liberty Life is going to continue.' I'm not sure that they really believed all that, but quite honestly it was the total truth. Anyway, they were very understanding, even sympathetic, and the deal we made with them was essentially to enable Stanbic to move their shareholding up to 50 per cent, reducing DGI down to 33 ⅓ per cent and Annexe to 16 ⅔ per cent. The DGI/Annexe combined 50 per cent interest was essentially a balance to the Stanbic stake, and Annexe agreed to vest its voting rights with those of DGI to entrench the position of joint control.

"The fundamental reason for the deal was to secure the commitment of Stanbic to the future of Liberty Life. The essential key, however, was the fact that I at all times during my lifetime retained an equal voting right in Liberty's affairs. In terms of control, the deal brought Stanbic's and my own interests into an exact matching position.

"Under the previous regime, I always had the casting vote, which actually gave me total control of the Liberty Life Group. I gave up that casting vote deliberately, and the new agreement was that so long as I am capable, and so long as I wish, to be Chairman of Liberty Life, I have the right to be so, and also Chairman of any of the Group's subsidiaries of which I wish to be Chairman. However, on my demise or retirement, the right to appoint the Chairman reverts to Stanbic.

"The reason behind that was basically a function of my personal estate planning, so that, when I was out of the way, Stanbic would forever have responsibility for Liberty Life. And that suited me perfectly. My position was, and always will be so long as I control DGI, I would have the right to two Board seats on all the main public companies in the Liberty Life Group, and as long as I am fit and well, I have the right to be Chairman. But Stanbic was now standing ready to take over full responsibility for the major financial institution that Liberty Life has become when the need arises, and that gave me a great deal of comfort, for a major institution of the highest reputation and standing was now available to take my place and ensure total continuity for Liberty Life.

"The actual transaction in all its detail was a very complex one as it effectively involved an internal Scheme of Arrangement, whereby additional shares in LCC were issued to Stanbic to give them 50 per cent, and in consequence brought Michael Rapp and myself down proportionately, DGI to 33 ⅓ per cent and Annexe to 16 ⅔ per cent. In return, Stanbic issued 6,7 million new Standard Bank shares, one-third to Annexe and two-thirds to DGI. These shares were issued at R9 a share, and there was some R25 million of cash in addition, making a total of some R85 million. As a result Michael and I, or rather Annexe and DGI in the above proportions, ended up with a 10 per cent interest in Stanbic."

Stanbic, having bought 25 per cent of Liblife Controlling Corporation for R2 million in 1978, found itself paying, and paying very happily indeed, some R85 million for a second 25 per cent tranche only five years later. Comments De Villiers: "I was always convinced in my own mind that sooner or later our stake would increase, but I did not expect it to be as soon as 1983."

And Gordon and Rapp, having, let it be noted, taken enormous personal financial risks in 1978, found themselves, only five years down the line, totally free of debt and very wealthy indeed.

The Stanbic stake in the Liberty Life Group, valued at the market value of its effective 12 million shareholding in Liberty Holdings was, at the end of 1988, worth nearly R500 million. This amounts to over 20 per cent of the entire market valuation of Stanbic itself, and represents an incredible capital gain over the R87 million cost, of which the bulk, R85 million, had been paid only five years previously.

De Villiers and Mackenzie were completely behind the second Liberty Life deal, but Stanbic's London parent, Standard Chartered plc, was very much less enthusiastic. Of all the major United Kingdom banks it was one of the most conservative and risk averse, and its highly orthodox approach was part of a strategy to fend off potential takeover raiders. Its Chairman at that time, Lord Barber, a former Chancellor of Britain's Exchequer, was ultra-conservative, and very, very establishment. Lord Barber and the Standard Chartered Board were very much opposed to mixing banking with life insurance; they could therefore see no good reason, and very little logic, in Stanbic getting even closer to Liberty Life.

Another complicating factor was that, at precisely the same time that the negotiations over Liblife Controlling were coming to a head, so was the great battle for effective control of South African Breweries, in which Donald Gordon was seen, perfectly correctly, to be a prime mover – if not, indeed, the prime mover in many eyes. And the Breweries deal was rocking the boat, and upsetting the South African establishment – much of it represented on the Stanbic Board, on which Liberty Life was represented by Gordon himself.

The upshot was that when Barber and Michael McWilliam, the erstwhile managing director of Standard Chartered, flew post-haste to Johannesburg to, as Gordon puts it, "try to kybosh the whole Liberty Life deal", they found pockets of sympathetic support on the Stanbic Board. "The problem was that the whole of the Stanbic Board was involved, one way or the other, in the Breweries affair. At one extreme were Ian Mackenzie, the Chairman, and Henri de Villiers, then the chief executive, who were seen very much as Liberty Life men, and at the other Mike Rosholt, Chairman of Barlows, and deputy chairman of Stanbic and a senior director of Breweries and very much regarded as an Old Mutual man. He was a director of Old Mutual and Barlows itself was very much in the Old Mutual orbit. In addition, Old Mutual was particularly agitated about the whole Breweries affair – particularly their Chairman, Jan van der Horst, who was also a director of Breweries. And there was I, right in the middle and rocking the boat. I was inescapably in the forefront in the Breweries affair, dipping my toes into areas of the establishment to which I had certainly not been invited, although I was trying, not very successfully, to distance myself as far as possible from the row!"

The scene was set for a right royal confrontation, and one duly followed. But Mackenzie ("If it hadn't been for him, the whole Liberty Life/Stanbic deal probably would have been aborted," says Gordon) and De Villiers dug their toes in, aided by two quite important circumstances. One was that, as by far the most influential of all of Standard Chartered's overseas interests, Stanbic had long enjoyed a degree of freedom of action not normally accorded to the overseas "branches" of the major British banks. Stanbic, as almost any Johannesburg banker will confirm, was a good deal "freer" of London control than its counterpart, Barclays (now First National). So the stubborn and spirited stand of Mackenzie and De Villiers against Barber carried a great deal of weight. The other circumstance was that, quite simply, Standard Chartered's long-term commitment to South Africa, and thus to Stanbic, was less than total, as subsequent events would soon show. So why battle over something that would prove of relatively minor concern in the long run – or in the very short run – as in fact matters turned out? (Although there were, to be sure, very real financial considerations behind Standard Chartered's 1987 decision to withdraw from South Africa.)

In the event, after "four or five highly emotive and frequently acrimonious hours", as Mackenzie recalls, Barber caved in, although he remained highly critical of the R9 per share price tag put on the new Stanbic shares to be issued to DGI and Annexe, deeming it to be far too low. So the second-stage deal went through, and Liberty Life became jointly controlled by Stanbic and Gordon. Control as such was never exercised by either Stanbic or Gordon, but remained subject to Donald Gordon's veto, and Annexe's obligation at all times to vote with DGI and Gordon.

So Gordon's position remained essentially unchanged, and Stanbic would have to wait until his demise or retirement before they could call the shots at Liberty Life. But the ongoing integrity of a great emergent financial institution had been firmly secured.

A side effect of the deal was that the issue of new Stanbic shares to DGI and Annexe served to dilute Standard Chartered's shareholding in Stanbic to approximately 51 per cent, while the holding of the Liberty Life Group, including DGI and Annexe, in Stanbic rose to some 10 per cent.

Shareholders were told, in the Chairman's Statement for 1983: "Since 1978, when control of the Liberty Life Group returned to South Africa, approximately 51 per cent of the ordinary share capital of Liberty Holdings has been held by Liblife Controlling Corporation. In that year Standard Bank Investment Corporation acquired a 25 per cent interest in Liblife Controlling, with the balance held by DGI Holdings (50 per cent) and Annexe Investments (25 per cent). Last October the shareholdings in Liblife Controlling were rearranged to enable Stanbic to acquire a further 25 per cent, bringing its position to one of joint control of the Liberty Life Group. This arrangement has substantially strengthened the association between Stanbic and and the Liberty Life Group."

The Directors' Reports of both Liberty Life and Liberty Holdings noted: "Mr I Mackenzie and Dr C B Strauss were appointed directors of the company on 16 November 1983."

Stage three in the Stanbic/Liberty Life story, which marked the beginning of Standard Chartered's withdrawal from South Africa, followed only two years later, in 1985. Stanbic then made a rights issue, which the British parent decided not to follow, but instead to renounce the major portion of its rights entitlement in favour of Liberty Life. That was relatively simple, but the associated deals were complex, and vitally important. And there was – almost – a major legal complication.

"The deal had already been announced", recalls Michael Katz, "and very soon after I received phone calls almost simultaneously from Liberty Life and Stanbic to the effect that each had received urgent, hand-delivered letters to their respective Chairmen from Dr Robert Burton, then Registrar of Financial Institutions. The letters were identical, brief, and very much to the point. The nub was one pithy paragraph which said: 'This transaction violates the Banks Act and/or the Insurance Act and is therefore null and void.'

"We were in a quandary in that the deal had been announced and our share prices had reacted firmly upwards; if the deal were indeed to be set aside the consequences would be very serious. And it was the Thursday before Easter. Anyway, in consultation with both Liberty Life and Stanbic, we decided to ask the Johannesburg Stock Exchange for suspensions of the listings of the shares of both groups. I then phoned Robbie Burton and pointed out that we fundamentally disagreed with him, that we would prepare a memorandum over the weekend, and would he arrange a meeting with the then Minister of Finance, Owen Horwood, as soon as possible.

"Burton's argument, simplified, was that the Acts stipulated that only one financial institution could be the recognised 'bank controlling company' of any particular bank at any one time. Since the Old Mutual, with its then 18 per cent shareholding, was in that position with regard to Stanbic, they, Old Mutual, could be allowed to hold up to 30 per cent, but Liberty Life could not be permitted, in terms of the Acts, to go above 10 per cent without Ministerial approval. Our argument, even more simplified, was that there was nothing in the Banks Act regarding only one 'bank controlling company' per banking institution, and that the Insurance Act, which was indeed more specific, did not apply in this case.

"On the Tuesday after Easter, we went to see the Minister. As we walked in, he said: 'Mr Katz, I think you will agree that Liberty Life has violated both the letter and the spirit of the Act.' I replied: 'With great respect, Minister, I disagree with both assertions,' and we then demonstrated that on the Act as it then stood Liberty Life fell within its rights. This was accepted and the official objections were withdrawn.

"Section 28 D of the Banks Act has since been amended to provide that only one financial institution can be recognised as the 'bank controlling company' of any bank. So once again Liberty Life set a major precedent."

Back, then, to the simple facts, as given to shareholders in the Group Chairman's Statement with the 1985 Annual Report.

"During the year Standard Bank Investment Corporation Limited (Stanbic), the listed holding company of the Standard Bank Group, embarked on a rights issue of preferred ordinary shares to augment the capital of its banking subsidiaries. As a consequence of this move arrangements were concluded with Standard Chartered Bank plc, the former United Kingdom holding company of Stanbic, whereby Standard Chartered renounced the major portion of its rights entitlement in favour of Liberty Life. [This was in terms of an agreement entered into between Standard Chartered, Liberty Life and Stanbic at the time of the 1983 Stanbic/Liberty Life transaction.]

"As part of this transaction and in order to rationalise and further consolidate the holdings of the Liberty Life Group in Stanbic to the status of an associated company, Liberty Life in April 1985 acquired a further 6,7 million ordinary shares in Stanbic. Subsequent to the year end and following a further share issue by Stanbic, the Liberty Life Group acquired an additional 1,9 million preferred ordinary shares in Stanbic. Liberty Life now owns approximately 21,5 per cent of Stanbic's issued equity share capital which is only exceeded by the 38 per cent interest held by Standard Chartered.

"Our relationship with the Standard Bank Group, today South Africa's leading bank group, continues to develop excellently and important mutual benefits arising from the relationship are increasingly being achieved."

Conrad Strauss also welcomed the closer links, but from a slightly different perspective. Looking back on the deal a few years later, he said: "I think the deal must be viewed in the light of the evolution that was taking place in the South African financial sector. The closer association between ourselves and Liberty Life was in a sense defensive – from our side at any rate, maybe not so much theirs – because we were being left out as other strong group formations were taking place. The movement was initiated largely by the Old Mutual, with Nedbank, and Sanlam with its own group banks. We felt that for us to be competitive in the broadest sense we should become involved in the development of a financial congeneric where we had major influence. Hence this third Liberty Life deal which, with all its ramifications – and those were typical of what I regard as Gordon's skills as a financial engineer – was just what Stanbic needed at that time."

Gordon takes up the story again: "Simultaneously with the Stanbic rights issue, in order to rationalise the situation because Michael Rapp and I were large individual shareholders in Stanbic, and to bring Liberty Life up to a 20 per cent equity accountable interest, it was decided that DGI and Annexe would dispose of their 6,7 million Stanbic shares to Liberty Life. We were paid in Liberty Life 9 per cent convertible preference shares, Series E – 1 072 000 shares issued at R60 per share, plus R24,2 million cash. The consideration was divided in the ratio of two to one in favour of DGI and Annexe respectively. We did not, however, give up our rights in the Stanbic rights offer, which was a one-for-five offer of preferred ordinaries at R12 per share. We took up our rights for cash. Liberty Life consequently brought its stake in Stanbic up to 21,5 per cent, which enabled Liberty Life to equity-account the Stanbic interest from then on."

Of major importance in view of subsequent events was that Liberty Life, as part and parcel of the deal, was granted "first right of refusal" over Standard Chartered's remaining 38 per cent holding in Stanbic should the London company eventually decide further to reduce its stake in South Africa. And – a matter which was later to become a major source of contention – this "right of refusal" only applied to enable Liberty Life to achieve the maximum legally permitted 30 per cent level in Stanbic; thereafter, any "surplus" shares had to be dealt with by agreement between Liberty Life and Stanbic. This aspect of the agreement was backed up by a "Chairman to Chairman" letter in which Ian Mackenzie undertook to use his "best endeavours" to ensure that the understanding about the placing of excess shares would be honoured and, in particular, to ensure that "interests adverse to those of Liberty Life" should not be permitted to hold more than 20 per cent of Stanbic.

As an aside, but an important one in view of the tussle with Old Mutual that was to come a couple of years later, Gordon recalls that Liberty Life's move upwards in its Stanbic shareholding, from some 10 per cent to the 21,5 per cent achieved in 1985, was very strongly opposed at the time, as Katz's recollections have made clear. At the time of the 1983 deal, Old Mutual held 18 per cent of Stanbic against Liberty Life's 10 per cent. Gordon had discussed, with Old Mutual's Jan van der Horst, a possible "swop" of their Stanbic holdings for Liberty Life's interest in South African Breweries at their crucial dinner meeting in Johannesburg in 1983.

The next event occurred in the United Kingdom late in 1986, when Lloyds Bank made an unwanted and highly emotive takeover bid for Standard Chartered Bank. This, obviously, had no direct impact on Liberty Life, but it was the catalyst that triggered Standard Chartered's decision finally to disinvest from South Africa, and hence to stage four in the Liberty Life/Stanbic epic.

First, however, let us go back a short period in time. While the battles in 1983 were finally settled the way Gordon wanted, Lord Barber remained ostensibly less than happy, particularly over the price of R9 per share at which the Stanbic shares had been issued to DGI and Annexe.

It obviously rankled, and Gordon recalls: "Barber, quite unreasonably, was upset with Liberty Life over the price, and when I was in London a few months after the deal, by which time the Stanbic shares had indeed risen sharply, he again raised the issue over lunch, inferring strongly that Liberty Life had negotiated too tough a deal with Stanbic as the shares had almost doubled in value since the announcement of the transaction. I strongly refuted the allegation and said that the price rise to about R17 a share just went to prove what a first rate deal it was for Stanbic, and how right Mackenzie and I had been in putting Stanbic and Liberty Life together. He replied quite caustically and in my view unfairly, saying: 'Fine, a good deal for you, but not so hot for us.'

"I stuck to my guns but was unable to convince him. Certainly the stock market has proved him totally wrong, because on the criteria of relative price, Stanbic seems to have got the better of the deal. But Liberty Life had achieved its seemingly impossible objective of becoming the undisputed dominant shareholder in Stanbic. And the long-term future and integrity of Liberty Life was firmly secured well beyond the current generation to the mutual benefit of both these great institutions. And this, of course, was the primary rationale of the transaction in the first place."

More importantly, the deal with Liberty Life had also made a major contribution to Stanbic being now indisputably accepted as the leading South African commercial bank, and its higher rating is clearly reflected by its share price.

Against the background of Lord Barber's assessment of Stanbic's strategy, it is not surprising that he was unwilling, later on, to take the excellent advice that Gordon proffered to him in 1986 when the unwelcome Lloyds Bank bid loomed large on Standard Chartered's horizon.

"It was pretty obvious, early in 1986, that Lloyds Bank was about to move on Standard Chartered", Gordon recalls, "and Barber and McWilliam unbent sufficiently to enlist my aid and advice. After careful consideration and a good look at the relevant numbers, I suggested to them that Standard Chartered, with Liberty Life's support, should acquire control of Sun Life Assurance Society in the UK, in which TransAtlantic had already built up a 26 per cent interest. The objective of this would be to simulate the interrelationship between a bank and a life insurer as had been so successfully established between Stanbic and Liberty Life in South Africa.

"On the assumption that TransAtlantic would support the proposal and accept Standard Chartered's shares in exchange for its 26 per cent of Sun Life, this should ensure success for a full takeover bid that would be envisaged following the acquisition by Standard Chartered of the TransAtlantic holding. Not only would success be virtually certain, provided the terms were reasonable, but the transaction would also translate into a TransAtlantic cross-shareholding in Standard Chartered that would provide them with a strong pivotal shareholder and a comfortable buffer against any unwanted takeover attempt.

"Lord Barber and his colleagues wouldn't listen to this heresy, as he was totally unconvinced of the strategic benefits of banks and life insurers working together, even though the alliance between Liberty Life and Stanbic in South Africa had been so successful."

In the end result, the Lloyds Bank bid was repelled, but at great cost, and the tactics adopted to achieve this pyrrhic victory will have an adverse effect on Standard Chartered's development for some time. It is an amazing irony and twist of fate that during December 1988, Lloyds Bank acquired 57 per cent control of Abbey Life, a life assurer in whose establishment Gordon had played a major role in the early sixties.

The Lloyds Bank/Abbey Life transaction was structured broadly in a very similar manner to that suggested by Gordon to Barber for the acquisition of control of Sun Life by Standard Chartered less than three years earlier. Had Barber had the prescience and the confidence to pioneer this trend in the UK, having learned from the precedent of Stanbic and Liberty Life in South Africa, the future of Standard Chartered could have been very different. Although Standard Chartered had fended off the Lloyds approach, it was apparent that more drastic steps would have to be taken, and the sale of assets was one obvious option. If this were to happen, that embarrassing (in terms of South Africa's ever-growing political isolation) 38 per cent stake in Stanbic was a prime candidate for disposal.

Rumours grew in strength in the early months of 1987, but it was not until July that matters finally came to a head.

In London's *The Times* of 21 July 1987, its banking correspondent, Richard Thomson, ran what seemed an authoritative, if not inspired, piece under the headline: "Standard seeks Stanbic sale", and accompanied by a picture of Sir Peter Graham, who had recently succeeded Lord Barber to the bank's hot seat.

"Standard Chartered, the London-based international banking group, is actively looking for buyers for its 38 per cent stake in Stanbic, the South African bank. Hill Samuel, the merchant bank acting for Standard, has been discreetly sounding out possible purchasers including Liberty Life, the South African insurance group.

"The disposal of such a politically embarrassing investment by Standard Chartered could be the prelude to a large capital-raising exercise or a merger with another bank. Although the South African involvement did not deter Lloyds Bank from bidding for Standard last year, South Africa has become an increasingly emotive issue in the international business community.

"The sale, which should net Standard around £80 million, would also help to cover the British bank's substantial bad debt provisions while improving its balance sheet. Standard is badly in need of extra capital, with lower equity and primary capital ratios than any of the big four clearing banks.

"The disposal would still leave Standard with around £750 million in cross-border lending to South Africa, however.

"The decision to sell Stanbic highlights the uncertain future of Standard, whose chairman is Sir Peter Graham. Mr Robert Holmes a' Court, the Australian businessman, last week joined Sir Y K Pao as a deputy chairman of the bank. Both men helped to rescue Standard from the Lloyds bid and each holds a stake of nearly 15 per cent in the bank. Moreover, Lloyds is now free to renew its bid for Standard if it wishes.

"With foreign banks and industrial companies steadily withdrawing from the country, any buyer of the Stanbic stake is likely to be South African. Under an agreement dating from 1985, Liberty Life has first option on Standard's interest in Stanbic in the event of a rights issue or a large disposal of shares. Liberty Life already owns 21,5 per cent of the South African bank.

"Under South African law, however, no one may own more than 30 per cent of a bank without the prior approval of the South African Reserve Bank, the country's central bank.

"Standard has been under less pressure from anti-apartheid campaigners than Barclays Bank was, but commercial considerations have become increasingly important. Analysts expect group pre-tax profits to remain virtually unchanged this year. But a boost in its provisions to 25 per cent to 30 per cent of bad debts, as other banks are doing, would cost Standard around £395 million, slashing more than £50 million off expected interim pre-tax profits."

The subject was rapidly taken up in Johannesburg, and *The Star* of 21 July followed Thomson's piece, adding that Stanbic's Conrad Strauss said that it would be inappropriate for him to comment on the developments, but quoting him as saying: "During the Lloyd's affair last year, Standard Chartered made it clear that it wanted to reduce its interests in South Africa, but it is not for me to comment on what other groups do with their assets."

Meanwhile, Strauss had been in consultation with Liberty Holdings' Farrell Sher. Also on 21 July, Sher telexed an internal memorandum to Gordon, who was then in London: "Stanbic putting out advert to press and JSE to be advertised tomorrow:

"The Board of Stanbic wishes to draw the attention of shareholders to the following announcement released in London by Standard

Chartered today: "In response to press comment concerning the future of its shareholding in Stanbic, a Standard Chartered spokesman said: 'This matter has been the subject of periodic review since Stanbic ceased to be a subsidiary of Standard Chartered in 1985 and is currently being re-examined. Unless a further restructuring of the investment is decided upon, no further public comment will be made.'"

*Business Day* took up the story on 22 July, under the headline "Liberty is set to move on Stanbic". "Liberty Life is the obvious front-runner to pick up London-based Standard Chartered's 39 per cent holding in Standard Bank Investment Corporation, which is probably up for grabs.

"The deal could come soon because Standard Chartered is said to be keen to dress up its balance sheet before its half-yearly report-back on 18 August by making adequate provision against its Third World debt exposure of almost £900 million.

"Liberty Life, in terms of an agreement, has first option on Standard Chartered's £270 million stake in the SA banking group.

"Liberty Life Chairman Donald Gordon told *Business Day* in London last night: 'I am aware Standard Chartered are looking into the matter of their shares in Stanbic. I think everyone knows that.

"'But we have certainly not been formally offered the shares to date. Before any transaction, they would have to offer the shares to us as we have pre-emptive rights.'

"It is believed Standard Chartered's merchant banker, Hill Samuel (London) has been sounding out other possible buyers in SA, but obviously any proposal would have to have Liberty Life's agreement.

"Gordon confirmed this to *Business Day* last night when he said Liberty Life could hold up to 30 per cent, but it also had the right to approve of where the balance of the shares Standard Chartered sold went – in order to ensure they did not fall into 'unfriendly hands' and upset the cordial relationship between Stanbic and Liberty Life."

Those comments of Gordon to *Business Day* pretty accurately set the parameters for the intense behind-the-scenes bargaining, bickering and just plain bloody in-fighting that went on for the next two-and-a-half weeks, before the London *Financial Times* was able to report the wrapping up of the deal on 8 August, under the headline: "Standard Chartered Bank sells £155m stake in S African arm."

"Standard Chartered Bank, the London-based international bank, yesterday sold its 38 per cent stake in Standard Bank Investment Corporation, its South African associate, for £155m in what is the largest divestment ever from the country.

"The Anti-Apartheid movement, which has been operating a worldwide boycott against Standard since May, welcomed the sale. 'The Bank has finally realised that big business and support for apartheid do not mix,' it said.

"However, Standard's group managing director, Mr Michael McWilliam, said the decision to sell the stake to a group of South African investors had nothing to do with politics. It was taken for financial reasons.

"The Bank would be taking large losses on its exposure to Third World debt, when it announced its interim figures on 18 August, and this would result in a 'substantial reported loss'.

"By selling off the South African stake, Standard will go some way towards restoring its capital position. However, Mr McWilliam said 'it would be quite misleading to say it was the whole solution'. The Bank would have to look at other options, including a rights issue and selling off other parts of the group.

"The deal had been designed to allow Standard to take as much money as possible at the commercial rand exchange rate, rather than the less beneficial financial rand rate.

"Stanbic is declaring a special dividend, of which Standard will get R157,5m (£47,8m) as well as its R8,7m share of the interim dividend – all payable at the commercial rand rate. It will also be paid R558m at the financial rand rate.

"Mr McWilliam said the deal gave Standard R19 a share, compared with the R21 that Stanbic's shares had been quoted at before they were suspended on the Johannesburg Stock Exchange last week. Even so, Standard will be suffering a loss of £36m on the disposal compared with the shareholding's book value.

"In Johannesburg, analysts said that the Reserve Bank's agreement was given as a sweetener to encourage Standard to maintain its banking ties with South Africa.

"The special dividend will deplete Stanbic's capital and there will be a rights issue to restore it. This is being underwritten by Liberty Life and Gold Fields of South Africa.

"Once the rights issue has been completed and Standard's 38 per cent shareholding transferred, ownership of Stanbic's equity will be as follows: Liberty Life, 30 per cent; Old Mutual, 20 per cent; Goldfields, 10 per cent; Rembrandt, 10 per cent; Standard Bank Pension Fund, 5 per cent; and the public, 25 per cent."

The official announcement, dated 11 August and signed by H P de Villiers as Chairman and C B Strauss as group managing director, wrapped up all the loose ends:

"It was announced on 7 August 1987 that an agreement had been reached for the sale to South African institutions of the 38 per cent shareholding in Standard Bank Investment Corporation held by Standard Chartered plc of London.

"The directorate, management and staff of Stanbic regret that the equity relationship between the two groups, which dates from the foundation of The Standard Bank of South Africa in 1862, has come to an end. It is a matter for satisfaction, however, that our long-standing and cordial business, operating and personal associations with Standard Chartered will continue. We welcome the fact that three-quarters of our shares are now held by strong and stable South African institutions.

"Stanbic management has for many years been totally independent of Standard Chartered and we shall not change our operating structure or our methods as a consequence of the new arrangement. We shall keep our name, and our solid capital structure is intact. The excellence of our systems and services has gained us a prominent place among the world's best banking and financial services organisations. Furthermore, we recognise that as a major force in the life of South Africa we have a responsibility to society that extends beyond the confines of our industry. Our social responsibility programmes will therefore remain in place and the principles of non-racialism and non- sectarianism will continue to guide our affairs.

"We regard our changed circumstances as an opportunity for continuation of the growth and development that over the past 125 years have made us South Africa's premier banking and financial services group."

That all reads very well, of course, as most public statements do, but now let us go back and look at some of the battles that had been fought in reaching that happy solution.

We will start with Strauss, commenting on the main parties involved. "First, going back to an agreement that was entered into in 1983 between Standard Chartered, Liberty Life and various players in the Liberty Life Group and Stanbic – those in the nature of things were the main parties involved. While the other big shareholders were concerned – and Old Mutual was the only other substantial shareholder – they were not part of any agreement. They may well have had concern, but in terms of the formal process laid down in that 1983 agreement, Old Mutual was not a party.

"So the moment Standard Chartered decided they wanted to reduce their shareholding, back in June, which was what I had expected anyway, their first port of call had to be Liberty Life, in terms of that agreement. Liberty Life then had first refusal up to its statutory limits and my reading of the situation was that above those limits, that is a total shareholding of 30 per cent, the balance of the disposal had to be in consultation with the Stanbic Board. But the agreement also indicated that certain Liberty Life interests had to be taken into account in the disposal of the surplus; obviously, in this context, Liberty Life would not be happy to see a strong position created by a major competitor in the disposal of those shares. As I saw it, above Liberty Life's legal limits, the disposal was a matter for consultation between the Stanbic Board and Liberty Life, with due consideration being given to Liberty Life's feelings about other shareholders."

While it may not have suited the Stanbic Board, and certainly it would not have pleased Old Mutual, one of Liberty Life's first steps was to see if the authorities would, in fact, allow it to exceed that statutory maximum of 30 per cent. "After all," Gordon points out, "the rule had been previously more often breached than it had been complied with. First there was Sanlam and Trust Bank, then Old Mutual and Nedbank and finally Barclays, Anglo and Southern. Why shouldn't we go up to 40 per cent or 50 per cent if we wanted to, and we had the right to take up the shares?"

As Strauss sees it: "I don't think the Stanbic management would have encouraged that approach, because the proposals were in no sense a rescue operation. In the past, whenever the legal limits were exceeded, it was specifically a rescue – of Trust Bank by Sanlam, and of Nedbank by Old Mutual. We wouldn't have liked to have been tarred with that particular brush. And overall, so far as placing the shares was concerned, as someone put it very eloquently, it was not the task of the Stanbic Board to look after Donny Gordon's interests, or to look after the Old Mutual's interests, or Rembrandt's. They'd all been around long enough, and could look after themselves. The obligations of the Stanbic Board were to look out for the interests of the widows and orphans out there, not the big battalions, even if we did have to live with them afterwards." In the event, although Liberty Life argued, and argued hard, with Pretoria, the authorities stood their ground; 30 per cent was to be Liberty Life's maximum holding – and no "cheating" by pushing surplus Stanbic shares "upstairs", to Liberty Holdings and other Group companies.

Gordon's biggest concern was to see that the Old Mutual's shareholding did not grow to 25 per cent (his own situation in the United Kingdom with Sun Life made him keenly aware of the value of that figure, and of the "blocking" rights that went with it). But if, as was being suggested, all the big shareholdings – in practice, that of the Old Mutual – were increased in the same proportion as Liberty Life's in rising to 30 per cent, then the Old Mutual's would in fact go to over 26 per cent. The argument, Sher recalls, waged fierce and loud – with unkind phrases about "perpetuating an oligarchy" being hurled at Gordon and De Villiers, and returned, with interest, to Van der Horst – but eventually Old Mutual recognised the moral, if not the legal, force of Mackenzie's Chairman to Chairman letter on interests adverse to Liberty Life's, and acknowledged that they, Old Mutual, did perhaps fall into that category.

Once that was conceded, the issue of shareholdings was fairly easily settled, and fell into the background. The next battles were fought over Standard Chartered's overriding need to get as much cash as possible, and as much of it out to the UK at the commercial rand rate, as it could. In this context, the fact that Hill Samuel in London, and its erstwhile South African end, Corbank, saw their prime task as representing Standard Chartered's interests only, and not the deal as a whole, exacerbated the problems, and made for difficulties.

Here, personalities entered the picture. Richard Crick, at one time Hill Samuel SA's managing director, but now handling the London end of the deal, frequently, it is said, "muddied the waters". Laurie Korsten, who had taken over Hill Samuel SA and renamed it Corbank, is "a bit of a prima donna", and managed to "ruffle a lot of feathers". One major row, at least, between Crick and De Villiers (normally a very quietly spoken gentleman) is well documented, and tempers frequently ran uncomfortably high.

But there were lighter moments. There was one meeting in the

Liberty Life Boardroom, with six of the protagonists present, arguing over a money issue – who pays what expenses, Standard Chartered or Stanbic? De Villiers handed Gordon a fat envelope, which some present assumed was full of bank notes; they were wrong, however, for he was merely passing over tickets for the next night's events at the Standard Bank's spanking new tennis arena.

For Sher, it was like old times. "We worked like hell, all hours, and the adrenalin was pumping. It was just like the old Liberty Life in full swing again, something I'd begun to miss as we became more and more the big institution. It was a big deal, the biggest 'disinvestment' from South Africa yet. It was about R760 million. Eventually, we got it all together, and we had a deal in place. At the end, however, it was a relatively minor issue – the question of expenses and the transfer duty that was payable by the buyers – that nearly caused the whole thing to crash.

"On Thursday 6 August, we'd worked all night. Liberty Life people, Standard Merchant Bank and Corbank, and everything was settled except for the expenses issue. Emotions were running high, and it looked as if we'd have to start again. I reported to DG, who wasn't at that meeting, and I finally tumbled into bed at about 2 am.

"At around 4.30 am on the Friday my phone rang. It was DG, summoning me to a meeting at his house at 5 am. I got there to find Michael Katz, Alan Romanis and Roy McAlpine there as well – absolutely old times all over again. DG had thought up a formula to solve the expenses problem – if Stanchart would undertake to pay the first R10 million, we, and the other major buyers of the Stanchart shares, would undertake to carry the rest, however much was involved (at that time we had no idea of the amount – on one set of assumptions, those costs could be up to R20 million). We thrashed it out, and it seemed that the formula would work fine. The shortfall, if any, could be absorbed by the underwriting fee.

"So by 7 am we were all in Stanbic's offices, in the Boardroom there. De Villiers and Strauss were there, and the merchant bankers. This time it was all settled, after not inconsiderable acrimony, and London accepted the deal and the compromise over the phone; an emergency Stanbic Board was called and it accepted as well; the deal was finally on. DG's statesmanlike gesture in guaranteeing any expenses above R10 million saved the day, and the whole deal, worth over R700 million, was back on course."

Prior to the dispute over expenses becoming a major issue, it had been Standard Merchant Bank that had come to the rescue by reformulating the scheme in such a way as to achieve the approval of all concerned, including the South African authorities. It was a highly ingenious application involving the development of an advanced computer programme that enabled any number of variables to be taken into account.

There was, of course, no hint of the background drama in the Chairman's Statement for 1987, in which Gordon simply reported an increased shareholding in Standard Bank Investment Corporation.

"It has always been our philosophy to concentrate our efforts on accumulating larger than average strategic holdings in leading corporations in respect of which we hope to achieve greater stability and more consistent results on the medium and longer term. In August 1987 the opportunity arose for Liberty Life to acquire an additional interest in Stanbic, South Africa's leading banking group, following the decision by Standard Chartered plc to dispose of its remaining 38 per cent interest in Stanbic. In line with our philosophy, Liberty Life increased its holding in Stanbic through the acquisition of a large block of Stanbic shares which was acquired from Standard Chartered in a complex financial transaction which was led by the Liberty Life Group and which also resulted in a substantial holding in Stanbic being acquired by the Gold Fields and the Rembrandt groups. Liberty Life clearly emerged as Stanbic's major shareholder as a consequence of this transaction with a holding of around 30 per cent.

"We regard this investment as being of fundamental importance to the Liberty Life Group and believe it will greatly cement our existing relationship with the Bank. I am confident that our interface will be of substantial benefit to both Liberty Life and Stanbic in the years ahead and will provide an important foundation from which stronger ties and synergies in business activity can be developed as the economy and the financial services industry in South Africa continues to expand."

Gordon's only regret in regard to his relationship with Stanbic was that his grand design of a broadly diversified financial services group, embracing Liberty Life, Stanbic and the United Building Society was not to be consummated. There is, sadly, no doubt that at higher levels of the bank and the building society there were substantial and serious personality conflicts, and the chemistry between the parties simply was not working. These things happen in the upper echelons of big business.

The grand alliance had in fact been agreed in principle, and Donald Gordon was scheduled to become Chairman of the United Building Society on Philip Sceales' retirement, which would facilitate the relationship. When it came to this all being put into practice, however, the cross-currents and conflicts of interest that arose made it impossible for Gordon to fulfil his proper role on the boards of both Stanbic and the UBS.

It was with great reluctance that under these circumstances he felt obliged to resign from the Board of the UBS and to deploy his energies and influence primarily in support of Stanbic, in which Liberty Life by this time had such a significant shareholding. Any other solution to Gordon's dilemma would have been unthinkable. But he still often muses as to what might have been.

# 15 First International Trust

One of the best – and best-known – examples of Donald Gordon's patience and far-sightedness in the investment sphere is the long-term stalking and eventual capture of First Union General Investment Trust (Fugit), South Africa's leading investment trust, which began its life almost contemporaneously with Liberty Life in 1957.

Fugit was operated and managed, under contract, by Union Acceptances Limited, a leading merchant bank that was founded by Anglo American and is now in the Nedbank stable. Both Anglo American and the Old Mutual, as well as UAL itself, had substantial shareholdings in Fugit, which was therefore regarded, by all except Gordon and his investment team, as being firmly and probably immovably ensconced in the Old Mutual/Nedbank sphere. A large number of other institutions were also fairly substantial Fugit shareholders, but their influence was relatively insignificant.

Before going on with the Fugit story, it is amusing to note that Liberty Life's first published portfolio of investments, that as at 31 December 1963, and disclosed for the first time in that year's Annual Report, showed a holding of 1 500 Fugit ordinary shares. The portfolio's total market value was R1 668 578, with equities contributing R250 493 to the total.

By 31 December 1964 the holding in Fugit was up to 4 250 shares, but the next year it dropped back to 1 260 shares, so there was obviously no long-range policy to acquire control of Fugit at that early stage! Indeed, after rising again to 9 260 shares in 1966 and to 9 649 in 1967, Fugit ordinary shares disappeared entirely from the Liberty Life portfolio in 1968 and 1969, the last years in which the full portfolio was published, although there was still a holding of 11 800 Fugit preference shares.

By late 1969, the Liberty Life investment department had identified Fugit as offering very good value in a generally depressed share market. As was common in those days, in the United Kingdom as well as South Africa, the ordinary shares of investment trusts normally stood at a sizeable discount to net asset value – that is, a discount to the market value of the underlying shares. This position world-wide prevails to this day, although many investment trusts have been devoured by predators bent on unlocking the discount. The rationale of this is that the net asset value can only be realised if the investment trust is wound up – or if full control is obtained, which would amount in practice to much the same thing.

Clearly, the market thought that neither of these criteria could possibly be met in this instance, hence Fugit traded at a substantial, but not abnormal, discount. Another factor was that investment trusts were very much out of fashion.

At the time of the launch of Guardbank, in partnership with the then Barclays Bank in 1970, Gordon had interested Arthur Aiken, its Chairman, to enter into a long-term joint venture to acquire a strategic stake in Fugit, in order to attempt to unlock the inherent discount in the market price of the Trust. Gordon was particularly interested in Fugit because of the quality of its portfolio and the irreplacable nature of some of the larger shareholdings.

The joint venture was embarked upon in the full knowledge that the exercise, if it had any chance of success, would be slow and painstaking graft; but on any construction the downside risk seemed minimal.

In the result, the completion of the objective of the exercise was only fully achieved on 2 December 1988, when Fugit, in its new guise as First International Trust, was effectively refinanced after a R484 million rights offer, at that time the largest ever concluded on the Johannesburg Stock Exchange.

The catalyst for this offer's success in an unfavourable stock market environment was that Fugit was to acquire Liberty Life's offshore assets and was to be reconstituted as the international investment vehicle for the holding of Liberty Life's high-quality international investment portfolio. A further attraction was the rand hedge attributes of those assets, which made it highly palatable for Fugit's minority shareholders to give up their claim to their share of Fugit's irreplacable equity portfolio.

Back to the mid-seventies. By then, after patient purchases stretching over several years, and without disturbing the market price trend to any significant extent, Liberty Life's investment team had acquired a substantial holding in Fugit of over 10 million shares, nearly 15 per cent of the total, for the account of the Liberty Life/Barclays Bank joint venture.

UAL's management was well aware that Liberty Life was buying, but the then managing director, Johan Nel, felt that, with some 10 per cent held by Anglo American, and another 12 per cent in the supposedly friendly hands of Old Mutual, UAL's own 15 per cent made the position fairly secure. In any event UAL held a long-term management contract, and he was not particularly worried. Liberty Life had further confused the issue by registering each alternate major purchase in a different nominee name, so that the full extent of Liberty Life's holdings was not apparent to UAL.

What was also not appreciated was that Anglo American's perception of UAL had changed. In 1976, UAL had become nominally independent and, although most outsiders still saw it as being within the Anglo American orbit, many Anglo American people felt differently. When Gordon approached Gavin Relly at Anglo American early in 1977 to enquire if they might be interested in disposing of their block of Fugit, the decision to sell at 60 cents was taken. Gordon was delighted at this support, and this formed the basis of much profitable and mutually satisfying business between Anglo American and Liberty Life over the years. UAL was informed by Anglo American in advance, but did not react, either positively or negatively.

Just prior to this, the Barclays Bank share of the joint venture had been acquired from them, as the bank, not unnaturally, shied away from the possibility of a confrontation. At this point, it was decided that the Liberty Life position should be disclosed to Johan Nel, who at first simply refused to believe the size of the Liberty Life build-up and refused Gordon's request for Board representation. Gordon told him, not too forcefully, that if he wanted proof this would be demonstrated in the election of directors at the forthcoming Annual General Meeting.

Gordon had decided on a gentlemanly, low-key meeting with Nel as he liked the man personally and did not want to upset him unnecessarily. But upset him he did as Nel began to accept the truth of the matter. The Old Mutual was perforce informed, and they reacted with understandable fury, partly on account of Liberty Life's cheek in invading what they considered their territory, but also at UAL for allowing the debacle to happen.

The in-fighting between the Old Mutual and Liberty Life had been rough over a long period, and both parties had always given as good as they got. However, for many years the Old Mutual regarded Liberty Life as an upstart interloper and refused to accept that it was here to stay as a serious and major player. Consequently, they could not legitimately complain about this new affront. Even so, a furious confrontation ensued in the stock market, initiated by the Old Mutual, and millions of Fugit shares changed hands at increasing prices. But this time South Africa's largest life insurer was totally outgunned by the size of Liberty Life's Fugit holding, and they eventually capitulated on their appreciation of the position by offering Liberty Life their Fugit shares. The move that precipitated the end of the battle was the pre-emptive acquisition by Liberty Life of another major block of Fugit shares, somewhat ironically from Prudential SA, at 80 cents per share, 10 cents over the market price at the time. Although the Old Mutual had first right of refusal over the Prudential's shares, Gordon gave the Prudential just one hour in which to accept or decline Liberty Life's special offer. Unfortunately for the Old Mutual, Cape Town was not able to react in time, and so lost this critical block of shares. This 80 cent price was subsequently offered to all the outstanding Fugit shareholders, after which Fugit, as a subsidiary, became a full member of the Liberty Life Group.

And so ended another major confrontation between Liberty Life and the Old Mutual, and an unwritten armistice was entered into, which was to last until 1983, when it was disrupted, hopefully for the last time, by the South African Breweries drama. All concerned have now come to realise that South Africa is a small country, and confrontation between its major institutions is simply not a starter.

With full control of Fugit in prospect, the issue was of sufficient importance for Ernest Bigland himself to fly out to the Board meeting of 2 March 1977, at which "Mr Gordon explained the background to the acquisition of approximately 14 000 000 Fugit shares in January/February 1977. Arising out of the aforesaid acquisitions and taking into account the Fugit shares previously owned by the company, it now owned 23 000 000 Fugit shares, equivalent to over 37 per cent of that company's issued share capital. In addition, other companies in the Guardian Liberty Group also owned Fugit shares and the total Group holding was currently approximately 43 per cent of Fugit's issued share capital.

"Mr Gordon further explained the background to certain rulings in regard to this transaction given by the full Committee of the

Johannesburg Stock Exchange and confirmed that the Johannesburg Stock Exchange had ruled that the Group might continue to buy Fugit shares in the market and even gain legal control without being obligated to make an offer to the body of Fugit shareholders. [This is still, in 1989, a principle that is occasionally questioned.] In view of this, and after Mr I G MacPherson had recused himself in view of his being a director of UAL it was agreed that the company continue to buy Fugit shares as and when favourable opportunities presented themselves." In spite of the JSE ruling, however, Liberty Life did in fact make an offer at 80 cents per share to all Fugit shareholders. Most accepted, to raise the Liberty Life holding in Fugit to around 70 per cent.

As we have noted, favourable opportunities continued to present themselves, and it was all over bar the shouting. Looking back, many years later, Geoff Richardson, UAL's present managing director, recalls: "We were all pretty steamed up at the time, and the general feeling was one of questioning whether Fugit really was Anglo American's worst investment. But we had to give Donald Gordon his due acknowledgement for masterminding a very astute move. Anyway, within a year we were doing the preference share placing for Liberty Life that paved the way for taking out Manufacturers Life and Sun Life – and hence DG's buy-back of control."

For the next twelve years, Fugit would remain essentially part of the Liberty Life Group's equity investment portfolio, although its net asset value per share had increased tenfold over that time frame to over 800 cents a share, from the highest price of 80 cents paid in 1977. This implied a massive capital gain running to nearly R500 million, which was turned to account when Liberty Life acquired Fugit's equity portfolio following the First International Trust reconstruction in 1988.

By the middle of 1988, the Liberty Life Group's overall stake was 92,5 per cent but the listing on both the Johannesburg and London stock exchanges had been maintained, and the shares were still quite freely traded.

In some ways, however, Fugit was a bit of an anachronism, and Donald Gordon doesn't like loose ends. "For a long time now", recalled Farrell Sher late in 1988, "DG had been considering what we should really do with Fugit. There was a view at one stage that Fugit should simply be liquidated, transferring its equity portfolio to Liberty Life and, of course, to the minority outside shareholders.

There was another view that perhaps we should buy out the minorities, or even incorporate its portfolio into Guardbank Growth Fund. Conceptually, DG has always felt that Fugit had its rightful place in the greater Liberty Life Group, rather than just being a pure investment trust."

Fugit took that rightful place on 1 September 1988, with a joint announcement by itself, Liberty Life and Liberty Holdings that spelt out the details of one of South Africa's largest-ever financial transactions. It detailed three separate proposals: "First, the disposal by Fugit of its entire equity portfolio to Liberty Life." That was a deal worth R646 million. "Second, the acquisition by Fugit of Liberty Life's offshore interests (TransAtlantic Holdings and Continental and Industrial Trust) and the consequent establishment of Fugit as the newly constituted listed international investment holding company of the Liberty Life Group." That leg involved over one billion rand – R1 086 million. "Thirdly, a proposed 75-for-100 rights offer to raise R484 million to be made by Fugit to its shareholders in which shareholders of Liberty Life and Liberty Holdings would also be given the opportunity to participate, in ratio to their indirect attributable holdings in Fugit." That would be the biggest rights issue ever made in South Africa, though it was barely half the size of the one made in the UK in 1987 by another of the offshore companies in the greater Liberty Life Group – Capital & Counties plc – but this was really a function of the low price of the rand against the pound sterling.

It is amusing to note that the joint announcement document was signed on behalf of First Union General Investment Trust Limited by Donald Gordon, Chairman; on behalf of Liberty Life Association of Africa Limited by Donald Gordon, Chairman; and on behalf of Liberty Holdings Limited, by Donald Gordon, Chairman.

"On 11 July 1988, the whole exercise really began in earnest," Sher recalls. "I was in London, and in the course of a phone conversation DG asked me when was I coming home. I said on 12 July, and he said, 'Fine, I want us to start working on a reconstruction and finally to sort out what we are going to do with Fugit.'

"I got back on the 12th, and right away we got down to a round of meetings. DG brought in a number of the senior Liberty Life people – Mark Winterton, Dorian Wharton-Hood, Steve Handler, Alan Romanis, Roy McAlpine, James Inglis and Joel Cane – and one evening we got down to a very useful think-tank. We were all going out for dinner together, but just before we were due to leave the office, DG came up with the simple but quite brilliant concept of moving the equity portfolio out of Fugit into Liberty Life and as a quid pro quo transferring Liberty Life's international interests into Fugit.

"That was the seed of the idea for the major reconstruction we effected late in 1988. The seed was sown, by DG himself, that night before we went out to dinner. Everyone was conscious of the need to do something about the increasing imbalance of shareholders' funds caused by the rapid growth of our offshore investments, which represented around 68 per cent of the total, and to do something with Fugit, but it was his idea, his creation, to move the international interests into Fugit, and to re-establish Fugit as the listed international vehicle for the Liberty Life Group." This strategy solved many problems in one fell swoop.

That was on 27 July 1988, and from then on the pace quickened appreciably. It might have taken twelve years to reach the decision to turn Fugit into First International Trust, but once the seed was sown, the corporate team swung rapidly into action. "DG asked us to prepare a comprehensive memorandum. We analysed the situation in great detail; all the pros, the cons, the difficulties, the problems, what consents we would need, what authorities would be involved. A lot of hard work, but that memo was delivered to DG on 6 August, with nearly all the snags ironed out or identified."

Between then and Wednesday 31 August, the concept was translated into the necessary documentation for that 1 September joint announcement, a process that involved outside advisers, the Reserve Bank, the Treasury, various UK authorities and both the Johannesburg and London stock exchanges. Gordon was unwinding at the famous High Rustenberg Hydro at Stellenbosch, in the Cape, but a mere telephone or telefax machine away, and they were all working at red-hot speed. "Security was a headache," says Sher, "but we've always prided ourselves at Liberty Life on tight security. There's never been a suspicion of a leak on any of the myriad deals we have done over the years. For this one, we used code names on all papers."

When all Group shares were suspended on the London and Johannesburg stock exchanges on Monday August 29, share price movements over the previous few weeks had been minimal – no leak whatsoever. Press speculation on the reasons for the suspensions was intense and widely varied – but completely inaccurate. Not one commentator came near to guessing the truth.

Once the announcement was made, it immediately became clear that, whilst the restructure was to the benefit of everybody concerned – shareholders in all the Group companies as well as policyholders of Liberty Life – the biggest beneficiaries would be the 2 500 or so outside shareholders of Fugit. But it was felt that these shareholders needed to be compensated for effectively renouncing their share of the extremely high quality Fugit portfolio. On relisting, Fugit rose from the pre-suspension price of R7 initially to R10 and later to R12, in effect a pure bonanza of R3 to R5 a share to the non-Group holders of some 4 million Fugit shares – and a price jump that underlined the tightness of the security, as well as the need for it. By March 1989, the First International Trust share price exceeded R15, an indication of the public enthusiasm for the share, and for the concept.

Asked why they gave all that money away, Sher replies: "Well, relative to the objective of using Fugit in the reconstruction – and it was by far the most suitable and sensible vehicle – it wasn't a large price to pay, particularly in view of the overall sums involved. The minorities were lucky, they just happened to be in the right place at the right time. And anyway, they were mostly people who had been Fugit shareholders for decades, and hence indirectly Liberty Life Group shareholders, for a long time." In any event, the deal had been done at the net asset value of all the companies concerned, so there was no real loss to anyone. And, of course, Liberty Life acquired an irreplacable equity portfolio in exchange.

Logistically, the exercise was a remarkable one. Fugit, or First International Trust Limited (FIT) as it was soon to become, was making that R484 million rights issue to raise the cash to bridge the gap between the assets it was buying for R1 086 million and those it was selling for R646 million, leaving itself with some R40 million of small change in the process for future developments. Liberty Life and Liberty Holdings were to pass on the bulk of their rights in the FIT offer to their own shareholders. In all, some 18 000 shareholders were concerned. A massive amount of documentation was involved, all of which was done in-house. "We used no merchant bank," says Sher, "everything was done by our own people, except that Standard Merchant Bank collected the money for us. It was a hectic five months, and I was very proud of the way our people performed."

"Nobody else could have done it with such efficiency in the tight timetable involved," adds Gordon.

The proposals were extremely well received by both the press and the market. Davis Borkum Hare's Richard Lomberg, writing in September, gave this assessment: "The proposed series of deals and rights offers is to be warmly welcomed because, not only does it add a new dimension to the market, it materially improves the scope for the development of both the local and offshore interests of the Group. We strongly encourage shareholders to take up their rights entitlements, at whatever level this occurs. The market, we feel, has failed to fully recognise the potential of the changes, or to accord Fugit the rating it deserves. Fugit is standing at a 28 per cent discount to the underlying asset value. With rapid profit growth likely as a result of the excellent performance of its investments, the fall in the rand against sterling, the favourable gearing in Conduit (Liberty Life's offshore holding company) and the probability of continued successful financial engineering, Fugit presents an excellent buying opportunity."

On 22 November, Martin & Co's Richard Jesse's evaluation was: "On a 20 per cent discount to the sterling NAV of the portfolio (the prevailing UK investment trust average discount) FIT translates through the financial rand to 1 013 cents, valuing the Letter of Allotment at 189 cents (current price: 170c). We regard FIT as a very high quality rand hedge investment, justifying core holding status. In periods of particular rand exchange rate weakness the discount to the sterling NAV is likely to close. Accumulate."

The massive issues went according to plan, and on 8 December 1988 a further joint announcement by the three principal companies read: "Shareholders are advised that 58 861 886 new ordinary shares of 25 cents each (99 per cent of the shares offered) were subscribed for pursuant to the rights offer made to shareholders of First International Trust, Liberty Life and Liberty Holdings of 59 435 111 new ordinary shares in First International Trust at a price of 815 cents per share to raise a total of R484,4 million for First International Trust. Liberty Life and/or its nominee have taken up the balance of the new ordinary shares in First International Trust in terms of the underwriting agreement.

"Following the completion of the rights offer, Liberty Life (including policyholders' interests) now owns approximately 57 per cent of the issued share capital of First International Trust, which has been reconstituted as the listed international investment holding company for The Liberty Life Group.

"As a consequence of the transaction, a net consideration of R477 million has been received by Liberty Life for shareholders' account. This amount has been invested in short and medium term money and capital market securities pending its disposition in permanent long term investments. This will result in a substantial increase in the level of investment income and in earnings after taxation attributable to shareholders of Liberty Life.

"Based on the current market price of R12 per First International Trust share, an unrealised surplus in excess of R35 million has accrued to the Life Fund for the benefit of policyholders and pension fund clients of Liberty Life following upon the acquisition of First International Trust shares allocated as part of the restructuring arrangements."

In the press release that accompanied the announcement, Gordon added this comment: "Given current economic conditions, we are extremely delighted at the successful conclusion of the rights offer which has resulted in First International Trust raising R484 million. This was the largest rights offer ever undertaken in South Africa, the next largest being Gencor's R410 million in 1984, followed by Nedbank's R345 million in 1986. The tremendous support received for the rights offer and the interest shown in the establishment of our new international holding company is a clear indication of the standing in which First International Trust is held by the investment community following the establishment of the company as the listed international investment holding company for The Liberty Life Group.

"The rights offer drew very substantial institutional support and has been taken up by the majority of the long-standing shareholders of First International Trust, Liberty Life and Liberty Holdings.

"In the eighteen working-day period during which the rights offer was open a total of 16,6 million rights changed hands, and First International Trust is now duly reconstituted with a wide spread of shareholders and provides the discerning investing public with an opportunity to participate directly in The Liberty Life Group's high quality offshore interests.

"We are particularly gratified that the reconstitution of First International Trust has provided the opportunity for significant participation of Liberty Life's policyholders and pension fund clients in our international investments which are now held indirectly through First International Trust."

That last paragraph underlines one of the key aspects of the whole deal. It was not merely the fact that, at 68 per cent of the whole, the Liberty Life Group's offshore assets were indeed causing severe imbalance, with the Group becoming increasingly to be regarded as a "rand hedge", rather than as the outstanding life assurance and financial services vehicle that it undoubtedly is.

Another aspect, that of "the participation of Liberty Life's policyholders and pension fund clients in the Group's international investments", had also become a matter of increasing concern. For unkind commentators were pointing out that Liberty Life's immensely successful offshore forays were all good and fine for shareholders, for whose account all of the international investments were held up to this point. But they were of no benefit at all to policyholders, who did not in any way participate in their success.

This had now been put right, and all concerned with the greater Liberty Life Group, in whatever capacity, could take both pride – and profit – from the financial skills that were making TransAtlantic and its associates an increasingly powerful force in the City of London.

As Davis Borkum Hare had noted in their market assessment cited earlier, the probability was that "successful financial engineering" would continue to play a part in the Group's affairs.

No transaction better encapsulates the skills of Donald Gordon. He is an exceptional financial engineer, and the repositioning of FIT demonstrated financial engineering at its highest level.

# 16 The Man from the Pru

The tenth of September 1986 was Liberty Life's twenty-ninth birthday in terms of its incorporation as a public company; 22 August was its twenty-eighth birthday as a registered life assurer. Back in those precarious early days, its toughest competitor and probably its biggest detractor had been the lordly and high-flying Prudential, South African scion of Britain's best-known life assurer, the great Prudential Assurance Company, of Holborn Bars, London. The famous "Pru", Britain's largest insurance company, was always the life insurance company for which Donald Gordon had the highest regard – and his admiration continues to this day.

As if in confirmation of this, at 31 December 1988, the largest single shareholding of the Continental & Industrial Trust, the London-listed investment trust subsidiary of TransAtlantic Holdings, was 3,8 million ordinary shares in the London-based Prudential Corporation plc. And this investment had performed very well since its acquisition soon after the Crash of 1987.

Prudential's South African salesmen, along with their rivals from Canada's Manufacturers Life and Sun Life, had in the early days referred derisively to "Liberty Life of Witbank" or "Liberty Life of Doornfontein" when attempting to persuade potential life insurance purchasers to stay with the establishment rather than risk trusting their hard-earned premiums to the upstart newcomer. The Canadians had had their come-uppance in 1972 and 1974, when their South African operations had been swallowed up by Liberty Life. But the proud Prudential had gone from strength to strength, and even to its own highly successful Johannesburg Stock Exchange listing in 1983.

On 3 September 1986 – just one week short of its twenty-ninth birthday – the voracious Liberty Life swallowed The Prudential Assurance Company of South Africa, in a giant R300 million deal that was its largest takeover to date. It was a deal which solidly consolidated Liberty Life's third place in the South African life insurance league, bringing it to within measurable range of its Cape-based mutual rivals, the Old Mutual and Sanlam.

Gordon's Chairman's Statement in the 1986 Annual Report admirably summed up the Prudential deal: "In September 1986 arrangements were concluded between the Liberty Life Group, the Prudential Assurance Company Limited (of the United Kingdom) and Prudential SA in terms of which, subject to the fulfilment of certain conditions precedent, Prudential SA would with effect from 1 January 1987 become a subsidiary of Liberty Life in terms of a merger between the two companies to be effected by way of an issue by Liberty Life of new convertible redeemable non-cumulative preference shares in exchange for the acquisition of shares in Prudential SA. In order to give effect to the merger Liberty Life will allot and issue with effect from 1 January 1987, 7 new Liberty Life convertible preference shares for every 100 ordinary shares in Prudential SA to be acquired pursuant to the merger. These new Liberty Life convertible preference shares will be issued at R140 per share and annual dividends of 500 cents per share in respect thereof will accrue from 1 January 1987. Based on Liberty Life's shareholding in Prudential SA at the date hereof it is anticipated that approximately 1,6 million new Liberty Life convertible preference shares will be issued of which 1,4 million will be issued to Prudential UK in respect of its 64,4 per cent interest in Prudential SA, as a result of which Prudential UK will hold an approximate 7 per cent equity interest in Liberty Life.

"The purpose of the proposed merger is to achieve economies of scale and to secure a deeper and more effective penetration of the South African life insurance market by the combined group which on 1 January 1987 will have total assets in excess of R10 billion. Both Liberty Life and Prudential SA have substantial depth in human resources in various areas of their respective operations and I am sure that these resources will, following the implementation of the transaction, complement each other and result in considerable benefits and opportunities for both companies and their staffs with resultant improvements in operating efficiency.

"Through its full-time representatives and insurance brokers Prudential SA markets a wide range of products for both individuals and groups in the South African insurance market, including conventional with-profit and unit-linked assurances, various types of retirement annuity contracts and a full range of group pension schemes. I am confident that the combined resources of the promotional and marketing divisions of Liberty Life and Prudential SA will result in enhanced penetration of the South African life insurance market. Prudential SA has an outstanding investment portfolio comprising, *inter alia*, a wide range of prime blue chip South African equities similar in quality to Liberty Life's holdings and a highly efficient and cost effective administration system utilising sophisticated computer systems. The company has a well-established position in the South African life assurance market and on its own record is the sixth largest life office operating in the Republic with total assets at 31 December 1986 of R2,37 billion.

"In order to give effect to the merger, Liberty Life has proposed a Scheme of Arrangement in terms of the Companies Act, 1973, and it is hoped that the scheme will be sanctioned by The Supreme Court of South Africa during March 1987.

"Liberty Life has undertaken to continue to adopt the policy which Prudential SA followed in relation to the determination of the amount and distribution of surplus to Prudential SA's with-profit policyholders in respect of policies which were effected prior to 1 January 1987 and their reasonable benefit expectations will, after such date, not be impaired.

"It is contemplated that in the medium term the respective businesses of Liberty Life and Prudential SA will be merged in accordance with the provisions of the Insurance Act, 1943, as amended."

Behind the scenes, of course, the deal was far more complex. Recalls Michael Katz: "The Prudential deal was a very interesting transaction. I was at a Margo Commission sitting when Donny phoned me – he had someone with him, could I come to his house? Well, Dorian Wharton-Hood [then managing director of Prudential SA] was there, and we started looking at the problems of Liberty Life taking them over. First, the Competition Board would be involved because its Act had recently been changed to bring within its purview any change of control of a financial institution; second, there was the Reserve Bank because of the very considerable exchange control implications; and thirdly there was the Registrar of Insurance because the acquisition of more than 25 per cent of Prudential SA would require his approval in terms of the Insurance Act.

"We had meetings with all three authorities within the next few days, and got approval in principle to go ahead. Apart from that, and its importance in terms of size in the line-up of the insurance industry generally, the Prudential SA deal was fairly straightforward from the legal point of view."

Press comment was generally enthusiastic. Peter Farley, in *The Star* of 4 September, wrote: "Liberty Life has leapt into a clear third place in the insurance league with yesterday's acquisition of the Prudential SA for an effective R300 million. The announcement yesterday ended a week of speculation after trading in the Prudential's shares was suspended for a day last week, in the wake of a jump in the price to 900c. The deal offers enormous synergy for both parties.

"The prime motivation for the deal, said Liberty Life Chairman Mr Donald Gordon, was to strengthen Liberty's depleted management resources. 'I cannot understate the shortage of top technocrats and qualified actuaries.' And though Mr Gordon denied this, analysts speculate the acquisition of one man – Pru MD Mr Dorian Wharton-Hood – was the main reason.

"The deal values the Pru shares at a shade under R10 each, identical to the ruling price on the JSE when the shares were again suspended yesterday morning.

"Mr Gordon emphasised this was not a disinvestment move by the Pru, though the Pru would be able to convert the new shares into cash in either 1992 or when the Liberty dividend reaches 500c a share.

"In the last full year Liberty paid 300c a share and Mr Gordon indicated the 500c target could be reached in the next three years. [This, in fact, occurred in the 1988 financial year, a full twelve months ahead of schedule.] So if the Pru wishes to convert its new equity into cash it may be able to do so by the end of this decade."

Brian Zlotnick, in *Business Day* on 4 September, wrote in a similar vein: "A week of intense market speculation surrounding the future of the Prudential SA ended yesterday with Liberty Life set to take over SA's largest independent life insurer by way of a R300m paper deal.

"However, contrary to the market's favoured view, the Pru's UK parent is not disinvesting from SA. It has agreed to exchange its controlling 64 per cent interest for new Liberty Life shares.

"The UK company lands up with only 6,7 per cent of Liberty Life's enlarged equity and effectively distances itself from SA in the sense that it will no longer have control or management say over an SA company.

"According to Liberty Life Chairman Donald Gordon the Pru's parent does not intend to dispose of its Liberty Life shares, so his statement implies that no money will be leaving SA as a result of the deal.

"Besides the benefits of economies of scale and increased market penetration flowing from the transaction, the combined group's total assets will be R11 billion. This will entrench Liberty Life's place firmly as SA's largest proprietary insurer and third-largest insurer. Morover, the combined annual net premium income should be about R1 billion and total income more than R1,5 billion.

"A motivating factor behind the deal is the effect the brain drain has had on Liberty Life. However, Pru MD Dorian Wharton-Hood says the company has no immediate staff problems. Gordon admitted yesterday: 'Liberty is looking a little thin in terms of senior management.' After an in-depth look at the Pru's management, he believed there were areas of tremendous compatibility.

"Once the transaction has been approved by all the relevant authorities, the appointment of Wharton-Hood and Mark Winterton (deputy Liberty CE) as joint MDs of the enlarged group should pave the way for a smooth merger. Eventually, new policies will no longer be issued in the name of the Pru.

"While the market was off-beam in speculating that the Pru's parent would disinvest, it was on target in identifying Liberty Life – which already has 4,1 per cent of the Pru's equity – as the predator."

Before the deal was finally wrapped up, Liberty Life had further increased its stake by purchasing another 20,3 per cent from Lifegro Assurance, the fifth largest assurer in South Africa, who in frustration at being upstaged in its own nefarious plans to bid for Prudential SA had indicated its intention to act as a spoiler. Gordon quietly disposed of that problem by buying Lifegro out. Culturally and philosophically, Liberty Life was clearly the only possible home for the Prudential of South Africa; and, of course, Brian Corby, the UK Prudential chief, and Donald Gordon had become friendly over many years of contact on the London scene, another valuable by-product of Liberty Life's international strategy.

London took a different view on the disinvestment issue, with *The Times*, on 4 September, running the headline: "Prudential pulls out".

"The Prudential Corporation is effectively to pull out of South Africa through an agreed takeover of Prudential Assurance Company of South Africa, its quoted subsidiary, by Liberty Life, one of the country's biggest insurance groups.

"Liberty Life is making a preferred ordinary share offer which values Prudential SA at R304 million and which will result in the groups merging operations from next January. Prudential, which had a 64 per cent stake in Prudential SA, will end up with a 6,7 per cent interest in Liberty Life, and it intends to keep this. The new Liberty Life shares, valued at R140, will pay a fixed annual dividend of R5.

"Mr Brian Medhurst, managing director of Prudential's overseas division, said the decision to merge with Liberty Life had resulted from political developments in South Africa which had seen many senior insurance personnel leave the country."

By 7 September, the Johannesburg *Sunday Times* had had a little more time to consider the issues, and David Carte and David Southey ran the headline: "Liberty pips Lifegro to the Pru".

"Liberty Life's sensational R300 million snatch of Prudential SA this week places it within medium term reach of the size and power of Old Mutual and Sanlam.

"Donald Gordon's meticulously planned and executed coup adds R3 billion to Liberty's assets, lifting them to R11 billion. Liberty's move has caused some nervousness in Southern and Lifegro lest Mr Gordon should turn his sights on them in the race to catch Old Mutual and Sanlam.

"All he would need is the consent of the ultimate controllers – Anglo American in the case of Southern and Rembrandt in the case of Lifegro. Mr Gordon has excellent relationships with both Anglo and Rembrandt.

"But Mr Gordon says he is not interested in more insurance acquisitions until the merger with Prudential SA shakes down. The merger lifts the value of Liberty's investments by 23 per cent to to R9,8 billion, its life funds by 42 per cent to R6,4 billion, and estimated distributable profit by about 14 per cent to roughly R80 million.

"In clinching this takeover, Liberty Life pipped Lifegro to the post. Lifegro also wanted a marriage with Prudential SA and built up a strategic stake shortly after its listing. Now it will be able to convert its stake into a capital profit of more than R15 million.

"Mr Gordon says: 'It is a great deal for Liberty Life, but a good one for Prudential SA as well. It's a very good fit. We were the only ones with whom they could have felt culturally at home.' Mr Gordon stresses that 'neither Liberty Life, nor Prudential UK wished to be associated with disinvestment'.

"However, Prudential UK can tell anti-apartheid campaigners at its meetings that it no longer controls a South African company. Instead, it will have a 6,7 per cent stake in Liberty Life.

"Mr Gordon says the takeover was the culmination of cordial relations with Prudential SA in the past two years. The price – effectively 980c a Prudential SA share – was fair as the Prudential SA price was 650c a few weeks ago. 'We could have saved a couple of million by going for a finer price, but when you deal with people of the calibre of Prudential UK you don't play silly beggars.'

"The two parties are stressing that the major benefit of the merger is that it bolsters the management of both companies. Liberty Life admits it was short on management. It acquires a top insurance marketer in Prudential SA managing director Dorian Wharton-Hood, who becomes a joint managing director of Liberty Life alongside Mark Winterton.

"Mr Gordon says Mr Wharton-Hood will 'fill a hole' left by the departure of Liberty Life managing director Monty Hilkowitz for Australia. Mr Wharton-Hood says he will work happily alongside Mr Winterton. 'I'll get on with the selling while Mark looks after the administration and the technical actuarial stuff, which is not really my turf.'"

Peter Farley returned to the topic, with a far deeper insight into the facts, after talking to Wharton-Hood, it would appear, in *The Star* on 8 September. His headline was: "It was a close call for the Pru-Liberty deal".

"Just how much cloak and dagger intrigue is involved in the behind-the-scenes activity of a major merger like the Liberty-Prudential deal? Enough to almost scupper the whole thing, according to Prudential MD Dorian Wharton-Hood.

"Although Liberty Life had approached the Prudential UK many times over the years with a view to buying the South African operation – their overtures had always been rejected. That was until July 1986.

"Wharton-Hood was involved in routine discussions in London with Pru chief executive Brian Corby when Donald Gordon – also in London – called with yet another approach. This time the Pru decided to see what Liberty Life had to offer, but with no intention of rushing into a deal. Long-term strategic forecasts showed that the Prudential SA would eventually have to find a local partner, either to ensure growth of business or if political pressure forced the Prudential UK to pull out. And as Liberty Life was the only company they were interested in talking to it made sense to see what was on offer. Liberty Life needed people, particularly in the higher echelons, so the synergy was available.

"What ensued was a series of highly secret meetings between Gordon and Wharton-Hood. So secret that not even the senior management of the respective insurance companies were told.

"That was the case until a week ago last Wednesday when the Prudential SA share price started rising. Someone had got wind of the talks. The share was suspended – which will still have to be investigated – and everything moved into top gear."

What had happened, as a very well authenticated story related by Gordon has it, was that someone in the investment field saw Gordon and Wharton-Hood getting out of Gordon's car in Pretoria at the offices of the Registrar of Financial Institutions. That "someone" was reputedly Bruce McInnes, once Gordon's personal assistant before he left Liberty Life to make his own fortune by revitalising Hudaco, an industrial conglomerate with a high profile on the South African scene. McInnes, having seen the two chief executives together in the company of Michael Katz, might well have put two and two together.

Another version is told by Farrell Sher. "As Donald and Dorian walked out of Dr Japie Jacobs' private door at the Reserve Bank in Pretoria, they almost bumped into Johann Rupert, then a merchant banker, who said triumphantly: 'I know what you two are up to.'"

*The Star* continued: "Corby flew out from London and the discussions were widened to include the senior people in each camp. And that is where the trouble started. While both Gordon and Wharton-Hood were excited by the prospect, they had no idea how those down the line would react. Almost to a man, at different meetings last Saturday, they opposed the idea of the takeover.

"Wharton-Hood says that in the preceding days he had been agonising over the fact that he had to keep it secret – even from his inner cabal at the Prudential SA. And, in many ways, his worst fears were realised.

"More persuasion ensued, backed by Corby's support for the deal and convincing arguments that the deal was in the best interests of all concerned. Much of the problem on the Prudential SA side stemmed from its platform of being the major independent and the fact that the deal would mean the end of the Prudential SA.

"However, come Monday and the Prudential SA management were reluctantly moving behind the deal. But more surprises were in store. Early Tuesday afternoon Wharton-Hood and Corby were waiting for a copy of the terms to come from Liberty Life. What actually arrived were different from those agreed in principle.

"Opposition from within Liberty Life had forced Gordon to change the terms. Corby and Wharton-Hood immediately went to Liberty Life to call it all off. However, an eleventh hour negotiating session not only got the talks back on the rails, but also produced an agreement for Corby to take back to London.

"Approval by the Prudential UK was a formality and the deal was through – at incredible speed for a transaction of this nature – but only by the skin of its teeth."

Farley was surprisingly – almost embarrassingly for both Gordon and Wharton-Hood – close to the truth. The deal had indeed almost foundered on the rock of senior management opposition – surprisingly, perhaps, even more from the Liberty Life side than from within the ranks of Prudential SA. Ultimately, Gordon had had internally to resort to the device of a "free and open" vote, which looked thoroughly democratic but which also exposed those of his top managers who opposed the transaction.

Nevertheless, oppose they did. To the extent that, on the vitally important issue of price, they actually had their own way. The "opposition" stoutly refused to allow Gordon to pay the equivalent of over R11 per Prudential SA share that he had tentatively agreed with Wharton-Hood and Corby. Those preliminary terms were essentially eight Liberty Life convertible preference shares for every 100 Prudential SA shares.

A reduction to around R10 per share, or seven for 100, received a reluctant consensus from Gordon's executives. In Gordon's view, this was still something of a compromise, for there were still some who thought Liberty Life was paying "over the odds" for Prudential SA. Says Gordon, philosophically: "The truth or otherwise of this will take decades to be proved; and most of the players, myself included, will be happily retired by then."

Mark Winterton was particularly vociferous in insisting that

Liberty Life was overpaying. This had a strong influence on Gordon and the other senior executives, as Winterton was not only deputy chief executive as well as managing director, but was also a highly experienced actuary who had been involved in most of Liberty Life's insurance acquisition deals over the past fifteen years. He had spent most of his working life with Guardian Assurance in London before being seconded to Liberty Life in 1970. Winterton was also the senior executive whose personal position would be the most affected, as he would be accepting the proposal that Wharton-Hood would be coming in as joint managing director, although Winterton, as incumbent, would be the more senior of the two.

It was at this stage, with the deal looking decidedly uncertain, that Gordon and Corby decided to employ a most unorthodox strategy. It was risky, but it worked. They agreed that the executives of both their companies be locked together into the Liberty Life Boardroom. At the start, they were addressed in turn by Corby and Gordon, who then withdrew with the instruction to the executives that they were not to leave the Boardroom until all differences had been ironed out.

Hours later, and after separate working lunches for each group of executives, the smiles on the faces of most of those emerging wearily from the Boardroom told it all – the strategy had been successful. Gordon afterwards often wondered how Corby had explained to his London Board the manner in which all those seemingly irreconcilable differences and perceived problems between the two sides had eventually been resolved.

Even so Gordon was forced, much to his embarrassment, to reduce the price, even at the risk of losing the deal. Some on the Prudential SA side still feel, perhaps a little uncharitably, that this "wrangling" on price was a deliberate negotiating ploy on Gordon's part. That is not his style: he is a tough, even an outstanding, negotiator, but he doesn't chisel; in this case he had no option. Winterton confirms that he and other top Liberty Life executives were so unhappy that they would have refused to back the merger without a reduction in price. Gordon was left with a clear choice – reduce the price, or scupper the whole deal.

The other issue that riled – and still riles – a number of very senior Liberty Life men is the emphasis, in both press comment and in Gordon's own statements at the time, placed on Liberty Life's need to expand top management. Certainly, Wharton-Hood was an important acquisition, and he is personally well accepted; but there were more than a few noses out of joint.

Monty Hilkowitz's loss – defection, as it was seen by Gordon at the time – did indeed leave a gap, perhaps even a yawning chasm, at the top of Liberty Life. As managing director he was the "Crown Prince" and when he went – and when, perhaps even more importantly, Michael Rapp moved to London as well, albeit to mastermind Capital & Counties' enormous expansion drive – Gordon certainly had problems.

Winterton, Hilkowitz's appointed successor – first as deputy managing director, and then as deputy chief executive and managing director – is an outstanding administrator, but he is not a marketing man, as was Hilkowitz. And he had anyway made it abundantly clear that he intended to retire when he reached the age of 60 in 1992. Gordon himself had temporarily had to resume the role of chief executive that he had given up to Hilkowitz, but the marketing gap remained. Even so, many senior Liberty Life people were less than delighted to be informed by the press that Wharton-Hood, and with him, the top executives of Prudential SA, were being bought just to fill the hole. To a large extent, however, this did not happen, as during the traumatic few months following the deal many key Prudential SA executives were head-hunted and moved elsewhere. In an economy so short of seasoned executives as is South Africa's, this was understandable, but most regrettable.

Hilkowitz had long been a key figure at Liberty Life. Back in 1978, when the *Financial Mail* brashly asked Gordon: "What about succession?" his reply was: "If, for example, I were to fall under a bus? There are certain situations that one must not lose sight of. One of the major shareholders, in fact the second largest individual shareholder, is Michael Rapp. Then, the deputy chairman is Ernest Bigland."

The *FM* countered: "But he has just retired from active life in the UK?" Gordon: "Yes, but nonetheless he remains deputy chairman. But the individual with the greatest financial stake after me is Michael Rapp, who is a highly intelligent, highly dedicated, able executive in his own right. There are also many others who could hold the reins, either alone or as a team. Monty Hilkowitz has recently been appointed chief general manager, embracing responsibility for all admin and marketing functions."

The *FM*'s pen portrait of Hilkowitz, in 1978, is worth repeating in view of the fact that, with Bigland's death and Rapp's relocation to London, he had indeed had to take up the "reins", as Gordon had put it.

"Tall, lean, good-looking and very, very, relaxed, Monty Hilkowitz, at the age of 38, has just been promoted to chief general manager of Liberty Life. On being congratulated on his appointment and being told that he seemed to be taking it very much in his stride, his reaction was typical: 'Yes, I am excited; but you know, when one has lived with a company for so long one has a reasonable idea of what it is all about.'

"A Free Stater, born in Vrede on 20 July 1940 ('It was a Saturday, at 8 in the morning') Hilkowitz is essentially a calm man, a very precise man. He was educated at, and matriculated from, Bellville High. Like the boss, Gordon, he is one of the very few in the top echelons of Liberty Life who did not go to university. 'But I am an actuary. In fact I wanted to be a doctor. But, when I left school it was decided that I would work for a while to earn enough to put myself through university. Somehow I got involved in actuarial studies and never got around to going to university – or to being a doctor.'

"He started with Southern Life when he left school, and stayed there for ten years, qualifying as an actuary in 1966. Then, in 1967, he joined Swiss Reinsurance, in Johannesburg: 'That was a quantum leap in my career. A short while later I became responsible for the SA life reinsurance operations of SwissRe and, after three years there, promotion was clearly a matter of leaving SA if I wanted to stay with the company. I wanted to stay in SA – so, DG and I started talking. He was looking – those days, he was always looking – and so was I.'

"The upshot of all the looking and talking was that Hilkowitz joined Liberty Life on 1 November 1970 as assistant general manager, sales and marketing: 'And really my job up to this promotion has never been anything else. I came in to run sales and marketing, reporting to Donald Gordon, and that is what I'm doing today.'"

There are those, both within and outside Liberty Life, who maintain that Hilkowitz's eventual resignation was directly related to an *FM* crack about his tennis prowess: "He also plays tennis – better than DG." The canard is totally untrue: Gordon's tennis may be keen and highly competitive, but he has not yet fired anybody for beating him. Monty Hilkowitz is a Cancerian, as is Donald Gordon, and, so far as tennis is concerned, Hilkowitz had a ten-year age advantage.

If any further proof is needed, a letter (which also admirably illustrates Gordon's puckish sense of humour) he wrote to the author after publication of that 1978 *FM* Survey should suffice. He wrote: "I must say, I was delighted to see how well the Liberty Life survey turned out in the end and even more so on the basis of being styled 'co-author'. I have looked in vain for this acknowledgement in the body of the text but was horrified to find that the only tribute to my real prowess was that Monty Hilkowitz played better tennis than I did! I think this bare-faced misrepresentation did much to discredit the credibility of the entire operation. I believe there is a very red-faced young man walking around Plettenberg Bay at the moment on this account, who is practising like mad to make it a self-fulfilling prophecy!! Quite seriously, it really was a magnificent effort and I have heard nothing but complimentary remarks from everyone who has read it. Thank you enormously for your co-operation, help and understanding, and I look forward to getting together with you on chapter two before too long."

Hilkowitz was confirmed as Crown Prince in the 1981 Annual Report. Gordon's Chairman's Statement noted: "Finally, in order to relieve the heavy burden that I have borne as Chairman and chief executive over many years, it was decided that Michael Rapp and Monty Hilkowitz be appointed as managing directors of Liberty Holdings and Liberty Life respectively, which, I believe, will substantially improve the effectiveness of our operations and at the same time will be seen as providing opportunities for talented men to play a meaningful part in the operation of the Liberty Life Group."

It was only five years later, in the Annual Report for 1986, that Gordon was constrained to report: "On 30 June 1986 Mr Monty Hilkowitz resigned as managing director of Liberty Life and from the Boards of various Group companies on which he served in order to take up a senior executive position in Australia. I wish to thank Mr Hilkowitz for his long and valuable services to the Group since he joined Liberty Life in 1970."

Why did Hilkowitz quit after sixteen highly successful years, and – even more surprisingly to many of his colleagues – at the cost of sacrificing some R12 million in total to which he would have been entitled in 1988, to say nothing of the substantial income flow that his interest in DGI Holdings was already producing?

In appreciation of his considerable services to Liberty Life, Gordon, notwithstanding the legal agreements and the precedent he was creating, did in fact leave Hilkowitz with a significant proportion of his shares in DGI Holdings, despite the fact that he did not stay the mandatory ten-year course from the time of the buy-back from GRE in 1978. But Hilkowitz did serve over sixteen years at Liberty Life in total, and 'that's a lifetime by most standards,' observes Gordon ruefully.

In an interview early in 1987, settled in his new and challenging job in Australia but back in Johannesburg for a visit to his family, Hilkowitz was frank, but scrupulously fair. "I have an enormous number of deep personal friendships with people at Liberty Life; I will always miss that and I'll never be able to replace it – it's just too deep. I don't think that even yet I fully understand my relationship with Donald Gordon; any criticism that I might have is totally insignificant in relation to the enormous respect and regard that I have for Donald as well as a genuine affection built up over sixteen years of a very intense relationship. I also have the greatest admiration for his financial acumen.

"There were a number of factors. The year before I resigned I attended a senior executive programme at Stanford University [the last Liberty Life executive to go on such a course!] and had time to think about things generally. Where I was going, where my career was going and where South Africa was going. No one issue made me leave. Contrary to what some people said it was not the political situation or any other one circumstance. Basically, I was not very settled in my job, good though it may have looked to be managing director of Liberty Life. I was forty-six at the time and if I had left it a few years longer it would have been substantially more difficult to start up a new career. Also there was Donald Gordon, who is an extremely competent and powerful person who casts a very big shadow and, as you know, it can be very difficult to grow in those circumstances, particularly when one's own ambitions are to be Number One.

"There were times when I felt that the only way I could grow was to face enormous inter-personal conflict. My relationship and regard for Donald were such that I would neither wish to, nor consider myself capable of, engaging in such conflict."

On balance, it seems clear that the loss, first of Hilkowitz, and then of Rapp (to London, although, of course, by no means out of the Group), were factors that motivated Gordon to make his final – and successful – approach to Corby. And the timing, with disinvestment very much in the air, was also important. Gordon, in his 1987 Chairman's Statement, was disarmingly frank about that aspect of what he terms "... the misguided sanctions and disinvestment programme initiated by the Western world which constituted the catalyst that enabled Liberty Life to acquire major strategic interests in prestigious and core South African enterprises such as the Standard Bank Group, the Premier Group and the South African subsidiary of Prudential Assurance Company of London."

There can be little doubt that the undoubted marketing and public relations skills of Wharton-Hood had appeal for Gordon. Asked at the press conference to announce the Prudential SA deal how much of the motivation for the deal stemmed from the acquisition of Prudential SA's chief executive, Gordon quipped: "I love him very much, he's a marvellous chap!" But not everybody present from Liberty Life was amused.

Only a couple of weeks later, Gordon would announce an even larger deal – the R400 million flotation of Liberty Investors Limited (Libvest). Its prospectus, dated 15 October 1986, showed Libvest to be the investment holding company through which joint control (with Stanbic, of course) of the whole Liberty Life Group was exercised. The shares were in great demand, a clear reflection of the prestige of the Liberty Life Group in the eyes of the South African investing public. The Libvest issue was vastly oversubscribed, pulling in an unprecedented R2,2 billion of public money. Its successful launch on the JSE in November 1986 made a fitting climax to a year that had seen great progress in all the divisions of Liberty Life's far-flung empire.

# 17 The TransAtlantic Adventure

Donald Gordon has always been internationally minded; he has always taken a far broader view than that of the relatively narrow confines of the South African economy – an economy which unfortunately has fallen out of pace with the dynamically growing Western world.

Indeed, he stressed this very strongly in Liberty Life's 1987 Chairman's Statement. Under the heading "Liberty Life's international strategy" he spelt out his philosophy:

"Insurance by its nature is essentially an international business and most of the great companies of the world in this sector have built their stability, strength and international dominance by establishing international networks across the globe and their home-based industry has prospered on account of this essential exposure and risk diversification.

"From the earliest days of its corporate existence and being a late-comer to the life insurance field, Liberty Life was totally convinced that its future lay in establishing itself as an international insurance and financial services group rather than remaining a small regional insurance company confined to South Africa in a market already dominated by a number of large mutual insurers.

"Immediately following its listing on the Johannesburg Stock Exchange in 1962, more than twenty-five years ago, Liberty Life became dedicated to achieving international status and in this way it sought to elevate its position in both the international and South African environments. Today internationalisation of insurance and integration of world financial markets has become a world-wide phenomenon and other major South African insurers are now making moves in this direction.

"South Africa's financial services industry is poorer for the lack of positive and direct international interaction, particularly in the life insurance industry which has nonetheless proved to have an exceptionally high degree of expertise. To a not insignificant degree this sophistication and innovative ability demonstrated over the past two decades, has been stimulated by Liberty Life and its marketing and investment culture due to its internationally orientated approach arising from world-wide connections and actual experience dating back more than a quarter of a century.

"As early as 1962 Liberty Life played an important role in the formation of Abbey Life Insurance Company in the United Kingdom. This company is today the largest listed British life insurance company formed since the Second World War and was destined to spearhead the revolution in the life insurance industry in the United Kingdom in a similar manner to Liberty Life's role in the South African market. It is no coincidence that the interaction of our early international aspirations has played such a significant role in the development of perhaps the two most sophisticated life insurance markets in the world today – the United Kingdom and South Africa.

"From the outset Liberty Life worked assiduously towards its objective of creating a truly international insurance group utilising the investment-driven marketing approach which has become the hallmark of Liberty Life's success. This process was effectively interrupted for a period of fifteen years from 1964 until 1978 during which period Liberty Life became a member of the London-based Guardian Royal Exchange Group which, regrettably, in 1964 persuaded Liberty Life to dispose of its interest in Abbey Life. The direct thrust of our aspirations was temporarily blunted and our efforts were channelled more directly into the wider Guardian Royal Exchange Group world-wide strategy in which Liberty Life played an important role.

"Following the re-acquisition of South African control of the Liberty Life Group in 1978 whilst maintaining a strong business and personal association with Guardian Royal Exchange which still continues, the impetus of our previous direction was rapidly reaffirmed resulting in 1980 in the formation of TransAtlantic Insurance Holdings Limited, later to be shortened to TransAtlantic Holdings plc, as the vehicle for Liberty Life's international development. The objectives of this company were based on achieving a similar formula of success involving the synergistic blending of life insurance protection with innovative investment strategies in which real estate and growth equity investment were major components in an inflationary era."

The capital strength of TransAtlantic Holdings, which has grown at an unprecedented rate, is demonstrated and reinforced by its relatively modest borrowings. It would, on the basis of total shareholders' funds, position TransAtlantic in the top forty of all United Kingdom-listed companies were TransAtlantic listed on The Stock Exchange, London. TransAtlantic is thus undoubtedly one of the strongest financial holding companies operating in the London market and its presence and achievements continue to gain recognition and credibility in the City of London and in other financial capitals as one of the important participants in the dramatic restructuring of the international financial services industry.

Given all that, it is therefore rather surprising to note that, apart from founding Abbey Life in the UK in 1962 and selling out in 1964, Liberty Life had no overseas investments whatsoever until 1980. A large number of propositions were investigated by Gordon and his senior colleagues during the sixties and seventies – particularly in the United States and in Canada – but nothing substantial came to fruition. That, of course, as Gordon has explained, was during the Guardian Royal Exchange era when, as a subsidiary of the UK concern, Liberty Life's freedom to act innovatively was severely constrained.

Once freedom had been restored the overseas development was explosive from mid-1980, but in a totally controlled and structured manner. From very modest beginnings, TransAtlantic's assets had grown to £1,3 billion by 31 December 1988. The company, now listed on The Luxembourg Stock Exchange, had capital employed of £1,3 billion by the end of 1988 – from nothing to over one billion pounds sterling in just over eight years – a truly spectacular achievement of financial engineering necessitated by the rigorous foreign exchange constraints applicable in South Africa. TransAtlantic was in fact incorporated on 24 June 1980 – to coincide precisely with Donald Gordon's fiftieth birthday. Its initial capital of £20 000 was contributed by Liberty Life, and was used essentially for preliminary expenses.

During the first full year of TransAtlantic's operation, DG was to establish his *modus operandi* for the company. A pattern was developed of visits to the UK to coincide with the Board meetings of GRE and to attend to the business of TransAtlantic. After the acquisition of Capital & Counties, his schedule was modified slightly to incorporate its Board meeting cycle as well. In the past seven years of the association with Capital & Counties, Gordon missed only one full Board meeting – and none of TransAtlantic's. In the past eight years, he has spent an average of 100 days a year in the UK, normally involving seven separate visits and including the full month of June, in which month most of TransAtlantic's corporate activity usually takes place. (That Wimbledon and Ascot, which embrace two of DG's favourite relaxations, also take place during that month is completely coincidental, of course.)

Until 1985, there was no office, no secretary and no motor car – let alone a chauffeur. Most of the administrative duties were undertaken by a secretarial company called Stonehage, which for a while became affiliated to TransAtlantic. During this period, the company's affairs were overseen on a part-time basis by non-executive UK-based directors of TransAtlantic. In 1985, Michael Middlemas was appointed Liberty Life's international director. At first, he was based in Johannesburg, but commuted frequently to London while engaged in absorbing the intricacies of the broader Liberty Life Group.

At the beginning of 1986, Middlemas was relocated to London to establish the first full office of TransAtlantic in St Andrew's House, Broadway, close to Westminster Abbey, Buckingham Palace and the Thames Embankment. His first staff appointment was of David Fischel, an ex-colleague of his from his Touche Ross days, who was to take local control of the affairs of TransAtlantic as Group financial director when Middlemas resigned in September 1987.

In the early stages of TransAtlantic, Gordon was heavily involved in cementing existing relationships, establishing connections and absorbing the financial environment and City culture – and, most importantly, in building up a stake in The Sun Life Assurance Society. A great deal of time and attention was devoted to nurturing banking relationships and putting into place banking facilities to finance the acquisitions of an increasing number of Sun Life shares. It was only with the advent of Middlemas, who was of course fully schooled in the trappings of the City of London, that things began to change, and there is little doubt that the provision of proper facilities contributed substantially to the increased momentum of TransAtlantic's development from then on.

Essentially, in those early stages, the entire operation was financed with borrowed monies and, as interest rates were relatively high, the actual interest payable was substantially greater than the income received on the low yielding Sun Life shares. Much time was spent consulting solicitors, brokers and merchant bankers: Lord (Simon) Garmoyle and Ken Costa, of Warburgs; and Robin Baillie and Sir Peter Graham – then respectively managing director and Chairman of Standard Chartered Merchant Bank. Graham ultimately assumed the Chair of Standard Chartered Bank itself until his retirement in 1988. Warburgs were later to be dropped as merchant bankers after Peter Grant, Chairman of Sun Life, threatened to remove Sun Life's business from Warburg's stockbroking arm, Rowe & Pitman, if they continued to advise TransAtlantic; and Warburgs did not muster sufficient courage to resist this pressure. Robin Baillie, after retiring from his executive role at the merchant bank, joined the Board of TransAtlantic late in 1988.

It was around September 1981 that good fortune smiled upon the fledgeling enterprise. Then, following a suggestion from Basil Landau (a close personal friend of Gordon and then an executive director of General Mining Union Corporation [Gencor]) to his Chairman, Ted Pavitt. Pavitt called upon Gordon at his office with an interesting proposal. Gencor, it transpired, had a dominant 29,6 per cent stake in a UK company called Capital & Counties, which company had run into severe difficulties in the UK property crash of the seventies. It was now energing from this traumatic period but, so far as Pavitt was concerned, TransAtlantic and Liberty Life were far better suited to running a listed property company in the UK than was Gencor.

Pavitt suggested that Gencor would be happy to exchange its interest in Capital & Counties for shares in TransAtlantic provided suitable terms and conditions could be devised – and TransAtlantic was acceptable to the Capital & Counties Board. After an examination of the accounts of Capital & Counties, Gordon's conclusion was that the company had great potential.

Gordon immediately began serious negotiations with Pavitt, whom he knew well as a fellow director at the United Building Society, South Africa's largest such institution. There had also been a profitable connection between the two men through Clydesdale Collieries, a listed coal mining company which Liberty Life controlled until 1984, and which Gencor managed. When control of Clydesdale was acquired by Gold Fields of South Africa in exchange for an issue to Liberty Life of 10 per cent convertible preference shares in Gold Fields, the relationship with Gencor had come to an end. The deal, however, gave Liberty Life a substantial stake in Gold Fields of South Africa and made it one of the largest shareholders in that prominent mining house, now, in 1989, deeply embroiled in the controversial bid by Anglo American's offshore arm, Minorco, for UK listed Consolidated Gold Fields in London.

After a period of intense negotiation, running up to the end of 1981, and some tough but friendly bargaining, agreement in principle was reached for Gencor's Capital & Counties shares to be acquired by way of a restructure of TransAtlantic, the effect of which would be that almost 50 per cent of the expanded share capital of the nascent TransAtlantic would be issued to Gencor in exchange. Approximately one-half of these TransAtlantic shares would be placed in the London market for cash for Gencor's account. The deal was conditional on TransAtlantic establishing a reasonable rapport with the Board and management of Capital & Counties.

A number of meetings was arranged with all the executive directors of Capital & Counties and it soon became clear that they saw great synergy in a relationship with TransAtlantic, backed as it then was by Liberty Life's proven property expertise. This important transaction was finally consummated, to become effective from 1 January 1982. It proved to be a turning point in the affairs and aspirations of TransAtlantic, and even more so in the fortunes of Capital & Counties.

Dennis Marler, its then managing director and the present Chairman, was particularly enthusiastic, and his support was fundamental to the great success and advancement that was to be the pattern of the unprecedented progress of Capital & Counties over the next seven years – to the point where the company is now widely regarded as the premier retail property developer in the United Kingdom.

It is illuminating to compare the attitude of co-operation found at Capital & Counties with the obstructive negativism in the relationship with the Board of Sun Life. One can only speculate on what great strides might have been taken had Sun Life adopted a similar stance from the beginning. Gordon comments: "The difference would have been phenomenal. What a tragedy it was that there was not a more enlightened and forward-thinking leadership in Sun Life during those vital eight years that have been squandered in bickering and in-fighting. And I think of the opportunities that have been lost by the unconstructive tactics of people unable to visualise the benefits of co-operation, and who sadly lacked the self-confidence to rise to the challenges. In addition, there are the unnecessary costs and the misdirection of the energies of senior staff on defensive tactics, as well as the general adverse effect on staff morale.

"I well remember Dennis Marler saying to me, prior to TransAtlantic bidding for control of Capital & Counties in 1985: 'Donald, we can't live in this grey area of your 29 per cent holding – it is neither fish nor fowl. We would prefer to know just where we are – either in the TransAtlantic group or out of it. We would much prefer the former, but only on the basis of your total commitment.' I responded defensively: 'Dennis, while we have only 29 per cent, you are working for us. Once we buy control, we will be working for you.'"

Gordon, by this time, had ample experience of the sometimes dubious advantages of control; his changing approach to the imperatives and psychology of "control" was developing even then, but had not yet completely crystallised in his own mind.

In the event, it was apparent that Capital & Counties had such incredible potential that the prospect of acquiring control was simply, as part of increasing TransAtlantic's exposure to the company, too good to be resisted. The rest is fast becoming history. An era of carefully controlled dynamic growth began for a company destined to make a significant and lasting contribution to the environment in which it exists. This is what great corporations are all about – and it is part of the enduring fascination of real estate, and the permanency of tangible and real assets.

In the case of Capital & Counties, an era of potential greatness and progressiveness. In that of Sun Life, a classic case history of futility and negativity. "Hopefully this, too, will pass," muses Gordon as the world passes into 1989.

He first spelt out his international philosophy in his Chairman's Statement for 1980. Over the years, the words have changed a little; the logic not at all. "The South African insurance industry has traditionally been substantially influenced and in many respects dominated by the major foreign multinational insurers which have operated over a long period in the Republic by way of subsidiary or branch operations and South Africa has never for this reason been fully involved (other than with our immediate neighbours) in the mainstream of world insurance with all its implications. Other comparable countries such as New Zealand, Australia and Canada, have been far more successful in terms of their involvement in the international ramifications of world insurance.

"The Liberty Life Group has always held the conviction that insurance is an international business and that the South African insurance industry has reached the stage of development and technical advance in terms of which a move towards greater international involvement will have substantial benefits for the South African economy from a strategic point of view and will secure the advantages of economies of scale, fundamental spread of risk and other benefits inherent in such a development. It is also contended that geographical diversification, particularly into an insurance sector as important as the United Kingdom and North American markets, is an essential ingredient for the long-term well-being of the South African insurance industry in which the Liberty Life Group plays a very important role.

"In view of the favourable opportunities presenting themselves in 1980, moves were initiated to secure these objectives. In February 1980, Liberty Life acquired a 25 per cent interest in the Montreal Life Insurance Company for a consideration of Can $4,5 million, which investment was later absorbed by TransAtlantic. Montreal Life is a Canadian life assurer within the GRE group, and at the end of 1980 had assets of some Can $180 million."

Although this acquisition was not expected to have any material effect on Liberty Life's earnings in the short term, it was nonetheless hoped that the interaction of ideas within the framework of the proposed arrangements with Montreal Life would lead to considerable experience being gained of North American life insurance technology, which would in turn be applied to the benefit of Liberty Life and the South African life insurance industry as a whole.

In the event, this first step in pursuit of Liberty Life's international ambitions did not work out, with the North American insurance market proving an extremely hard nut to crack, particularly as a 25 per cent interest in a small Canadian life office did not really provide the incentive to deploy important human resources, especially in a geographic location 10 000 miles from base. In addition, the previously very strong links with Guardian Royal Exchange, once the 75 per cent shareholder, had been significantly weakened by 1980, and the effort involved was just not commensurate with the potential reward. The holding in Montreal Life was sold back to GRE a few years later, and the proceeds were utilised to further TransAtlantic's ambitions.

The most crucial and important investment of all, the one that set the pattern for TransAtlantic's move into the United Kingdom, was initiated during the latter part of 1980, when TransAtlantic acquired a substantial core shareholding in Sun Life Assurance Society Limited, one of the largest proprietary life insurers in the UK. In currency translation terms, Sun Life was substantially larger than Liberty Life, being broadly comparable on the basis of assets with South Africa's two largest offices, the Old Mutual and Sanlam. In October 1980, it was announced that TransAtlantic had acquired 10,2 per cent of the equity of Sun Life. Since that date it had acquired further shares in that company with the result that by 6 March 1981, approximately 19 per cent of the equity capital of Sun Life had been purchased at a total cost of £27,5 million. This holding constituted TransAtlantic as the dominant and the largest single shareholder in Sun Life.

At that stage the investment in Sun Life was financed by way of medium-term multi-currency facilities with a number of major international banks pending the finalisation of more permanent long-term financial arrangements. The facilities themselves were initially arranged with the backing of Liberty Life. Within a relatively short period, this backing became unnecessary, as TransAtlantic's internal strength grew inexorably.

TransAtlantic rapidly became a free-standing company in its own right. With the Gordian knot of its parent's apron strings severed, TransAtlantic soon took on its own personality, and this was reinforced by the gradual formation of its own, independent, Board. Liberty Life's dominance and influence were slowly allowed to loosen as TransAtlantic assumed its own position of importance on the UK financial scene.

It was not intended that Liberty Life would involve itself in the management of Sun Life and it had not at that stage sought to obtain Board representation. However, it was hoped that a meaningful measure of co-operation would be established in the future to the mutual benefit of both Sun Life and TransAtlantic.

Eight years down the line, and with TransAtlantic's holding in Sun Life now over the 29 per cent level, the meaningful co-operation and Board representation which had been so assiduously sought for so long, seemed, at last, to be becoming a reality. This dramatic breakthrough was presaged in the 1987 TransAtlantic Chairman's Statement.

"Some progress has been achieved regarding the efforts to advance the undoubted opportunities for co-operation between the TransAtlantic group and Sun Life and to achieve an acceptable accommodation with their Board. The Sun Life Chairman and I have recently had a number of constructive discussions concerning our various objectives and we shall continue to seek solutions to the long-term benefit of Sun Life in respect of which we both have essentially similar aspirations. I reiterate my hope that in the foreseeable future the current impasse can be satisfactorily resolved." The chronicling of the events leading up to the climax of the Sun Life saga, and the attainment of TransAtlantic's initial objectives, is set out in the following chapter.

Going back once again, Donald Gordon had reported on developments on the international front in his 1981 statement. "Liberty Life's international interests have been greatly advanced during the year with the restructuring of our overseas holdings under a major new United Kingdom holding company, TransAtlantic Holdings, which holds Liberty Life's increased 21 per cent strategic interest in Sun Life, involving an outlay of £29 million, as well as the 29,6 per cent interest in Capital & Counties, which was to be acquired with effect from 1 January 1982. Capital & Counties is one of the leading property companies operating in the United Kingdom with underlying real estate assets of approximately £200 million at that time." The Sun Life shareholding was to become the foundation for the restructuring of Liberty Life's offshore investments under TransAtlantic, but Capital & Counties would in due course become the more important investment in terms of financial involvement.

The consideration paid for the 29,6 per cent interest in Capital & Counties was the issue to the vendors of 29 million shares in TransAtlantic priced at £1 per share, which placed a value of 128 pence per share on the Capital & Counties shares acquired. This compared favourably with the net asset value disclosed in the Capital & Counties' interim statement at 29 September 1981 of 182 pence per share. The acquisition of a substantial stake in a major listed United Kingdom property company was consistent with TransAtlantic's declared policy of making strategic long-term investments in companies in the United Kingdom and North America in life insurance, real estate and related investment fields and had resulted in TransAtlantic establishing itself with a relatively strong capital base of some £59 million.

This high capital base had effectively arisen following the Trans-

Atlantic restructuring by way of Liberty Life capitalising £30 million of the value of the TransAtlantic shareholding in Sun Life by assuming £30 million of TransAtlantic's borrowings in a new intermediate holding company established by Liberty Life named Conduit Insurance Holdings Limited. A further £29 million resulted, as we have seen, from the allotment of 29 million shares at £1 per share to the vendors of Capital & Counties shares.

Hence the capital base of TransAtlantic had, with the aid of some fairly rudimentary financial engineering, quickly reached relatively significant proportions. As part of the restructuring arrangements, Conduit had undertaken to place 15 million of the Capital & Counties vendors' shares with UK, and international, institutional and private investors. Of these shares, Conduit itself acquired around 9 million, and the balance were placed appropriately to achieve a reasonable spread of shareholders for TransAtlantic. Gencor remained with around 14 million TransAtlantic shares. Conduit's acquisition was financed from bank facilities that had been negotiated for Conduit itself, and the effect of the transactions was such as to constitute Conduit as the holding company of TransAtlantic, with a shareholding of the order of 66 per cent of TransAtlantic's equity by the end of 1982. Donald Gordon and Michael Rapp joined the Board of Capital & Counties as representatives of TransAtlantic.

Looking back, Gordon notes that already, in 1981, the Liberty Life Group was beginning to parallel, in the United Kingdom, the development trail that it had already blazed in South Africa. "We already had in TransAtlantic a major core life insurance interest in Sun Life, and there we were, with Capital & Counties, adding the nucleus of a major property arm. The Capital & Counties deal, incidentally, was a classical financial exercise in that we made our acquisition of a major stake in it without any cash being utilised; we issued TransAtlantic shares and in so doing broadened that company's base and introduced important new partners."

Further big strides were taken in 1982, as Gordon recorded in his Statement for that year. "TransAtlantic was completely restructured during 1982 following the acquisition early in the year of the 29,6 per cent interest in Capital & Counties plc, which company holds real estate investments of over £200 million in its own right. The acquisition of Capital & Counties was financed by the allotment of £29 million of new equity in TransAtlantic which resulted in non-

Group shareholders now owning approximately 34 per cent of TransAtlantic's equity."

TransAtlantic in 1982 increased its interest in Sun Life from 21 per cent to almost 24 per cent of the issued share capital thereby consolidating its position as the most significant and largest single shareholder in that company.

At the date of the latest published accounts at 31 December 1988, Sun Life had total assets of over £6,7 billion and investment reserves for the 1988 financial year of £1 043 million. Based on the rates of exchange ruling at the year-end, this made Sun Life significantly larger than Liberty Life itself (this is not strictly true in real terms, but derives from the very low rate of the South African rand against the British pound). Sun Life has been operating in the United Kingdom since 1810 and is involved in the full spectrum of life insurance and pension activities there. The company is listed on The Stock Exchange, London, with a market capitalisation at the 1988 year end of around £550 million. Dividends were increased by 15 per cent for the year, somewhat less than the average of over 20 per cent of earlier years.

During 1983, the capital of TransAtlantic was augmented by £32,25 million as a result of the issue for cash of 21,5 million new shares at 150 pence per share. Of the new shares, 20 million were subscribed for and taken up by Lincoln National Life Insurance Company of Fort Wayne, Indiana, for £30 million. The balance of 1,5 million new shares was subscribed for by Conduit, in order to maintain the control position in TransAtlantic.

Lincoln National is a subsidiary of Lincoln National Corporation which had assets of over $10 billion, and at the time was the fifth largest listed life insurer in the United States, writing more individual life insurance than any other publicly-held group in North America. It was also a market leader in reinsurance.

At the end of 1983, the Liberty Life Group's interest in TransAtlantic had been reduced to 50,4 per cent compared with 66,2 per cent at the end of 1982, as a result of the dilution involved in the introduction of Lincoln National as a major shareholder.

The flirtation with Lincoln National was relatively brief. The Americans became disenchanted with the conservatism of the London market and with the gradualistic strategy of TransAtlantic in developing its position in Sun Life. The cultural difference between TransAtlantic and the high-pressure Lincoln National was not a formula by which the objectives of either party could be achieved satisfactorily, and there was also some sensitivity in regard to TransAtlantic's relationship with South African-based Liberty Life.

Another major factor was that Morgan Grenfell, to whom Gordon had introduced Lincoln National for independent advice, saw great potential in the advent of a major US life company into the London market, and led them into another acquisition which meant that they would be in conflict with the aspirations of TransAtlantic. Until 1988, when John Craven assumed the leadership of Morgan Grenfell, relations between TransAtlantic and Morgan Grenfell were soured by this incident.

So the relationship between TransAtlantic and Lincoln National was amicably severed, and Conduit re-acquired the TransAtlantic shares held by the Americans. From the Group Chairman's Statement for 1984:

"The Liberty Life Group's overseas investments held through TransAtlantic Holdings now represent a very significant factor in Liberty Life's operations. In July 1984 the Group acquired the shareholding in TransAtlantic formerly owned by Lincoln National Life Insurance Company on attractive terms as a result of which Liberty Life increased its interest in TransAtlantic to 75 per cent of its issued share capital from 50,4 per cent previously.

"TransAtlantic's property subsidiary, Capital & Counties, held real estate investments worth over £230 million at the end of March 1984 and is showing great promise by concentrating and focusing on the development of regional shopping centres, a field which in the United Kingdom environment has substantial potential and in which Liberty Life also has extensive expertise.

"The increase in TransAtlantic's consolidated capital and reserves from £145 million at 31 December 1983 to £184 million at the year end, was due primarily to an increase in the market value of Sun Life and Capital & Counties which rose in value during the year by £38 million to reflect a total appreciation of £95 million from their original acquisition cost.

"The portion of this appreciation attributable to Liberty Life's 75 per cent interest in TransAtlantic and the substantial changes in the parity of the rand against sterling during the year are the major components accounting for the significant uplift in Liberty Life's non-distributable reserves of R107,6 million to a total of R343,7 million at 31 December 1984." Another important leg was added for the first time to the international portfolio in 1985, when a major quoted investment trust entered the fold. This marked a further parallel to Liberty Life's South African pattern. In the Republic, the Liberty Life Group controlled First Union General Investment Trust Limited (later to become First International Trust), the country's largest investment trust. In the UK, it was now in the process of absorbing Continental & Industrial Trust.

The Chairman's Statement for 1985 noted: "During 1985 TransAtlantic's assets, particularly in rand terms, increased dramatically from R470 million (£204,5 million) at 31 December 1984 to R1 846 million (£500,2 million) at the financial year end while both earnings and dividends paid continued to increase. The total capital employed in TransAtlantic, including capital contributed by minority shareholders and long-term offshore loans, at 31 December 1985 was £460,9 million, much of which has been achieved by way of the uplift of the dynamic appreciation in value of TransAtlantic's original investments in Sun Life and Capital & Counties with relatively negligible financial support from Liberty Life's resources in South Africa. The decline of the rand obviously increased the relative size of the offshore operations in the Liberty Life Group financial statements. The magnitude of TransAtlantic's undertaking, however, is large by any standards and its total shareholders' funds of £330,8 million would rank it easily in the league of the largest 100 listed United Kingdom companies.

"The principal event during the 1985 year affecting the international interests was the acquisition of control of Capital & Counties plc in which TransAtlantic has held a 29,6 per cent interest since 1981. An opportunity to acquire an additional holding of 3,7 million shares at 225 pence per share in this successful company was accepted in June 1985. As a consequence of this, a mandatory offer, in terms of the takeover rules applicable in the UK, for the entire issued ordinary share capital and convertible loan stock in Capital & Counties was embarked upon. This offer resulted in TransAtlantic increasing its interest in Capital & Counties to 90 per cent of its ordinary shares and 92 per cent of the convertible loan stock in issue.

"Acceptances under the offer which was declared unconditional on 18 July 1985 amounted to 43,2 million ordinary shares (56,3 per cent). These shares were vested in a newly formed subsidiary of TransAtlantic, T C Investments Limited, and the holding was increased to 45 million ordinary shares by subsequent acquisitions and a transfer from TransAtlantic which retained the balance of its Capital & Counties shareholding and the convertible loan stock. This constituted the new subsidiary, T C Investments, as an intermediate holding company with a 58,6 per cent holding in the ordinary shares of Capital & Counties. A consortium of major international investors subsequently acquired an aggregate 40 per cent interest in T C Investments."

Half of this minority interest was taken up by a company associated with the Rembrandt Group, and now controlled by the international company, Richemont. This was a significant vote of confidence in the future of TransAtlantic as that company had been one of the placees of the TransAtlantic shares arising out of the acquisition of the original 29,6 per cent holding in Capital & Counties.

The close association with the Rupert family and the Rembrandt Group had commenced some years earlier when Johann Rupert returned from the United States where he had spent some considerable time with Lazard Freres, preparing himself for his move into merchant banking in South Africa in 1979. A great friendship developed between the young Rupert and his much older mentor, Donald Gordon, which has since involved the entire Rupert family, including the founding father of the Rembrandt Group, Dr Anton Rupert, its present Chairman.

Richemont is now TransAtlantic's second most important shareholder, with a shareholding in excess of 20 per cent. The relationship is further cemented by Liberty Life being a major shareholder in both the Rembrandt and Richemont companies. Through Gordon's efforts in 1988 Rembrandt became a 10 per cent shareholder in Standard Bank Investment Corporation following the final disinvestment by Standard Chartered Bank of their interest in their South African subsidiary.

"The TransAtlantic Group at the year end", continued the 1985 Chairman's Statement, "held 91,4 per cent of Capital & Counties' issued ordinary share capital and its effective interest was thus 68 per cent, allowing for the 40 per cent minority shareholders' interest in T C Investments.

"During the year TransAtlantic also increased its holding in The Continental & Industrial Trust plc – a leading investment trust listed on The Stock Exchange, London – to 25 per cent, involving a total investment of approximately £27 million."[This prominent investment trust had been established and controlled by Schroders Bank, who were also Capital & Counties' merchant bankers, and who were very supportive of TransAtlantic's desire to acquire an investment trust to round out TransAtlantic's total strategy, modelled on that of Liberty Life.]

"The important investment in Sun Life Assurance Society, valued at £120 million at 31 December 1985, remained unchanged during the year. The dividend distribution has again been increased by 20 per cent in the 1985 year."

Ever since TransAtlantic commenced its acquisition of a strategic stake in Sun Life, the strategy of the Sun Life Board had been to maintain a dividend growth of at least 20 per cent each year – in 1984, the dividend growth rate was 23 per cent. The object of this strategy was clearly to improve Sun Life's rating and with that to maintain as high a share price as possible in order to discourage TransAtlantic (or any other unwelcome predator for that matter) from contemplating a bid. On a short-term view, the Board of Sun Life was successful in this objective; however, from TransAtlantic's point of view it also had the welcome effect of transforming its income flow. In the early stages, interest paid on TransAtlantic's borrowings was substantially greater than the income arising from the Sun Life shares held. Given the high rate of dividend growth, this situation soon reversed itself, and made the holding of the Sun Life shares a far more comfortable exercise.

However, it was clear to Gordon that the development of Sun Life's business could not sustain a 20 per cent compound dividend growth rate indefinitely, and his fears were that, in their efforts not to let the rate of dividend growth drop, the financial strength of Sun Life could be seriously weakened. On the other hand, he saw that this factor would itself inevitably bring Sun Life to the negotiating table in the long run. So his usual infinite patience, a hallmark of Donald Gordon's negotiating strategy, and one he developed from his contact with his mentor, Ernest Bigland, would see the tide gradually move in TransAtlantic's favour. There is little doubt that this was an important factor in the somewhat more compromising approach that Peter Grant was beginning to display in 1987 and early 1988.

A major change in the relationship between Liberty Life and TransAtlantic came in 1986, when the holding in TransAtlantic was reduced to below 50 per cent as one of the effects of a major rights and other share issues.

"During 1986 the number of TransAtlantic ordinary and preferred ordinary shares in issue was increased from 97,5 million to 172,5 million as a result of three separate issues of shares. First, in May 1986 an issue of 50 million preferred ordinary shares at 275 pence per share by way of a rights issue and offer for subscription raised £137,5 million; second, in July 1986 an issue of 4,3 million preferred ordinary shares at 275 pence per share to shareholders in The Continental & Industrial Trust who accepted the share alternative included in the offer for their shares, increasing capital by a further £11,8 million; and third, on 31 December 1986 an issue of 20,7 million ordinary and preferred ordinary shares to the 40 per cent minority shareholders in T C Investments, the intermediate holding company formed to hold the shares in Capital & Counties acquired under the offer in 1985, which transaction further augmented capital by £56,9 million and increased the effective interest of TransAtlantic in Capital & Counties to almost 92 per cent.

"In order to broaden TransAtlantic's shareholder base and to reinforce its independence from Liberty Life, a major portion of Conduit's rights entitlement in TransAtlantic (mentioned in the previous paragraph) was placed with a wide spread of United Kingdom and international institutional and private investors. The effect of the aforementioned rights issue being disproportionately taken up and the other issues of shares to third parties was to increase TransAtlantic's shareholders' funds to £560 million and to widen the spread and the number of shareholders to over 650 with a view to ultimately facilitating a future listing on The Stock Exchange, London. Accordingly, Conduit permitted its controlling interest in TransAtlantic to be diluted from 75 per cent to 49 per cent to achieve a more broadly based international profile which we believe to be in the best long-term interests of the Group in the current environment."

This had the effect of precluding Liberty Life from consolidating TransAtlantic into its balance sheet, and TransAtlantic thereafter was accounted for as an associated company, which reduced Liberty Life's total accounted assets by some R1,7 billion in that one year. However, the advantages of TransAtlantic no longer being controlled by Liberty Life, in terms of political and strategic considerations, were the overriding factor. It is not inconceivable that in certain circumstances Liberty Life's strategy would be conducive to a further dilution of its interest in TransAtlantic to whatever level might be appropriate to allay any negative impact associated with the South African connection.

Notwithstanding the substantial contraction of some R1,7 billion in the consolidated assets of Liberty Life in the 1986 year resulting from the deconsolidation of TransAtlantic, total assets of Liberty Life nevertheless reached the R10 billion mark on 1 January 1987 – the date on which The Prudential Assurance Company of South Africa became a wholly owned subsidiary of Liberty Life.

The achievement of the R10 billion milestone was three years ahead of Gordon's prediction (that the R10 billion mark would be achieved by 1990) made in September 1982 at Liberty Life's twenty-fifth anniversary celebrations, when total assets had just reached the R2 billion mark. This represented a fivefold rise in a little over four years, and once and for all time silenced the sceptics who had dismissed Gordon's 1982 prediction as "pure fantasy".

The investment in TransAtlantic was equity accounted in 1986 in respect of the 49 per cent holding, but nonetheless accounted for around 50 per cent of the shareholders' interests reflected in Liberty Life's financial statements at that time. This aspect is primarily due to the dynamic organic growth achieved in TransAtlantic's underlying investments and related currency translation surpluses and was a major component accounting for the high level of non-distributable reserves reflected in both the Liberty Life and Liberty Holdings balance sheets.

In Gordon's 1986 Chairman's Review of the ever-growing international interests, he comments: "The Liberty Life Group's international interests are held through TransAtlantic, a 49 per cent owned associated company which at the end of the 1985 financial year was a 75 per cent subsidiary of Liberty Life. This United Kingdom holding company was initially established by Liberty Life in 1980 for the purpose of making selected investments with long-term potential in the life assurance and real estate sectors and in other fields related to the financial services industry. During 1986 TransAtlantic has made significant progress towards its declared medium term intention of obtaining a listing on The Stock Exchange, London."

Barely a year later, Gordon would spell out in detail the problems besetting the desired London listing, and the reasons for instead settling for the "second prize" of a listing on The Luxembourg Stock Exchange. "On 26 October 1987, TransAtlantic's ordinary and preferred ordinary shares were listed on The Luxembourg Stock Exchange to provide the present 750 shareholders and prospective shareholders with a more broadly based market for trading their shares. This significant move was made in the light of the known reluctance of The Stock Exchange, London, to grant a listing to a company whose principal business consists of the holding of substantial shareholdings in other listed companies, other than a company which would qualify as an investment trust or investment company under their current listing regulations.

"In the circumstances, rather than to embark on a major restructuring of the TransAtlantic group, which may well have involved a delisting of Capital & Counties and, in the opinion of the Board, would have greatly inhibited the flexibility of the Group, it was reluctantly decided for the time being to defer an application for a London listing for TransAtlantic. It still remains, however, an important objective to obtain a listing of TransAtlantic shares in the United Kingdom in addition to our Luxembourg listing as soon as conditions become appropriate."

But patience is one of Gordon's strongest characteristics and the "Battle of Sun Life" and its companion, "The Debate with the SEL", will continue to preoccupy him as he attempts to satisfy the SEL that its perceptions in regard to TransAtlantic not being properly qualified for a full London listing are incorrect.

In 1986, TransAtlantic succeeded in doubling both profit before taxation from £11,9 million to £24,4 million and capital and reserves from £249 million to £519 million. To have established these new levels in one year was a major achievement, particularly when one considers that this was not accomplished at the expense of any dilution in earnings or net assets per share, which both also recorded excellent progress. Clearly, the rate of development of TransAtlantic was now in full spate, with all aspects of the business operating in top gear.

In his 1986 Review, Gordon also noted: "Capital & Counties, a 92 per cent subsidiary of TransAtlantic, is being developed in a committed and positive way in the United Kingdom and internationally and is currently concentrating on its major United Kingdom shopping centre developments." This is yet another parallel with South Africa, where Rapp & Maister pioneered regional shopping centres with Sandton City and Eastgate, which provided the core foundation for Liberty Life's high-quality real estate portfolio. "The results of Capital & Counties for the year were up to expectations with profits after taxation increasing from the equivalent of £8,9 million to £10,8 million, resulting in a 21 per cent increase in earnings per share on an annualised basis and a 10,4 per cent property revaluation surplus increasing net assets per share by 15 per cent on a fully diluted basis from 280 pence to 322 pence per share.

"During the year under review TransAtlantic acquired 89 per cent control of the Continental & Industrial Trust, an approved investment trust listed on The Stock Exchange, London with highly liquid assets of approximately £150 million. An extremely conservative investment policy was followed with the major proportion of the company's portfolio being disposed of at the time of acquisition of control and the proceeds temporarily reinvested mainly in short-term gilts and other liquid assets pending reinvestment in conformity with its objectives in terms of its new modified investment policy."

Despite the Crash in stock markets the world over in October 1987, Gordon was able, in his Chairman's Statement for that year, to report further remarkable progress. "The year saw strong growth in both TransAtlantic's earnings and dividends per share, the former growing by 29 per cent and the latter by 33 ⅓ per cent, easily surpassing the equivalent 1986 increases of 26 per cent and 20 per cent respectively. Pre-tax profits of TransAtlantic advanced from £24,4 million to a new record of £39,1 million, an increase of over 60 per cent.

"Net assets per TransAtlantic share increased from 301 pence to 336 pence, an improvement of 12 per cent. Given the sharply lower levels of international financial markets, this result can be regarded as highly satisfactory. Taking into account the low exposure to equities, the net asset value growth emanated mainly from the positive effect of £188 million of new capital introduced into Capital & Counties mainly from United Kingdom and international investors during 1987 and from its quality real estate portfolio which performed particularly well, achieving a capital surplus on revaluation of the order of £62 million for the year."

In 1988, the financial results were even more impressive, with profits before taxation reaching £52,5 million. More importantly, total shareholders' funds had reached a level of £1 012 million, with capital employed also passing the billion pound sterling milestone to reach £1,29 billion at the year end. Sun Life had contributed its normal increased dividend, but the real impact on TransAtlantic's financial results was the burgeoning and dynamic progress made at Capital & Counties.

This company was rapidly moving itself into the category of the most exciting listed property company in the UK, with its efforts being concentrated on the retail sector of the property market, particularly in regional shopping centres on and around the M25 ring road encircling the greater London conurbation. These developments, at Thurrock Lakeside, Watford and Bromley, strategically placed surrounding London, an area traditionally having relatively poor major shopping amenities, have, in the view of Capital & Counties, quite outstanding potential.

The most exciting prospect of these, on which building operations commenced in September 1988, is Thurrock Lakeside, planned for 1,2 million square feet of retail shopping at a cost of over £300 million. It is projected to have an enormous impact on Capital & Counties' future. The other two major developments at Watford and Bromley are equally exciting, but are on a somewhat smaller scale than Thurrock.

In the case of Bromley, a 43 per cent participation in the project was disposed of late in 1988 on excellent terms to General Accident for a contribution of £110 million towards its cost, a deal negotiated on the basis of a guaranteed yield of around 5,5 per cent to General Accident on completion. A similar participation was retained by Capital & Counties, with the local Council retaining the balance. A smaller 25 per cent participation is held in the Watford project, and Capital & Counties' partner there, the Sun Alliance Assurance Company, has a larger participation in this unique development in the central area of Watford.

A number of other retail developments are being undertaken, resulting particularly from the acquisition of the properties relating to the Lewis' Limited stores group in 1988. All these projects are scheduled to come on stream during 1990 and 1991, the first being Thurrock, which is planned to be in full operation by the end of 1990.

Notwithstanding the current concentration on regional retail development, Capital & Counties' retail division is also extremely busy with innumerable developments of strategic sites, mainly in south-east England, with a much lesser accent on central London sites, which have already benefited from the full impact of the property boom of the past few years, and are areas which, in the view of

Capital & Counties, could be beginning to level off in terms of rental improvement.

The real estate controlled by Capital & Counties could well increase threefold over the next few years, for a tenfold increase from the company originally acquired by TransAtlantic in 1981. Having learned the lessons of the seventies, it is now Capital & Counties' policy for all real estate in hand to be funded on an efficient long-term basis, as well as to provide finance to take advantage of opportunities that arise from time to time.

On this basis, and with Donald Gordon's long-time colleague, Michael Rapp, now fully integrated into Capital & Counties as executive deputy chairman, the prospects for Capital & Counties are extremely bright. And, as Capital & Counties is at this stage the dominant component in TransAtlantic, the future for that company is equally exciting.

The incorporation of Continental and Industrial Trust as a subsidiary of TransAtlantic in 1988 by virtue of its owning 42 per cent of the ordinary shares and 65 per cent of the voting preference shares, and supplemented by a voting agreement with Conduit, which owned an additional 29 per cent stake, properly reflects the broader TransAtlantic group's massive financial strength, with liquid resources, including liquid short-dated gilt-edged stock, of £138,3 million out of total assets of £155,1 million.

Thus the prospects for the greater Liberty Life Group's United Kingdom ventures, through TransAtlantic, have far exceeded Donald Gordon's most optimistic expectations. Even now, the interest held by Liberty Life, following its dilution at the TransAtlantic level, and also due to the advent of First International Trust, nonetheless still accounts for around 50 per cent of the net equity of the Liberty Life Group. It is entirely thanks to these massive overseas assets that the listed shares of the Group – Liberty Holdings, Liberty Life itself and Liberty Investors – recovered so strongly on the Johannesburg Stock Exchange to levels above those ruling before the October 1987 Crash, within a year of that event.

On any basis, this dynamic UK company, TransAtlantic, must rank as Liberty Life's, and Gordon's, finest achievement, especially if one considers the relatively hostile environment in which it operates and the relatively short time frame in which all these momentous developments have taken place. The investments in TransAtlantic and in Continental and Industrial Trust, notwithstanding that Liberty Life has relinquished direct control of its erstwhile offshore subsidiaries, still constitute Liberty Life, with its important interest in First International Trust, very much of a "rand hedge" stock, a highly desirable quality in South African investment terms in these difficult times. And this in turn impacts on Liberty Holdings and Liberty Investors, both of which have their stakes, direct and indirect, in Liberty Life and First International Trust, as major assets.

# 18 The Sun Life Saga

On 19 October 1988, the Sun Life Assurance Society announced the news of the appointment to its Board of Michael Rapp and Lord Douro, both nominees of Liberty Life's London associate, TransAtlantic Holdings. At the same time, two nominees of Union des Assurances de Paris Internationale (UAPI), Jean Peyrelevade and Jacques-Henri Gougenheim, its Chairman and managing director respectively, were also appointed. TransAtlantic's Chairman, Donald Gordon, was not himself able to accept nomination to the Sun Life Board as he was still a director of GRE, which in the London financial hierarchy is by far the more prestigious and important institution.

This announcement marked the end of an epic six-year struggle, mostly behind the scenes but occasionally in the open, between Donald Gordon and Peter Grant, the Chairman of Sun Life. This was not essentially a battle between two individuals, but more of a conflict of philosophies and cultures: between the introspective and hidebound attitudes of the City of London business establishment and the more open and entrepreneurial approach of the new breed of dynamic overseas businessmen, of which Gordon is a shining example.

It was a long, hard and sometimes acrimonious tussle. It was also an episode that strongly underscored many of the qualities that have contributed to Gordon's outstanding success. Foresight, superior negotiating skills, toughness, mental agility and long-range planning. And, above all else, patience and tenacity. The Sun Life saga fully confirms the truth of Benjamin Franklin's famous dictum: "He that can have patience can have what he will."

It all began in 1980, when, as an essential platform in Gordon's long-cherished plans of expanding Liberty Life into an international player on the financial services scene, he formed TransAtlantic Insurance Holdings Limited, which later became TransAtlantic

Holdings plc. TransAtlantic would spearhead the drive into the United Kingdom, and for this a meaningful stake in a major UK life assurer was the fundamental core from which the whole strategy would evolve.

Diligent research, by both Liberty Life's back-room boys in Johannesburg and its advisers in London, narrowed the field down to three potential targets, of which Sun Life, the UK's fourth largest life insurance company, was the preferred option.

Then, in June 1980, Lady Luck came into the picture. Gordon received private information that the Kuwaiti Investment Office, which had for several years been pumping that Middle Eastern state's surplus oil profits into the London stock market, had decided for reasons that have never been divulged to reduce its exposure to the UK insurance sector. This might mean that its laboriously acquired 9,7 per cent stake in Sun Life, the biggest single shareholding in the company at that time, could be for sale. Gordon immediately instructed Julian Benson, of Laing & Cruickshank and an early director of TransAtlantic, to approach the Kuwaitis and ascertain how the land lay. Benson reported excitedly over the telephone to Gordon in Johannesburg that the entire holding could be acquired at a price of 270 pence per share. "But Julian, that's more than 10 per cent over the market price," I countered, "offer them 240 pence." "You can't do that with the Kuwaitis; they are a law unto themselves in London," was Benson's plaintive response. "Are you telling me that you can't bargain with them? That's preposterous," riposted Gordon. After a somewhat acrimonious exchange on the rules of the game, Gordon managed to convince a reluctant Benson that he should go back and negotiate with the Kuwaitis. After the fourth try, Benson came back to Gordon to report jubilantly that he had bought the block at 240 3/8 pence per share, a very considerable improvement on that first offer of 270 pence. Benson certainly earned his brokerage that day – and TransAtlantic had a firm foothold in the Sun Life door in Cheapside.

Gordon lost no time in trying to capitalise on the situation. In July 1980, he telephoned Philip Walker, the then Chairman of Sun Life. "I'm Donald Gordon, of TransAtlantic; you probably know we are the largest shareholder in your company. I would like to pay my respects and meet you to talk about the future." Walker was obviously less than happy, but he set up a meeting for Gordon with Sun Life's managing director, Richard Zamboni.

Gordon recalls that it was a fairly frosty meeting. "Although I was a director of the Guardian Royal Exchange, and therefore, or so I thought, fairly 'respectable', Zamboni made it patently clear that our investment in Sun Life was unwelcome. Nevertheless, I put forward various proposals, the most important of which involved Liberty Life's expertise in unit-linked insurance, a field that Sun Life had yet to enter."

That did not go down very well either, and Gordon soon afterwards returned to Johannesburg. Not until some five weeks later, on 15 August 1980, did he hear anything concrete from Zamboni.

"Dear Mr Gordon, As I mentioned to you on the telephone last week, I have only just returned from an overseas holiday which commenced the day after our meeting. However, I have now had an opportunity to discuss your proposals with my Chairman, Mr Philip Walker, and I am writing to let you have our conclusions.

"It will probably not come as a surprise to you to learn that in the present political climate investment in South Africa could have certain marketing disadvantages and would not, therefore, be in the best interests of the Society's shareholders. Conversely, you might feel that this same factor could affect the potential value of any sizeable holding which Liberty might take in the Society.

"We are an office of long and high standing and one which has developed dynamically in many directions in recent years and we have every confidence in the management expertise which we have developed especially in the investment, actuarial and marketing fields. This does not mean that we have nothing to learn from other experienced people, but in our opinion any substantial capital arrangement would not be justified in order to obtain such benefit.

"I enjoyed meeting you on your last visit to London, but I must conclude now that there would be no point in holding a further meeting on this subject."

For many, the above letter – the very first in Gordon's private file headed "Sun Life Assurance Society plc – Directors' Correspondence" – would have been the complete brush-off. But Gordon just does not brush off that easily. It is also worth noting that Zamboni's first letter set the pattern for Sun Life's attitudes over the years that were to follow. First, that the South African connection is commercially dangerous and, second, that you, Liberty Life, a relative upstart in life insurance, have very little to teach us, "an office of long and high standing".

TransAtlantic continued to buy Sun Life shares whenever they came on offer at a reasonable price on market weakness, and in this way Gordon kept up the pressure on Zamboni and Walker. By October 1980, TransAtlantic was able to announce, in compliance with the rules of The London Stock Exchange, that it had 10,2 per cent of the equity of Sun Life.

Walker took this a little more seriously, and on 3 November he wrote his first letter to Gordon.

"Dear Mr Gordon, Our managing director, Mr Zamboni, has kept me informed of the conversation which he had with you just before his departure for America, and subsequent correspondence and telephone calls on the subject of your investment in our Company. I am sorry that I was not available at the time of your visit, and consequently missed seeing you. I have noted with interest your acquisition of the Kuwait shareholding, and that you have now become the largest single shareholder in Sun Life. Mr Zamboni conveyed to me your kind invitation to visit you in South Africa, and perhaps at some future date, I may be able to take you up on this. Unfortunately, I have no present plans to visit your country, so that it is more likely that you will be visiting England again before I shall be out there.

"If and when you decide to come over here, I shall be very pleased if you will let me know, so that I will not again miss the opportunity of making your acquaintance and discussing with you matters of mutual interest."

Gordon replied on 11 November, noting that he and his colleague, Michael Rapp, would be in London towards the end of November. The four – Walker and Zamboni, Gordon and Rapp – met late that month, and the discussions were surprisingly constructive, although the atmosphere was cool. "Even so, I felt that we were getting somewhere," recalls Gordon, "and that they were beginning to take us seriously. Things went so well that Walker agreed to come out to Johannesburg early the next year in order to take matters a few steps further."

The share purchases continued, relentlessly, all the time putting more and more pressure on Walker. By the end of February 1981, approximately 19 per cent of the equity capital of Sun Life had been purchased at a total cost of around £27,5 million.

It was against this background that Philip Walker and his wife travelled to South Africa. Gordon's files contain a very interesting memo on a "Discussion with Mr Philip Walker, Chairman of Sun Life, on Tuesday, 24 February 1981". The sometimes quite amusing repartee conceals the tensions that must have been present as the two chairmen fenced skilfully.

"The conversation started with Gordon courteously enquiring from Walker how his favourite company in the UK was doing. (He was, of course, referring to Sun Life and not to GRE in this context.) Walker responded that, in view of the position, it would be improper for him to disclose anything at all, particularly in regard to dividend policy and the like. At some stage in the conversation Gordon did indicate that he could ask the questions at an annual general meeting, which could be a lot more awkward (this somewhat teasingly).

"Gordon then indicated to Walker that having achieved certain of his personal objectives in the South African market, he was rather anxious to succeed in building something really worthwhile on the international financial services scene. He believed that Liberty Life/TransAtlantic had the experience and the connections, the dynamism and the will. It was with this in mind that TransAtlantic decided to take a major position in the UK life insurance industry. By reason of an ironic quirk and twist of fate, Sun Life had been the company which had come in for Gordon's attention out of a small choice of likely candidates. The fact that TransAtlantic was able to pick up 10 per cent of the shares from the Kuwaitis was a major factor in this. It would seem to Gordon that there was tremendous synergy in Liberty Life and Sun Life working together, and that Liberty Life could contribute an enormous amount to the ongoing development of Sun Life.

"Walker enquired as to whether it was still Gordon's intention to acquire a maximum of 20 per cent of the equity, to which Gordon replied that he would be happy to do that for a reasonable length of time as there was no serious strain in carrying the investment, even at the relatively low dividend yield. However, if Gordon were to fulfil his ambitions in this, TransAtlantic should try to do something a little earlier, rather than later. Walker indicated that TransAtlantic's acquisition of nearly 20 per cent (he had checked on this and Gordon confirmed that TransAtlantic had around 12 million shares) had made the staff and the Board rather jittery and that clearly it was in the company's interests for this situation to be stabilised. Gordon agreed and revealed that TransAtlantic had developed at least a dozen possible scenarios, some of which could well be appropriate to the circumstances, and could satisfy the overall concerns of Sun Life.

"Gordon also asked Walker whether, as far as investments in South Africa were concerned, he had heard of the Prudential, whose vast interest in South Africa did not seem to militate against their success in the UK. Nonetheless, Gordon took Walker's point about South African investment and indicated that he hoped this problem would disappear in the course of time.

"In any event, Gordon said, there were ways in which these objections could be overcome. Certainly, Liberty Life's record with staff and its policy to remunerate staff at a level above the general market in exchange for above-average service and dedication, and also the philosophy of Liberty Life to reward the efforts of senior staff by way of all types of incentives were matters of which he was extremely proud.

"The atmosphere of the discussion was relatively affable – far more so than in London – and in the end Walker indicated to Gordon that he had not come to South Africa to negotiate and his intention was basically to have a holiday. However, Gordon would not be stonewalled. He extracted an undertaking that any approaches TransAtlantic might make – accepting that the ball was in TransAtlantic's court to make such proposals – would be looked at fairly.

"Gordon asked Walker if he could give him a profile of the important directors of the Sun Life and Walker indicated that the more important directors were basically the merchant bankers. Gordon asked about the Lazards connection and Mr Grant [the first mention of the man who would become DG's principal adversary] and Walker said that most of the directors had an equal voice in the Sun Life although to a large extent he had a very important influence in view of the fact that he had come in as Chairman and had automatically assumed the role of executive Chairman. He was very proud of the success he had had in developing Sun Life to its current position. Gordon indicated to Walker that should they do any arranged deal, that it would be essential that he would be prepared to stay on for a few years to help with the transition. Walker said that he felt reasonably fit and energetic. The whole interview terminated in an affable fashion, and for the last half hour Michael Rapp was in attendance."

So by February 1981, Walker and Gordon were on first-name

terms and, in the months that followed, the chances of an "accommodation", or even an "understanding", sometimes looked quite promising.

Following discussions on 18 March, while Gordon was in London, a letter dated 27 March: "Dear Philip, I found our discussions last week extremely useful and constructive and I hope you will seriously consider all the positive implications involved. I believe we have the nucleus of a proposal which could lead to a great advance in the development of both Sun Life and Liberty Life thereby achieving most of our logical aspirations.

"As you will recall, I indicated that I would be revisiting the United Kingdom towards the end of April and I am now setting up my plans for this visit. I would like to call on you on Wednesday 22 April and if this is convenient, I would much appreciate your setting a suitable time. I look forward to seeing you and sincerely hope that we can progress our discussions in a constructive manner."

Such hopes were soon to be dashed by an arm's-length, if not downright frosty, reply dated 3 April, in which Walker effectively closed the door. His final paragraphs read: "In these circumstances we do not feel we could put your suggestions to our shareholders either with any positive recommendation in view of the complex individual considerations arising, or with any assurance of obtaining from them a favourable reaction.

"We do not seek to dispute your right to seek control of this company if you are prepared to pay a price which will persuade the shareholders to part with their shares. However, nothing I have said in this letter should be taken as expressing any opinion on the economic value of your suggestion."

It would be a fascinating – if somewhat pointless – exercise to attempt, with hindsight, to evaluate the "economic value" of Gordon's proposal to Walker, but there is little doubt that an arrangement such as was then proposed would have had immense impact on the UK life insurance scene, and beyond it, over the past decade.

Gordon's response was predictable. Dated 15 April 1981, it read: "Dear Philip, I would be less than honest if I did not express some disappointment at the inability of your Board to react favourably to the positive and exciting proposals which I put before you last month, which in my opinion would have represented a fundamental advance in the fortunes and future prospects of Sun Life, its policyholders, shareholders and staff, as well as to our own interests in South Africa. In the circumstances, I have little option but to accept the view of your Board for the present time.

"I would mention that I am somewhat surprised at your inability to differentiate between a cosmetic and pragmatic approach and although I fully concede that some people may express the views that you have outlined concerning South Africa, it is nonetheless an indisputable fact that most major British insurance companies have subsidiary companies or important interests in South Africa – including the Prudential, Commercial Union, Royal, Guardian Royal Exchange, Legal & General, Sun Alliance, Eagle Star and many others. It would not appear that their South African connection has in any way impeded their progress and I can assure you from personal knowledge that none of these companies have any current interest in withdrawing from the Republic.

"In the light of your letter, we are obviously reviewing our position and in the interim it does seem somewhat pointless for us to meet next Wednesday."

Gordon's 1981 views on the "South African connection" are somewhat optimistic in 1989 terms and, of the seven companies he named, three have subsequently partially or wholly withdrawn from the country, including Prudential SA, which Liberty Life itself acquired in 1987.

It did not take Gordon long to review his position, and he convened another meeting early in July, at which TransAtlantic's merchant banker, Lord Garmoyle (now the Earl of Cairns), of Warburgs, was also present. It, too, was fruitless, as were a number of further meetings held during the following year. Philip Walker's letter of 3 April 1981 had effectively ended all negotiations, and although some frosty contact was maintained, it also marked the practical end of the Walker/Gordon impasse. In this period TransAtlantic attended only one annual general meeting, and at that refrained from voting its shares on any issue. But a new era was dawning. It was heralded by a letter dated 18 August 1982.

"Dear Mr Grant, I have read with considerable interest of your proposed appointment as Chairman of the Sun Life with effect from 31 December 1982 and take this opportunity of congratulating you on this appointment.

"On behalf of Liberty Life, I would like to assure you of our positive support in the furthering of the interests of Sun Life with the dual objective of enhancing our very substantial investment and our desire to adopt a constructive and positive stance.

"I do hope over the years to come, we shall have the opportunity of co-operating together in the best interests of our mutual affairs."

Thus, in his very first "sighting shot" across the bows of Sun Life's incoming Chairman, Donald Gordon made two things very clear to Peter Grant. First, the inescapable fact that Liberty Life had a "very substantial investment" in Sun Life; and second, that the name of the game was "co-operation".

Right from the start, the two men maintained a correct, indeed, sometimes even a cordial, personal relationship. They are of an age, even if their backgrounds could hardly be more diverse. Asked how he got on with Grant, Gordon is at first rather cautious. "Personally, we got on alright, even fine. I neither like him nor dislike him – I have no particular feeling one way or the other."

They had many exploratory lunches, at the Savoy or the Ritz, and many memorable dinners, at the Connaught, Boodles or Waltons. "I give him full marks for his very diligent attitude in maintaining personal contact. Our personal relationship has never in any way been other than pleasant and we have always been thoroughly courteous to each other. We have had some enjoyable and some interesting evenings together. However, not once was any other person from Sun Life present, and it was clear that all their executives were prohibited from any contact with TransAtlantic whatsoever.

"We must have discussed and debated, analysed and argued hundreds of proposals to overcome the impasse, most of them emanating from me. Every angle to induce Sun Life to co-operate was explored – and diplomatically disposed of. It became patently obvious to me that Grant's tactics were to stonewall our initiatives until he could find a way to 'see us off'. But two can play that game, and I too began to use our contacts to probe and to try to find his Achilles' heel. I knew that this would inevitably appear if I was patient long enough – or lived long enough!"

For the next four years, the titanic debate between these two protagonists continued behind closed doors. TransAtlantic had rapidly built up its stake to over 25 per cent, a level which confers "negative control" in the sense that it enables the holder to block certain proposals requiring special resolutions. Gordon continued to put forward various variations on his earlier themes, and to press for the Board representation that is normally granted to such a large shareholder, particularly one who had specifically, at that time, foresworn any intention to bid for control. Gordon has always averred that "going for control" of Sun Life was always TransAtlantic's worst option, and that he would only go the route of total confrontation if absolutely forced into doing so. Grant stonewalled, forever hiding behind the commercial dangers of the unwanted and unpopular South African connection, and maintaining, with somewhat specious logic, that Board representation for TransAtlantic would lead to back-door control of Sun Life.

Eventually, late in 1986, the impasse came into the open. Hard on the heels of yet another round of face-to-face discussions, the Sun Life Board on 8 December 1986 put forward proposals for the formation of a holding company, ostensibly to free the group from certain UK legal restrictions affecting the expansion of its financial services operations. The proposals were broadly in line with trends in the UK life insurance industry at that time, in that other major companies were going much the same route as they expanded from "pure" life insurance into full-scale financial services operations.

In general terms, and on the face of the matter, the proposals were inoffensive, and they made a certain amount of commercial sense, although they failed to spell out just what the proposed diversification into financial services would involve. However, they included provisions which seemed designed to allow the Board of the new Sun Life holding company much greater flexibility, particularly in relation to the issue of further ordinary shares. This could have the effect – and was probably so designed – of diluting and even emasculating TransAtlantic's dominance without any further reference to Sun Life's shareholders, and certainly without TransAtlantic's approval. In addition, provisions were included which clearly could have reduced TransAtlantic's position, and which would have allowed for the introduction of further major shareholders into Sun Life to balance out TransAtlantic's influence, without TransAtlantic's compliance or approval.

Since the proposals involved a Scheme of Arrangement under Section 425 of the 1985 Companies Act, they required the support of a Court meeting, there to be passed by special resolution. The necessary Extraordinary General Meeting had been called for 7 January 1987, and Grant's proposals required to be passed by at least 75 per cent of the votes cast by the Society's shareholders.

Unfortunately for Grant, however, he had not regarded it as important to seek the prior agreement of his major shareholder, TransAtlantic. As Gordon recalls it: "Towards the end of 1986 proposals were put up by the Sun Life Board to form a holding company with the idea of operating Sun Life as a subsidiary of that holding company and, under its umbrella, entering into other areas of the financial services industry. Nothing wrong with that, nothing at all. The idea was to convert the shares held in Sun Life into shares in the holding company on a one-for-one basis. Fine up to there, but the snag was that the directors of the new holding company would have had the expanded power to issue new shares, for acquiring businesses or otherwise, the net effect of which could have been greatly to dilute our position.

"There was a lot of correspondence, a lot of to-ing and fro-ing, and a lot of legal adviser involvement. Ultimately we took the view, after much agonising, that despite some positive aspects, the overriding object of the scheme was permanently to weaken our position. So we informed Grant that we were going to vote against it. The special resolution didn't go through and the whole plan was abandoned."

With the row now out in the open, a very important exchange of letters followed. Gordon wrote a long letter to Grant on 20 February 1987. Some extracts follow:

"Having carefully reviewed the events of the past three months I would be failing in my duty not to express my concern and disappointment at the attitude and conduct of Sun Life in connection with the reorganisation proposals published in December 1986 which followed so closely after our discussion, initiated by you in your capacity as Chairman, with a view to achieving a closer relationship of our interests. These discussions were not pursued in view of your condition that TransAtlantic should disperse its Sun Life shareholding. This was simply not realistic and in the light of our earlier discussions I was surprised you even put it forward.

"The principle underlying the reorganisation proposals was not necessarily unacceptable to TransAtlantic but their form and the apparent motivation of certain aspects made them objectionable.

"I find distressing the attitude of the Sun Life Board in questioning the rights of shareholders to exercise their votes against proposals of the Board of which they do not approve. Much embarrassment could have been avoided if your major shareholders had been consulted in advance on proposals which would significantly have changed Sun Life's structure before going to the great expense of proposing them to the shareholders as a whole. I would have thought the precaution of prior consultation would have been particularly appropriate here in view of the cordial relationship that has developed between us in recent years and the fact that my confidentiality could not be in any doubt.

" . . . In particular, this potential dilution, your Board must have realised, could remove TransAtlantic's entrenched rights as a 25 per cent shareholder which, *inter alia,* guarantee that a special resolution cannot be passed without its consent. It is disappointing that your Board saw fit to effect such a change without consulting and seeking the approval of those it affects.

"In your circular to shareholders you state that 'Liberty have demonstrated very clearly that their interests are their own, and not those of other shareholders and of the Society as a whole'. It is of course the right and privilege of all shareholders to exercise their voting rights in their own interests. It is, however, the obligation of the Board of Sun Life to act in the interests of all shareholders and of the Society as a whole. The interests of all shareholders were affected by the defects in your proposals (although TransAtlantic as a major shareholder was affected more critically).

"In conclusion, I am saddened at the general conduct of Sun Life and its Board as represented by the Chairman in this unfortunate matter. Nonetheless, I would wish to reiterate that it has always been our objective to achieve a constructive accommodation with the Sun Life Board in the overall interests of the Society, its personnel and all its shareholders. This has been and continues to be our position.

"However, in all the circumstances, with its dominant shareholding in Sun Life, TransAtlantic now believes that the time may well have arrived to consider whether it should be represented on the Sun Life Board so that the unfortunate misunderstandings of the past few months can be avoided in the future. In this context I should tell you that we have under consideration the possibility of marginally increasing our shareholding to reinforce this view."

Not surprisingly, this very much less than conciliatory letter had been given very careful thought by DG and his advisers. It was, in fact, not posted, but was handed by Gordon to Grant after yet another of their "friendly" dinners, this time at the Connaught Hotel in London's West End. It brought forth a somewhat plaintive, but very tough, response.

Grant to Gordon, 5 March 1987. "Dear Donald, It was good of you to dine with me the other night and, as always, I enjoyed the stimulating conversation. You said you hoped we could stop writing letters to each other for a while and I agreed wholeheartedly.

"However, reflecting on the long letter which you then handed to me, I think I have no choice but to put on paper my great concern that still, after Michael Middlemas's [the then managing director of TransAtlantic] statement at the EGM, a lot of conversation, and now your 20 February letter handed to me that Friday evening, there is no detectable point of substance in your objections to our Scheme.

"Great care was taken in the drafting of the Scheme to look after your special interests as far as might be consistent with the interests of shareholders as a whole. Except from your goodself I have not heard a comment to doubt this statement. I know that shareholders, yourself excepted, were overwhelmingly in favour of that Scheme. I therefore have to deal with a situation where one shareholder with enough votes to obstruct is putting his own interests ahead of everything else, including other shareholders, policyholders and staff.

"This is not an attitude which we can accept and it is one which I must ask you to abandon. It is in your interests as well as those of other shareholders that this excellent company should continue to prosper. To that end your present approach makes all the more inappropriate your being represented on our Board. If you accept, as I think you do, that we have looked after your investment very well over these past five or six years and you wish to keep it, and you are of course very much entitled to do so, we will continue, I know, to look after it as well in the future. Should you decide, however, that the time has come to realise the holding, I indicated to you that there might be some interesting developments on which we might work together.

"Large institutions with many thousands of policyholders such as ourselves are neither suitable objectives for corporate raiders, nor appropriate targets for financial conglomerates. It is our duty to see that we protect the future in such manner as may be necessary."

With this exchange, the gloves were off – with a vengeance. Grant's remarks about "corporate raiders" and "financial conglomerates" were not at all well received. Gordon to Grant, 19 March:

"Dear Peter, I must apologise for not writing to you earlier and thanking you for the very excellent dinner we had together at The Connaught Hotel last month. I really enjoyed our getting together and hope that the occasion will be repeated before too long.

"I must also thank you for your letter of 5 March 1987 which I am afraid does not address any of the fundamentals of our recent disagreement and certainly does not accept the legitimate rights of shareholders in regard to a company in which they are invested, let alone the position of a major shareholder such as TransAtlantic in relationship to Sun Life.

"Consequently I have no further wish to continue this unhelpful correspondence which has proved to be totally unproductive and negative."

For TransAtlantic, it was one thing to use its 25 per cent plus shareholding to block a special resolution; but quite another to propose the election of directors to Sun Life's Board, for that required only a simple majority. To secure this, TransAtlantic would need support from other shareholders, or apathy by most of them, resulting in less than 25 per cent voting with the Sun Life Board.

"After that bleak exchange of correspondence," Gordon remembers, "we decided that we must test the waters, bring matters to a head by proposing our own directors and, in particular, see what institutional support we could muster, or what degree of apathy we could induce. The fact is that, in the City of London, the institutions do tend to stand together, to support each other in a crunch, and as a matter of practice do return supporting proxy votes. There is also a strong reluctance to be seen to be voting against the Board. And as the Board are the only people who actually have access to the proxies, people contemplating a proxy fight against an incumbent Board are at a great disadvantage. Another factor is the unwritten agreement – it's almost a cartel – that the big institutions always stand together. And, in any case, they mostly have cross-shareholdings that help keep the established managements in position."

For TransAtlantic at that stage, Board representation would have been a mixed blessing. "We were fully conscious of the fact that having directors on the Board of Sun Life would not necessarily be to our advantage. In the first place, it would seriously reduce our flexibility; once one is in the position of having directors on the Board, all sorts of conflicts of interest can arise. For just one example, it would enormously increase the difficulty of making a full bid for the company, should TransAtlantic be provoked into going that route. Three members on a Board of fourteen doesn't in any case have all that much impact. One knows that in the real world all the important decisions concerning a company are not taken in the Boardroom; they are decided informally before or after the Board meeting, and there one is presented with a virtual *fait accompli*. Normally, nobody disagrees or argues; nobody wants to rock the boat.

"So, basically, the decision to go ahead was taken mainly to test our power to influence institutional support, obtaining which, against another institution as powerful as Sun Life, would be almost unprecedented short of conditions of actual fraud by the directors. However, TransAtlantic was also conscious that had it won and got its people onto that Board, the other directors would over time have learned to trust and respect them. In the long run, this would have given TransAtlantic a greater influence over the direction of the company: this was, and still is, the important factor."

Perhaps Peter Grant realised that, too, for that would explain the stupendous effort he made to keep TransAtlantic out of his Boardroom at all costs, particularly as he had a Board which was not noted for its assertiveness; in fact, it was one which appeared to give him virtually a free hand.

Hence, on 20 March 1987, Middlemas wrote to Grant: "In the circumstances I am writing to you formally on behalf of TransAtlantic to propose that I, together with Mr Dennis Marler, Chairman of Capital & Counties plc, and Mr Michael Rapp, a non-executive director of TransAtlantic and executive deputy chairman of Capital & Counties plc, be invited to join the Sun Life Board. I am sure you will agree that all of the above, having regard to their background and experience, will be able to make a significant contribution to the deliberations of your Board."

After that, the fat was really in the fire. Gordon: "The immediate result was that we saw a campaign of vilification, innuendo, circulars and newspaper advertisements and articles on a scale that was quite staggering, and absolutely unprecedented for such a relatively unimportant issue. The whole affair became a major test so far as Mr Grant was concerned and it was perceived as such by the City. Never before had the simple nomination of three thoroughly worthy gentlemen to the Board of a public company stirred such a furore;

and never before, I fully believe, has a public company expended the best part of one million pounds, or more, of shareholders' funds on a less worthy cause." (TransAtlantic was never able to persuade Grant to disclose the precise figure, but he did concede that it was more than £500 000.)

Grant, in his desperation to win the contest, went to quite unprecedented lengths, one of the most unusual of which was to send, to every shareholder of Sun Life, a tape-recording soliciting their support.

"Hello – this is Peter Grant, the Chairman of Sun Life Assurance Society. Thank you for listening to this tape, and giving me the welcome opportunity of telling you personally more about why my fellow directors and I need your support in defeating proposals put forward by Liberty Life of South Africa to appoint three of their nominees to the Sun Life Board.

"As I explained in my recent letter to you accompanying the Annual Report, your directors are unanimous in believing that Liberty's proposals are against the interests of shareholders, policyholders and staff alike.

"Liberty has no entitlement in law to appoint directors to your Board, and is seeking to do so against the views of your directors. Putting it bluntly, Liberty is trying to get control of your company through the back door, and it must not be allowed to succeed.

"In asking you to vote against Liberty's proposals, I want to draw your attention particularly to Sun Life's outstanding performance, which is summarised on the inside front cover of my letter. Our record of achievements speaks for itself.

"If we are to succeed in retaining our independence, and the ability to build on our successes of the past decade for the benefit of all shareholders, it is vital that you vote against Liberty's proposals.

"The proxy card enclosed with my letter clearly indicates how your Board recommends that you should vote. Please complete and return the card as soon as possible. Doing this will not prevent you from attending the Annual General Meeting on 13 May and voting in person if you wish. If you are able to come, you will be most welcome.

"I do hope that what I have said has convinced you of the urgent need to vote against Liberty's unwelcome proposals. But if you have any questions, please call me at my office on (01) 606 7788 and I will do my best to help you.

"Thank you for your support and for listening to me."

Grant's costly campaign was effective and "Liberty's unwelcome proposals" were heavily voted down. (In actual fact, the proposals were TransAtlantic's, but Grant always used the South African connection to muddy the waters whenever possible, even to the extent of constantly referring to Liberty Life "of South Africa" rather than the correct title – "Association of Africa".)

"Grant's major task", says Gordon, "was to get people to take the situation seriously, to get sufficient people coming to the table to vote on the basis that in this grave emergency their Board needed support. They obviously needed at least 26 per cent of shareholders to support them, which would represent one-third of the total vote excluding TransAtlantic. And this, given normal shareholder apathy, was a high total to motivate. Hence Grant's high profile and emotional campaign. And, of course, the conventional wisdom in the City is that one votes in favour of the Board. In this particular instance TransAtlantic finished up with very few votes apart from their own – and incidentally, due to a clerical error, we voted less than we actually had. The resolution for the appointment of our three directors was beaten by some 47 per cent of votes cast against it, with only 27 per cent in favour. Even so, and in spite of a powerful campaign – one which would have done justice to a US presidential election – less than half of the total votes were cast in favour of the Board.

"Even so, Grant latched on to this as a famous victory and a major defeat for us. He would rub this in at every opportunity – the fact that we had absolutely no outside support, and no institutional support, as he saw it – and he never allowed us to forget it. I think his attitude perhaps stimulated us to not to allow such a thing to happen again; it might well have helped us to win the vastly more important 1988 proxy battle."

Relative calm returned to the relationship, with Grant feeling, at least temporarily, a bit more secure. But TransAtlantic's 25 per cent stake remained a reality, and a threat. So, in September 1987 fresh proposals were brought to the table: this time, uncharacteristically, by Grant. "Around September", recalls Gordon, "he came to see us, at TransAtlantic's office in London. He always came to my office, I really don't know why – I don't believe I have ever met with him in his."

Grant's proposals centred on a new holding company which would buy TransAtlantic, and bring Capital & Counties into the equation, as well as new outside partners – the leading French insurer, the state-controlled Union des Assurances de Paris (UAP), was mentioned for the first time. Jardines, of Hong Kong, and The Equitable of America were also mentioned. The net effect would be that Sun Life's business base would be broadened considerably, and it would end up with two or three big shareholders instead of only one, each balancing out the others.

Grant proposed that: "Sun Life should offer to buy the whole of the equity capital of TransAtlantic for shares and cash. For the UK holders the consideration would be shares underwritten for a cash alternative. For Liberty the consideration would be shares and cash in such mix as the end structure of the transaction might require. Sun Life would make the offer via a new holding company.

"Capital & Counties would be sold back to Liberty and to its present shareholders and if desired to Sun Life shareholders. Sun Life would subscribe for an amount of new shares to give Sun Life, say, 20 per cent of C&C's enlarged capital. The votes on Sun Life's 20 per cent would form part of Liberty's controlling block. Michael Rapp as deputy chairman of Capital & Counties would join the Sun Life Board.

"A French insurance group (UAP) and Jardines would each subscribe for Sun Life capital to become 12-15 per cent shareholders each; the French paying cash and Jardines by way of a convertible note, resulting in Sun Life having a material (say £150-£180 million) investment in Jardines. On privatisation of UAP, Sun Life would subscribe £50 million to its core shareholding. Sun Life's new investments in C&C, Jardines and UAP should be at least as profitable as its existing business."

On this basis, TransAtlantic would have finished up as one of three major shareholders in the new Sun Life Corporation. Says Gordon: "We examined the proposals carefully, but clearly they had no real commercial merit from TransAtlantic's point of view, other than the fact that they would weaken its position. TransAtlantic then countered, working along similar lines but on a far more structured and commercial basis, and came back with proposals which could have had the effect of bringing at least one new outside shareholder into 'the game play'." At any stage, one new participant only was the maximum TransAtlantic would consider. More than one was totally unviable.

This counter-proposal, put forward early in October, was headed: "Revised proposal to achieve an elegant solution to the problem existing between Sun Life and TransAtlantic".

Although it had been very carefully considered and structured, and could well have worked, it was again totally rejected by Grant. But at least the parties were once again negotiating on a serious basis. TransAtlantic was never quite sure of the reasons for the apparent change of heart, but the long-term question mark over Sun Life's ability to maintain its much vaunted 20 per cent annual dividend growth rate could well have been a factor. This explanation was to a large extent validated when the increase in Sun Life's dividend was reduced to 15 per cent for 1988 – the lowest level of increase for almost a decade. Of course, Grant's preoccupation with the dilution of TransAtlantic's position was always a major motivator.

These proposals, counter-proposals and further refined proposals formed the basis around which intensive and extensive talks and negotiations would revolve for the best part of a year – until September 1988.

Potential outside partners, apart from UAP, who would eventually be the "sole contender", included Jardines and the American Equitable group (a front-runner at one time, until they put forward terms that Gordon describes as "almost insulting to Sun Life, never mind to TransAtlantic"), the Belgian Groupe AG, and the Italian Agnelli family insurance interests. It seemed at times that Grant was acting with some desperation, frantically seeking any way of getting off the TransAtlantic hook.

Jacques Gougenheim, the managing director of UAP International (UAPI), paid a courtesy visit to Johannesburg to meet Donald Gordon and to assess the implications of UAPI becoming involved with Sun Life, notwithstanding the dominant stake held by TransAtlantic in that company. Discussions were very positive – perhaps too positive for Peter Grant – and on many aspects consensus was reached on an acceptable compromise in regard to Sun Life's future involving the inclusion of UAPI as a substantial shareholder.

John Hignett, of Lazard Brothers, London, attended the meetings (as also did Peter Greenfield, now retired from GRE and a director of TransAtlantic) and obviously reported back to Grant on their outcome. This resulted in a visit by Grant himself to Johannesburg a few weeks later, when discussions continued in the same vein, Gougenheim having returned to Paris and Hignett to London.

It seemed, at this stage, that the impasse was at last capable of resolution. However, the full Board of TransAtlantic, when it later met in London, was somewhat sceptical, feeling that Grant's sudden change of heart was not totally credible. It was agreed that TransAtlantic would await further documentation of the deal before committing itself irrevocably to the latest approach. This seemed acceptable to all parties, and promised to leave TransAtlantic with a 25 per cent stake in Sun Life, with Sun Life taking a similar shareholding in either TransAtlantic itself or in Capital & Counties.

But the documents themselves, as finally submitted, were in a number of material respects at variance with Gordon's expectations on certain essentials. So TransAtlantic again came to the inescapable conclusion that the whole transaction was a strategy that had the poorly concealed intention of diluting the TransAtlantic shareholding and emasculating its entrenched rights.

In a strong letter to Grant on 13 July 1988, Gordon indicated his reaction in no uncertain terms and made it perfectly clear that TransAtlantic was not prepared to go along with the proposals so long as the negative and devious attitudes continued. In a detailed analysis, Gordon contended that from every point of view the deal, as documented, was unacceptable to TransAtlantic. He also objected vehemently to the fact that, as was clear from the documents, for months past Sun Life and UAPI had been involved in the preparation of detailed documentation and strategies, while TransAtlantic had pointedly been excluded from these vital deliberations which could affect the whole future of Sun Life.

There were meetings in London, Paris, Brussels, Rome and New York, but in the end Grant decided to go it alone, obviously with the approval and support of UAPI, with unilateral proposals for a deal between Sun Life and UAPI that were completely unacceptable to Gordon and TransAtlantic.

Gordon first heard of these proposals following a telephone call from the financial editor of the London *Evening Standard* on the morning of 12 September 1988. There had evidently been an informed leak in the business pages of the previous day's London *Sunday Times,* outlining very closely the substance of the proposed transaction. Gordon had to respond that as he had not yet heard any details of the deal, it was difficult for him to comment.

He did, however, tell the *Evening Standard* that in future he would probably need only to talk to UAPI, rather than Peter Grant, and this suited Gordon as "the French were nice people". This knee-jerk reaction of Gordon's was destined to have a substantial impact on how events would now unfold. Sitting in TransAtlantic's London office that Monday afternoon, Gordon was pondering what should be done. He was seriously contemplating telephoning Jacques Gougenheim in Paris – whom he had of course met in Johannesburg the previous May.

At that precise moment, a call came through from Gougenheim. He was telephoning to thank Gordon for the complimentary remarks he had made about UAPI in the *Evening Standard*. And as he, Gougenheim, was the only member of UAPI known personally to Gordon, he took the remark as a compliment. Gordon grasped the opportunity to ask Gougenheim why he had not previously discussed the unilateral proposals with him, particularly as they had had such full discussions on all the issues in Johannesburg.

Gougenheim responded by claiming that the terms that had been negotiated with Grant were so attractive to UAPI that the opportunity was one that could not be missed. Gordon countered by asking whether UAPI had considered the possible repercussions should the proposals be rejected, adding that, taking into account TransAtlantic's 26 per cent shareholding together with the Belgian Groupe AG's 7,5 per cent and other shareholders who would be unhappy, there was in his view a very strong possibility that the proposals would be voted down by the shareholders. Further, the bid premium in the Sun Life share price would disappear on the consummation of the deal and the shares would trade lower as the prospect of a bid for Sun Life finally evaporated.

Gougenheim said that Sun Life's advisers had assured them that there was not the slightest possibility of that happening. Gordon persisted, asking Gougenheim if he had fully considered the implications should their advisers prove wrong, reiterating his opinion that the vote would be adverse. "Well," said Gougenheim, "that would merely confirm what we have long suspected – that the French are not particularly welcome in London."

Gordon reflects: "I have no doubt in my mind that this talk led to the negotiation by Lazards for Groupe AG to enter into a 'put and call' option, first with Lazard Freres, and later ceded to UAPI, over their 7,5 per cent shareholding in Sun Life. This involved UAPI in a high take-up price, which although widely guessed at, has never been officially disclosed."

To achieve this option substantial pressure had been brought to bear on Groupe AG by the French business establishment. The sale of its Sun Life stake must have been difficult for Groupe AG to swallow in view of the fact that they had been subjected to a defeat by UAP in the takeover battle involving Royale Belge the previous year. *C'est la guerre,* however, and European business politics prevailed.

From then on, the campaign by both TransAtlantic and Sun Life for shareholders' support was in full flood. To a large extent, this was fought out in the media, which entered the fray with great enthusiasm and commitment. "I was personally spending many hours a day speaking to the press and explaining our position, and in this respect I believe that TransAtlantic got the better of the exchanges. These culminated in the virtually unanimous barrage of press criticism against the proposals that appeared in the newspapers on the morning of the Sun Life Extraordinary General Meeting."

The UK was in the throes of a postal strike at the time and, for some reason, Sun Life had given effectively only minimal statutory notice – a matter of seventeen days in all. This gave TransAtlantic an extremely hectic time in trying to make up for the initial impression created by the press in both London and Paris that the deal, being agreed by Sun Life and UAP, was a foregone conclusion. The early press reaction on both sides of the Channel was to the effect that Sun Life had succeeded in closing out TransAtlantic's position once and for all. This even included an explicit cartoon in London's *Financial Times* which showed Gordon having the door closed in his face by a triumphant Grant, helped by Peyrelevade, the UAP Chairman. And, because of the postal strike, direct postal communication by TransAtlantic with the general body of Sun Life shareholders was made impossible by the short timeframe available.

That Gordon and TransAtlantic succeeded so well in bringing the weight of the media over to their side by the morning of the EGM was a great achievement, but Grant also helped quite considerably, by shooting himself in the foot.

A matter of substantial press criticism, and one of considerable surprise to the City, was the timing of Grant's entering into a £200 000 service contract with the Sun Life, and almost simultaneously arranging a similar contract for himself with an American investment banking group, Paine Webber. This occurred following Grant's retirement from Lazard Brothers, and was regarded by the media and the public as being "well over the top" for a chairman who was neither fully an executive chairman nor a full-time executive of either of the companies concerned. A £200 000 per year salary package was virtually unknown in London's insurance industry in 1988, even for highly experienced chief executives in companies much larger than Sun Life. Such a level of remuneration was just not on for a merchant banker recently turned life insurer. The idea of greatly augmenting this with a second part-time appointment was anathema to the industry and to the City, and all the justified criticism certainly did nothing to further Grant's cause with Sun Life's shareholders.

All this press activity might well have turned the tide and, for the first time in living memory, the cosy insurance voting cartel was breached, with several institutions actually taking the unprecedented step of being openly seen to be voting against the Board of an establishment life insurance company. Many, less courageous, merely abstained from voting. Others "voted with their feet", by selling their shares. Significantly, notwithstanding the major importance of the issues at stake, the total number of shares polled was considerably less than the number polled in the vote on the much lesser issue of the appointment of directors, eighteen months earlier.

But we have run ahead of our story, and need to backtrack. In summary, Grant's proposals were: First, that Sun Life would issue to UAP International, the unlisted non-domestic subsidiary of UAP, 13,18 million new shares. Hence, UAPI would hold 18,2 per cent of Sun Life's enlarged equity. Second, in return, Sun Life would receive 7 412 000 convertible warrants which could, after five years, be converted into 15 per cent of the equity of UAPI, or else be redeemed at face value. Third, there would, in addition, be a one-for-seven rights issue at £6 per share to raise £62 million that would be used to finance joint ventures into Europe with UAPI.

Gordon and his advisers were distinctly unimpressed. "The real thrust of the situation from Sun Life's point of view", he recalls, "was to be allowed to participate with UAP in the development of new business in Europe, which frankly none of us believed had any commercial logic at all. We just couldn't conceive of a situation where there was good business that UAP would be prepared to share and to bring Sun Life into the European equation. Fine for UAP, which anyway was big enough to swallow Sun Life almost without trace, for it would be getting a firm footing in the UK insurance market – which, incidentally, is very highly regarded from the European viewpoint. But Sun Life, we thought, was getting remarkably little in return – 15 per cent, maybe, of an unlisted subsidiary of the giant state-owned UAP."

Responsible London stockbroking opinion viewed Grant's proposals with similar misgivings. Typical was the comment of one leading London stockbroker: "Sun Life has finally produced its 'elegant' solution to its South African problem and simultaneously found an apparently credible way into the 1992 insurance Olympics. But a cross-holding with UAP, France's largest composite insurer and number two in Europe, is not what the speculators wanted Sun Life to announce.

"This deal clearly reflects the unequal bargaining power of Sun Life and UAP. Sun Life had limited options in Europe. The UK market is 'suffering increasing competition and declining margins' (their words) and they needed geographic diversification to support long-term earnings growth. They lack the capital, the manpower and the time to either buy or build something in Europe, and a strategic link was the remaining option. They also needed to dilute Liberty Life's 26 per cent stake.

"UAP has got a remarkably good deal. In return for a modest deferred stake in its non-French operations it gets access to Sun Life's product development skills, its computer systems and its management skills. That is clearly what it wanted."

A leading merchant bank was much tougher. Under the heading: "Vote against the proposal", they said: "The proposed deal with UAP has two elements, expansion into Europe and cross-shareholdings. We support Sun Life's laudable aim to expand its business and would support an even larger rights issue to do this.

"We believe that the proposed terms of the share issue to UAP International are abominable and calculate that they are severely deleterious to Sun Life's shareholders.

"As an entry fee to joint ventures with UAPI's small, barely profitable Italian and Spanish, mostly non-life, subsidiaries, the dilution implicit in the share issue makes no commercial sense.

"Seen against a background of antagonism between the management of Sun Life and TransAtlantic the proposed deal could be understandable, but that does not make it sensible."

Despite this strong support of their own view that there was "no commercial logic" to Grant's proposals, the Board of TransAtlantic was reluctant to declare itself firmly. "We didn't want to be seen as wreckers, or as taking a negative approach. And we hoped, right up to the end, that Grant would see sense and modify the proposed deal along the lines we were suggesting. We put great pressure on Lazards, who were advising both Sun Life and UAP, to modify the terms, but to no avail."

So the row raged on in the London financial press – and, far more importantly – in the City's institutional boardrooms, as both sides lobbied long and hard for voting support at the critical Extraordinary General Meeting of Sun Life that Grant had called for Thursday 29 September 1988. It was one of the most interesting corporate rows that the City of London had seen for a long time – certainly one involving the true "Establishment", the financial institutions.

On Monday 26th, after much burning of the midnight oil in TransAtlantic's London Broadway headquarters over the weekend, Gordon's men issued a press release outlining eighteen matters on which TransAtlantic sought further information "before deciding on its voting intentions" at the forthcoming EGM.

Commenting on this release, another influential stockbroker wrote: "Although this might read like the Cheapside equivalent of Luther's Wittenberg Theses, it provides food for thought for all Sun Life shareholders and the EGM promises to be an exciting event."

And exciting it was, with Thursday morning's *Financial Times* setting the scene. "Sun Life. It may be just conceivable that someone apart from the Sun Life Board and UAP would benefit from the deal to be considered at today's EGM. But if so, Sun Life has certainly made little effort to prove it, and precious few of the group's institutional shareholders appear convinced. Stamping the deal with the revered numerals 1992 does not mean that the two companies' plans for European co-operation would prove either workable or wise. And it requires a significant leap of faith to believe that 15 per cent of an unquoted subsidiary of a nationalised French insurance company is worth the same as 18,2 per cent of Sun Life.

"All that does not mean, of course, that the institutional shareholders – many of whom are in the same line of work as Sun Life – will not have an attack of occupational solidarity and support the Sun Life management. And the voting intentions of the largest shareholder, Mr Donald Gordon of Liberty Life, appear to have changed several times in the past week. On the face of it, it is difficult to see why shareholders should back a deal born of personal animosity more than commercial or financial logic. If they do, they will have only themselves to blame for allowing UAP a look-in to Sun Life on the cheap."

Although the *FT*'s view was encouraging, Gordon still went to Thursday's meeting with a relatively open mind. "Grant's response to our eighteen points had been completely unconvincing," he says, "but nonetheless I was still hoping for a last minute change of heart. I went to the EGM determined to state our case explicitly, and TransAtlantic's Board had determined that the way we voted would hinge on Grant's response at the actual meeting."

The facilities for the EGM were totally inadequate. This vitally important meeting in fact took place in three separate rooms, linked together by inadequate video facilities and a poor public address system. Gordon had to hold a microphone in one hand while trying to deal with his notes with the other. Eventually, Len Berkowitz, of TransAtlantic's solicitors, Linklaters and Paines, had to hold the microphone for him – perhaps the most highly-paid microphone holder in history.

The TransAtlantic party was forced to take seats in a corner facing the entire Sun Life Board, who sat scowling at short range at Gordon as he spoke into a video camera so placed as to make it difficult to give a fair presentation of TransAtlantic's case. The best seats, of course, had been reserved for the large Sun Life team of advisers. TransAtlantic's counsel immediately objected and gave notice that, as the meeting was in three rooms and not in one, it could not in law be regarded as a meeting, thus setting the grounds for a post-meeting legal action should this prove necessary.

In the event, this precaution was not necessary, so let us return to that Friday's *Financial Times* for its ball-by-ball account of that historic meeting – a meeting at which one man's determination and perseverance prevailed over a major City institution. "Chairmen in clash over Sun Life/UAP alliance. A public clash between Sun Life Assurance and its biggest shareholder TransAtlantic Holdings ended in suspense yesterday, as the two groups awaited the outcome of a crucial shareholder vote on Sun Life's plans for an alliance with UAP, French state-owned insurer.

"The result is expected at 8 am today. The vote followed a two-hour extraordinary meeting at Sun Life's London headquarters yesterday, called a fortnight ago to seek shareholders' approval for the scheme.

"Attended by about 200 shareholders who overflowed from the Boardroom into nearby offices and corridors, the meeting had to be conducted in three separate rooms linked by closed circuit television.

"In spite of the congestion, only two small shareholders and one institutional fund manager spoke up to intervene in what became a confrontation between Mr Donald Gordon, TransAtlantic Chairman, and Mr Peter Grant, Chairman of Sun Life.

"Mr Grant, appearing diffident and reserved but rarely flustered by Mr Gordon, took only 17 minutes to dispose of 18 questions challenging the deal tabled earlier this week by TransAtlantic, which controls 28,4 per cent of Sun Life. 'I'm not apologetic at all for the deal, which I think is a very good one,' Mr Grant said.

"Mr Gordon spoke for 45 minutes, often losing his audience [because of the inadequacy of the communication equipment], before finally making it clear that TransAtlantic would vote against Mr Grant's plans to bring in UAP as an 18,2 per cent shareholder as a prelude to life assurance joint ventures in Italy and Spain, while Sun Life may eventually take 15 per cent of a UAP subsidiary.

"Attacking the deal, Mr Gordon accused Sun Life's Board of what he called 'a dictatorial attitude'. If the deal went ahead he said 'our voting rights would be totally emasculated'. Nothing would convince him that the share swop was credible, he stated."

The TransAtlantic group was particularly incensed at the £4,5 million indicated as the costs of the proxy battle, and Gordon pressed Grant as to who was to bear this astronomical sum, especially given the fact that it represented a high proportion of Sun Life's net equity. Grant asserted that this sum should be weighed against the market capitalisation of Sun Life, a concept that Gordon vociferously rejected out of hand as having no basis in any form of accounting or financial logic.

"All indicators about the poll pointed last night to a close result, amid signs that Sun Life's Board has failed to secure the unanimous support of the other British insurers which speak for about 14 per cent of the shares.

"Two insurers, Sun Alliance with 5,2 per cent and Prudential with 2,6 per cent, have swung their votes behind Mr Grant. Sun Alliance has close ties to Sun Life.

"Opposing the scheme, however, were fund managers at Royal

Insurance, the biggest UK-based non-life insurer, with 0,7 per cent, and the Lucas Industries staff pension scheme. A measure of the difficulties faced by insurers in deciding their stance is that Commercial Union is understood to have deliberately abstained from the vote."

An insurmountable problem for TransAtlantic was to find out just exactly who had voted for, or against, and who had abstained. This was a jealously guarded secret known only to the Sun Life Board. This is an unfair advantage which is an unfortunate feature of UK company law, and one which acts as a great deterrent to shareholders contemplating a vote against the Board.

Then came a Reuters' news flash at 8 am the next day. "Life insurer Sun Life Assurance Society plc said its shareholders had rejected a plan to link with French insurer Union des Assurances de Paris.

"It said in a statement that 20,75m votes representing 35,1 per cent of the issued ordinary share capital rejected the proposal, while 16,55m (28 per cent of the shares) voted in favour."

So, although only 9 per cent of the "outside" shareholders actively supported TransAtlantic, as for technical reasons TransAtlantic could only vote 26 per cent, a massive 37 per cent abstained from voting.

Late the previous evening, Gordon had bumped into Grant, who was with some of UAP's advisers, at London's famed Berkeley Hotel. "I enquired of him the outcome of the proxy vote and expressed my amazement and concern that it had taken so long to be declared. Grant refused to tell me, but said he would telephone me the following morning before 8 am, prior to the announcement on the Stock Exchange. I could not deduce the reason for this reluctance and assumed that it had something to do with the admissibility of the votes applicable to the Groupe AG shareholding, to which our counsel had indicated objection earlier at the EGM."

Later the next day, TransAtlantic issued another press release. "Mr Donald Gordon, Chairman of TransAtlantic, commenting on the result of the meeting of Sun Life shareholders to approve the proposed alliance with UAP International (where the resolution was defeated by a margin of 4,2 million votes out of a total of 37,3 million votes cast – 63 per cent of total shares in issue) said: 'We have consistently stated that we are not against the concept of expansion in Europe and see the merit of increasing the company's capital base.

Moreover, we have always taken the view that we would be happy to see UAP as a significant shareholder of the company on appropriate terms.

"'We would be prepared, if called upon, to help in reformulating suitable proposals for submission to shareholders and to support Sun Life in the development of its business to the best of our ability.

"'The new situation will, we believe, substantially improve the prospects of our being involved in the future direction and fortunes of Sun Life.

"'We agonised long and hard as to whether we should vote for or against the proposal. Both options offered advantages. In the end, after full review, we decided to vote against the proposals put forward because we believed the terms negotiated by the Board to be unfair to Sun Life and certain of the proposed voting arrangements with the Sun Life Board to be unacceptable on fundamental principles of shareholder democracy. TransAtlantic was also concerned that part of the motivation of the proposals was to dilute TransAtlantic's shareholding which has recently been increased to 28,4 per cent from approximately 26 per cent.'"

TransAtlantic did not have to wait long to see UAP become "a significant shareholder" in Sun Life. Later that same Friday, a Sun Life release read: "Sun Life has been informed by UAP that it has today purchased in the market 6 305 000 shares in Sun Life, representing 10,7 per cent of the issued share capital.

"The Board of Sun Life welcomes this purchase which was made with its knowledge and approval. In the course of preparing the proposals considered at yesterday's EGM, Sun Life developed an excellent relationship with the UAP Group, and looks forward to developing commercial links with them in Europe.

"The Board of Sun Life welcomes the constructive announcement today by TransAtlantic Holdings of its positive attitude to UAP as a significant shareholder, and to the Board's strategy to develop into Europe. This strategy now has the clear support of the overwhelming majority of Sun Life shareholders.

"The Board looks forward to close relationships with its two major shareholders."

Grant was neatly turning two unrelated press releases to his own advantage, but it really did not matter any more.

The 10,7 per cent bought by UAP in its "dawn raid" in the market (which some, perhaps unkindly, think was facilitated by Sun Life's seemingly deliberate delay in announcing the results of the previous day's vote) brought its total holding to precisely the 18,2 per cent it would have had if the original deal had gone through. But at a substantially greater cost in cash terms! Looking back to his accidental meeting with Grant at the Berkeley the previous evening, Gordon has no doubt but that the delay was deliberate, as dawn raids normally take some time to organise. Certain selected shareholders were given the opportunity of disposing of their holdings at an inflated price of over £12 per share. TransAtlantic was extremely unhappy about this unnecessary delay and questioned whether it was justifiable or equitable."

Saturday's London *Daily Mail* then proceeded to ask a very pertinent question. Under the banner headline: "The Sun goes down on General Grant", writer Michael Walters asked: "Should Peter Grant go? That was the question round the City last night as investors pondered the news that shareholders in Sun Life, one of the proudest names in British insurance, had voted down their Board's plan for a cosy cross-shareholding scheme with a French insurer.

"Mr Grant, the Sun Life Chairman, has won few friends in this campaign. He was the architect of perhaps the most important scheme put to Sun Life shareholders for many a long year. They threw it out. Mr Grant was last night putting on a happy face, trying to gloss over the yawning hole in his credibility, and settling back to stay in his £200 000 a year part-time post. There was no question of Mr Grant's resignation, said his public relations man [the felicitously named Tony Good, of Good Relations].

"No-one was looking for a fight yesterday. But Mr Grant had been tagged firmly as a lame duck leader for Sun Life at the end of an eventful day in which control effectively passed to the two largest shareholders, South African backed TransAtlantic Holdings and French group Union des Assurances de Paris. That, of course, is what Mr Grant was most keen to avoid.

"Sun Life shares rose smartly yesterday to mark their Chairman's eclipse. Mr Grant has lost his game and though he may stay, prudent shareholders may think this the time to say goodbye."

But Grant showed no signs of saying "Goodbye" and so, with this major victory behind him, Gordon wrote to him on 17 October 1988. "Now that the Extraordinary General Meeting is behind us and the dust has settled, I think it is appropriate for me to respond to you following on our discussion last Wednesday."

At that discussion Grant had, at long last, unconditionally invited Gordon to nominate two representatives to the Sun Life Board. "As I have indicated to you it is not feasible for me at this stage to join the Sun Life Board in view of my other obligations, nor do I believe that my presence would be particularly helpful. Taking all factors into account it seems that the optimum benefit would accrue to Sun Life if we were to indicate the availability of Lord Douro and Michael Rapp for invitation to the Sun Life Board and hope that these nominations would be acceptable."

Despite his stunning defeat and the fact that certain sections of the London press had called for his resignation, Grant stubbornly dug his toes in. He replied the same day, accepting the nomination of Lord Douro, but politely opposing that of Michael Rapp – solely on the grounds of his South African nationality – for the time being, and asking TransAtlantic for an alternative nomination.

Gordon, not unnaturally, was infuriated. His very cool and studied reply of 18 October first pointed out that the nominations of Michael Rapp and Lord Douro had only been made after very mature consideration, and were designed to provide the highest possible contribution to the deliberations of the Sun Life Board. He stressed that Michael Rapp was a man of considerable quality and ability and had been his closest colleague for over two decades. Gordon also pointed out the considerable difficulty of his position in regard to a pointed rebuff of a colleague of whom he clearly had such a high opinion. He next objected to Grant's raising the South African issue yet again, noting that Grant had earlier, in his June proposals, indicated that he would then have been prepared to invite Rapp onto his Board.

Finally, after reminding Grant of the considerable contributions made over recent decades by other ex-South Africans to the UK life insurance industry, Gordon indicated his intention – doubtless with complete sincerity – to throw the whole issue back into the melting pot by withdrawing both nominations.

Faced with this implacable determination and after a few more heated words over the telephone, Grant finally changed his mind and bowed to the inevitable. On 19 October he wrote again to Gordon, gracefully welcoming the two new directors – Rapp and Douro – to Sun Life's Board, and graciously confirming an arrangement with Gordon to lunch on the morrow to introduce Grant to Douro.

By late November 1988 it had become inescapable to the TransAtlantic Board that the future of Sun Life would need to be settled by TransAtlantic and its somewhat involuntary partner, UAP International. Their aggregate shareholding, with TransAtlantic holding almost 30 per cent and UAPI over 18 per cent, was approaching 50 per cent of Sun Life's equity. Both had taken the opportunity of marginally increasing their Sun Life holdings on London stock market weakness.

The emotion and trauma of the unbecoming row leading up to, and culminating in, the Sun Life EGM on 29 September, and the dawn raid that followed the next morning, was gradually becoming diffused, and the time was approaching for frank communication between the chairmen of TransAtlantic and UAP in regard to their respective future intentions.

The relationship between the two men, from totally different cultures and backgrounds, was far too new and tenuous for any firm proposals to be put forward in connection with the problematic life insurance company – Sun Life – of which they now found themselves as major shareholders. There was TransAtlantic with its near 30 per cent holding and UAP International with over 18 per cent, with the obvious intention of increasing this closer to the TransAtlantic level in the fullness of time. By January 1989, this process was already in train, and on 18 January UAPI announced that its Sun Life holding had been increased to 19,24 per cent. By early July 1989, its interest had been increased to over 22 per cent, boosting the aggregate stake of UAPI and TransAtlantic to 52 per cent.

And so the Sun Life saga, after raging over so long a period, was early in 1989 moving inevitably towards its day of resolution, which hopefully would end the era of trauma and uncertainty which had blighted this great life insurance company for so long, preventing it from achieving its full potential.

For Liberty Life, and for Donald Gordon, an era of ever-increasing influence outside the narrow confines of the Republic of South Africa is now in sight. More than thirty years of highly successful endeavour have been crowned by the recognition that the major South African financial institution that Gordon has created is now a power to be reckoned with internationally.

# Appendix Corporate Profile and Year-by-year Summary of Progress

Part of the Liberty Life Association of Africa's Annual Reports for 1987 and 1988 are quoted below: first, the Group's own "Profile", as seen by management after thirty years of unbroken progress and success, and second, an encapsulated history, which sets out the bare bones of some of the events that are enlarged upon in this volume, in a year-by-year summary.

## CORPORATE PROFILE

Founded in 1958 with a capital of R100 000, Liberty Life Association of Africa Limited, with shareholders' funds at the end of 1988 of over R3 billion and total assets of R14,8 billion is today the largest proprietary life office and the third largest life assurer in the Republic of South Africa. Liberty Life's shares are listed on The Johannesburg Stock Exchange and The International Stock Exchange, London.

Liberty Holdings Limited, the listed holding company of The Liberty Life Group, has been listed on The Johannesburg Stock Exchange since 1968 and owns an effective 52,2 per cent of the equity of Liberty Life, the Group's main operating company.

Liberty Holdings, and consequently The Liberty Life Group, are jointly controlled by Liberty Investors Limited and Standard Bank Investment Corporation Limited.

Liberty Life's primary objective is to create a high-calibre international insurance-based financial services group to provide its clients with superior service in its areas of expertise.

Liberty Life specialises in a sophisticated approach to life insurance and pension funding largely based on the direct linkage of equities and quality real estate to policyholders' benefits with the object of reducing the ravages of inflation. Liberty Life's innovative abilities were the catalyst for revolutionising the life insurance industry in this regard over the past quarter of a century.

In 1987 Liberty Life acquired The Prudential Assurance Company of South Africa Limited and has a 61 per cent controlling interest in Charter Life Insurance Company Limited in which Guardian National Insurance Company Limited, a listed subsidiary of Guardian Royal Exchange of the United Kingdom, owns the balance of the shares. Liberty Holdings has a 44,4 per cent holding in Guardian National, one of South Africa's leading property, casualty, personal lines and marine insurance companies.

The Liberty Life Group also owns 59,2 per cent of the issued share capital of First International Trust Limited, which is a long-term investment holding company, listed on The Johannesburg Stock Exchange, which was reconstituted in the final quarter of 1988 as the international holding company for The Liberty Life Group's off-shore interests. First International Trust owns 49,3 per cent of TransAtlantic Holdings PLC, a United Kingdom registered investment holding company which has total capital employed of over £1 billion (R4,3 billion) and was listed on The Luxembourg Stock Exchange in October 1987. TransAtlantic's major interest in the international life insurance industry is a 29,8 per cent strategic holding in Sun Life Assurance Society PLC, a major insurer operating in the United Kingdom life and pension markets, which is listed on The International Stock Exchange, London. First International Trust also owns 29,5 per cent of the equity of The Continental and Industrial Trust PLC, a leading London-based listed investment trust. TransAtlantic also has a direct 41 per cent interest in Continental which it controls. TransAtlantic's major subsidiary, Capital & Counties plc, in which it owns a 65,4 per cent (fully diluted) interest, is a significant property development company based in the United Kingdom which is also listed on the London Stock Exchange.

Liberty Life's other strategic investments include an interest of over 30 per cent in Standard Bank Investment Corporation Limited, the leading South African banking group, and approximately 34 per cent of Premier Group Holdings Limited, a major South African food-based conglomerate. Premier Group Holdings has, in turn, a 35 per cent interest in The South African Breweries Limited, South Africa's largest beverage and consumer-orientated group.

Liberty Holdings also has interests in a number of other companies, the main business of which includes:

- investment management for The Liberty Life Group and other institutional clients;
- mutual fund management;
- the construction, development and management of real estate;
- the broad financial services industry.

Taking into account off-balance sheet investment portfolios and real estate managed on behalf of self-administered pension funds, directly managed associated companies and mutual fund interests, total assets under The Group's direct control exceed R23 billion.

## THIRTY-YEAR PROGRESS OF THE LIBERTY LIFE GROUP

**1958**

Liberty Life in August 1958 is registered to undertake life insurance business in the Republic of South Africa with a capital of R100 000. The first life policy is written in October.

**1960**

The first retirement annuity products are introduced to the South African life insurance market.

**1962**

Liberty Life is granted a listing on The Johannesburg Stock Exchange, the first life insurance company to be listed. Total assets exceed R1 million – a tenfold increase over its original capital base in only three years.

Liberty Life plays a leading role in the formation of Abbey Life Insurance Company in the United Kingdom, destined to become a major participant in the introduction of linked life insurance to the United Kingdom. Abbey Life is now the largest listed life insurer formed since the Second World War.

African Life acquires a 23 per cent interest in Liberty Life for R300 000. The price paid, R10 per share, is a near fourfold increase on the opening listing price of six months earlier.

**1964**

Guardian Royal Exchange Assurance of London acquires a 75 per cent controlling interest in Liberty Life. Liberty Life's premium income passes the R1 million mark.

**1965**

Liberty Life, in partnership with two other South African financial institutions, launches South Africa's first mutual fund and introduces the concept of life insurance policy benefits linked directly to mutual funds.

**1967**
Total assets exceed R10 million. Liberty Life introduces the variable investment participation (VIP) principle which establishes a direct link between policyholders' benefits and the investment portfolio of the company, allowing Liberty Life to relate its policyholders' benefits directly to the potential of its own investment portfolio, particularly in relation to equities to protect against inflation.

**1968**
Liberty Holdings (formerly Guardian Assurance Holdings [South Africa]) is formed to consolidate the South African interests of The Guardian Royal Exchange Assurance Group by acquiring the entire issued share capital of Guardian Assurance Company of South Africa and 75 per cent of the issued share capital of Liberty Life. Liberty Holdings is listed on The Johannesburg Stock Exchange in December 1968 following a record public subscription.

**1969**
Liberty Asset Management (Libam), the investment management arm of The Liberty Life Group, is launched.

**1970**
Guardbank Management Corporation formed in conjunction with Barclays National Bank (now First National Bank) as the management company of the GuardBank Growth Fund.

**1971**
Liberty Life introduces the Liberty Property Bond series of policies which for the first time makes available effective linkage of policy benefits to the growth and hedge potential of major multi-million rand property investments owned by The Liberty Life Group.

**1972**
Liberty Life acquires the South African life insurance operations of Manufacturers Life Insurance Company of Canada, thereby increasing its asset base to over R100 million.

**1973**
Liberty Life acquires control of Real Estate Corporation, a major South African listed property company.

**1974**
Liberty Life acquires the South African life insurance operations of Sun Life Assurance Company of Canada, thereby further substantially augmenting its asset base and career agency force.

**1975**
Liberty Life acquires control of Clydesdale (Transvaal) Collieries.

**1976**
Liberty Life acquires the entire issued share capital of Rapp & Maister Holdings, one of South Africa's leading listed property-owning and development companies, which had been associated with Liberty Life for many years. Liberty Life's annual income exceeds R100 million.

**1977**
Liberty Life gains control of First Union General Investment Trust, South Africa's premier listed investment trust, thereby enabling Liberty Life to acquire large holdings of key South African industrial and financial equities.

**1978**
Control of The Liberty Life Group returns to South Africa when Liblife Controlling Corporation is formed by Liberty Life's founders together with Standard Bank Investment Corporation to acquire a controlling interest in Liberty Holdings from The Guardian Royal Exchange Group which retained an 11 per cent interest.

**1980**
Liberty Life introduces a staff share incentive scheme whereby every member of staff is afforded the opportunity of acquiring a minimum of R2 000 of equity in Liberty Life by way of a long-term share incentive scheme with substantial elimination of downside risk. This scheme was the first such scheme in South Africa to include all races.

TransAtlantic Holdings is established in London as the vehicle for Liberty Life's international development and acquires an important interest in Sun Life Assurance Society of the United Kingdom. This makes TransAtlantic the largest and dominant shareholder in Sun Life.

**1981**
Liberty Life is granted a listing on The Stock Exchange, London.

TransAtlantic Holdings, in exchange for an issue of shares,

acquires a 29,6 per cent interest in Capital & Counties, a major United Kingdom property company involved in large-scale real estate development.

Liberty Life introduces to South Africa the "Lifestyle Protector" – a unique policy designed to maintain the purchasing power of future premiums.

**1982**

Liberty Life celebrates its 25th anniversary and Liberty Life Centre, the new corporate headquarters in Braamfontein, Johannesburg, is opened.

**1983**

Liberty Life takes the lead in introducing The Liberty Universal Lifestyle series of policies to South Africa, which today represents a major feature of Liberty Life's new business thrust.

Liberty Life, in association with Johannesburg Consolidated Investment Company and Anglo American Corporation, acquires joint control of Premier Group Holdings which, in turn, acquires a 35 per cent interest in The South African Breweries.

Standard Bank Investment Corporation, in exchange for a large issue of its shares, increases its interest in Liblife Controlling to 50 per cent involving joint control of The Liberty Life Group with its founders.

**1984**

Liberty Life disposes of control of Clydesdale (Transvaal) Collieries to Gold Fields of South Africa in exchange for a significant shareholding issued by Gold Fields of South Africa to Clydesdale shareholders.

**1985**

TransAtlantic acquires control of Capital & Counties following a take-over bid on The Stock Exchange, London.

Liberty Life becomes a registered financial company in respect of Standard Bank Investment Corporation and increases its stake to over 21 per cent, following Standard Chartered Bank relinquishing control to a level of 39 per cent.

**1986**

The VIP Lifestyle Annuity policy, designed to apply the flexible "Universal" concept to retirement planning, is launched in South Africa.

TransAtlantic gains control of Continental & Industrial Investment Trust, a significant authorised investment trust listed on The Stock Exchange, London.

**1987**

Liberty Life celebrates its 30th anniversary. Premium income exceeds R1 billion for the first time, with policyholder benefits exceeding the R750 million mark.

The Prudential Assurance Company of South Africa becomes a wholly-owned subsidiary of Liberty Life with effect from 1 January 1987.

Liberty Life increases its interest in Standard Bank Investment Corporation to over 30 per cent following the final disposal of the interest held by Standard Chartered Bank. This makes Liberty Life the largest shareholder in South Africa's leading bank.

Liberty Life's market capitalisation achieves the R3 billion level for the first time and total assets of Liberty Holdings and Liberty Life each exceed R11 billion.

Liberty Life records 25 years in which it has raised its dividend each year and has averaged 34 per cent compound growth over the period – a feat claimed to be a record unsurpassed by any listed company in the Western world over a 25 year period.

**1988**

The first dividend, of R13 million, is received from Liberty Life's offshore investments.

Construction work commences on a major extension to Liberty Life Centre.

The dividend paid to shareholders exceeds R100 million for the first time, and investment income exceeds R1 billion.

Record new business production reaches R247 million of recurring premium income, a one-hundredfold increase on the figure for 1967, when R2,3 million was recorded.

First Union General Investment Trust (Fugit) is restructured by the exchange of its equity portfolio for Liberty Life's offshore investments. This involved the successful conclusion of a R484 million rights issue, the biggest ever in South Africa, and the renaming of Fugit as First International Trust Limited (FIT) as the international holding company for the Liberty Life Group's offshore investments.

TransAtlantic increases its interest in Sun Life to 29,9 per cent and, after successfully preventing the Board from implementing certain corporate proposals, obtains representation on the Sun Life Board for two of its nominees.

Construction commences on three major regional shopping centres on or adjacent to the M25 Ring Road encircling the Greater London conurbation.

# Index